Advertising Media

A Managerial Approach

Advertising Media

A Managerial Approach

Anthony F. McGann
University of Wyoming

J. Thomas Russell
University of Georgia

Second Edition   1988

Homewood, Illinois   60430

This book was set in Century Schoolbook by Better Graphics, Inc.
The editors were Jeanne M. Teutsch and Merrily D. Mazza.
The production manager was Irene H. Sotiroff.
The drawings were done by Jay Bensen, the Artforce.
R. R. Donnelley & Sons Company was the printer and binder.

ISBN   0-256-05988-8

Library of Congress Catalog Card No. 87–81340

Printed in the United States of America

2 3 4 5 6 7 8 9 0 DO 5 4 3 2 1 0 9

Advertising media are an integral part of marketing and advertising strategy. In recent years, increases in media time and space costs have led to sophisticated planning, analysis, and evaluation of media purchases. This revised text offers an introduction for future media planners and salespeople and an overview of advertising media for those responsible for managing a total advertising program.

In *Advertising Media: A Managerial Approach* we view the media process from three perspectives. First, we consider the advertiser's marketing strategy, budgeting acumen, and corporate goals. Second, we examine the media themselves. The unique character of the various media as business and social institutions shapes the advertising messages they carry. Finally, we discuss the role of the advertising agency, which is responsible for planning and carrying out the basic function between media and client.

In the past, advertisers have sometimes regarded media-planning decisions as complementary, but secondary, to the creative aspects of advertising. Journalism advertising programs, with historical roots in news editorial training, understandably tended to emphasize writing, production, and art. Media planning was often taught as a portion of some other course, and little attention was given to developing the student's expertise or to directing graduating students to jobs in the area. Business schools did not teach courses in media decisions and, until recently, largely ignored any serious consideration of advertising media. Advertisers and advertising agencies tended to evaluate prospective employees on the basis of their portfolios rather than on their media and marketing expertise.

In recent years, this view of advertising media changed dramatically. As the investment in advertising time and space passed the $100 billion mark in the United States and nears the $200 billion level worldwide, advertisers increasingly sought to manage these expenditures more efficiently. Journalism schools found that they simply cannot place students who have no solid foundation in media planning and have changed their curricula accordingly.

In business schools, marketing department faculties see advertising as an increasingly attractive career for their students. As a result, course offerings are expanding in the expected areas of faculty expertise: advertising management, media, and strategy. It is unrealistic to think that marketing departments will offer substantial numbers of "creative" courses in the foreseeable future. Perhaps the best evidence of the growing importance of advertising in business schools can be seen in the current membership of the American Academy of Advertising (AAA). The AAA was founded in 1958 as an organization devoted to the study and advancement of advertising education. In its early years, members came largely from journalism faculties; today 60 percent of the Academy's 400 members come from business school faculties.

This book fills the need for a text devoted to helping students learn the important managerial decisions involved in planning, buying, and evaluating advertising media. We accomplished this goal in a way that also assists instructors and reflects the importance now given the subject in journalism programs and business schools and by practitioners.

In contrast to others in the area, this revision reflects our conviction that the study of advertising media should emphasize three areas:

1. The marketing management foundations of the media function.
2. The technical, economic, managerial, and multinational character of advertising media.
3. The quantitative nature of management problems related to the media function.

The text's three parts generally correspond to each of the three emphasized areas.

Chapters 1 to 5 relate basic marketing principles to the advertising media function. Our research indicates that every accredited journalism advertising program either requires or strongly suggests a marketing minor for advertising majors. Consequently, this first section assumes a rudimentary knowledge of basic marketing. Not to do so would eliminate the book from consideration by marketing departments and most leading journalism advertising programs.

Chapters 6 to 11 discuss the characteristics of each of the mass media as advertising vehicles. We emphasize the use of various media as components in the overall marketing and promotional program and keep descriptive material to a minimum to avoid duplicating similar material provided in most introductory advertising texts. Chapter 12 highlights the global nature of contemporary advertising media decisions. It provides a framework for sound managerial thinking about media in other countries and illustrates important media applications overseas. These chapters also emphasize new and future technologies as they relate to marketing and advertising, including satellite communication, the vertical blanking interval potential, two-way communication, and the disappearance of distinctions between print and broadcasting.

The last four chapters emphasize management of the media function. Chapter 13 discusses media selection and allocation methods that are increasingly necessary for the successful media planner. Chapter 14 furnishes an example media platform, while Chapter 15 shows how to develop and measure the effectiveness of media schedules. Finally, Chapter 16 summarizes the future of the media, including employment opportunities.

A special word of thanks goes to Ernest Larkin, University of Oklahoma; Nancy Stephens, Arizona State University; Bob King, The Citadel; and Gil Churchill, University of Wisconsin—Madison. Throughout this revision, they furnished the benefit of their experience, insights, examples, and encouragement.

This revision could not have been completed without the secretarial expertise of Karol Griffin, Susan Gabriel, and Teresa Curry.

Finally, a word of thanks to our patient families whose understanding and encouragement were vital to the completion of the revised book. Our wives, Esther and Judy, and children, Celeste, Christopher, Kevin, Angelica, Kelly, and Kenneth, were especially unselfish and deserve special thanks.

A.F.M.
J.T.R.

ACKNOWLEDGMENTS

Throughout the writing of this revision, we have benefited from the help and advice of many advertising professionals and academicians. We wish to acknowledge the contribution of the people and firms who have been so helpful.

Joseph M. Alle, Account Executive, Foster and Kleiser

Claudia Allen, Vice President/Sales, Gannett Outdoor of Colorado

Edward I. Barz, Senior Vice President, Simmons Market Research Bureau

Charles O. Bennett, Vice President-Communications, Audit Bureau of Circulations

Carlos Boettger, Advertising Director, *The Rocky Mountain News*

Joan E. Bolen, The Advertising Council, Inc.

Shelly Cagner, Arbitron Ratings Company

Joel J. Cooper, Account Executive, Zeller & Letica, Inc.

Virginia A. Daly, Editor, Adweek's Marketers Guide to Media

Chris Dickens, Deputy Chairman, Media and Business Affairs, European HQ, Young & Rubicam International

Sheryl Fradkin, Director of Marketing and Operations, Colorado Homes and Lifestyles

Robert C. Gardner, President, *Marketing & Media Decisions*

Kathryn Kucharski Grubb, Managing Editor, *Journal of Advertising Research*

Lynn Halbardier, Manager, External Communications, Specialty Advertising Association, Inc.

Rebecca H. Holman, Vice President and Director of Consumer Studies, Young and Rubicam, Inc.

Barbara W. Hruska, Direct Marketing Educational Foundation, Inc.

Frank E. Keller, National Sales Manager, Outdoor Division, Donrey Outdoor Advertising Company

Otis Kirchhoefer, Editorial Director, Standard Rate and Data Service, Inc.

Terri Luke, Promotion Manager, A.C. Nielsen, Inc.

Kenneth J. Markey, Assistant Brand Manager, Adolph Coors Company

Richard R. Marlowe, Naegele Outdoor Advertising, Inc.

Daphne Mosher, Time, Inc.

Melissa S. Newman, Media Director, Levy & Asch

Barb Pittman, Associate Media Director, Tracy-Locke, Denver

Walter E. Reichel, Executive Vice President, Director, Media and Program Department, Ted Bates Worldwide

Maureen Sweeney, Time, Inc.

Leonard S. Spinoso, Vice President–Finance, Newspaper Advertising Bureau, Inc.

James P. Thavis, Executive Vice President, U.S. Suburban Press, Inc.

Patricia Vance, Director, Corporate Relations, Broadcasting Publications, Inc.

Alice Vantrease, Creative Marketing Services

William N. Wilkins, President, Institute of Outdoor Advertising

CONTENTS

Evaluation. Step 5: The Media Schedule. The Finances of Media Buying: *The Advertising Agency. Agency of Record. The Independent Media Buyer. The Media Representative.* Summary.

Television Industry Overview. Television as an Advertising Medium: *Television Dayparts. National and Local Television Advertising. Types of Sponsorship. Syndication.* Factors to Consider in Buying Television: *Inflation. Clutter. The Fragmented Audience.* The New Technology: *Cable Television. Other Forms of New Television Technology.* Buying Television: *Prime-time Network Buys. National Spot Buys. Local Buys. Television Rate Structure. Television Discounts and Special Features.* Television Ratings: *Nielsen Television Index (NTI). Nielsen Station Index (NSI). Other Television Research.* The Outlook.

General Characteristics of Radio: *AM Radio. FM Radio.* Formats. Networks: *Wired Networks. Structure of Wired Networks. Major Problems of Network Radio. Nonwired Networks.* Radio as an Advertising Medium: *Strengths. Weaknesses.* Rate Structure in Local Radio: *Format. Coverage Area Ratings. Daypart. Commercial Time.* Sources of Rates and Audience Data: *Spot Radio Standard Rate and Data Service. Estimator Books. Syndicated Audience Services. Intermedia Approaches to Buying Radio.* The Outlook: *Implications of Radio Deregulation. Research.*

General Characteristics of Newspapers. Newspapers as an Advertising Medium: *Categories of Newspaper Advertising. Major Advertising Considerations for Newspapers.* Newspaper Rate Structure: *National Rates versus Local Rates. Units of Purchase. Open Rate versus Flat Rate. Short Rate versus Rebate. Run-of-Paper and Special Rates. Combination Rates.* Auditing the Newspaper Audience. The Outlook: *Move to the Suburbs. Local Market Research. The Newspaper as a Delivery System. The Shopper. The Youth Market. Economic Forces. The Electronic Newspaper.*

Consumer Magazines: *Cost and Revenue Patterns. Selectivity.* The Numbers Game. Why Advertisers Buy Magazines: *Strengths. Weaknesses. Buying by the Numbers.* Sources of Magazine Circulation Data: *Independent Auditing Companies.* Rate Cards. Syndicated Research Services. *The Syndicated Magazine Services. The Gold Standard.* How Advertisers Buy Magazines: *Where? What Format? How Much? Common Magazine Discounts.* The Magazine Network. Scheduling Magazine Advertising. The Guaranteed Circulation. The Future of the Consumer Magazine. Business Magazines: *Marketing Strategy for Business Publications. Competition from Other Media. Circulation.* Farm Magazines:

Forecast of Changes in Agriculture. Marketing Strategy for the Farm Press. Structure of the Farm Press. Appendix.

Marketing Considerations. Creative Considerations. The Media Platform. The
Media Platform: *Section I, Overall Objectives. Section II, Media Strategy. Section III, Media Tactics. Section IV, The Media Schedule. Section V, Summary.*
Media Plan—National Client: 1. Media Objectives. 2. Media Strategy: *Target
Audience. Data Source. Coors Comparison to Premium Category Competition.
Geography. Market Analysis Allocation. Spending Methodology Allocation. Response Function.* 3. Media Rationale: *Media Mix. Television Dayparts. Optimum 4-Week Effective Weight for Branded Advertising. Maximum 4-Week
Effective Weight for Branded Advertising.* 4. Media Plan: *Scheduling Guidelines. Quarterly Scheduling Priorities. Quarterly Scheduling. Timing Seasonality. Category Seasonality.* Media Plan—Regional Client: Media Objective.
Media Rationale. Media Plan—Local Client: Media Objective. Media Rationale.

Supervising the Actual Media Purchase. Guidelines for Successful Negotiation.
Intermedia Equivalencies. Monitoring the Advertising Campaign: *Verification
of Broadcast Advertising. Verification of Print Advertising. Makegoods, Rebates, and Rip-Offs.* Adjusting the Schedule during the Campaign: *Changes in
the Competitive Environment. Changes in the Editorial Environment. Changes
in the Client Organization.* Evaluating the Efficiency of the Media Plan: *Definition of Efficiency? Communicative Efficiency of the Media Plan. Sales Efficiency
of the Media Plan. Beyond Sales Response. Sales Efficiency of the Media Plan.
Beyond Sales Response.* Appendix: Examples of Firms Providing Advertising
Media Research: Broadcast: *A. C. Nielsen Company. Arbitron Ratings Company. Birch Radio.* Print: *Simmons Market Research Bureau, Inc. Mediamark
Research Inc. Mendelsohn Media Research, Inc.*

The Marketing Revolution: *External Marketing Constraints on the Media Planner. Internal Marketing Constraints on the Media Function. Factors Largely
Controlled by the Media Planner.* The Management Revolution: *Media Planning and the Management Function. The Media Function as Managed by
Executives Outside the Advertising Department. The Media Function and the
Corporate Advertising Department. The In-House Agency.* Technology and
Managing the Media Function: *Advertising and the Changing Media Environment.* Technology and the Media-Planning Environment. Educational Training for Media Planning. Education for a Career in Advertising. Employment
Opportunities. The Future.

CHAPTER ONE

Advertising Media and the Marketing Process

What's important today is the value per consumer reached.*

William E. Phillips,
Chairman and CEO, Ogilvy and Mather

A student who knows what gross rating points are,
what a double truck bleed page is or what a scatter plan is,
along with a liberal arts background, may be more cost
effective in an entry level position.†

Howard Bell,
President AAF

THE MANAGEMENT PROCESS AND ADVERTISING MEDIA

This text discusses advertising media from a managerial perspective. Management has been defined as the process by which the objectives of an organization are achieved. This process includes the functions of planning, organizing, staffing, directing, and controlling.

We emphasize the management functions as they are applied to advertising media:

Planning is the process for determining what is to be achieved. Our discussion of planning will focus on the determination of advertising media objectives.

Organizing includes both allocating resources and setting up procedures for accomplishing objectives. Here, allocating funds to the

---

* *Marketing and Media Decisions,* University of Illinois, June 1985, p. 60.

† James Webb Young address, University of Illinois, November 1985.

advertising budget and distributing these funds among the available media are paramount. The organizing function depends on a thorough understanding of each advertising medium.

Staffing advertising media tasks is discussed from the standpoint of work assignments and from the perspective of the human skills most relevant to success in those tasks.

Directing is the process of putting a plan into action. Media plans are implemented by the purchase of advertising space and time.

Control is the collective name for the processes used to ensure that the advertiser's objectives are realized and costs are held within the allocated budget.

Students often visualize advertising as a set of activities unrelated to the other functions of business. Such a separation is unfortunate and artificial. Almost all advertising takes place within an organization, either a business or a nonprofit enterprise. To highlight this real-world connection between advertising media and other organizational activities, we will introduce you to the many ways in which functional business disciplines such as accounting, finance, and marketing play out their assigned roles in the management of advertising. Because of the strong tie between marketing and advertising media, Chapter 1 focuses on this relationship.

This text assumes that you have had an introduction to advertising course at a principles level. Chapter 1, then, reviews key concepts in advertising management that assist in the general tasks assigned to marketing management. To oversimplify, such tasks are attempts to stimulate demand. In addition, Chapter 1 suggests ways in which other business disciplines give the advertising campaign, and the media employed in that campaign, direction, boundaries, and integration with the other decisions made by the advertiser's organization.

THE MARKETING CONCEPT

In 1985, the Board of Directors of the American Marketing Association approved a revised definition of marketing. They said:

> Marketing is the process of planning and executing the conception, pricing, promotion and distribution of ideas, goods and services, to create exchanges that satisfy individual and organizational objectives.[1]

This new definition is quite compatible with socially responsible organizational behavior. Philip Kotler calls such an orientation the "societal marketing concept" and defines it as:

---

[1] *Marketing News,* March 1, 1985.

the organization's task [which] is to determine the needs, wants and interests of target markets and to deliver the desired satisfactions more effectively and efficiently than competitors in a way that preserves or enhances the consumer's and society's well-being.[2]

You can see that this widely accepted definition of socially responsible marketing contains three elements: customer satisfaction, organizational satisfaction, and long-range social responsibility. A fourth factor, integration of effort, is the method by which an efficient organization combines these three elements in its everyday activities.

Consumer Orientation

Although businesses look at their activities in a number of ways, all of these approaches can be classified into two categories: those that emphasize business needs and those that emphasize customer needs. The marketing concept was revolutionary in that it focused on customer needs and customer satisfaction. Before business accepted the marketing concept, typical firms emphasized the satisfaction of business needs. Thus, profits, sales, production efficiencies, and other criteria dominated. Under the marketing concept, these criteria remain important, but they are secondary to the establishment of customer satisfaction.

In the management of the advertising media function, consumer preferences for media represent the single, most important "given." It is highly unlikely that advertising decisions and advertising itself will, in the short run, change consumer preferences for a particular newspaper, magazine, or television show. Rather, the advertising community accepts consumer preferences for media as they exist, assuming that those preferences can be discovered. Then, the advertising decision maker attempts to purchase media in a way that is consistent both with client needs and with consumer reading, listening, viewing, and traveling patterns.

Satisfaction of Organizational Objectives

The marketing concept insists on the satisfaction of organizational objectives. Students (and others) often give enthusiastic recognition to the real benefits that result from a focus on consumer satisfaction. Unfortunately, this enthusiasm does not spill over to the other major elements of the marketing concept. Decision makers who fail to recognize the importance of organizational objectives become vulnerable to organizational disappointments—even failure and disappearance. Thus a company may define itself as being in the business of satisfying consumer beverage

---

2 Philip Kotler, *Marketing Management: Analysis, Planning, and Control,* 5th ed. (Englewood Cliffs, N.J.: Prentice-Hall, 1984), p. 29.

preferences. However, if it doesn't satisfy the need for organizational profit, then it won't be in the business of selling beverages very long. The logic of a business enterprise is to earn a profit. Profit permits the enterprise to remain in business and to accomplish the objectives for which it was established. Not-for-profit enterprises substitute some other objective for the profit motive (for example, the election of a political candidate or the solution to some social problem such as roadside litter).

Regardless of the nature of the organization, organizational needs must be met or the group forfeits its reason for existence. If a corporation cannot earn profits or if a nonprofit organization cannot accomplish its objectives, there is no reason for the enterprise to continue.

Again the media function must be brought into consonance with the need for satisfying organizational objectives. In the nonprofit enterprise, promotional activities must be performed and media for these activities managed in a way which optimizes the satisfaction of the organization's objectives. This is not to say that only traditional media can be purchased in some particular product or service class. In some Third-World countries, for example, pharmaceuticals are advertised by voice from loudspeaker trucks since a large proportion of the population can't read. Media management in for-profit corporations must be an efficient component of advertising activities. In addition to reflecting consumer preferences for media and being thoroughly integrated with the other aspects of the marketing effort, media management must contribute to corporate profitability and to organizational success.

Integration of Effort

Of course, the management of advertising media does not occur in a vacuum. For that matter, the management of advertising is itself highly interrelated with other marketing and business activities. Sound management theory requires that the marketing activities of an organization be thoroughly integrated. But it also requires that the decisions in other areas be consonant with customer satisfaction. Virtually all a firm's decisions have implications for the marketing function and for customer satisfaction. For example, a decision to reduce the cost of a quality control program may raise the cost of the warranty service and lower the level of customer satisfaction. Also, decisions about customer credit extensions, new product development, channels of distribution, and especially advertising can materially alter levels of customer satisfaction. Throughout all areas of business, marketing must be integrated with other activities such as finance, production, personnel, and accounting. And decisions made in these areas must be integrated with the marketing concept.

Just as marketing needs to be interrelated with other business areas, the components of marketing need to be integrated within this discipline.

Almost every introductory marketing textbook examines the four major areas of marketing: product, price, physical distribution, and promotion. Within promotion, most include not only personal selling but also the impersonal kinds of demand-stimulating activities generally thought of as advertising. Integration of effort requires that advertising activities be consistent with other marketing activities.

Within advertising, the media function itself must be integrated to be effective. Media buyers must recognize not only the media consumption decisions consumers make, but also the need to integrate these consumption preferences with all the other marketing aspects of the client's product. For example, a specialty good that is produced in small quantities, carries a high retail price, and is distributed through exclusive distribution channels (e.g., a Rolls-Royce) requires highly selective advertising media support. Such media support is different from that needed for general consumer products, such as groceries, commodities, and other shopping- and convenience-type products.

Long-Range Social Responsibility

Advertising activities are one important way corporations and other organizations attempt to satisfy their long-range social responsibility. Some major advertisers, such as Sears, withdraw their advertising support from television programs they consider in poor taste or socially irresponsible. Many other corporations, including Exxon, Mobil, Xerox, and IBM, choose particular advertising media to practice what they regard as corporate social responsibility. For example, they sponsor cultural events, entertainment, and TV programming.

The advertising industry itself has been in the forefront of efforts to solve social problems with advertising (see Figures 1–1 and 1–2). Advertising industry associations have been pioneers in attempts to resolve problems of discrimination, pollution, and disease.

Managing the media function is also an opportunity for public service. Just as in product advertising where media cost efficiencies must be matched with consumer media consumption patterns, so too in public interest advertising, consumer markets and consumer patterns must be matched with organizational objectives in a cost-efficient manner.

THE MARKETING CONCEPT AND EXTERNAL FORCES

If management could operate in a vacuum, the marketing concept would be relatively easy to apply. In the real world, however, such a vacuum does not exist and forces beyond the organization's control make practicing the marketing concept more difficult (see Figure 1–3). A discussion of

FIGURE 1-1

No matter what blood type you are, if you're a donor,
you're the type this world can't live without. Please give.

American Red Cross

Reprinted with permission of The Advertising Council, Inc.

FIGURE 1-2

TO THE AVERAGE AFRICAN FAMILY, THIS IS A FEAST.

A feast an African family must live on for days. All because of the most severe drought in history. Which has triggered an extreme African famine.

Last year alone, over one half million Africans died of starvation. And this year, a half million more will do the same. This cycle will continue until we do something to bring it to a halt. And we can.

The next time you pay for a meal, think for a moment. And help pick up the tab for those who really need it. Please give what you can to the Red Cross African Famine Relief Campaign.

I'M PICKING UP THE TAB.

Enclosed is:
○ $4 to feed a child for one month
○ $24 to feed a family for one month
○ $96 to feed a village for one month

✚ American Red Cross

NAME _____

ADDRESS _____

PHONE _____

Send to: The American Red Cross
African Famine Relief Campaign
National Headquarters, Washington, D.C. 20006

A Public Service of This Publication

FIGURE 1–3 How External Forces Interact with the Marketing Concept

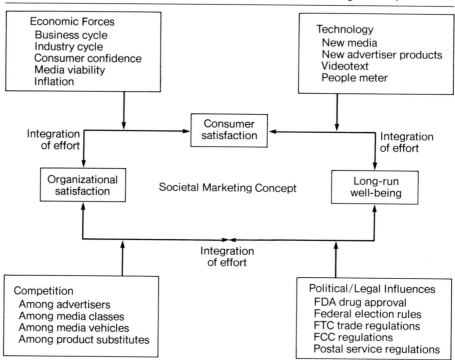

some of the more important external forces and their influence on marketing management follows.

Economic and Technological Forces

During economic boom periods, even poorly managed companies have a good prospect of making some profit. General levels of economic activity are high, and sellers enjoy economic benefits in the marketplace. From the individual consumer's standpoint, jobs are plentiful, wages are good, and economic well-being characterizes the majority. Advertising (at least in the United States) tends to flourish during boom times. But macroeconomic activity levels vary, and this implies that economic downturns regularly follow periods of economic expansion. During these downturns (depressions are the most serious type—economic recessions are a more frequent and less devastating type), only carefully managed enterprises survive.

In periods of economic contraction, advertising budgets also tend to contract. Dunkle and Kwan, in a 40-year study, showed that advertising and gross national product are highly and positively correlated.[3] Thus, in periods of economic downturn, advertising expenditures in general and the activities associated with media purchasing tend to fall off.

In addition to the general economic influences of expansion or recession, two specific forces—inflation and technology—have a significant impact on advertising decisions.

Inflation works its pernicious influence in many ways. During periods of continued secular price inflation, consumer confidence and purchase levels erode. The ability of companies to satisfy consumer expectations is impaired because increases in costs often require retail price increases. And when companies purchase media advertising, inflation in media space and time prices imposes a damper on how efficiently the advertising function can be executed.

Product innovation (particularly the development of new products based on a new technology) has a positive effect on the general level of economic activity. New products not only satisfy consumer needs in ways previously unavailable, but to some extent, they also satisfy the human desire for variety.

In addition, recently developed technology offers some dramatic prospects for improving advertising efficiency. While a full discussion of this technology will be reserved for later chapters, we should point out that new methods of designing, producing, and distributing messages may revolutionize the ways consumers acquire information. For example, the traditional distinctions between print and broadcast media may disappear in the next decade. Consumers may be able to view on television information now carried in newspapers, and subsequently print any portion of this "electronic newspaper" they wish to retain for future reference. This sort of technological innovation not only would revolutionize production and channels of distribution but would also require major changes in how newspaper advertising efficiencies are computed.

Competitive Pressures

One of the most abiding characteristics of marketplace activity is the presence of competition. Companies conduct their marketing activities in a competitive setting. Consumers can substitute one product for another; they can spend their leisure time reading any of a wide variety of magazines, viewing any of a broad assortment of television programs, or engaging in many other activities. Except for the regulated monopolies, competition seems to be everywhere. When competitive pressures diminish in our society, governmental agencies, acting in the public interest,

---

[3] As reported in F. M. Nicosia, *Advertising, Management, and Society* (New York: McGraw-Hill, 1974), p. 186.

take steps to heighten competition. In this way, they seek to improve both industrial efficiency and consumer welfare.

From the standard of managing media activities, competition among media is highly important. In one sense the manager of advertising media activities functions as a "consumer" of advertising space and time. This person (even though acting on behalf of an advertising client) attempts to purchase certain advertising coverage at minimum cost. In this endeavor, competition among enterprises in a single medium, for example among several radio stations, can improve the efficiency of the media purchase. Similarly, competition between major media classes, for example between magazines and television, can also be the basis for improved efficiency in the media function.

Political and Legal Influences

Virtually all business activity takes place within a framework of politics and law. The activities we think of as marketing are quite extensively constrained by our system of law. In particular, the Uniform Commercial Code and the federal antitrust statutes carefully specify permissible marketing activities.

Advertising is an especially regulated activity within marketing. Standards of truthfulness and candor are carefully spelled out by both federal and state law. In addition to making literally truthful statements, advertisers must use great care to avoid claims that tend to deceive audiences, even when these claims are literally or technically true. Further, advertisers are prohibited from making claims that have not been substantiated.

Since the lawmaking process in this society takes place within the political arena, advertisers must be energetic in pointing out the advantages that advertising creates for consumers. One good example is the possibility that advertising reduces retail prices.[4] Another is that advertising, according to George Stigler, is an "immensely powerful instrument for the elimination of ignorance."[5] And, of course, one of the most fascinating areas of marketing in the nonprofit sector is the advertising associated with political campaigns themselves. At present, political advertising is less regulated and has more lenient standards for "claim substantiation" than most other types of advertising. We are tempted to think that the advertising media function is separated from questions of politics and law. However, this is not the case. In corrective advertising,

---

[4] Robert L. Steiner, "Marketing Productivity in Consumer Goods Industries—A Vertical Perspective," *Journal of Marketing* 42, no. 1 (January 1978), pp. 60–70.

[5] George J. Stigler, "The Economics of Information," *Journal of Political Economy* 69, no. 3 (1961), pp. 213–25 at p. 220.

regulators, such as those at the Federal Trade Commission, have gone so far as to specify the particular media that must carry a corrective message. And, for better or worse, certain media are barred from carrying advertising for certain types of products. For example, it is no longer legal to advertise cigarettes on television. In addition, self-regulation by advertisers prevents the advertising of distilled spirits on television. Publishers, of course, have long exercised their rights under the First Amendment to reject advertisements of certain companies and advertisements for certain products.

We can see that these constraints complicate the already complex process of choosing advertising media efficiently. Nevertheless, those of us who are responsible for the advertising media function must be sensitive to the legal and political ramifications of our activities.

INTEGRATED ESTIMATION OF DEMAND

It has been said that the function of advertising is to shift demand schedules upward and to the right. This is a technical way of saying that the function of advertising is to stimulate demand (see Figure 1–4). By

FIGURE 1–4 Stimulation of Demand by Promotion

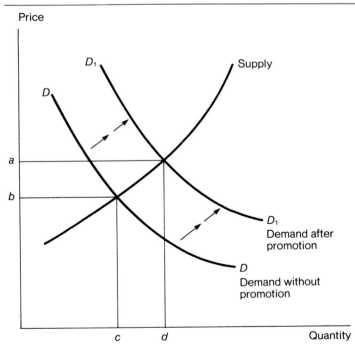

and large, the claim is accurate. The economic result is that advertising increases prices, quantities sold, or both. However, in important instances advertising is designed to destimulate, or decrease, demand for some product or service. An example of such demarketing is advertising that encourages people to stop smoking. Nonetheless, whether used for traditional marketing purposes or for the somewhat newer demarketing objectives, advertising's role is primarily one of influencing demand for products and services.

If advertising's role in altering demand is to be successful, decision makers must understand that demand is the product of the many forces we have just outlined. In very simple terms, the demand for some product or service is a function of consumers and their wants or needs; advertisers and their wants or needs; the competitive environment; and the more general economic, political, and legal milieu. In this textbook we focus not on altering political or legal processes directly or, for that matter, on altering consumer wants or needs in fundamental ways. At least in the short run, we accept the premise that such changes are beyond the direct control of the advertiser. Our focus is directed toward carefully measuring these forces and combining these aspects of demand with efficient production of advertising messages. Inherent in advertising efficiency is the notion of efficiently selected and used advertising media.

Advertising and Product Demand

The ultimate goal of most advertising is to stimulate demand for a particular brand. In formulating an advertising campaign, however, it is important for advertisers to fully understand the types of demand they are dealing with. This section deals with the various types of demand and the campaigns that might be used to stimulate them.

Generic Demand.   Before brand promotion can be effective, there must be some generic demand from consumers. An advertising campaign for Chevrolet must consider both the demand for Chevrolets and the demand for cars in general. Any brand advertising has elements of generic promotion. However, in some circumstances (for example, if a single firm dominates the market), the goal of the advertiser's campaign is to sell the product in general rather than his brand only.

Assume that brand Y has an 85 percent share of the market; brand X, 5 percent; brand Z, 5 percent; and the remaining 5 percent is spread among several smaller firms. Firm Y can compete on a brand basis and attempt to gain a small share of market from each of these other firms (and risk antitrust problems). Or it can promote the product to nonusers or light users, recognizing that it can expect approximately its same 85 percent share of any new sales.

A declining industry sales trend may also indicate the need for a generic campaign. If sales are declining for all brands, cooperative efforts are sometimes used to stimulate generic demand. In other cases, the largest seller in an industry unilaterally engages in generic advertising (e.g., the Campbell's campaign featuring the "Soup is Good Food" theme). This approach recognizes that brand competition is pointless if the generic demand is soft. Of course, generic campaigns are also used in industries whose sales are not declining. Both the Florida and California Fruit Growers (Sunkist) cooperatives use generic themes in addition to promoting their individual brands.

Brand Demand. Most consumer advertising is directed toward increasing the demand (sales) for a particular brand. Many critics charge that advertising creates temporary changes in brand preferences without causing permanent growth in the market. In fact, advertising does both. In certain industries, particularly those where usage is almost universal, brand switching is a dominant objective of advertising. On the other hand, most industries show growth in some brands and an increase in sales for all brands. At least a portion of this generic growth is normally attributed to brand advertising.

Direct and Indirect Demand. Most consumer products are used and promoted for the utility they provide consumers. The advertising function is very different for products whose demand depends on the utility they offer other products. Industrial goods usually fall into the indirect demand category. For instance, textile sales depend on consumer demand for finished apparel; consequently, Du Pont does a great deal of consumer advertising for its synthetic fabrics although it does not manufacture wearing apparel.

The demand for a product with an indirect demand usually demonstrates a positive correlation with the demand for the end product with which it is associated. However, sometimes the opposite is true. For instance, manufacturers of automotive parts (excluding those selling to new-car makers) find that as the demand for new cars decreases, the demand for replacement parts increases.

Advertising Elasticity of Demand. Like other marketing decisions (most notably, decisions regarding price), advertising may be addressed to audiences whose demand is elastic or inelastic. When demand elasticity is expressed and measured as a function of advertising, we speak of advertising elasticity. In symbolic form, the coefficient of advertising elasticity, E_a, can be calculated using the equation

$$E_a = \left| \frac{Q_1 - Q_0}{Q_1 + Q_0} \div \frac{A_1 - A_0}{A_1 + A_0} \right|$$

where

Q_0 = Sales before the advertising change
Q_1 = Sales after the advertising change
A_0 = Advertising before the change
A_1 = Advertising after the change

when

$E_a > 1$, demand is advertising-elastic
$E_a < 1$, demand is advertising-inelastic
$E_a = 1$, demand is of "unit-elasticity"; in this condition, total sales revenue is a maximum

To review, then, recall that advertising is practiced within the general confines of the marketing concept and the orientation that the marketing concept implies. Also, recognize that the marketing concept operates within an external environment. Although marketing attempts to alter demand, demand is a function of forces beyond the direct control of the marketing manager. We now turn to the relationship between the marketing concept and the marketing plan.

Example: Calculation of Advertising Elasticity

As the promotions manager for Etherial, a recording studio, you are responsible for estimating advertising elasticity of demand for a new album cut by one of the firm's artist groups, the Stone Hogs. This new album, titled "Pigs in a Blanket," is tested in two markets. As far as you can determine, except for advertising expenditures, all factors that influence album sales (demography, air play, etc.) are identical in both markets. In Market A, advertising is set at $50,000; in Market B, advertising is $75,000 for the test market period. Album sales in A are $130,000 and in B, $170,000 for the test. What is the apparent advertising elasticity of demand?

$$E_a = \frac{\$170,000 - \$130,000}{\$170,000 + \$130,000} \div \frac{\$75,000 - \$50,000}{\$75,000 + \$50,000}$$

$$= \frac{\$40,000}{\$300,000} \div \frac{\$25,000}{\$125,000}$$

$$= .133 \div .200$$

$$= \underline{\underline{.665}}$$

Therefore, demand is advertising-inelastic. Changes in sales revenue are proportionally less than changes in advertising expenditures.

THE MARKETING CONCEPT AND THE MARKETING PLAN

In simplest form, the marketing plan is the statement of how the market-ing manager intends to implement the marketing concept. To be more precise, it is the plan by which the marketing manager attempts to coordinate issues of Product or service, Price, Place (the physical distribu-tion system for bringing the product or service to the market place), and Promotion efforts. These are called the "4 Ps" of marketing. Marketing plans, then, are relatively detailed statements about how the manager will attempt to integrate efforts to satisfy customers and meet organiza-tional objectives.

Product Management

The management of products has long been a focus of organizational activity. Brand managers have attempted to bring products with certain characteristics to the marketplace—"good" or "satisfactory" products, "inexpensive" products, or "durable" products. And such product charac-teristics have long been part of the marketing manager's emphasis. Product management has also been an area in which the marketing concept has been imperfectly applied. From the consumer's viewpoint, a product is an expected bundle of benefits, and managerial emphasis on a product's technical aspects may fail to supply the benefits.

As consumers, we make purchases in the marketplace because we expect these purchases to help us solve problems. Therefore the brand or product manager should probably abandon some of the earlier ways of looking at products and services. Products have been traditionally cate-gorized as either commodities or differentiated goods. Here theory sug-gested that differentiated goods (usually branded goods) were amenable to advertising's support, whereas commodities were not. Yet recent busi-ness history tells us that commodities can sometimes be successfully advertised. Chickens of a particular producer, wines from a particular country, coffee beans from a particular region, and even so ordinary a product as table salt have responded well to advertising (see Figure 1–5).

The notion of a product life cycle also suggests different ways in which advertising can accomplish its assigned tasks. For example, in introducing new products to the marketplace, sellers frequently find that initial advertising expense (per unit of goods sold) is very high. In this case, simpleminded cost/benefit analyses of advertising will indicate that sellers are spending too much on advertising. However, a competent marketing manager recognizes that initial investments in promoting new products pay handsome returns if and when the products reach the growth stage. Then, during product maturity, advertising has a powerful

FIGURE 1–5 Branding a Commodity

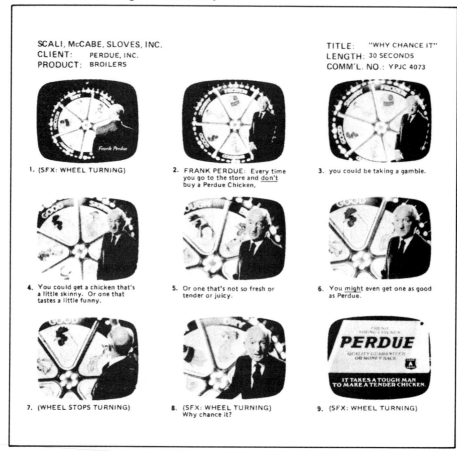

A well-known face in the Northeast Corridor, Frank Perdue talks chicken.

SOURCE: "The Wishbone Offense: Branding a Commodity," *Marketing and Media Decisions*, May 1985, p. 84.

and sustaining role in product sales and competitive success. Finally, advertising can be efficiently employed even in the final stages of the product life cycle. At these stages, advertising can be used to clear inventory of outdated or discontinued merchandise, thus materially increasing the profitability of such products.

Price Strategy

The price of a good is itself exceptionally important information to both sellers and consumers. For most branded products, prices are set by managers in one of three ways: in relation to competition, in relation to costs, or in relation to demand. While a full discussion of price theory is beyond the scope of this book, advertising campaigns ought to be cognizant of the pricing mechanism the product manager used. Often an understanding of the price-setting mechanism permits the construction of effective advertising copy and illustrations. For example, advertising copy for J.C. Penney's blue jeans and other sports clothing makes direct use of the company's competition-oriented pricing mechanism. In addition, account executives should recognize that the pricing structure used may play a material role in setting advertising budgets based on the product's impact on profits. Budget size directly influences media purchases.

Physical Distribution Systems

Like pricing, the physical distribution of goods and services is an important aspect of marketing and a topic that this book cannot treat fully. However, advertisers and other decision makers should recognize that a product's ultimate success can depend on carefully managed physical distribution systems and the channels of distribution used to bring goods to the marketplace. Students (and some real-world executives) often think that the overwhelming bulk of advertising must be directed to audiences of prospective consumers. Such an emphasis creates the serious risk of neglecting members of a channel of distribution, who are themselves intermediate markets for goods and services. This can be a serious mistake. Many relatively ordinary products in the packaged goods industries are highly successful because they are supported by advertising directed to the channel of distribution. Failures in the absence of such advertising support are, unfortunately, also numerous.

Promotional Plans

Organizations' promotional plans are often divided into two major types: the sales force plan and the advertising campaign. A small minority of organizations use only one or the other. That is, some organizations rely exclusively on a personal selling force, and others concentrate their entire promotional effort on advertising. Most commonly, however, advertising and personal selling enhance each other's effectiveness. Therefore, sales force managers need to have some knowledge of the advertising campaign at an early stage in its development in order to develop and coordinate effective sales presentations. On the other hand, information gleaned by a field sales force can be an invaluable contribution to the advertising strategy, including the development of effective ad copy. A canny sales force can provide advertisers (and those responsible for producing advertising media schedules) with current, accurate information about the media consumption habits of sales prospects. To do this, the salesperson simply reports prospects' comments about broadcast media programs, their sources of product information, and the journals they subscribe to. Advertising constructed with the benefit of information like this can help salespeople avoid truly "cold" calls. In addition, such advertising helps the salesperson handle prospects' objections and thereby contributes to the overall effectiveness of the sales force. Figure 1–6 is a recent version of a classic statement about the relationship between advertising and sales force effectiveness.

ADVERTISING CAMPAIGNS AND ADVERTISING MEDIA

Advertising campaigns have four important elements: the allocation, the copy plan, the media plan, and the plan for evaluating their effectiveness. The allocation is the statement of the overall funds available for the advertising effort. Recall that there are several major ways in which real-world advertisers solve the problem of determining how much money to devote to advertising. These methods include the percentage of sales, the percentage of forecast sales, or competitive equivalencies, the "all-you-can-afford" method, the so-called objective and task methods, and several other more difficult but more theoretically correct marginal and mathematical modes.

Research confirms what some have suspected all along—namely, that even large corporations set advertising budgets in a slapdash fashion. One study of a group of the largest U.S. advertisers found that almost half never used either computer models or quantitative models for their ad budgeting activities.[6]

While budget allocation is neither the primary focus of this text nor the primary responsibility of those who plan for and coordinate media buys, it should be noted that most companies underutilize their information and analytical talents when it comes to setting an ad budget figure. As a result, their budgeting practices are frequently suboptimal. Many organizations would benefit greatly by using mathematical approaches to setting the ad allocation. People with quantitative training (and in advertising jobs they tend to be people who have worked in the media function) have an obligation to point out to senior decision makers (for example, brand managers, marketing executives, chief executive officers, and members of boards of directors) that optimal advertising effort depends on correctly allocating funds to the advertising function. Thus, while this function is not a direct part of their day-to-day jobs, quantitatively competent media people have opportunities to improve the

---

[6] A. J. San Augustine and W. F. Foley, "How Large Advertisers Set Budgets," *Journal of Advertising Research* 15, no. 5 (October 1975), pp. 11–16.

FIGURE 1-6 How Advertising Prepares the Way for the Salesperson

"*I don't know who you are.*

I don't know your company.

I don't know your company's product.

I don't know what your company stands for.

I don't know your company's customers.

I don't know your company's record.

I don't know your company's reputation.

Now—what was it you wanted to sell me?"

MORAL: Sales start **before** your salesman calls—with **business** publication advertising.

McGRAW-HILL MAGAZINES
BUSINESS • PROFESSIONAL • TECHNICAL

efficiency with which organizations make investments in advertising (see Figure 1–7.) The budgeting process will be discussed in detail in Chapter 4.

Selecting Themes and Messages—The Copy Plan

The copy plan in an advertising campaign is really a schedule of what things need to be said, to which people, at what times, in what ways, through which media. The emphasis in a copy plan, though, is on designing effective messages—messages that will accomplish the advertising objectives set out in the marketing plan. To accomplish this task, "creative" people in advertising have traditionally borne the burden of developing, designing, and testing copy, illustrations, scripts, music, and other audio and visual aspects of advertisements. And copy messages that were

---

FIGURE 1–7   Does Effective Use of Media Really Matter?

In a study of 2,000 advertising agency executives and 3,000 executives in advertiser firms, Korgaonkar, Moschis, and Bellenger divided each sample into two groups: Those responding for "successful" advertising campaigns and those responding for "unsuccessful" campaigns. The answers to five questions about media importance are shown below.

| | Percentage of Respondents Who Agreed | | | |
| | For Successful Campaigns | | For Unsuccessful Campaigns | |
Statement	Agency Execs	Advertiser Execs	Agency Execs	Advertiser Execs
The characteristics of the media audience were congruent with the characteristics of the customers.	95.9%	94.6%	87.0%	69.5%
The product was advertised in the right media at the right time and place.	97.9	85.9	80.3	56.7
The product was advertised in the appropriate media.	99.5	98.4	87.7	82.9
The selection of media was based mainly on cost considerations (reverse scoring).	26.3	51.0	42.1	69.2
The selection of media was based on careful analysis of demand factors.	85.1	79.9	66.7	40.3

SOURCE: P. K. Korgaonkar, G. P. Moschis, and D. N. Bellenger, "Correlates of Successful Advertising Campaigns," *Journal of Advertising Research* 24, no. 1 (February/March 1984), pp. 47–53; and P. K. Korgaonkar and D. N. Bellenger, "Correlates of Successful Advertising Campaigns: The Manager's Perspective," *Journal of Advertising Research* 25, no. 4 (August/September 1985), pp. 34–39.

once based on whim are now subjected to research inputs and precampaign evaluation.

It is tempting to think that creative aspects of campaigns can be divorced from media functions. However, it is dangerous to succumb to this temptation. The creative aspect of virtually all advertising messages is necessarily influenced by the medium that carries the message. Thus, it is not traditional to use color illustrations in newspaper advertising. (Today, this tradition is changing as sophisticated newspaper publishers are able to offer one- and four-color illustrations.) Illustrations that are appropriate in certain up-scale consumer magazines are inappropriate in advertising to children. Radio, which relies exclusively on audible messages, plays a different role in a campaign's creative design than television, with its ability to present visual images. A well-designed and executed advertising campaign thoroughly integrates the so-called creative aspects (the copy plan) with the so-called quantitative aspects (the media plan). The copy plan frequently includes three types of objectives.

1. *Audience identification.* A major step in developing a copy strategy is to determine who you are trying to reach. Various means of identification can be used, including demographics, psychographics, and lifestyle studies. These are discussed in detail in Chapter 5.

2. *Copy Themes.* The product analysis previously discussed is used to determine how product benefits can be used in specific advertising themes. It is crucial that the advertising campaign be built around a central persuasive idea, giving continuity to various advertisements that will be used throughout the campaign. Often the theme becomes a slogan that continues from one campaign to another ("Volvo. A Car You Can Believe In"). At other times, the theme is a background idea that is promoted but not specifically stated.

3. *Specific Selling Ideas.* A final step in the copy objectives is to determine how specific advertisements will be handled. What types of illustrations will be used? To what degree will color be used? How will advertisements adapt the central theme in the various media? All of these questions must be addressed before the actual production of advertising is undertaken.

The Media Plan

The media plan is the major emphasis of the rest of this book. Managers engage in the major activities of planning, organizing, directing, controlling, and staffing, and management of the media function is no exception. In the media plan, carriers for advertising messages are selected, compared, priced, evaluated, and generally brought into conformity with the advertising goal. The objectives of media plans are often separated into three major parts:

1. *Target Audience(s)*. The media planner must first identify his audience. Normally audience identification in media planning lacks some of the flexibility open to the creative department. Audience identification for media purposes must conform to the information available about the media. Often this limits the media planner to demographic-oriented information.

2. *Media Characteristics*. The media planner must coordinate his effort with the creative objectives. Media must be selected not only on the basis of their cost efficiency in reaching the target market but also according to their ability to deliver the creative message. But compromise is a two-way street, and creative approaches often have to be adapted to particular media vehicles. A discussion of the individual media can be found in Chapters 6–12.

3. *Other Promotion*. Regardless of whether the advertising agency or department is directly involved in the production of collateral promotional material, various promotional and advertising elements must be closely coordinated.

   a. *Public Relations.* If the advertiser wants to conduct a formal public relations program, the program should convey the same basic message as the advertising. Although the format will be different and news values will be emphasized, the same marketing and/or advertising goals applicable to the advertising should apply in the public relations area.

   b. *Point-of-Purchase.* In-store point-of-purchase material is the last promotional opportunity for the product. It is also a means of instigating impulse buying. In either case, point-of-purchase material should tie in with media advertising so consumers will connect the two.

   c. *Collateral Material.* In many cases, collateral material such as brochures, specialty items, and calendars are prepared as part of the total promotional effort. These items should complement the overall sales effort by promoting the basic theme and objectives of more visible promotional endeavors.

Stating Campaign Objectives

Real-world advertising campaigns are often deficient in the statement of their goals or objectives. (The terms *goals* and *objectives* are used interchangeably here.) Those in advertising sometimes prefer imprecise objectives—maybe because they are apprehensive about their ability to achieve more precisely stated goals. Advertising goals can be stated at three levels: the communications level, the sales or marketplace level, and the owner or profit level.

Communications Level. At the communications level, the objectives of advertising campaigns can be stated in terms of brand awareness, brand recall, inclusion of the advertised brand in an evoked set of brands for the product class and certain other measures of favorable attitude toward the advertised good, or inclination or intentions to purchase it. In addition, advertising objectives at the communications level can include changes in these measures, although the statement of an objective as a change implies a "before-after campaign" measure of that variable.

Sales Level. At the sales or marketplace level, advertising objectives can be stated in absolute values, for example, sales of X million units or Y million dollars. They can also be expressed as desired changes in those values; for example, a sales increase of so many thousand dollars per month during the period of the campaign. Finally, they can be expressed in competitive terms such as brand share, market penetration, ranking among the competitors of an industry or a product class, or in the case of mature products, surviving the onslaughts of recently arrived product substitutes.

Stating advertising objectives in sales or marketplace terms is desirable from a theoretical standpoint. Advertising expenditures, which are supposed to stimulate demand, *ought* to stimulate demand, and this stimulation ought to be measurable. However, many in the advertising industry resist stating advertising objectives in these terms for two reasons. First, influences other than advertising affect sales levels, and this is a valid concern of advertisers. There are four marketing "Ps," not one. Thus a poorly designed product, a poorly distributed product, or an incorrectly priced product can fail in the marketplace even though the advertising campaign is superb. However, it is also (and unfortunately) true that some people in the advertising industry resist stating objectives in sales terms for a less defensible reason—they are generally unwilling to have clients evaluate whether they are doing what they say they would do. Thus, while an advertising account executive may tell a client that a successful ad campaign will do "wonders" for sales, that account executive may be reluctant to have the client evaluate whether the campaign has achieved those wonders.

Owner/Profit Level. At the owner level, advertising has consequences for company's profitability. Here the notion of profitability is used rather generally; it can be expanded to include the realization of objectives of not-for-profit groups. In the overwhelming number of cases, though, the acid test of business effectiveness is the generation of long-term profits for owners. Therefore, it is theoretically correct to describe profits as a function of business effectiveness. This effectiveness certainly includes, for most organizations, the effectiveness of advertising activities. While some have studied the link between advertising investments and profitability,[7] it is unrealistic to assume that effective advertising is always associated with high profits or, in the case of publicly held firms, with the price of common stock shares. The effectiveness of business functions other than advertising (such as production, finance, and other aspects of marketing) all play a role in determining organizational profitability or success. Thus, while there are indications that effective advertising is associated with high profitability, advertisers properly resist the notion that the advertising function should bear the entire burden for organizational success.

Russell Colley proposed another way of stating the goals of a particular advertising effort, and his method is widely used by advertisers. Called DAGMAR (for *D*efining *A*dvertising *G*oals for *M*easured *A*dvertising *R*esults), this method categorizes the communicative tasks of advertising into three groups: informative advertising, persuasive advertising, and reminder advertising. For each kind of task, specific audiences and results are stated. Although this method has been in use for a generation, it remains popular. It focuses attention on the necessity for precise objectives against which to measure the effect of advertising.

Budget Constraints

The advertising budget decision produces an upper limit on the funds that can be expended to purchase advertising media during an advertising campaign. Advertising allocation is one of the obvious constraints imposed on the media function in a campaign, but other budget constraints are also relevant to the management of the media function.

Client Considerations. First, the client (or other decision maker) may have specified communication objectives that call for devoting specific proportions of the total budget to several of the major media. Media planners should be prepared to provide information about alternative media choices when these are warranted, because a decision to accomplish certain types of communication objectives can imply the maximum which can be allocated to each of the utilized media. Also, mathematical

[7] F. K. Reilly, A. F. McGann, and R. A. Marquardt, "Advertising Decisions and Stockholders' Wealth," *Journal of Advertising Research* 17, no. 4 (August 1977), pp. 49–56.

models sometimes allow very efficient media to "run away" with the media selection process, counter to all reason or judgment.[8]

Properties of Media.   Second, because all media are not equally efficient, a given proportion of the total advertising budget may have to be spent in a particularly efficient medium. This too imposes constraints on the media function.

Making Use of Discounts.   Finally, budget constraints can be more flexible than they originally appear if the advertiser-advertising agency combination is financially able to take advantage of cash discounts and other incentives for prompt payment. The net effect of such incentives can be to increase the advertising budget allocation.

Suitability of Medium.   One of the most fascinating and demanding tasks faced by those responsible for the advertising media function is the matching of advertiser needs with media characteristics. In this task, they match the characteristics of particular media (e.g., television's ability to combine sight and sound) with the advertising to be carried. More important, they also match the audiences of the various media with the target segments the advertiser wishes to reach. The problem here is not lack of data. Rather, media planners face what at first seems to be a flood of information. However, after that information has been sifted and graded with regard to quality and applicability, the exact information they need often seems unavailable. Publishers and (to a lesser extent) broadcasters are quick to furnish those who buy media with the characteristics of their audiences. In particular, the print media furnish voluminous information about the demographics of their readers. In the marketplace, however, demographics are often only moderately correlated with the purchasing behavior an advertiser is interested in. For example, the most frequent purchasers of an over-the-counter pharmaceutical may be persons aged 55 and over. However, this correlation between a demographic variable such as age and the purchase of a particular product is only part of the story. Other factors having to do with demographics, as well as other attitudinal and financial data, can play a determining role in the decision to buy a particular pharmaceutical product. The methods by which media planners combine demographic and other information about audiences with the needs of the advertiser for precise market segments will be discussed in greater detail

---

[8] F. M. Bass and R. T. Lonsdale, "An Exploration of Linear Programming in Media Selection," *Journal of Marketing Research* 3 (May 1966), pp. 179–88.

later. However, we must say at this point that simpleminded attempts to match media characteristics, audience demographics, and advertiser objectives for market segmentation are virtually predestined to produce less than optimal media purchases.

COORDINATING MEDIA FOR BEST EFFECT

The next aspect of the media plan is intermedia coordination designed to produce an optimum total advertising effect. Synergism says that, because of the interaction of the parts, the whole is sometimes different from (either greater or less than) the sum of the parts. Nowhere is this truer than in advertising campaigns that use more than one medium. Synergistic effects are possible in multiple media for several reasons. First, the audiences for one medium may overlap those for another. For example, automobile passengers who pass an outdoor billboard might be members of the audience for a television show later that evening. Thus, simply counting the audiences for each medium may overstate the size of a particular audience.

Second, subsequent exposures to a particular advertising message don't have the same effect as the first exposure. Research literature suggests consumers may need three or more exposures to an ad before they can reliably recall salient information from it. Evidence also suggests that, beyond this threshold, additional exposures (particularly those coming from different sources) can produce a geometrically increasing effect on consumer awareness and intentions to purchase.

In recent years there has been greatly heightened interest in combining traditional media concerns with an overall marketing strategy. Advertising agencies such as BBDO, Ogilvy and Mather, Benton & Bowles, Campbell-Ewald, and others have designed new organizational structures and communications systems to more fully integrate the media function with the marketing plan. As one agency executive puts it:

> The transformation of the media discipline is sparking the emergence of a media person who can not only decipher minute cost advantages between late fringe and early morning television spots, but a trained thinker who can intuitively understand the difference between marketing shampoo to a glamour girl or to an intelligent, active woman who indulges in health and beauty needs.[9]

In summary, management of advertising media activities occurs within the framework of an organization's advertising and marketing

---

[9] Laurel Cutler, Vice President, Leber, Katz as quoted in Rebecca Fannin, "Toying with How to Wed Marketing with Media," *Marketing and Media Decisions*, June 1985, p. 60.

efforts. These, in turn, occur in a particular competitive, economic, and political setting. The marketing concept, which has contributed greatly to a new and profitable focus on the consumer, can also be used to enhance the efficiency of advertising and its major components: creative plan and media strategy.

REVIEW QUESTIONS

1. What are the five major management functions?
2. Describe the marketing concept.
3. Two specific economic forces, inflation and technology, have had a significant impact on advertising decisions. Give an example of the effect of each force on advertising decisions.
4. How is efficiency influenced by competition among media?
5. Give an example of advertising used to "demarket" a product.
6. State the difference between advertising to direct demand and to indirect demand.
7. What is a target audience?
8. In a particular year, the Yummy Yogurt Company spent $100,000 on advertising and enjoyed sales of $1 million that same year. The following year, the company increased its advertising budget by 10 percent, and sales increased by $104,000. Assuming that advertising effects did not carry over from year to year, what is the apparent elasticity of demand? (Hint: compute the elasticity of demand coefficient.)
9. How can competition among media enterprises (say, several radio stations) improve the efficiency of the media purchases that an ad agency makes?
10. Find a product or service in the "real world" where it appears that advertising reduced the retail price. Does this situation appear unusual or typical? Why?
11. Select and describe actual examples where each of the other three marketing Ps (price, place, product) have a direct influence on product promotion.

SUGGESTED ADDITIONAL READING

ALSOP, RONALD. "Watchdogs Zealously Censor Advertising Targeted to Kids." *The Wall Street Journal,* September 5, 1985.

BAIG, EDWARD C. "Trying to Make Beef Appetizing Again." *Fortune,* November 25, 1985, p. 64.

BELK, RUSSELL W., and RICHARD W. POLLAY. "Images of Ourselves: The Good Life in Twentieth Century Advertising." *Journal of Consumer Research* 11 (March 1985), pp. 887–97.

BERNSTEIN, S. R. "What Is Advertising? What Does It Do?" *Advertising Age,* November 21, 1973, pp. 8+.

"Brokers Go All out on Advertising." *Business Week,* September 21, 1981, p. 68.

CASILLO, ROBERT. "Dirty Gondola: The Image of Italy in American Advertisements." *Word & Image* 1, no. 4 (1985), pp. 330–50.

COEN, ROBERT J. "Ad Spending Fails to Equal Predictions." *Advertising Age,* May 12, 1986, p. 76+.

DAVENPORT, JOHN. "Stigler's Message." *Fortune,* March 4, 1985, pp. 73, 176.

FANNIN, REBECCA. "Toying with How to Wed Marketing with Media." *Marketing and Media Decisions,* June 1985, pp. 60–64.

FRIEDMAN, MONROE. "The Changing Language of a Consumer Society: Brand Name Usage in Popular American Novels in the Postwar Era." *Journal of Consumer Research* 11 (March 1985), pp. 927–38.

JERESKI, LAURA K. "The Wishbone Offense: Branding a Commodity." *Marketing and Media Decisions,* May 1985, pp. 80–84, 176.

KORGAONKAR, PRADEEP K., and DANNY N. BELLENGER. "Correlates of Successful Advertising Campaigns: The Manager's Perspective." *Journal of Advertising Research* 25, no. 4 (August/September 1985), pp. 34–39.

KORGAONKAR, PRADEEP K., GEORGE P. MOSCHIS, and DANNY N. BELLENGER. "Correlates of Successful Advertising Campaigns." *Journal of Advertising Research* 24, no. 1 (February/March 1984), pp. 47–53.

LOWRY, BRIAN. "New Zealand Lamb Joins Branding Trend." *Advertising Age,* September 1, 1986, p. 27W.

MEYERS, JANET. "Beef, Pork Gird for Meaty Battle." *Advertising Age,* October 20, 1986, p. 2.

MILLER, MARK C. "The Critical Pursuit of Advertising." *Word and Image* 1, no. 4 (1985), pp. 319–24.

MORRISON, ANN M. "Cookies Are Frito-Lay's New Bag." *Fortune,* August 9, 1982, pp. 64–67.

PASKOWSKI, MARIANNE. "The Flag, Apple Pie . . . and High Life." *Marketing and Media Decisions,* May 1985, pp. 60+.

SCARRY, ELAINE. "Willow Bark and Red Poppies: Advertising the Remedies for Physical Pain." *Word & Image* 1, no. 4 (1985), pp. 381–408.

SHETH, JAGDISH N., and BRUCE I. NEWMAN. "The 'Gender Gap' in Voter Attitudes and Behavior: Some Advertising Implications." *Journal of Advertising* 13, no. 3 (1984), pp. 4–16.

TRACY, ELEANOR J. "Black-and-White Magic in Chicago." *Fortune,* September 2, 1985, p. 47.

CHAPTER TWO

The Advertising Media Research Process

Washington, D.C., residents are heavy consumers of sleeping tablets, breath mints, and before-dinner drinks. They are below-average buyers of U.S. Treasury bonds.*

Bernie Whalen

Good advertising decisions depend on good advertising research. In order to learn what products and services consumers want, what factors contribute to effective advertising copy, what regional differences account for various food preferences, and a host of other important business and marketplace conditions, advertisers require accurate, timely, relevant, affordable information. Nowhere is the need for good research clearer than in advertising media decisions.

DIVERSITY IN MARKETS AND AUDIENCES

Contemporary markets are characterized by their great variety and variability. Differences in the consumption of goods can be found among regions, income levels, occupational categories, sexes, household types and sizes, and personality types.

Equally diverse are the ways in which people accept or reject the communications media that convey advertising messages. For example, heavy users of yogurt are also heavy consumers of classical music radio broadcasts. However, in New York City, this national trend is interrupted. There, yogurt users are more likely to be found in the audiences of progressive rock music radio stations. The 1985 A. C. Nielson Company Report for network television indicated that "Dallas" ranked tops among U.S. households, but it did not make the list of top 15 shows

---

* "Research Firm Gathers Product-Usage, Media Exposure on Local Markets," *Marketing News,* January 6, 1984.

among teenagers or preteen children.[1] Adult men selected "60 Minutes" as their favorite network program. Adult women, teenagers, and children aged 2 to 11 included the "Bill Cosby Show" in listings of favorite programs. The number one network program in Washington, D.C., that autumn was "Dallas," while in Dallas (Texas) the favorite was "Dynasty." The long-running "Tonight Show," hosted by Johnny Carson, ranked second in Philadelphia but only tenth in Boston among all network programs. Research to reveal these and other pertinent facts is essential to good decisions about advertising media.

THE SCIENTIFIC METHOD

In this chapter, you will see how the research process relates to good advertising media decisions. Most of those who work with advertising media are consumers or users of research as well as doers of research. In this chapter, we tell you how to use research results and describe the process by which good research is produced. This information should help you increase your understanding of the research process and improve your ability to use research results effectively.

Making decisions about advertising media is greatly facilitated by certain intellectual disciplines collectively called the "scientific method." In this method, the overall research process is divided into four basic stages:

1. Defining the problem.
2. Collecting pertinent facts.
3. Analyzing these facts.
4. Deriving and implementing a solution to the problem.

The scientific method requires that decision makers understand the use of models. This chapter's organization is based on the four stages of the scientific method. The chapter also covers the nature and uses of models in the course of managing the advertising media process.

Statement of Research Purpose

When done as part of decision making, research is purposive. That is, it is undertaken to solve some practical problem in a more efficient way. In Chapter 1, you read of the importance of knowing the customer in the process of implementing the marketing concept. In fact, it is virtually impossible to apply the marketing concept unless you know the con-

---

[1] *Nielsen Report on Television* (Northbrook, Ill.: A. C. Nielsen Company, 1985).

sumer, and marketing research is the most important means by which to gain this knowledge.

In managing the advertising media function, the problem is to maximize advertising's impact within a fixed budget. This statement of the problem is more clearly evident in the media function than in other business areas. One bedeviling problem in conducting marketing research is that managers often have trouble correctly specifying the problem. Business case histories are replete with instances where managers incorrectly stated the problem. In these cases, research is costly and irrelevant, and resources expended in the research process do not contribute to solving the primary problem.

Stating the problem in media decisions is not always simple. It is, nevertheless, a basic axiom that the research process cannot be correctly applied to advertising media situations without a clear statement of the problem to be solved. Most often, this statement is composed of two factors: specific statement of the advertising objective to be accomplished and complete specification of the constraints to be imposed on the solution.

In managing advertising media, the statement of the problem typically requires managers to understand three concepts: the cost of information, the value of information, and the role of a research hypothesis.

The Cost of Information.   In research processes that solve business problems, one frequently overlooked issue is the cost of information. Information is necessary to analyze available alternatives and frequently to formulate a statement of the problem. For either of these purposes—forming a hypothesis or analyzing alternatives—the collection of relevant information is a cost-incurring activity. That is, resources are expended in the collection of information. By looking at the major kinds of information, we can better understand the nature of the costs associated with their collection.

Primary Data.   In business decision making, information is traditionally divided into two categories: primary data and secondary data. **Primary data** are facts collected by the decision-making organization for its particular needs. An example of primary data might be the information an advertising agency collects by itself to construct a demographic profile of the customers for a client's product. Figure 2–1 shows primary data collected by the Denver Research Institute to measure the life style dimensions of readers of *Colorado Homes and Lifestyles,* a Denver magazine.

Primary data can be subdivided into two categories. One category comprises the data that the organization collects for the purpose of mak-

**FIGURE 2-1   Recreational Activities of Respondents in Past
12 Months**

Activity	Percentage of Respondents
Listened to recorded music	91.3%
Read books for pleasure	90.3
Attended live theatrical events	69.5
Attended art show or gallery	69.4
Engaged in photography	64.8
Snow skied	52.2
Bicycled	45.2
Played golf	32.2
Played tennis	31.6
Boated or sailed	24.1
Played racquetball, handball, or squash	22.4
Collected stamps, coins, etc.	18.6
Water skied	12.9
Skin or scuba dived	9.5
Piloted a private plane	5.4
None of the above	0.7

SOURCE: Denver Research Institute, "A Survey of Reader Characteristics for *Colorado Homes and Lifestyles*," May 1984, p. 7. Reprinted with permission of *Colorado Homes and Lifestyles* magazine.

ing a particular decision or set of decisions. We call this category decision-specific or problem-specific primary data. The second category includes facts collected by the organization (or possibly by the organization's client, in the case of an advertising agency) in the course of normal business activities. This kind of primary information, which we call general primary information, comes from such sources as billing records, advertising budgets, client sales records, and corporate income tax returns.

In the case of general primary data, the important costs of information are the marginal costs of retrieving, analyzing, and interpreting these data in light of the problem at hand. For example, information on a client firm's corporate income tax returns may be useful in solving an advertising problem. But only the human and other economic resources required to *reanalyze* certain aspects of the tax returns would be relevant costs for this kind of information—not the entire cost of preparing the returns.

Analyzing problem or decision-specific primary information requires greater amounts of manpower and capital. Here, the actual cost of the information includes not only the cost of the analysis but the costs of designing the data collection effort and collecting the information in useful form. Later in this chapter, some of the costs associated with the collection of primary information will be identified in greater detail. For now, you need only recognize that the costs of problem or decision-specific primary information are higher than the costs of general primary information.

Secondary Data. **Secondary data,** the other major kind of data, are those facts collected by others. Secondary data include the information published by trade associations and governmental agencies such as the Bureau of the Census. Secondary data also include information collected by commercial research firms for subsequent sale to subscribers. From the standpoint of the "user" organization, data collected by Simmons Market Research Bureau and the A. C. Nielsen Company are secondary data.

Three examples of secondary data directly related to advertising media issues are shown in Figure 2–2. They represent the kind of secondary research data that media planners might use in making decisions.

The Value of Information. Like virtually every other business process, advertising media research requires the comparison of relevant costs with relevant benefits. In advertising media research (and, for that matter, in many of the business research applications), the benefit gained from the research process is called the value of information. This benefit, or value, is expressed on two levels: the value of perfect information and the value of imperfect information. The latter is often called the value of information under conditions of uncertainty. In the following example, we use the concepts of value of perfect information and value of information under uncertainty to illustrate the process of setting a maximum value on research information.

An Example: JAZZY Cologne. Assume that the Larkin-Pisani advertising agency is preparing an advertising campaign for a client who wishes to market a woman's cologne, called JAZZY, primarily to women 18 to 34 years of age. The fragrance is described as being too grown-up and sophisticated for the "bubble-gum" set and too precocious to appeal to middle-aged women.

The JAZZY Problem. Those working on the JAZZY account are trying to decide whether to augment their magazine advertising with a microencapsulated (scratch-and-sniff) sample of the fragrance. The cost of adding these sample patches to magazine advertising already budgeted for the campaign would be $25,000.

The account people at Larkin-Pisani are uncertain about how women in the target market will respond to the scratch-and-sniff sample. On the plus side, getting women to experience a new fragrance has always been an important part of successful new product introduction in this industry. On the other hand, microencapsulated samples are not perfect represen-

A.   Family household income

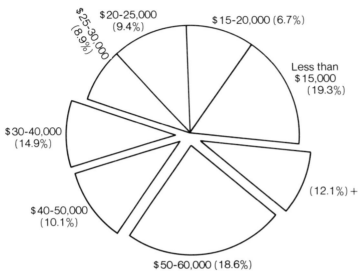

Students are accustomed to consuming. Fifty-six percent come from
households with incomes of $30,000 or more. The mere fact that they
are in college evidences their aspirations of continued consumption.

SOURCE: *1985–86 College Newspaper Directory and Rate Book,* American Pas-
sage, p. 16.

**B.   Daily and Weekly Newspapers, Financial Publications, Sunday
Supplements, and Sunday Comics Audience**

	Men 18+		Women 18+	
	Readers per Copy	Readers (millions)	Readers per Copy	Readers (millions)
Daily newspapers market group:				
1–10	1.1	15.8	1.1	15.8
11–50	1.1	17.2	1.1	17.2
51–100	1.1	9.0	1.1	9.0
Total (1–100)	1.1	42.0	1.1	42.0
Weekly newspapers:				
Grit	1.93	1.7	2.71	2.4
National Enquirer	1.53	7.1	2.29	10.6
The Star	1.20	3.7	2.20	6.9
Financial publications:				
The Wall Street Journal	1.47	2.5	.68	1.2
Barron's	2.73	.7	1.19	.3

B. Daily and Weekly Newspapers, Financial Publications, Sunday Supplements, and Sunday Comics Audience *(concluded)*

	Men 18+		Women 18+	
	Readers per Copy	*Readers (millions)*	*Readers per Copy*	*Readers (millions)*
Sunday supplements:				
Family Weekly	.75	9.1	.85	10.2
Parade	.84	18.2	.87	18.7
Sunday	.93	20.4	.98	21.6
N.Y. Times				
Magazine	1.41	2.0	1.37	1.9
Sunday comics:				
Metro Sunday				
Comics	.58	13.0	.56	12.4
Puck–The Comic				
Weekly	.55	9.6	.57	9.9

SOURCE: Ted Bates, "Instant Media Facts 1981–1982," p. 66.

C. College Student Print Media Habits: Weekly Readership Comparison

Percentage of total students

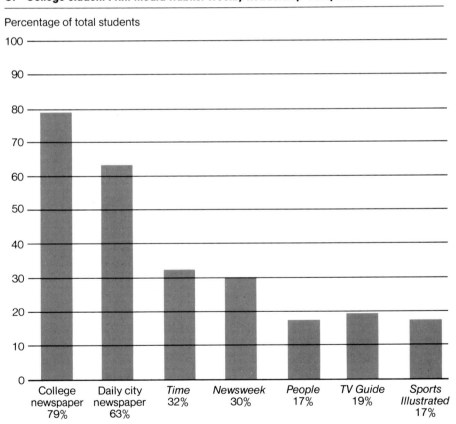

Read any of the above in past 7 days

SOURCE: The College Market/Profile of Students as Consumers, CASS Student Advertising, Inc., 1980, p. 9.

tations because fragrances change when combined with a wearer's particular skin chemistry. Further, scent samples carried in magazines are probably inconsistent with the prestige price levels the client intends to use. Focus group tests at the agency revealed that women thought a cologne sent through the mail on a paper tape was probably an inexpensive fragrance. To oversimplify their real responses, we assume that women either respond favorably or negatively to the samples attached to magazine advertisements.

JAZZY company executives estimate that a favorable response to the scratch-and-sniff sample will add $100,000 to net profit. However, they are pessimistic about the chances of a favorable response and set the probability at only .25.

Decision Analysis for JAZZY. For analysis purposes, the two choices available for the campaign can be called "strategies," and the reactions of women in the target segment can be called "states of nature." The four possible results, or outcomes, are the product of multiplying each strategy by each state of nature. These outcomes are listed below:

1. Don't use scratch-and-sniff patch; women respond negatively. This produces a result of $0.
2. Don't use a scratch-and-sniff patch; women respond favorably. This produces an opportunity loss of $100,000 in net profits.
3. Use scratch-and-sniff patch; women respond negatively. This produces a loss of $25,000, the marginal cost of the microencapsulization campaign. (Actually the losses could be greater if women who would otherwise have bought JAZZY are turned off by the patches. For purposes of this example, the loss is limited to the cost of an ineffective addition to the magazine campaign.)
4. Use scratch-and-sniff patch; women respond favorably. This produces a gain of $100,000 in net profits.

This problem, along with associated probabilities of occurrence, can be displayed in a diagram called a two-state decision tree, shown in Figure 2–3.

Expected Value under Uncertainty. The expected value of each strategy is found by multiplying the two outcomes of that strategy by the probability that each will occur. The expected value of *not* using the scratch-and-sniff patch is:

$$EV_0 = (.75)\,(\$0) + (.25)\,(-100,000) = -\$25,000$$

Similarly, the expected value of using the patch is:

FIGURE 2–3 Two-Stage Decision Tree

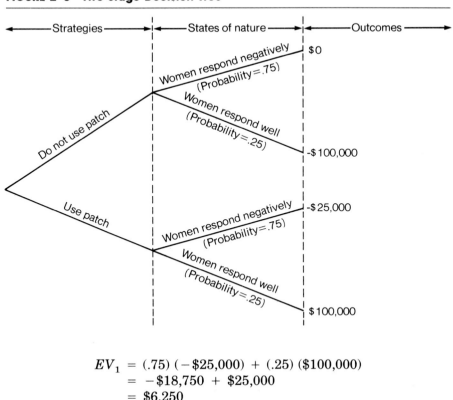

$$EV_1 = (.75)(-\$25,000) + (.25)(\$100,000)$$
$$= -\$18,750 + \$25,000$$
$$= \$6,250$$

Thus, the decision to use a scratch-and-sniff patch, which results in an expected net profit contribution of $6,250, should be made even though the company executives think there is only about a one-in-four chance of a favorable response from women in the target age group. The other decision, not to use the patch, has an expected loss of $25,000.

Expected Value of Perfect Information.   Keep in mind, though, that the probability of occurrence for each state of nature was produced by JAZZY executives' guesses, also called "subjective probabilities." These guesses are based not only on uncertainty but also on wisdom, experience, and judgment. In the real world, subjective probabilities can be important. However, if the Larkin-Pisani agency could perform research that would tell, *with certainty,* whether women's responses would be favorable, then the *"perfect"* information could be used to choose the best strategy.

Note that the concept of the **value of perfect information** assumes no change in probabilities and outcomes. It simply computes the gain from always choosing the correct strategy.

To compute the **expected value of perfect information** (or EVPI), it is necessary to reverse the decision tree in Figure 2–3, as has been done in Figure 2–4. Then, the outcomes for the best strategy are multiplied by their probability of occurrence.

If the Larkin-Pisani people had performed research that yielded perfect information about women's response to the patch, then company and agency could simply choose the best strategy. If women responded favorably, the patches should be used. If women responded negatively, the patches should not be used. The expected value of perfect information (EVPI) in this problem is the sum of the relevant outcomes times their probabilities.

From Figure 2–4:

$$EVPI = (.75)\,(0) + (.25)\,(\$100{,}000) = \$25{,}000$$

How much should **JAZZY** executives be willing to pay for research that will produce "perfect" information? The **value of perfect research** (VPR) is equivalent to the difference between the expected value of

---

FIGURE 2–4 Reversed Decision Tree

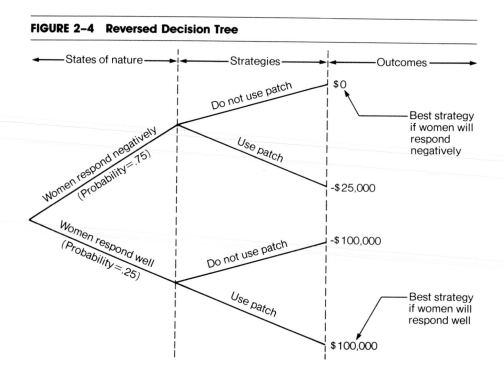

perfect information and the expected value under uncertainty of the best strategy. In this example:

$$VPR = EVPI - EV_1 = 25,000 - \$6,250 = \$18,750$$

It should be stressed that VPR ($18,750 in the JAZZY problem) is the *maximum* sum decision makers should be willing to pay for research-produced information. Since real research is virtually never perfect, it produces information that is less than perfect. Thus, real-world executives should be willing to pay only a portion of VPR, since some uncertainty will still be present.

Operational Hypotheses

Assuming that the decision maker has calculated (or estimated) the expected value of perfect information and has set this figure as the upper limit of what should be spent on research, the first step in the research process is to state the problem in "research" form. In this form, the statement of the problem is called a hypothesis.

The Nature of a Hypothesis. Hypotheses are assumptions, or tentative statements, about states of nature. In the preceding JAZZY problem, one hypothesis would be: "Women will respond well to a scratch-and-sniff appeal for JAZZY." Hypotheses in advertising decisions often involve tentative statements of a numerical nature; here the true numerical value of the state of nature is called a parameter.

Of course the scientific method requires more than assumptions (or hypotheses) for proper decision making. Hypotheses must be tested carefully and found to be true (more precisely, found to have an acceptably high probability of correctly describing the relevant state of nature) before the prudent decision maker incorporates them into decision making.

Hypothesis Tests. Hypotheses may be tested in a number of ways, but under conditions of uncertainty the most appropriate tests in advertising research are statistical ones. The usual method is to state the advertising problem in the form of a null hypothesis. In this form, the tentative assumption about the state of nature is that any statistical relationship is due to the unrestricted operation of the laws of chance. Subsequent research efforts are then combined with sampling statistics. These are "calculated values that represent the probable deviations of sample characteristics from [parameters]."[2] Sampling statistics, then, provide the

---

2 Frederick Williams, *Reasoning with Statistics* (New York: Holt, Rinehart & Winston, 1968), p. 7.

decision maker with an objective, rigorous test of the null hypothesis, and technically speaking, the procedure is to test the null hypothesis. If it can be rejected on the basis of analysis that uses sampling statistics, we infer that the research (or alternative) hypothesis is correct. The research hypothesis is the logical opposite of the null hypothesis. An example of a pair of hypotheses (null and research) is:

Null H_o: There is no significant difference between the sales response generated by an advertisement placed in *Sports Illustrated* and the sales response generated by the same ad placed in *McCall's*.

Research H_r: There is a significant difference between the sales response to identical ads placed in *Sports Illustrated* and *McCall's*.

Practical Hypotheses. To be of practical use in advertising decisions, problems must be stated in the form of operational hypotheses. Such hypotheses must possess two characteristics:

1. They must be "falsifiable."
2. The variables named in them must permit operational measurement.

The first characteristic, falsifiability, is necessary for any scientific hypothesis testing. Thus, the statement, "Ad A will eventually produce acceptable sales," is not falsifiable. If the ad does not produce acceptable sales this week, it might do so next week, or next month, or next year. If a statement cannot be disproved using agreed-on methods, it cannot serve as a hypothesis in advertising research.

The second condition, measurable variables, simply means that we must state the hypothesis precisely enough so that subsequent measurements will lend themselves to the application of sampling statistics. "Repeat purchase rate" is a variable amenable to quantification, and we can measure this variable among a sample of customers to several decimal places. "Positive feelings about the Exxon Corporation" may or may not be a measurable variable, depending on our ability to measure such feelings with accuracy.

Construction of Models. In advertising research, particularly for problems involving advertising media, models are often used to assist the manager. A model is a simplified abstraction of selected properties of a real-world phenomenon. Managers construct and use this simplified representation of reality because it permits them to focus attention on the most important aspects of the problem at hand.

Other industries sometimes use physical models. A wave tank, which replicates the action of real ocean waves, may be used in the design of beach structures or supertankers. In advertising, the most frequently employed models are symbolic and may be either verbal or mathematical, depending on the type of symbols used to construct them. An example of a verbal model is:

> Purchase some advertising space in magazine A, and twice as much advertising space in magazine B, in a way that maximizes the total advertising weight of both vehicles, provided that the cost of both does not exceed $3,000.

The same representation, expressed in the form of a mathematical model, would be:

$$\text{Maximize } Z = A + 2B$$

Subject to:

$$A > 0$$
$$A + 2B \leqslant \$3,000$$

Here Z is the symbolic notation given to the variable, advertising weight.[3]

Mathematical Models. In this example, the correct application of either the verbal or the mathematical model will produce the same "answer." However, mathematical models possess certain characteristics that make them particularly useful in the solution of advertising problems. These characteristics include precision, internal logic, and amenability to adjustment. By precision, we mean that a mathematical model can be constructed with less ambiguity than would probably be the case for a similar verbal model. By internal logic, we mean that the decision maker using a mathematical model is imposing the helpful discipline of logic on the process. The fallacy of $2 + 2 = 5$ is quickly recognized by all. Mathematical models also simplify the common process of adjustment; in the above example, an adjustment might take the form of changing $2B$ to $1.5B$. Both the nature of the change and its consequences are highlighted through the use of mathematical models. In this book, we emphasize mathematical models.

Types of Media Models. For problems in advertising media, it is useful to distinguish four classes of mathematical models based on their linearity and certainty: linear, nonlinear, deterministic, and probabilistic. Models that employ constant proportions between variables are

---

[3] In algebraic notation, the statement $A < x$ means A is less than x. The symbol $\geqq$ means greater than or equal to, and the symbol $\leqq$ means less than or equal to. A beginning algebra text and one of the better dictionaries will have a more complete listing of algebraic inequality notations.

called **linear,** and those using varying relationships are termed **nonlinear.** Because of computational and measurement difficulties, advertising decision makers emphasize linear models, and these are also the focus in this book. Figure 2–5 illustrates linear and nonlinear models.

Models based on certainty are called **deterministic** models. An example of a deterministic model is the media-buying model $(Z = A + 2B)$ used previously. Alternatively, models based on conditions of uncertainty are termed **probabilistic** models. For example, a model that uses the concept of expected value under uncertainty (the "EVs" of the JAZZY example) is a probabilistic model, as are virtually all of the models that utilize sampling statistics.

In actual practice, advertising media models used to allocate funds among the media purchases in a campaign and those used to choose media are commonly linear and deterministic.

In contrast, research to solve problems regarding the response produced by advertising commonly uses probabilistic models. Among this class of models, linear forms are more frequently used than nonlinear, though the use of the more complex nonlinear variety is (and should be) growing. In later chapters, we will discuss the application of probabilistic models to problem solving in advertising media.

FIGURE 2–5   Examples of Linear and Nonlinear Advertising Functions (Models)

A. Rate card for the *Tattler*

Rate per column-inch $20

B. Rate card for the *Bugler*

1–50 column-inches	$20/col. in.
51–100 column-inches	$18/col. in.
101–200 column-inches	$16/col. in.
201–500 column-inches	$10/col. in.

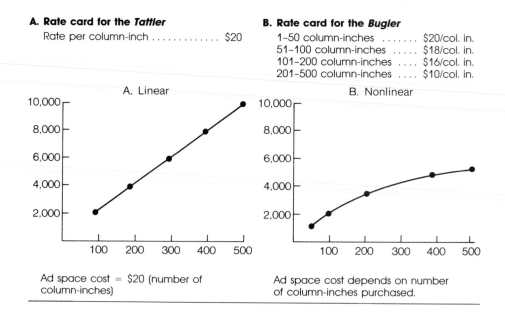

A. Linear

Ad space cost = $20 (number of column-inches)

B. Nonlinear

Ad space cost depends on number of column-inches purchased.

Choosing an Optimum Model. When faced with an advertising media problem, some managers (and some students) are a bit bewildered about how to proceed. This bewilderment can produce unfortunate choices and results. Sometimes the decision maker simply avoids choosing among models by making a snap judgment. We call this the "Custer's 7th Cavalry approach." It produces sudden, dramatic, and often regrettable results. Another method is to simply take a mathematical model "off the shelf," preferably a very complex model, and force the problem into it. We call this the "procrustean solution," after the giant of Greek mythology who seized travelers and tied them to an iron bed. When the traveler was too short for the bed, he was stretched until he fit; when the traveler was too tall, Procrustes cut off his legs. Travelers thus detained might well have objected to the cost of this "solution," based on a model (bed) that was not appropriate to their needs. Similarly, the procrustean method of model selection in advertising research is often associated with suboptimal results.

Characteristics of an Optimum Model. An optimum model in advertising or other business decisions highlights the crucial elements in the "reality" of the problem. Its elements recognize the presence or absence of certainty and linearity in this reality. The costs associated with its use are justified by the economic benefits of the information it produces. By recognizing these aspects of an optimal model and applying a modicum of logic, the advertising decision maker can select an optimal model for the problem to be solved. This process is diagramed in Figure 2–6. Recognize that the models listed are just examples. It is impossible for research to produce "perfect" information; its purpose is to produce better information than was previously available. In actuality, the cost comparisons for probabilistic models should really compare (EVPI − EV) with VAR, the value of the information produced by actual research.

Examples and Limitations of Computer-Assisted Media Model. In advertising agencies, the selection of media and the allocation of advertising weights among media is a relatively complicated process. However, computers can help decision makers effectively consider many numerically expressed alternatives. Many agencies and other advertising-related organizations have constructed proprietary models that process relevant information electronically. One example is the Telmar media selection model (see Figure 2–7).

All mathematical models are prey to certain limitations. For example, linear programming is one of the most widely used methods of optimizing the audience for an advertising campaign, within constraints imposed by budget and media choices. Yet, as Kotler notes, even this popular, useful model has important restrictions:

FIGURE 2–6 The Process for Selecting an Optimum Advertising Research Model

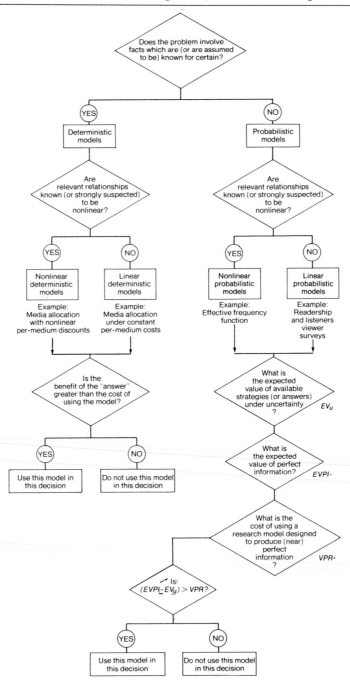

FIGURE 2–7

BRAND 2—BUDGET SETTING: GOAL 70% REACH
MEDIA OBJECTIVES

BUDGET GOAL: $500,000

NF GOAL(S):
REACH 70.0%

OPTIMIZATION
BASED ON: REACH

SELECTION PROCESS VIA MEDIAC MODEL

CUMV.

MEDIA	COST	REACH	AVG. FREQ.	GRP
1 BBB	48000	29.33	1.00	29
1 BBB	96000	37.71	1.55	58
1 AAA	150000	53.26	1.62	86
1 GGG	180000	57.16	1.72	98
1 AAA	234000	62.50	2.02	126
1 DDD	266000	64.58	2.12	136
1 BBB	314000	67.29	2.47	165
1 AAA	368000	69.92	2.77	193
1 FFF	391000	70.91	2.77	196

***RF GOAL(S) REACHED

BENCHMARK II SUMMARY AND ANALYSIS

USES MEDIA	COST
3 AAA	162000
3 BBB	144000
1 DDD	32000
1 FFF	23000
1 GGG	30000
9	391000

1. Linear programming assumes that repeat exposures have a constant marginal effect.
2. It assumes constant media cost (no discounts).
3. It cannot handle the problem of audience duplication.
4. It fails to say anything about when the advertisement should be scheduled.[4]

[4] Philip Kotler, *Marketing Management,* 2nd ed. (Englewood Cliffs, N.J.: Prentice-Hall, 1972), p. 688.

More generally, Day says that linear programming is not a panacea, but an invitation to hard work and rigorous thinking, and "should never be thought of as a way of turning a problem over to a mystical black box that gives instant solutions to thorny problems."[5]

Any model, to the extent that it abstracts irrelevant or tangential aspects of the real problem, has the capacity to distract the decision maker rather than enhance decision making. On balance, the advantages of models (especially precision, internal logic, and adjustability) are substantial. When combined with the power of computers to process and display the many alternatives available, decision makers must choose and use models carefully.

Collecting Information

We are now at the point in the research process where the problem has been correctly stated in the form of an operational hypothesis. We have analyzed the costs and value of research information and justified the need for more information. And we have tentatively selected an appropriate model or set of models. It is now time to collect the relevant facts that provide grist for the research mill.

Primary Data Collection. The first step in primary data collection should be to discover whether the needed information has already been gathered by the firm (or its agents). If general primary data are appropriate and on hand, the data collection process simply involves transferring the information within the firm.

Sampling. If decision-specific primary data are required, the two basic methods for gathering information are sampling and a census. In **sampling,** we collect information from a portion of the total relevant group. In statistical language, this group is termed a *population,* even when the group is composed of objects other than people. For example, costs of 30-second prime time television spots or magazines that offer split-run advertising are thought of as statistical populations. By collecting values from a portion of a population and subsequently applying sampling statistics, the decision maker is able to make probabilistic inferences about population parameters.

Census. The other method of collecting decision-specific primary data is the census. A **census** requires the collection of data from every mem-

---

[5] Ralph L. Day, "Linear Programming in Media Selection," *Journal of Advertising Research* 2 (1962), pp. 40–44.

ber (person or object) in the entire statistical population. Any time the size of the population is large, a census is almost always less efficient (that is, more costly) than a correctly drawn sample. The U.S. Census of Population (and the companion Census of Agriculture, Census of Manufacturing, etc.) is an imperfect census because it does not count *every* person and household (although census takers try to enumerate everyone and the percentage of people "missed" is relatively small).

Sampling and Survey Research. If data are to be collected by sampling, the researcher needs a strategy for selecting that portion of the population to be measured. When a probability distribution is employed to select subjects for measurement, the sample obtained is a probability sample. The basic random sample is a probability sample in which every member of the population has an equal chance of being measured. Other probability samples include stratified random samples and some cluster samples.

If a probability distribution is not used to select sample units, the sample obtained is a nonprobability or convenience sample. Collecting information from the first 100 people who write for a free catalog is an example of a convenience sample. So-called judgment and quota samples are most often nonprobability samples.

Probability samples are more difficult and more expensive to collect than convenience samples. True probability samples presume that a listing of the population can be produced, that a sampling plan based on a known probability distribution will be used to choose sampling units, and that the sampling plan is completed successfully. The last requirement precludes the real-world problems of refusals, not-at-homes, unlisted phone numbers, failure to return questionnaires or diaries, and panel mortality. However, true probability samples permit the correct application of powerful tools of statistical inference.

Convenience samples are cheaper and easier to produce. However, the absence of a probability-based sampling plan impairs the power of the inferences that are statistically derived. In practice, almost all sampling attempts to conform to the requirements for a probability sample, and nearly all real-world sampling departs to some degree from a true probability sample. Actual primary data collection is conducted to permit as close an approximation to true probability sampling as time, research funds, and the value of information permit. Sampling statistics are then applied as if a probability sample had been drawn. The decision maker recognizes that the "answers" developed are less certain than they would be if a true probability sample had been used.

Assuming that a probability sample of some type is desired, the next question might be, "How large a sample is required?" While a full discus-

---

FIGURE 2-8   Sample Size: Simple Random Sample

Permitted Error	Confidence Limits	
	95 Samples in 100	99 Samples in 100
1%	9,604	16,587
2	2,401	4,147
3	1,067	1,843
4	600	1,037
5	384	663
6	267	461
7	196	339

For a simple random sample, drawn from a very large population with replacement, the formula for sample size is:

$$n = \frac{Z^2\sigma^2}{h^2}$$

where

σ = Standard deviation
Z = Number of standard deviations
     for the specified confidence interval
h = Allowable tolerance for variation

---

sion of sample size can be found in many statistics and market research texts,[6] an indication of required sample sizes for a simple random sample is given in Figure 2–8.

An example of syndicated advertising research as it is affected by sample size can be found in the two major measurements of magazine readership. Both Magazine Research, Inc., and Simmons Market Research Bureau take samples of 15,000 persons for each of their six-month measurements. However, since only about 10 percent of the sample is likely to have read any particular magazine, the readership measurements for a single magazine are based on an effective sample size of about 1,500 persons. And when radio station KWKW measured the Los Angeles Latino market, it used a sample of 600 households headed by people with Spanish surnames.[7]

Secondary Data Sources.   Secondary data, you will remember, are data collected by another organization. Such data are purchased by the user organization. Figure 2–9 lists commonly used sources of secondary information in advertising media decisions.

---

[6] Gilbert A. Churchill, Jr., *Marketing Research* (Hinsdale, Ill.: Dryden Press, 1976), pp. 302–16.

[7] The Los Angeles Latino Market, Carranza Associates, 1982, pp. 1–8.

Data Quality.   Three important issues relate to the quality of data used in advertising decisions: **validity, reliability,** and **metricity.**

Validity.   By **validity,** we mean how well our information actually measures what it claims to measure. Suppose we ask survey respondents how much total income members of their household earn. Some respondents may provide actual income figures. But others may furnish erroneous data because they don't know the actual figure, because they inflate the actual figure to appear wealthier, or because they deflate the actual figure on the suspicion that the IRS might see the answer. To the extent that the measurement of any variable (e.g., household income) is contaminated by measurements of other variables (e.g., desire to impress interviewer or desire to thwart the IRS), it is an invalid measurement.

Reliability.   **Reliability** means the "repeatability" of a measurement. If it is repeatable with the same results, the measurement is reliable. Tests of data reliability, all based on correlation, include test-retest (where subjects' answers from two different measurements are compared) and alternative forms (where subjects are asked about the same thing in two or more different ways). And in a practical sense, it is impossible to have a valid measure that is not reliable.

Metricity.   **Metricity** is a property of data (or the measurement of data) that provides for a uniform scale interval. This property is not present in nonmetric data, the kind that categorizes or ranks things. For example, magazine readership studies categorize people as "readers" or "nonreaders," but this nonmetric measurement does not tell us how much difference there is within the reader categories. That is, what percent of "readers" read all of the magazine, half of it, etc. And a radio station's claim that "We're Number One" fails to specify how close the number two station is. In contrast, metric data are found in common advertising audience measurements. It is correct to say that an audience of 100 Gross Rating Points is exactly half the size of one of 200 Gross Rating Points.

   Metricity can also be represented in a geometric way. By this representation we mean whether or not numerical research data meet the following conditions:

$$d\overline{xx} = 0$$
$$d\overline{xy} = d\overline{yx}$$
$$d\overline{xy} \leq d\overline{xzy}$$

In other words, the distance from any point, x, to itself must be zero. The distance between two points, x and y, must be the same regardless of the direction of measurement. The distance between two points, x and y, must

FIGURE 2–9 How They Rank: 1985 Revenues of 44 Leading U.S. Research Organizations

Rank 1985	Rank 1984	Organization	Total Research Revenues* (millions)	Percent Change versus 1984	Research Revenues from Outside U.S. (millions)
1	1	A. C. Nielsen Co.	$517.0	+ 7.7%	$268.8 est.
2	2	IMS International	171.1	+ 11.4	86.9
3	3	SAMI	138.5	+ 17.0	—
4	4	Arbitron Ratings Co.	122.0	+ 15.3	—
5	8	Information Resources	75.1	+ 22.9	3.0 est.
6	5	Burke Marketing Services	73.1	+ 10.8	3.7
7	6	M/A/R/C	46.3	+ 23.0	—
8	7	Market Facts	37.8	+ 5.1	—
9	9	NFO Research	34.3	+ 16.3	—
10	10	NPD Group	33.1	+ 13.4	—
11	11	Maritz Market Research	30.0	+ 21.4	—
12	12	Westat	25.2	+ 3.3	—
13	13	Elrick and Lavidge	24.6	+ 5.6	—
14	14	Walker Research	20.7	+ 7.1	—
15	15	YSW/Clancy Shulman	19.5	+ 14.7	1.0
16	16	Chilton Research	19.1	+ 15.8	—
17	22	Simmons Market Research Bureau	16.5	+ 32.0	—
18	18	Louis Harris and Associates	15.8	+ 3.3	5.5
19	17	ASI Market Research	15.7	− 4.3	—
20	19	Opinion Research Corp.	14.5	0.0	—
21	21	Winona Research	14.4	+ 11.6	—
22	24	Decisions Center	13.8	+ 35.3	—
23	20	Ehrhart-Babic Group	13.8	+ 4.2	—
24	25	Harte-Hanks Marketing Services Group	11.7	+ 20.3	—
25	23	Data Development Corp.	10.9	+ 3.8	—
26	28	Custom Research	9.7	+ 12.8	—
27	29	National Analysts	9.6	+ 21.5	—
28	34	Mediamark Research	9.5	+ 23.1	—
29	27	Admar Research	8.9	− 4.3	—

be less than or equal to the distance from x, through any third point, z, to y. (This last is known as the triangular inequalities rule.)

As a practical matter, research data are usually divided into four categories. These categories, their descriptions, and relevant classes of statistical tools are shown in Figure 2–10. Distinctions between metric and nonmetric data have important implications for media decisions. For example, one of the largest syndicated print research firms, Starch INRA Hooper, regularly furnishes information about how well a particular ad ranked in an issue of a magazine. Clearly such numbers represent ordinal quality data, and only nonparametric statistics are entirely appro-

FIGURE 2-9 *(concluded)*

Rank 1985	Rank 1984	Organization	Total Research Revenues* (millions)	Percent Change versus 1984	Research Revenues from Outside U.S. (millions)
30	33	Starch INRA Hooper	8.9	+ 18.5	—
31	26	McCollum/Spielman Research	8.8	− 6.4	—
32	32	Gallup Organization	8.6	+ 11.7	—
33	—	National Research Group	8.0	+ 73.1	.9
34	38	Response Analysis	7.6	+ 35.0	—
35	39	Decision Research Corp.	6.8	+ 23.6	—
36	30	Decision/Making/ Information	6.7	− 14.1	—
37	35	Market Opinion Research	6.5	− 5.0	—
38	—	Guideline Research	6.5	+ 18.0	—
39	37	Ad Factors Marketing Research	5.9	− 1.0	—
40	—	J. D. Power & Associates	5.8	+ 6.0	—
41	—	Lieberman Research West	5.3	− 2.6	—
42	—	Marketing Research Services	5.1	+ 59.0	—
43	40	Oxtoby-Smith	5.0	+ 2.7	—
44	36	Kapuler Marketing Research	4.8	− 19.5	—
		Sub total, top 44	$1,652.5	+ 11.5%	$369.8
		All other (56 CASRO companies not listed in top 44)	132.8	+ 10.9%	
		Total (100 organizations)	$1,785.3	+ 11.5%	$369.8

* Total revenues that include nonresearch activities, for some companies, are significantly higher. This information is given in the individual company profiles in the main article.

SOURCE: Reprinted with permission of *Advertising Age,* May 19, 1986, p. 85. Copyright Crain Communications, Inc.

priate for analyzing these ranks. Also, many of the behavioral measures of advertising performance, such as attitude or opinion change, are most likely to be measured in a way that produces nonmetric data.

Selecting Analytical Procedures. In addition to using a model that correctly reflects the presence or absence of certainty as well as the property of linearity, our analytical procedure should reflect the quality of our research data. As indicated in Figure 2–10 nonparametric statistical tools should probably be used when data are of only nominal or ordinal quality. Many analysts rely on a standard nonparametric refer-

FIGURE 2-10   Categories of Research Data Quality

Category of Data Quality	Properties	Examples	Appropriate Statistical Tools
Nominal	Numbers assigned only to classify; no arithmetic properties	0 = Present customer, past customer also 1 = Past customer, no longer customer 2 = First-time customer	Nonparametric or distribution-free statistics
Ordinal	Numbers specify ordered relations of some characteristics, without specifying the interval; rankings	1 = Most-preferred brand 2 = Second-choice brand 3 = Third-choice brand	
Interval	Numbers specify ordered relationships with arbitrary but equal intervals	Centigrade temperature, household income,	Metric statistics
Ratio	Same as interval, but scale has a "natural" or absolute zero point	TV Program Rating, number of minutes spent listening to radio, eye-pupil diameter	

ence, such as Siegel, for the details and limitations of these procedures.[8] The problems associated with using metric statistics or nonmetric data are illustrated below.

Assume that three magazine readers are asked to rank the following four magazines on the basis of their preference. This produces the following matrix of ranks:

	Reader 1	Reader 2	Reader 3
Cosmopolitan	1	3	4
Reader's Digest	2	2	2
Argosy	3	4	1
Literary Review	4	1	3

---

[8] Sidney Siegel, *Nonparametric Statistics for the Behavioral Sciences* (New York: McGraw-Hill, 1956).

If a decision maker wished to select the favorite magazine of the group represented by these three readers, he might be tempted to compute the average rank of each magazine, on the theory that the publication with the lowest average rank would be the overall favorite. In this case, *Reader's Digest* has the lowest mean rank (average = 2), and the other three publications are tied (at average = 2.67).

It is incorrect to compute average ranks, since ranks are ordinal data, while arithmetic averages are only appropriate for metric data. But to illustrate how dangerous it can be to apply an inappropriate technique, consider how many of the group represented by these three readers ever read *Reader's Digest,* if each only reads his/her favorite magazine!

Instrumentation. The final issue in collecting information is instrumentation: the questionnaire, interview form, or other document on which respondent answers are recorded. Obviously instrumentation is largely the concern in primary data collection efforts.

An acceptable data collection instrument should have four properties. These are:

1. Standardization of questions. All respondents should be asked the same question in the same way (provided the research design does not call for certain types of variability).
2. Assistance to interviewers and respondents. Areas of the instrument where questions can be expected to occur should contain clear instructions for resolving these questions.
3. Absence of demand characteristics. Questions and instructions should be carefully constructed to avoid leading the respondent to a particular answer.
4. Suitability for subsequent analysis. Instruments should be designed so that the subject's answers can be easily and accurately processed. Often this means the preparation of computer-compatible data records directly from responses. Figure 2–11 shows an example of a questionnaire designed for direct computer card punching. Small numbers on the right of the page indicate the positions in the computer record where each piece of data should be entered.

Data Analysis and Interpretation

If our advertising research has conformed to the process outlined in the foregoing portion of this chapter, we are now at the stage where the hypotheses will be tested and the test results reported to the person responsible for reaching a decision. Major steps in the testing process are presented below.

FIGURE 2–11 Questionnaire Designed for Computer Entry and Analysis

Statement	Definitely Disagree				Definitely Agree		
v. Once I find a brand I like, I stick with it	1	2	3	4	5	6	8
w. Eye make-up is as important as lipstick	1	2	3	4	5	6	9
x. Normally, I don't try new brands until they are well accepted by others	1	2	3	4	5	6	10
y. I rarely go out of my way to shop for groceries at the store with the lowest prices	1	2	3	4	5	6	11
z. I see no particular reason to avoid pre-servatives	1	2	3	4	5	6	12
aa. Health foods are not worth the extra costs	1	2	3	4	5	6	13
bb. I know a great deal about nutrition	1	2	3	4	5	6	14
cc. Breakfast is the one meal a person can most often skip without any bad side effects	1	2	3	4	5	6	15
dd. There are many prepared foods that are just as good as homemade or fresh foods	1	2	3	4	5	6	16
ee. Disinfectants should be used to get your house really clean	1	2	3	4	5	6	17
ff. I have to be careful what I serve members of my family because of health problems	1	2	3	4	5	6	18
gg. I prepare each meal to be nutritionally balanced	1	2	3	4	5	6	19
hh. So-called health foods are not any better for you than the well-known brands	1	2	3	4	5	6	20
ii. I buy more low calorie foods than most housewifes	1	2	3	4	5	6	21

4. Are you or anyone in your household now answering questionnaires or reporting purchases regularly for any other organization or company?

         Yes ( )[1]   No ( )[2]   22

4a. (IF "YES") What is the name of the company? _____ 23-25

5. This questionnaire has been completed by: "X" one:
   Female head of household ( )[1]   Male head of household ( )[2] 26
   Other household member (specify) _____ ( )[3]

> Now, please check over this questionnaire to be sure that you haven't overlooked anything. It is important that we have your answer to every question. Then, return it to us in the next three or four days in the enclosed, self-addressed and postage-paid envelope.

(END OF QUESTIONNAIRE)

Courtesy of Arbitron Consumer Research

Preparing Raw Data for Analysis.   With the data collection process completed, the next step is to prepare this information for analysis. To do this, we must first develop a procedure for handling missing data and wild codes.

Missing data are those portions of responses that are not complete and those responses that are completely absent from the data set. For incomplete responses, a decision must be reached about whether to exclude missing values from the analysis or to substitute a value, such as the average of the responses at hand. Completely absent responses are a part of the nonresponse problem; while these usually impair the statistical inferences of the hypothesis tests, they do not require immediate adjustments by the analyst.

Wild codes represent impossible or highly implausible values for a variable. Suppose we were measuring "years of formal education" and this variable ranged from 0 (never attended school) to 17 (our code for college graduate with some advanced graduate schooling). A value of 61, for some respondent, would represent a wild code item. Perhaps the keypunch operator transposed the code 16. In such an instance, comparing the wild code with the data collection instrument can produce the appropriate correction. All variables being analyzed should be subjected to wild code checks. Wild code values that cannot be corrected should be excluded from further analysis since they can (and often do) seriously distort the hypothesis test.

Recognizing Limitations.   No actual research produces perfect results, but reports of hypothesis testing sometimes conceal (or at least overlook) the imperfections. Analysts have a duty to provide decision makers, and decision makers have an obligation to insist on, a careful statement of the test's limitations. The major limitations, which should always be available to decision makers as part of the hypothesis test report, are:

1. Departures from metric data quality.
2. Departures from a probability sampling plan.
3. Departures from validity or reliability to the extent that these are known.
4. Departures from certainty implied by the use of a particular probabilistic model.

Explicitly stating these limitations is much more than "weasel-wording." Rather, it is a professional obligation in the process of using research to enhance the quality of advertising decisions.

Writing Useful Research Reports.   Research reports, which are the descriptions of hypothesis tests, are often not used (or only partly used) by decision makers. There are two basic reasons for this incomplete use. The decision maker may not have the required background to use the report, or the report may be flawed. This text will help you gain the required skills to use good research.

You can also eliminate (or reduce) the second cause of incomplete research utilization by making the research reports you produce useful. Useful reports have the following characteristics:

1. They conform to the scientific method. They marshal information in the same sequence as the research process they report.
2. They express matters clearly and avoid jargon. They present numerical information in clear tabular or graphic form. They use simple declarative sentences. And they include complete references and footnotes.
3. They acknowledge costs, justify them with expected benefits, and spell out limitations.

SOLVING PROBLEMS

To summarize, purposive research can be extremely helpful in reaching good decisions. Good decisions are workable solutions to real problems. It is possible to make a good decision without benefit of research, but the odds are against it; the decision maker who makes decisions without research is in effect making the quality of the decision a hostage to chance. In the process of solving advertising media problems where the alternatives and the constraints are numerous and the dollar value of the choices is very large, careful scientific research can greatly improve the percentage of good decisions.

REVIEW QUESTIONS

1. What are the four basic steps in the scientific method?
2. Distinguish between primary and secondary data and give an example of each type.
3. What is the name of the upper limit on the amount you would be willing to pay for research information?
4. You wonder whether magazine advertising is effective for a particular advertising client. Translate this problem into null hypothesis form.
5. A particular newspaper offers a 2 percent discount for prompt payment of advertising space bills. Is this a linear or a nonlinear discount?
6. What is the *average* research revenue of the 20 largest U.S.-owned research firms?

7. What is the quality of the data implied by the claim "We're number one"? What is the metricity?

8. In some research done among high school students, one of the respondents has a value of 91 in the age variable. Is this a "wild code"? What should be done about this value?

9. Why is good advertising research important?

SUGGESTED ADDITIONAL READING

"A Primer on the 2–12 Market." *Marketing and Media Decisions,* September 12, 1985, p. 102.

ALRECK, PAMELA L., and ROBERT B. SETTLE. *The Survey Research Handbook.* Homewood, Ill.: Richard D. Irwin, 1985.

ASSMUS, GERT; JOHN U. FARLEY; and DONALD R. LEHMANN. "How Advertising Affects Sales: Meta-Analysis of Econometric Results." *Journal of Marketing Research* 21 (1984), pp. 65–74.

BOOTE, ALFRED S. "Interactions in Psychographics Segmentation: Implications for Advertising." *Journal of Advertising* 13, no. 2 (1984), pp. 43–48.

FABIAN, GEORGE S. "Ad Agency Research Departments Now Help Clients Develop Marketing Plans, Strategies." *Marketing News,* January 22, 1982, p. 4.

FISHER, ANNE B. "Coke's Brand-Loyalty Lesson." *Fortune,* August 5, 1985, pp. 44–46.

FREDRICKS, JOAN. "Observe These Rules When Designing Questionnaires." *Marketing News,* January 22, 1982, p. 18.

"Keeping an Eye on Media Habits." *Marketing and Media Decisions,* July 1985, pp. 129–32.

LASTOVICKA, JOHN L. "Sampling Designs for Sample Surveys of Advertisers." *Current Issues and Research in Advertising,* 1985, pp. 89–94.

LISSANCE, DANIEL M., and LELEAND E. OTT. "What Every Young Account Representative Should Know About Creative Research." American Association of Advertising Agencies (undated).

"Research Business Review." *Advertising Age* Special Report, May 19, 1986, pp. S1–S60.

RICHMAN, TOM. "Peering into Tomorrow." *INC,* October 1982, pp. 45–48.

SCHUMER, FERN. "The New Magicians of Market Research." *Fortune,* July 23, 1983, pp. 72–74.

STOUT, PATRICIA A., and JOHN D. LECKENBY. "Measuring Emotional Response to Advertising." *Journal of Advertising* 15, no. 4 (1986), pp. 35–42.

TULL, DONALD S., and GERALD S. ALBAUM. *Survey Research: A Decisional Approach.* New York: Intext Press, 1973.

WEISS, DOYLE L.; CHARLES B. WEINBERG; and PIERRE M. WINDAL. "The Effects of

Serial Correlation and Data Aggregation on Advertising Measurement." *Journal of Marketing Research* 20 (1983), pp. 268–79.

WILLIAMS, MONCI JO. "The Baby Bust Hits the Job Market." *Fortune,* May 27, 1985, pp. 122–27.

WILSON, R. DALE, and KAREN A. MACHLEIT. "Advertising Decision Models: A Managerial Review." *Current Issues and Research in Advertising,* 1985, pp. 99–188.

Advertising Measurement

Chapter 2 was devoted primarily to advertising research *methodology*. It combined general principles of the scientific method with decision-making theory to provide a framework for advertising research. In this chapter, attention shifts to advertising research measurement, for it is important to know not only how advertising research should be designed but also what advertising variables to measure, when these variables should be measured, and how best to measure them.

IMPORTANT ADVERTISING MEASURES

What are the most important advertising research measures? Diane Schmalensee recently surveyed the advertising research literature and found that the top priority advertising questions could be grouped into three categories:

1. Theories of individual responses to advertising. For example, how do consumers respond to advertising? Is there a link between advertising and consumer behavior?
2. Measures of individual responses to advertising. For example, how should individual consumer response to advertising be measured? How do alternative measures compare?
3. Advertising operating concerns, such as optimal media choices, concept and copy tests, and optimal repetition levels.[1]

How Advertising Works

Can we develop one grand overall theory to explain how advertising works? Expert opinion varies. Some think that searching for such a theory is academic busy work, while others see such effort as a unifying force in the discipline and industry. But almost everyone agrees that

---

[1] D. H. Schmalensee, "Today's Top Priority Advertising Research Questions," *Journal of Advertising Research* 23 (April–May 1983), pp. 49–60.

advertising "works" as a part of the general process of consumer behavior.

Measuring Individual Responses

The process of measuring individual responses to advertising is often divided into two activities: measures of learning and measures of involuntary or physiological response. Learning can be divided into cognition, affect, and conation. Each of these divisions, along with their common measures, is shown in Figure 3-1.

One aspect of these measures is that they are produced, in part, by the interaction of the research or researcher with the consumer being polled in a semantic or verbal mechanism. This interaction can confound the research intent in ways that range from gross contamination by demand characteristics to subtle language nuances that separate the questioner's intent from the respondent's reply.

Physiological Measures. To avoid the demand characteristics of semantically based measures, researchers use a group of involuntary bodily responses in gauging responses to advertising messages. They may monitor brain waves, galvanic skin response (such as the so-called lie detector), eye pupil diameter, heart rate, and eye movement when subjects are exposed to advertising stimuli. This approach can yield precise measurements, and it removes a degree of semantic ambiguity.

Each of the physiological measures has a literature as well as a group

FIGURE 3-1 Stages of Learning and Common Measures

Stages of Learning	Common Measures
Cognition	Recall
	Recognition
	Belief
	Awareness
	Comprehension
Affect	Attitudes about product
	Product preferences
	Congruence of product with self-image
	Internalization of product message
Conation	Intention to try product
	Intention to adopt product
	Intention to purchase
	Actual product purchase

SOURCE: Adapted from D. H. Schmalensee, "Today's Top Priority Advertising Research Questions," *Journal of Advertising Research* 23 (April–May 1983), p. 53.

of champions and adherents. Unfortunately, greater measurement precision is offset by greater uncertainty about the *meaning* of the results. For example, a classic study employing eye pupil diameter changes by Eckhard Hess and James Polt found that "normal" female subjects displayed the largest pupil dilation (increase) of any group in the experiment and, further, that normal female subjects' pupils increased most in size (+23 percent) when viewing pictures of a nude male. The researchers concluded that the observed increase in pupil diameter reflected a response to interesting or pleasant subject matter.[2] Implicit in the findings is the suspicion that the researchers would have obtained different results if they had asked female subjects which pictures were interesting or pleasant. While the increase in pupil size is incontrovertible, the interpretation of this outcome is ambiguous. The subjects may have been responding to novelty, other illustrations used in the experiment, and elements other than the central figure in the illustration.

Operational Issues

Operating concerns in advertising research involve those decisions made on a daily or frequent basis. Ivory-tower researchers may be uninterested in research about operating issues and may prefer research projects devoted to the development of theory. But real-world advertising depends on the measurement of operating variables in order to deploy financial, creative, and managerial resources in the production of effective advertising. Figure 3–2 enumerates both the questions to be asked and the suggested approaches to answering these operating questions in advertising.

Need for Repetition.   One answer to the first question can be found in the work of Herbert Krugman. His research indicates that three advertising exposures may be the optimal advertising frequency.[3] Fewer than three exposures provided an insufficient base for consumers to learn about the product or message. More than three exposures produced boredom, irritation, and other counterproductive responses. While the optimum frequency may vary in response to a host of other variables (such as consumer involvement with message or product, media used, creative execution, and extent of clutter), a general finding is that some number of exposures greater than one but less than "a lot" represents the most effective level of repetition.

---

[2] E. H. Hess and J. Polt, "Pupil Size as Related to Interest Value of Visual Stimuli," *Science* 132 (1960), pp. 349–50.

[3] H. E. Krugman, "Memory without Recall, Exposure without Perception," *Journal of Advertising Research* 17, no. 4 (August 1977), pp. 7–12.

FIGURE 3–2 Operating Concerns in Advertising

A. Questions to be answered:
  1. What is the minimum number of repetitions required for impact? At what point does advertising wear out?
  2. What are the effects of nonverbal elements of advertising and how can the effects be measured?
  3. Under what conditions should which media (medium) be used, considering audience involvement and issues of media measurement?
  4. How can advertising concepts and whole advertising campaigns (as opposed to single commercials or executions) be measured?
  5. What consumer characteristics affect consumers' response to advertising?
  6. What is the ideal relationship between market share and share of voice?
  7. How should communications budgets be allocated over advertising, sales promotion, personal selling, and corporate communications?
  8. What are the uses for and impact of corporate communications?
B. Suggested approaches:
  1. Empirical work and experiments
  2. Review of how firms now make these decisions
  3. Critical review of existing research on corporate communications (including definition and taxonomy)

SOURCE: Schmalensee, "Today's Top Priority Advertising Research Questions," *Journal of Advertising Research* 23 (April–May 1983)

Nonverbal Elements and Involvement. The second question, relating to nonverbal elements in an ad, can be researched in several ways. Krugman's support for "recognition" as a practical measure of advertising impact is one way because recognition measures capture both verbal and nonverbal elements in the message. A second way is to measure not only verbal but also visual recall, as Burke does when it collects data for "related recall." Here, the measurement includes recollection not only of specific copy points but also of specific visual elements in the advertisement

Concept Testing. Concept testing for individual advertisements as well as for entire campaigns is an integral part of the evaluative pretesting process and is described in detail later in this chapter.

Buyer Characteristics. Consumer characteristics have a justifiable fascination for advertisers. Differences in the characteristics of two or more groups is often the basis for creating market segments, while differences in the characteristics within a target market can furnish valuable clues about how to design and deliver the advertising message. Consumer characteristics that distinguish market segments and suggest advertising design decisions include demographic variables (e.g., age, gender, geographic location, size of household, marital status, formal education, employment status), media exposure and consumption patterns, and purchase histories for a wide variety of goods and services. Companies that sell syndicated advertising research (e.g., Simmons Market Research Bureau) are traditional sources of information about consumer characteristics. Of course, primary research projects can also produce this information.

Market Share and "Share of Voice." The relationship between market share and "share of voice" has been studied with some success. **Share of voice** is defined, in practical terms, as the proportion of all advertising messages for a product class that are accounted for by advertising messages for a particular brand in the product class.

A widely accepted rule is that market share is proportional to marketing effort. This rule is sometimes called the **fundamental theorem of market share.** A firm that spends x percent of its industry's total marketing expenditure should hold an equal percentage of the industry's sales. However, several factors intervene and prevent the theorems for market share from becoming purely mechanical computations. Such factors include price, product, quality, effectiveness, and elasticity. Of these, the quality of the advertising messages, the effectiveness with which they are delivered, and the advertising elasticity of demand most directly influence the relationship between share of voice and market share. Thus, a company that spent 15 percent of its industry's total advertising budget, but had advertising message quality that averaged 10 percent above average, and a media effectiveness that was 8 percent better than normal might be expected to hold:

$$\text{Market share} = (.15) \text{ (industry ad expenditures)}(1.10)(1.08)$$
$$= 17.82\%$$

In a similar way, firms that have lower-than-average message quality and media effectiveness will reduce market share from a value proportional to expenditures.

Advertising Budget Impact. Advertising budgets are crucial to the media function. They are the core of financial activities in advertising and the subject of the following chapter.

Corporate Communications. Corporate communications are different from product communications. Thus, they can be distinguished from familiar advertising we associate with goods and services. Corporate communications in the context of Figure 3–2 means messages whose primary purpose is to alter the external environment in which the company operates. Intended audiences for these messages may be opinion leaders, lawmakers, regulators, competitors, labor unions, or the general public. Such communications have strategic purposes and are expected to influence sales only as a secondary effect over time.

Perhaps the best way to gauge the effect of corporate communications over time is to track the firm's stock price. Various tests, experiments, and comparisons of stock price can lead to estimates of the actual benefit produced by corporate communications. The point here is that if corporate communications have the claimed qualities (e.g., strategic impact, improved external environment, etc.) then a large number of reasonably intelligent investors operating in a reasonably efficient stock market will collectively recognize these qualities and bid up the price of the stock.

Pretesting Research for Advertising Messages

It is important for an advertiser to know what effect an advertisement or campaign will have before the message is delivered to the intended audience. Research undertaken for this purpose is usually called **"copy testing,"** even when done for broadcast advertising. Two aspects of copy testing research are especially important to grasp: the principles of sound copy testing and the methods by which copy testing is done.

Recently, a group of major advertising agencies banded together to develop industry-wide standards for good copy testing research. Called the PACT group (*Positioning Advertising Copy Testing*), these agencies developed a consensus statement on the rule of copy testing and a set of nine principles for how this research should be conducted. These are presented below.

PACT Principles

1. A good copy-testing system provides measurements relevant to the objectives of the advertising.
2. A good copy-testing system is one that requires agreement about how the results will be used *in advance* of each specific test.
3. A good copy-testing system provides *multiple* measurements, because single measurements are generally inadequate to assess an advertisement's performance.
4. A good copy-testing system is based on a model of human response to communications—the *reception* of a stimulus, the *comprehension* of the stimulus, and the *response* to the stimulus.
5. A good copy-testing system allows for consideration of whether the advertising stimulus should be exposed more than once.
6. A good copy-testing system recognizes that the more finished a piece of copy is, the more soundly it can be evaluated, and requires, as a minimum, that alternative executions be tested in the same degree of finish.
7. A good copy-testing system provides controls to avoid biasing effects of the exposure context.
8. A good copy-testing system is one that takes into account basic considerations of sample definition.
9. A good copy-testing system is one that demonstrates reliability and validity.

Copy-Testing Methods.   Seven frequently used methods of copy test-ing are presented below:

Day-After Recall (TV)
Description:
1. Advertisement placed in regular programming, preferably in a high-rated show.
2. Telephone screening next day to find program viewers and deter-mine the percent of those who:
    a. Recall seeing the commercial for the advertiser (total recall).
    b. Can describe commercial well enough that it can be identi-fied as the test commercial (proved recall).
    c. Can describe the commercial but cannot be specifically pin-pointed to test ad (related recall).

Measures:
1. Recall (total, proven, and related).
2. Playback—based on coding of respondents' descriptions of the commercial.
3. Verbatim descriptions.

Cost:
   High. Must include cut-in charges and media cost in addition to research cost.

Evaluation:
1. The best available method for measuring attention due to com-pletely natural viewing situation.
2. Playback material usually only fair and frequently dominated by visual element rather than copy points.
3. Verbatims helpful in spotting misperceptions.
4. No diagnostics and no emotional response.
5. Little or no ability to customize questioning.
6. Hard to use for low-incidence target audience.
7. Broad exposure of test ad beyond research sample.
8. Recall measure is imprecise measure of intrusiveness, which tends to penalize commercials depending on visual response and mood.
9. Scores influenced by programming.

Invited Viewing (TV)
Description:
1. Target audience contacted by telephone and recruited to watch a low-rated show.
2. Advertisement placed in the show.

3. Respondents contacted next day to obtain:
   a. Total recall.
   b. Proven recall
   c. Related recall.
   d. Playback.
   e. Some diagnostics.
4. Different suppliers may add other questions and measures of:
   a. Personal relevance.
   b. Persuasion.

Cost:

Moderate. Media cost must be added but is low due to low-rated show on independent channel.

Evaluation:
1. Good measure of attention.
2. Playback material usually only fair and frequently dominated by visual elements rather than copy points.
3. Verbatims helpful in spotting misperceptions.
4. Diagnostics questionable due to very small number who answer these questions.
5. Fair ability to customize questioning.
6. Usable for many low-incidence target audiences.
7. Modest exposure of test ad beyond research sample.
8. Recall measure not quite as good quality as in day-after recall due to sensitizing viewers in recruiting.
9. Scores influenced by programming.

Cable Invited Viewing (TV)
Description:
1. Target audience contacted by telephone and recruited to watch show on unused cable channel.
2. Advertisement placed in the show.
3. Respondents contacted next day by phone to obtain:
   a. Recall.
   b. Playback.
4. Commercial reexposed on unused channel and diagnostic measures obtained (usually an optional addition to test).

Cost:

Moderate. No additional media expense.

Evaluation:
1. Good measure of attention.

2. Playback material fair and frequently dominated by visual elements rather than copy points.
3. Verbatims helpful in spotting misconceptions.
4. Diagnostics good.
5. Fair ability to customize questioning.
6. Representativeness of sample questionable because respondents must be cable subscribers. Generally unsuitable for continued use on low-incidence target audience.
7. Minimal exposure of text ad beyond research sample.

Theater Testing (TV)
Description:
1. Respondents invited to theater by postcard or telephone.
2. Commercial exposed in program.
3. Recall and playback measures obtained after program is over through a self-administered questionnaire. (One service obtains recall by telephone three days later.)
4. Commercial reexposed without program context.
5. Attitude, persuasion, and diagnostic questions asked through self-administered questionnaire.
6. May include later telephone contact to measure recall.

Cost:

Low to moderate.

Evaluation:
1. Covers broadest range of measurements within a single test design, but does not stand out as good way to measure any one.
2. Playback material poor due to respondents' reluctance to write sufficient descriptions on self-administered questionnaire.
3. Little ability to add customized questioning.
4. Difficult to use on low-incidence target audiences.
5. Subject to group interaction effects.
6. No exposure beyond research sample.
7. Appropriate choice for small budget campaigns where multiple testing is too expensive.

Central Location Testing (TV)
Description:
1. Respondents recruited through intercepts in shopping mall.
2. Shown or played advertisement (may or may not be presented in program or editorial context).
3. Playback, attitude, persuasion, and diagnostic questions asked.

4. If presented in context or in clutter, may obtain an immediate recall score.
5. No standard syndicated service available, so tests follow customized designs.

Cost:

Low.

Evaluation:
1. Best method for measures of comprehension and attitude as well as diagnostic measures.
2. Poor measures of attention.
3. Most easily adapted to unusual target groups and net impression objectives.
4. No exposure beyond research sample.

Tip-in-Tests (Print)
Description:
1. Advertisement tipped into advance copy of current magazine.
2. Target respondents contacted at home or in shopping mall to place magazine.
3. Telephone or personal interview conducted following day to obtain recall, playback.
4. May include diagnostics after reexposure during the interview.

Cost:

Moderate.

Evaluation:
1. Good exposure context provides good measure of attention.
2. Reexposure permits good diagnostic measures.
3. Difficult to administer for low-incidence target groups.
4. Performance affected by issue size (some suppliers offer correction factors.

Simulated Driving Test (Radio)
Description:
1. Respondents invited to participate in "driving test."
2. While involved in simulated driving experience, commercial is exposed on "car radio."
3. Respondents recontacted later to obtain recall and playback material.
4. In some designs, recall and playback are obtained immediately after exposure, and the commercial is reexposed to obtain diagnostics and attitude measures.

Cost:
    Moderate.

Evaluation:
1. Fairly good measures of recall and playback.
2. Other measures good in reexposure designs.
3. Difficult to administer for low-incidence target groups.
4. No exposure beyond research sample.

Variables Measured in Advertising Research

The variables actually measured in advertising research are arranged in six categories: general measures, general audience measures, general market measures, print audience variables, broadcast audience variables, and cost-of-audience measures.

General Measures. **General measures** are adapted to various advertising data but are not unique to them. One of the most commonly used general measures adapted for advertising is the index.

Indexes. A common comparison used in media is the index. An **index** compares several media on the basis of an arbitrary standard. For example, if the national rating for "Cheers," 18, is assigned an index number of 100, then the indexes based on selected local market ratings of "Cheers" would be as follows:

	Local Market Ratings for "Cheers"	Index
Atlanta	20	111
Houston	18	100
Los Angeles	22	122
New York	16	89

We arrive at these figures by dividing our base (i.e., the national rating) of 18 into each local market rating and multiplying by 100 to remove the decimal. The rating in Atlanta was 11 percent higher and the rating in Los Angeles was 22 percent higher than the national average. The index number for Houston was exactly at the national average; the rating in New York was 11 percent below average.

General Audience Measures. **General audience measures** are those used in most media audience evaluations and are often used for intermedia comparisons. In most cases, general audience measures are unique to the advertising/marketing functions. These terms are extremely important for later discussions of media planning.

Reach is the number of *different* people who are exposed to the advertising or to the vehicle in which the advertising appears. Reach can be expressed in number of people, number of households, or percentages of a population or market. The terms *coverage, unduplicated audience,* and *cume* are used as synonyms for reach. Cume, short for "accumulated audience," refers to the number of different people (or households) a medium reached during a specified period. Cume is most commonly used in broadcast media audiences.

Effective reach is the number of exposures to an advertisement necessary to achieve the campaign objectives. Some research indicates that less than three exposures will not allow adequate recall. However, too many exposures are inefficient in that incremental recall after 7, 8, or 10 exposures during a purchase cycle is very small.

The broadcast media are almost always purchased in "packages," or groups of commercials, rather than on a show-by-show basis. **Gross rating points (GRPs)** are a measure of scheduling impact calculated on a weekly or monthly basis. GRP can be figured in two ways:

1. Sum the ratings of the individual show carrying the commercial (assuming one commercial per show).

Show	Network Rating
"Family Ties"	21.1
"Cosby Show"	25.6
"60 Minutes"	22.1
"Golden Girls"	21.1
	89.9, or about 90

2. Multiply reach by frequency. (See definition of *frequency* that follows in this section.) Here reach is expressed as a percentage of population rather than a whole number. If we assume that the four shows listed above had an average reach of 22.5 percent of TV households, then the formula would be:

$$22.5 \times 4 = 90$$

The obvious question is, "Why use the second formula when it is so simple to add up the ratings?" If we want to know only the GRP level for a particular schedule, we would use the addition method. However, the latter formula precisely identifies the interaction that exists between reach and frequency:

$$\frac{\text{GRPs}}{\text{Reach}} = \text{Frequency} \qquad \frac{\text{GRPs}}{\text{Frequency}} = \text{Reach}$$

The media planner must have access to the reach and frequency estimates to use these formulas. The sources of such data are numerous and are discussed later.

It is also helpful to be able to calculate frequency estimates for combinations of media. We will provide a simple means to estimate frequency using the following data:

	Target Audience		
	Reach Percent	Frequency	GRPs
Television ads	30	4.0	120
Magazine ads	20	2.0	40

In this example, reach is expressed as a percentage of the prospects in the target market exposed to television and magazine vehicles carrying the ad. Often, media people simply sum the GRPs and let the matter drop. In fact, ads in the two media did earn 160 GRPs. But notice that by limiting this analysis to GRPs, you ignore (or assume away) the problem of audience duplication.

It is probable that some viewers of the television ads also saw the magazine ads. If so, the true total reach (or unduplicated audience) is less than the sum of the reach for each medium. To estimate the true reach, we use a simple adjustment process:

First, assume no audience overlap between media by summing the reach for each medium. This step sets the maximum value for the combined reach, and in the example above we get 30% + 20% = 50%.

Second, subtract from the maximum combined reach the probable audience overlap. A general guideline indicates that the reach for the highest reach medium (i.e., television, 30 percent) in the market is a reasonable estimate of the TV reach among magazine readers. In our example, 30 percent × 20 percent, or 6 percent of the total target market saw the ads in both television and magazines. Now recall that reach is synonymous with unduplicated audience, and therefore it would be imprecise to double-count this 6 percent in the audiences for each medium. Therefore, we subtract the duplicated portion of the audience, 6 percent, from the value calculated in the first step, or 50% − 6% = 44%.

Since frequency is equal to GRP/Reach, we can now use our estimate of combined reach to improve our estimate of the true combined frequency. In our example:

$$\text{Frequency} = \frac{160}{44} = 3.64$$

Of course, the same process of subtracting probable duplicated audience components from values for maximum reach can be applied to combinations of two or more vehicles in a single medium and to combinations of more than two media. These problems employ exactly the same approach, though the calculations are somewhat more complex.

Duplication is the number or percentage of people who will see an advertisement or campaign in two or more vehicles. Audience duplication in a multimedia advertising campaign can be difficult to estimate.

Composition is the mixture of audience characteristics found in the audience for a medium or vehicle. Composition also refers to the percentage of some medium's total audience made up of a market segment.

A concept similar to frequency is **audience turnover,** or simply turnover. Turnover measures the number of average audiences that saw the medium during a specific period. Using the data provided in Figure 3–3, the calculations are as follows:

$$\text{Turnover} = \frac{\text{Cume}}{\text{Average audience } \frac{(290)}{4}} = \frac{120}{72.5} = 1.66$$

Note that in the case of both frequency and turnover, the calculation results in an answer between 1.0 and N (N = Total exposure opportunities, in this case 4.0). However, frequency and turnover are inversely related.

Frequency is defined as the average number of times the audience reached is exposed to a medium or an advertisement during a specified period. Figure 3–3 calculates a simple frequency problem for a local television show.

In Figure 3–3 we see that 120,000 different people accounted for 290,000 exposures (or duplicated audience). Thus, on average, the members of the audience saw the show 2.42 times during the four-week period studied. Note that by the fourth week, everyone in the audience had seen the show.

FIGURE 3–3 Audience Frequency Calculation

Week	Total Audience (000)	Cume (000)
1	70	70
2	70	30
3	75	20
4	75	
	290	120

Gross impressions is a term used to enumerate the size of the duplicated audience. It expresses the number of times any person has been exposed to an advertising message or campaign. It is similar in spirit to the more familiar gross rating points, but it states the duplicated audience as the product of reach (in people) and the average frequency, or:

$$\text{Gross impressions} = \text{Reach (people)} \times \text{Frequency}$$

In broadcast, gross impressions (also called gross audience) is the sum of the average quarter-hour persons for all spots in a particular schedule.

General Market Measures.   General market measures include **designated market area** (DMA), a specification of each of over 200 unduplicated television marketing areas in the United States. While some DMAs are comprised of more than one county, each U.S. county is assigned to only one DMA. Related terms are Metro Survey Area, which generally corresponds to the Metropolitan Statistical Area used by the Department of Commerce, and Total Survey Area, which includes the MSA plus those counties outside that receive moderate strength (0.5 MV/M) radio signals from at least two AM stations licensed in the market.

Print Audience Measures.   Primary variables for print audience measurements are extremely important in judging the relative value of print media options. Most often these measures are associated with magazines.

Recall is the process by which consumers notice, remember, and are able to report some or all of an advertising message. Recall is traditionally used to measure magazine advertising and is calculated in several, slightly different ways. **Unaided recall** is produced without prompting (e.g., by a "recent reading" readership survey). **Aided recall** is produced with the help of a copy of the publication being studied (e.g., by a "through-the-book" survey). **Day-after recall** is measured during the day after exposure. **Claimed recall** is simply a respondent's assertion that he saw the advertisement. **Related recall** occurs when respondents can provide descriptions of specific portions of the advertisement.

Primary readers are those readers of a publication who are members of a household that purchases or subscribes to the publication. In the aggregate, these readers are called the primary circulation of the publication.

Pass-along readers are those readers of a publication who are not members of the purchasing or subscribing household. They are also called secondary readers and, in the aggregate, secondary circulation.

In-home readers are those who read the average issue of a publication in their home.

Out-of-home readers are those who read the average issue of a magazine in a place other than their own home.

Readers per copy is the average number of readers of one copy of a publication. One disputed estimate of readers per copy placed the figure for the edition of *Playboy* delivered to overseas military installations at 13.

Average issue readership (AIR) is an estimate of the number (or percent of a target) of people in a target market who will see or read any given issue of a publication. This estimate is obtained from a readership survey. If this estimate is obtained from a survey of readers of the publication during the last issue period, it is also called the last issue readership.

Through-the-book is a readership measurement technique that calculates readership estimates by showing respondents either actual copies or "skeletonized" copies of the publications being studied.

Recent reading is a readership measurement technique that obtains its estimate without referring to any specific issues of a publication and without showing the respondents anything more about the publication than a masthead card.

Opportunity to see (OTS) is a measure of those who read at least some of a particular issue of a publication. Since not every reader sees every advertisement, it is more realistic to describe readers of a particular issue as those having OTS, rather than readers of a particular advertisement.

Cumulative readership is the number of people (often in a specified target market) who will see at least one out of two insertions in a single publication. The term is identical to the reach for an advertiser's messages in this publication.

Broadcast Audience Measures. **Broadcast audience measures** are used to estimate audiences during an entire schedule, specific dayparts, or at a given time. As national television advertising rates continue to increase, these measures become more and more crucial.

Rating is a broadcast audience term and is calculated as follows:

$$\text{Rating} = \frac{\text{Number of households "watching" a program}}{\text{Number of TV households in a population}}$$

A TV population normally includes either national households or households in a particular market. Ratings can also be calculated for people watching a program divided by the number of persons in the population. For radio ratings, the audience listening to a station is expressed as a percentage of the relevant population.

Share is a broadcast audience term that reflects the size of the audience for a particular program, expressed as a percentage of the total audience for the medium at the time of measurement. TV share is calculated as follows:

$$\text{Share} = \frac{\text{Number of households "watching" a program}}{\text{Number of households using television (HUT)}}$$

For radio share values, substitute "listening" numbers in the numerator and "households using radio" in the denominator. Person shares can also be calculated for both broadcast media.

Power share is a measure of the dominance of a television program within its daypart and time period. It is calculated as the number of share points by which the vehicle won or lost its time period, based on national ratings as measured by the A. C. Nielsen Company. An example follows:

> *"60 Minutes" (CBS); Week ending 11/2/86; 10/26 (plus 19); 10/19 (plus 18).* For all the talk about the "Rise and Fall of 60 Minutes," there is precious little evidence to suggest the program has entered the "Fall" stage. Not only does "60 Minutes" keep chugging along, recent numbers indicate it has hit full speed. On the October 26 and November 2 telecasts, the program popped season-best 40 shares. From September 14 to November 2, "60 Minutes" has averaged a 37 share. From September 15 to November 3, 1985, "60 Minutes" had an average 35 share. The program has also stayed above the 7 P.M. to 8 P.M. fray between ABC and NBC, which is being won by NBC.[4]

Average time spent listening is a measure of the time an average person listens to a particular radio station. It is computed as follows:

$$\text{TSL} = \frac{\text{Average audience} \times \text{Number of quarter hours in daypart*}}{\text{Cume audience}}$$

* For example, the common radio daypart called Mon–Sun 6A.M.–Midnight has 504 quarter hours. Another daypart, Sun 7P.M.–Midnight, has 20, and so on.

Efficiency of target audience is the ratio of the total time spent listening by the target audience compared to that for the total audience. In other words:

$$\text{ETA} = \frac{\text{Target audience } TSL}{\text{Total audience } TSL}$$

Thus, an ETA value of greater than 1 indicates greater efficiency in the target audience than in the total audience.

Percent recycling is a radio audience measure that indicates the percentage of a station's listeners in one time period that also listen in another time period.

---

4 "TV Power Shares," *Advertising Age*, November 10, 1986, p. 79.

$$\text{Percent recycling} = \frac{\text{Cume audience that listens to both of two time periods}}{\text{Cume audience that listens to one of the time periods}}$$

Percent exclusive is the percent of a particular station's cume audience that listens to that station and no other. Percent exclusive is a measure of the portion of a station's audience that is not reached by any other station and is usually computed for a particular daypart, as follows:

$$\text{Percent exclusive} = \frac{\text{Station's exclusive cume}}{\text{Station's total cume}}$$

Away-from-home listening index is calculated in the following way:

$$\text{Index (AFH)} = \frac{\text{Station's AFH listening percentage}}{\text{The market's AFH listening percentage}}$$

This index relates the station's proportion of away-from-home audience to the typical away-from-home proportion for that market.

Average audience rating is the percent of a demographic group that viewed during the average minute of a particular program.

Average quarter-hour persons is an estimate of the average number of people who are listening to a station during any quarter-hour of a daypart.

Perhaps the most used device for comparing media is the **cost per thousand** (CPM) calculation. The formula is:

$$\text{CPM} = \frac{\text{Cost} \times 1,000}{\text{Circulation}}$$

Normally CPM is calculated on a weighted basis by media planners. The simplest weighting procedure is to calculate CPM on the basis of prospects rather than total audience. In reality, more sophisticated procedures are used in media planning with different audience segments given a weight equal to their importance as prospects.

Cost ranking is a ranking of the cost-per-thousand values for a list of publications.

The media buyer often compares different broadcast buys on the basis of the **cost per rating point** (CPP) of various schedules, as follows:

$$\text{CPP} = \frac{\text{Schedule cost}}{\text{GRPs}}$$

Media planners often use the cost per point calculation to compare the costs of reaching certain demographic target markets. This calculation, called the cost per demographic point, adjusts for wasted circulation and is used by the media buyer in much the same way as the weighted cost per thousand formula discussed earlier. Let's look at an example:

	Household Rating	Rating of Women 18+	Rating of Men 18+	Cost/30 Second
Daytime soap	7	5	1.2	$12,000

$$CPP = \frac{Cost}{Household\ rating} = \frac{\$12,000}{7} = \$1,711$$

$$Cost\ per\ demographic\ point\ (women\ 18+) = \frac{Cost}{Rating\ for\ women\ 18+} = \frac{\$12,000}{5} = \$2,400$$

$$Cost\ per\ demographic\ point\ (men\ 18+) = \frac{Cost}{Rating\ for\ men\ 18+} = \frac{\$12,000}{1.2} = \$10,000$$

The media planner uses the CPP to compare the efficiency with which different shows reach a target audience. The CPP is also used to determine how efficiently a single show reaches different demographic groups. In the above example, our soap opera does well in reaching women over 18, but as might be expected, it would be totally unacceptable as a vehicle for reaching adult males.

Spill-in is the portion of a television market's audience viewing "nonoriginating" stations. If 5 percent of the Denver television market is watching programs broadcast by WTBS in Atlanta, this figure represents the Atlanta station's spill-in to the Denver market. The opposite term, **spill-out,** is the portion of a television station's audience who view the broadcast from outside the originating DMA.

Combined Measures. One of the most useful types of advertising measurement combines (or cross-tabulates) at least two research measures. For example, it might be quite useful to know how many people in a target market read one or more Sunday newspapers, or what percentage of the household furniture buyers in the last year also subscribe to *Ebony* magazine.

This type of combined research can be attained through custom research studies. It can also be obtained from several advertising research firms who regularly report these data. Simmons Market Research Bureau is one well-known supplier of combined advertising data, and SMRB reports are available for 30 categories of purchases and 13 categories of media use. Figures 3–4 and 3–5 are examples of each SMRB report.

FIGURE 3–4 **SMRB Crosstabulation of Costume Jewelry Purchases with Selected Demographic Descriptors of Buyers** (costume jewelry bought and total amount spent in last 12 months, adults)

	Total U.S. (000)	Bought in Last 12 Months				Spent Less than $10			
		A 000	B % Down	C Across %	D Index	A 000	B % Down	C Across %	D Index
Total adults	164,927	15,352	100.0	9.3	100	3,303	100.0	2.0	100
Males	78,156	3,223	21.0	4.1	44	558	16.9	0.7	36
Females	86,771	12,129	79.0	14.0	150	2,745	83.1	3.2	158
18–24	28,686	2,603	17.0	9.1	97	705	21.3	2.5	123
25–34	38,660	4,447	29.0	11.5	124	923	27.9	2.4	119
35–44	27,652	3,065	20.0	11.1	119	665	20.1	2.4	120
45–54	22,514	2,376	15.5	10.6	113	328*	9.9	1.5	73
55–64	21,892	1,608	10.5	7.3	79	269*	8.1	1.2	61
65 or older	25,524	1,254	8.2	4.9	53	413*	12.5	1.6	81
18–34	67,345	7,049	45.9	10.5	112	1,628	49.3	2.4	121
18–49	106,223	11,239	73.2	10.6	114	2,438	73.8	2.3	115
25–54	88,825	9,887	64.4	11.1	120	1,916	58.0	2.2	108
35–49	38,878	4,190	27.3	10.8	116	810	24.5	2.1	104
50 or older	58,704	4,113	26.8	7.0	75	865	26.2	1.5	74
Graduated college	25,861	2,946	19.2	11.4	122	584	17.7	2.3	113
Attended college	27,231	3,186	20.8	11.7	126	578	17.5	2.1	106
Graduated high school	65,755	6,738	43.9	10.2	110	1,388	42.0	2.1	105
Did not graduate high school	46,080	2,483	16.2	5.4	58	753	22.8	1.6	82
Employed males	54,185	2,478	16.1	4.6	49	362*	11.0	0.7	33
Employed females	41,876	7,120	46.4	17.0	183	1,490	45.1	3.6	178
Employed full-time	82,854	7,441	48.5	9.0	96	1,384	41.9	1.7	83
Employed part-time	13,207	2,156	14.6	16.3	175	467*	14.1	3.5	177
Not employed	68,866	5,755	37.5	8.4	90	1,452	44.0	2.1	105
Professional/manager	27,537	2,857	18.6	10.4	111	451*	13.7	1.6	82
Clerical/sales	26,625	3,713	24.2	13.9	150	734	22.2	2.8	138
Craftsmen/foremen	12,051	434*	2.8	3.6	39	30†	0.9	0.2	12
Other employed	29,848	2,594	16.9	8.7	93	636	19.3	2.1	106
Single	33,826	2,919	19.0	8.6	93	675	20.4	2.0	100
Married	102,816	10,224	66.6	9.9	107	2,122	64.2	2.1	103
Divorced/separated/ widowed	28,285	2,209	14.4	7.8	84	507	15.3	1.8	90
Parents	59,203	6,830	44.5	11.5	124	1,567	47.4	2.6	132
White	143,976	14,135	92.1	9.8	105	3,062	92.7	2.1	106
Black	17,832	958	6.2	5.4	58	235*	7.1	1.3	66
Other	3,119	259†	1.7	8.3	89	6†	0.2	0.2	10

* Projections relatively unstable because of sample base—use caution.

† Number of cases too small for reliability. Shown for consistency only.

SOURCE: Simmons Market Research Bureau, Inc.: *1983 Study of Media and Markets*, p. 386

	$10–$24				$25 or More		
A	B	C	D	A	B	C	D
	%	Across			%	Across	
000	Down	%	Index	000	Down	%	Index
5,755	100.0	3.5	100	6,294	100.0	3.8	100
1,168	20.3	1.5	43	1,497	23.8	1.9	50
4,587	79.7	5.3	151	4,797	76.2	5.5	145
869	15.1	3.0	87	1,029	16.3	3.6	94
1,711	29.7	4.4	127	1,813	28.8	4.7	123
1,249	21.7	4.5	129	1,152	18.3	4.2	109
881	15.3	3.9	112	1,166	18.5	5.2	136
655	11.4	3.0	86	684	10.9	3.1	82
391*	6.8	1.5	44	450	7.1	1.8	46
2,580	44.8	3.8	110	2,841	45.1	4.2	111
4,339	75.4	4.1	117	4,462	70.9	4.2	110
3,840	66.7	4.3	124	4,131	65.6	4.7	122
1,760	30.6	4.5	130	1,621	25.8	4.2	109
1,416	24.6	2.4	69	1,832	29.1	3.1	82
892	15.5	3.4	99	1,470	23.4	5.7	149
1,023	17.8	3.8	108	1,585	25.2	5.8	153
2,976	51.7	4.5	130	2,373	37.7	3.6	95
865	15.0	1.9	54	865	13.7	1.9	49
906	15.7	1.7	48	1,211	19.2	2.2	59
2,740	47.6	6.5	188	2,890	45.9	6.9	181
2,806	48.8	3.4	97	3,252	51.7	3.9	103
840	14.6	6.4	182	849	13.5	6.4	168
2,109	36.6	3.1	88	2,194	34.9	3.2	83
946	16.4	3.4	98	1,460	23.2	5.3	139
1,464	25.4	5.5	158	1,515	24.1	5.7	149
163†	2.8	1.4	39	240†	3.8	2.0	52
1,072	18.6	3.6	103	885	14.1	3.0	78
1,054	18.3	3.1	89	1,190	18.9	3.5	92
3,916	68.0	3.8	109	4,187	66.5	4.1	107
784	13.6	2.8	79	918	14.6	3.2	85
2,814	48.9	4.8	136	2,449	38.9	4.1	108
5,228	90.8	3.6	104	5,846	92.9	4.1	106
336*	5.8	1.9	54	387*	6.1	2.2	57
192†	3.3	6.2	176	61†	1.0	2.0	51

FIGURE 3-5 SMRB Crosstabulations of Income with Special TV Programs and Events (Individual employment income special programs and special events on television: Almost certain to watch/watched last time shown, professionals and managers)

	Total U.S. (000)	$35,000 or more				$30,000 or more				$20,000–$29,999				$15,000–$19,999			
		A 000	B % Down	C % Across	D Index	A 000	B % Down	C % Across	D Index	A 000	B % Down	C % Across	D Index	A 000	B % Down	C % Across	D Index
All professionals and managers	27,537	5,675	100.0	20.6	100	8,358	100.0	30.4	100	8,465	100.0	30.7	100	3,825	100.0	13.9	100
ABC News Closeup	5,036	1,167	20.6	21.5	104	1,676	20.1	30.8	102	1,776	21.0	32.7	106	770	20.1	14.2	102
ABC Theatre of the Month	3,142	434	7.6	13.8	67	756	9.0	24.1	79	1,018	12.0	32.4	105	362*	9.5	11.5	83
Academy Awards	10,150	1,969	34.7	19.4	94	2,906	34.8	28.6	94	2,963	35.0	29.2	95	1,680	43.9	16.6	119
Academy of Country Music Awards	5,323	1,025	18.1	17.6	85	1,456	17.4	25.0	82	1,668	19.7	28.6	93	964	25.2	16.5	119
All Star Family Feud	3,731	425	7.5	11.4	55	678	8.1	18.2	60	1,034	12.2	27.7	90	730	19.1	19.6	141
American Movie Awards	3,015	390	6.9	12.9	63	603	7.2	20.0	66	753	8.9	25.0	81	514*	13.4	17.0	123
American Music Awards	4,177	576	10.1	13.8	67	941	11.3	22.5	74	1,055	12.5	25.3	82	706	18.5	16.9	122
Barbara Mandrell Special	5,226	898	15.8	17.2	83	1,375	16.5	26.3	87	1,670	19.7	32.0	104	734	19.2	14.0	101
Barbara Walters Special	6,435	1,099	19.4	16.9	82	1,589	19.0	24.5	81	1,977	23.4	30.5	99	1,147	30.0	17.7	127
Battle of the Network Stars	4,500	679	12.0	15.1	73	1,146	13.7	25.5	84	1,263	14.9	28.1	91	805	21.0	17.9	129
Bob Hope Special	7,232	1,472	25.9	20.4	99	2,163	25.9	29.9	99	2,318	27.4	32.1	104	923	24.1	12.8	92
Body Human	4,349	825	14.5	19.0	92	1,225	14.7	28.2	93	1,256	14.8	28.9	94	700	18.3	16.1	116
Bugs Bunny	4,533	858	15.1	18.7	91	1,260	15.1	27.5	91	1,351	16.0	29.5	96	555	14.5	12.1	87
Casper Christmas Show	2,194	332*	5.9	15.1	73	492	5.9	22.4	74	787	9.3	35.9	117	358*	9.4	16.3	117
Charles and Diana: A Royal Romance	1,777	734	12.9	15.4	75	1,164	13.9	24.4	80	1,464	17.3	30.6	100	904	23.6	18.9	136
Charlie Brown	6,041	1,080	19.0	17.9	87	1,482	17.7	24.5	81	1,912	22.6	31.7	103	1,062	27.8	17.6	127
Circus of the Stars	1,223	751	13.2	17.8	86	1,175	14.1	27.8	92	1,120	13.2	26.5	86	690	18.0	16.3	118
Cotton Bowl Parade	1,246	742	13.1	17.5	85	1,295	15.5	30.5	100	1,255	14.8	29.6	96	733	19.2	17.3	124
Country Comes Home	2,433	364*	6.4	14.7	72	613	7.3	24.8	82	772	9.1	31.3	102	319†	8.3	12.9	93
Country Music Awards	6,169	1,072	18.9	17.4	84	1,745	20.9	28.3	93	1,696	20.0	27.5	89	934	24.4	15.1	109

* Projections relatively unstable because of sample base—use caution.

† Number of cases too small for reliability. Shown for consistency only.

SOURCE: Simmons Market Research Bureau, Inc.: 1983 Study of Media and Markets, p. 79.

REVIEW QUESTIONS

1. What are the three categories of "most important" advertising research questions?

2. What is the major advantage and the major disadvantage to using physiological measures in advertising research?

3. What stage of learning is "product preference" likely to measure? What stage is "actual purchases" likely to measure?

4. What are the important measures of the cognition stage of learning?

5. Describe the adjustment factors that are used to fine-tune applications of the fundamental theorem of market share.

6. Summarize the PACT perspective on copy-testing.

7. The average national rating for a hypothetical TV show, "Those Amazing Weatherspoons," is 20. In Minneapolis, the show has a rating of 23. Express the Minneapolis rating as an index number using the average national rating as the base.

8. Define the following terms: reach, cume, duplicated audience, GRPs.

9. If, over a month, a TV show containing your client's commercial has an average audience of 20 percent of a market and a reach of 30 percent of that market, what is the audience turnover?

10. If 8 percent of the Dallas/Fort Worth market is viewing programs broadcast by WTBS in Atlanta, what is the Dallas/Fort Worth value for spill-in?

11. Using the data in Figure 3–5, how many adults in the United States graduated from college? How many of these college graduates spent $25 or more on costume jewelry in the last 12 months?

SUGGESTED ADDITIONAL READING

BOGART, LEO. "Executives Fear Ad Overload Will Lower Effectiveness." *Marketing News,* May 25, 1984, p. 4.

Journal of the Market Research Society 28, no. 2 (April 1986). Special Edition on Readership Research.

Journal of Media Planning 1, no. 1 (1986). Issue devoted to the papers delivered at the Symposium on Effective Frequency, Northwestern University, April 25, 1986.

KLEBBA, JOANNE M. "Physiological Measures of Research: A Review of Brain Activity, Electrodermal Response, Pupil Dilation and Voice Analysis Methods and Studies." *Current Issues and Research in Advertising* 2 (1985), pp. 1–74.

KOTEN, JOHN. "Car Makers Use 'Image' Map as Tool to Position Products." *The Wall Street Journal,* March 22, 1984, p. 35.

KRUGMAN, HERBERT E. "Point of View: Measuring Memory—An Industry Dilemma." *Journal of Advertising Research* 25, no. 4 (1985), pp. 49–51.

LEIGH, JAMES H., and ANIL MENON. "A Comparison of Alternative Recognition Measures of Advertising Effectiveness." *Journal of Advertising* 15, no. 3 (1986), pp. 4–12, 20.

MOORE, WILLIAM L. "Testing Advertising Concepts: Current Practices and Opinions." *Journal of Advertising* 14, no. 3 (1985), pp. 45–51.

"Right Hand Page, Far Forward." *Marketing and Media Decisions,* May 1985, pp. 72+.

Standard Definitions of Broadcast Research Terms 28, no. 2 (April 1986). Special Edition on Readership Research. National Association of Broadcasters.

STEWART, DAVID W.; CONNIE PECHMANN; SRINIVASAN RATNESHWAR; JON STROUD; and BEVERLY BRYANT. "Methodological and Theoretical Foundations of Advertising Copytesting: A Review." *Current Issues and Research in Advertising* 2 (1985), pp. 1–74.

SUMNER, PAUL. *Readership Research and Computers.* New York: Newsweek International, 1985.

WEINSTEIN, SIDNEY. "Advances in Brain Wave Analysis Allow Researchers to Test Effectiveness of Ads." *Marketing News,* September 17, 1982, p. 21.

Advertising Budgets

Although most executives indicate that computers are used in the advertising budgeting process, only about one third of them also analyze advertising-sales response functions. The majority of all executives believe that their company's advertising budgeting procedures need "some" or "much" improvement and many offer recommendations.*

Kent Lancaster and Judith Stern

At the financial heart of advertising activities is the advertising budget. The advertising budget greatly influences every other aspect of advertising, but its influence on the decisions and processes involved in advertising media is especially keen. Throughout this chapter, our discussion of budgets is divided into two major parts: how budgets are developed and used and how they should be developed and used. To accomplish this, we will explore the nature of budgets and the benefits of using them. Practical budgeting philosophies will be discussed and contrasted with theoretical standards. Major advertising uses of budgeted funds are then summarized. Finally, we will describe budgetary controls and their managerial applications.

WHAT IS A BUDGET?

Advertising is one of many business activities that requires funds. Thus, to oversimplify, financial management of advertising is the process of controlling the sources and uses of advertising funds. In this chapter, you will see that advertising budgets have much in common with budgets for other busines activities, such as manufacturing. You will also see that

---

* "Computer-Based Advertising Budgeting Practices of Leading U.S. Consumer Advertisers," *Journal of Advertising* 12, no. 4 (1983), pp. 4–9.

advertising budgets are different in some important respects from budgets for other business areas.

Advertising budgets are a fundamental tool for managing the large sums of money involved in advertising. In its simplest form, a budget is a plan. It describes management's intentions for future sources of funds and for future uses of these funds. All the other financial documents used by business today, describe what has already happened—budgets state what will occur in the future. We know that the future is uncertain and cannot be forecast exactly. Since budgets plan for actions to be taken in this uncertain future, they are subject to modifications over time. In fact, the farther the budget period extends into the future, the less fixed the budget is likely to be.

While it is important to recognize the uncertainties of future periods, it is equally important to recognize the value of planning the financial aspects of the future via budgeting. In general, the budgeting process yields several kinds of benefit to managers:

1. Budgets encourage (and even require) thinking ahead. The budgeting process not only reduces managers' concentration on reacting to events, but also stimulates the processes by which management can achieve better control over those events.
2. Budgets require coordination of managerial effort. In many enterprises, preparation of a budget is the process that most effectively draws together diverse interests and problems. Budgeting is often the process by which problems are resolved in light of what is best for the entire organization.
3. Budgets furnish performance standards. During and after the budget period, the budget can be used to evaluate, in relatively unambiguous quantitative terms, how effectively resources were expended and benefits realized.
4. Budgets are control devices. When properly used, budgets prevent small disturbances from becoming major problems or worse. In this sense, budgets are financial regulators; they prevent unanticipated problems from creating unchecked deterioration in financial matters.

TYPES OF BUDGETS

Flexible versus Appropriations Budget

Businesses use several kinds of financial plans or budgets. The first important distinction is between flexible and appropriations budgets. As its name suggests, a **flexible budget** usually permits variations in revenues, in expenditures, or in both. In contrast, **appropriations budgets** set a ceiling on the funds available for expenditure during the budget period. Many business activities are planned by flexible budgets, while appropriations budgets are common in government agencies and in the private sector for research activities and for advertising.

Cash versus Capital Budgets

An important distinction in business budgets is the length of the planning period. Financial management theory draws a fundamental distinction between budgets for a year or less and those for more than a year. Budgets for a year or less properly focus on plans for short-lived assets, chiefly cash. The most commonly used short-term budget is the cash budget. In contrast, budgets that plan for the management of assets having economic lives greater than one year are called capital budgets. Capital budgeting incorporates two important concepts into the planning. The first concept, the "time value of money," means that a dollar received in the near future is more certain, more useful, and therefore more valuable than a dollar received in the distant future. The second concept involves the "rate of return" that each capital asset is projected to furnish over time. Capital budgeting, then, is a process in which time-discounted rates of return are compared for competing capital projects within the constraint of the firm's cost of capital.

Advertising media budgets are almost always cash budgets of the appropriations type. In some respects, this practice is unfortunate, and suggestions for modifying the nature of advertising media budgets are presented later in the chapter. For now, let's examine how advertising budgeting is conducted.

HOW CAN CLIENT ORGANIZATIONS SET ADVERTISING APPROPRIATIONS?

The first step in cash budgeting is to plan for the sources and volume of the funds needed. In advertising budgets, the source of funds is the client organization. The volume decision, also called the advertising allocation, is usually done in one of five ways.

Percent of Sales. This method is the most popular for determining the advertising allocation, and it is especially prevalent among small and medium-sized clients. Allocations to advertising are calculated by selecting a percentage of sales revenue (e.g., 4 percent).

Percent-of-sales allocations are criticized by theoreticians who point out that this is a clear case of placing the cart before the horse. Advertising is supposed to stimulate demand for (and sales of) product. But here, past sales are used to set the level of advertising support for the future. Critics of this method argue that when times are good and sales are high, the method may allocate "too much" to advertising. While overallocation may cause advertising inefficiencies, the underallocation that occurs during hard times and periods of low sales will almost certainly result in insufficient levels of advertising.

Percent of Future Sales. One significant variant on the percent-of-sales for allocation is the substitution of "future" or forecast sales for past sales. This substitution neatly blunts the earlier theoretical criticism. Unfortunately, this method solves one problem by creating another— namely, the uncertainty of the forecast figure for sales. In addition, since future sales are a function not only of advertising but also of other decisions and external forces, the method incorporates some inevitable irrelevance. Logically, allocating advertising by some percent of carefully forecast future sales represents an improvement over the use of past sales. In practice, this method is less frequently used, probably due to clients' suspicions about sales forecasts.

Parity. Competitive parity means that the client allocates funds to advertising in the same way and at the same level as the competition. This method suffers from its own serious flaws and, depending on the method of imitation used, may also inherit other weaknesses. First, it is often difficult to discover what competitors are allocating to advertising, and therefore, attempts to follow competitors' decisions produce imperfect imitation. In other words, even if the method were prudent, it would be difficult to apply. Second, the method fails to recognize that companies in the same industry or product group have different advertising opportunities and efficiencies. Thus, to imitate others implies a passive, defensive managerial outlook, that is not consistent with either effective advertising decisions or business success. Finally, if competitors are using suboptimal advertising allocation methods, such as percent of sales, imitators inherit the inherent weaknesses.

Objective and Task. In this method, advertising objectives are precisely stated. Then (its proponents claim) the tasks necessary to achieve these objectives are described carefully. Next, the funds required for these tasks are specified. Finally, the task-required costs are added, and their sum is described as the advertising allocation.

Students first introduced to this method are inclined to be impressed by its logic, and the method is deductively logical. However, it is impractical because of two facts: it is almost impossible to know beforehand exactly what tasks (or activities) will be required to accomplish the chosen advertising objectives, and it is equally difficult to precisely determine costs for the task specified. To put the problem more philosophically, if an advertiser knew everything required to furnish the required inputs for the objective-and-task method, such as the selection of optimum objectives, there would be no need to follow the chronological steps of the method.

All You Can Afford. This method is the darling of advertising novices, who are understandably struck by its implied enthusiasm for their craft. It is our sad duty to dash some cold fact on that enthusiasm. First, what the client can "afford" is not necessarily correlated with the advertising opportunities available. Wealthy advertisers could overspend and poor advertisers underspend. Second, advertising is an important part of the marketing effort, but not the whole. Great differences exist among advertisers regarding the effectiveness of the advertising effort relative to that of other marketing efforts, such as product development or physical distribution. It is both simpleminded and dangerous for advertisers to assume that the benefits from added advertising always exceed the benefits from additional effort in the other marketing areas. Finally, and most fundamentally harmful, is the implied notion that advertising funds must come from surpluses within the advertiser organization. This notion produces an almost puritanical, invariably foolish, conclusion that it is not prudent to use external funds (say, debt) to finance advertising. The discussion of a capital budgeting approach to advertising allocation, found later in this chapter, will suggest a fundamentally different alternative.

How Do Advertisers Set Advertising Budgets?

It is instructive not only to see the methods by which real advertisers set advertising budgets but also to get a sense of the popularity of each method. In a recent study, Kent Lancaster and Judith Stern reviewed three earlier studies of how advertisers set budgets for advertising. In addition, they surveyed executives at the 100 largest consumer advertiser firms in the United States. These companies together account for over half of all U.S. advertising expenditures. The results of their study are summarized in Figure 4–1. These numbers show that over half the firms questioned use anticipated sales in their budget decisions and that only one company in five considers past sales. Further, the figure shows that objective-and-task methods have had the largest increase and that some measure of parity, in the form of either matching or outspending competitors, is used by one third of the sample firms.

FIGURE 4-1 How Advertisers Actually Set Advertising Budgets

	Percent of Respondents Using Each Method				
Method	San Augustine and Foley (1975)	Permut (1977) Media Allocation	Related Activities	Patti and Blasko (1981)	Lancaster and Stern (1983)
Quantitative methods	4	13	0	51	20
Objective and task	12	15	10	63	80
Percent anticipated sales	52	58	20	53	53
Unit anticipated sales	12	10	8	22	28
Percent past sales	16	33	5	20	20
Unit past sales	12	5	3	N/A	15
Affordable	28	43	63	20	13
Arbitrary	16	18	50	4	N/A
Match competitors	N/A	N/A	N/A	24	25
Outspend competitors	N/A	N/A	N/A	N/A	8
Share of voice/market	N/A	N/A	N/A	N/A	5
Previous budget	N/A	N/A	N/A	N/A	3
Others	20	3	15	N/A	12

Note: Totals exceed 100 percent due to multiple responses and rounding.

SOURCE: K. Lancaster and J. Stern; "Computer-Based Advertising Budgeting Practices of Leading U.S. Consumer Advertisers," *Journal of Advertising* 12, no. 4 (1983), pp. 4–9.

When Do Advertisers Set Advertising Budgets?

In addition to knowing about how advertising budgets are set, you should also understand the timing of advertising budget preparation. Figure 4–2 shows the budgeting calendar averages for the top 200 advertised brands and the time line along which various people and groups enter the budgeting process. The greatest number of large advertisers begin their budgeting process in June (24 percent) and make major media decisions in August. This figure also shows that over 60 percent of the agencies involved with these accounts are involved in the budget process from the outset, and almost as many accounts involve a media specialist from startup (58 percent). This figure contains powerful evidence that budgeting is outside the realm of advertising agency concerns or beyond the responsibilities of media professionals.

The final issue affecting the scheduling of advertising budgets is the timing of actual expenditures. Seasonal patterns in media audiences and other factors combine to create departures from a straight-line pattern of media purchases. Figure 4–3 shows the relationship between audiences and media purchases for four categories of advertising media.

This is how and when real-world advertisers and agencies perform the advertising budget-setting task. While the scheduling process works well, none of the budget-setting methods is free from defect. We now turn to a theoretically correct method for allocating funds to advertising.

FIGURE 4-2 Scheduling for the Advertising Budget Process

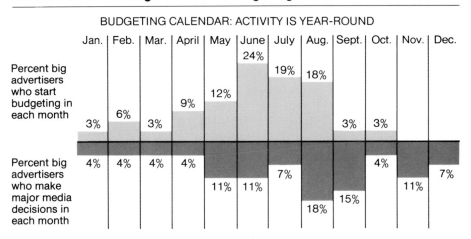

BUDGETING CALENDAR: ACTIVITY IS YEAR-ROUND

	Jan.	Feb.	Mar.	April	May	June	July	Aug.	Sept.	Oct.	Nov.	Dec.
Percent big advertisers who start budgeting in each month	3%	6%	3%	9%	12%	24%	19%	18%	3%	3%		
Percent big advertisers who make major media decisions in each month	4%	4%	4%	4%	11%	11%	7%	18%	15%	4%	11%	7%

WHEN KEY BUDGETING ACTIVITIES ARE PHASED-IN
(cumulative percent of cases from start-up)

	Agency gets into picture	Media specialist involved	Media recommend-ations	Media plan to marketing management	Total budget to marketing management	Total budget to top management
At start-up	63%	58%				
First month	87%	77%	21%	19%	27%	3%
Second month	97%	97%	50%	38%	57%	35%
Third month	100%	100%	89%	77%	87%	58%
Fourth month			100%	97%	94%	87%
Fifth month				100%	97%	94%
Sixth month					100%	97%
Seventh month						100%

(Shaded boxes indicate 60% or more)

SOURCE: "Decisions Survey among Top 200 Advertised Brands," *Marketing and Media Decisions*, Fall Special Edition, 1982, p. 143.

ALLOCATION THEORY AND ADVERTISING

The economic theory of allocating funds to business activities is perversely and deceptively simple. The decision maker simply sets the marginal cost of the activity equal to the marginal revenue or return earned by that activity. Under the assumption that the activity for which the allocation is being determined does not interact with other activities and decisions, the allocation level that produces the above equality (i.e., MC_i

FIGURE 4–3 Seasonal Fluctuations in Advertising Audiences and Media Purchases

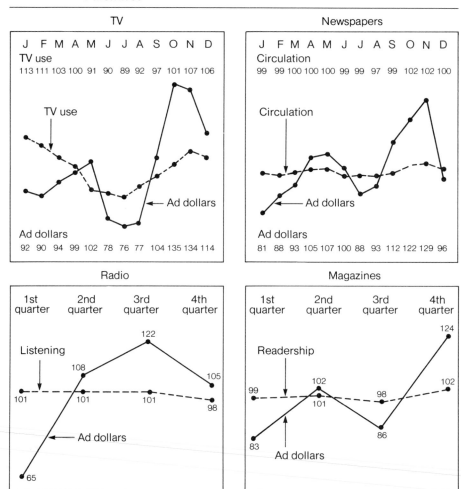

TV

J	F	M	A	M	J	J	A	S	O	N	D
TV use
113 111 103 100 91 90 89 92 97 101 107 106

TV use

Ad dollars

Ad dollars
92 90 94 99 102 78 76 77 104 135 134 114

Newspapers

J	F	M	A	M	J	J	A	S	O	N	D
Circulation
99 99 100 100 100 99 99 97 99 102 102 100

Circulation

Ad dollars

Ad dollars
81 88 93 105 107 100 88 93 112 122 129 96

Radio

1st quarter	2nd quarter	3rd quarter	4th quarter

122
Listening
108
105
101 101 101
98
Ad dollars
65

Magazines

1st quarter	2nd quarter	3rd quarter	4th quarter

124
Readership
102 102
99 98
101
86
83
Ad dollars

Note: Numbers shown are indexes, to a base of the annual average value.
SOURCE: *Marketing and Media Decisions,* Fall Special Edition, 1982, p. 141.

= MR_i) is the level that maximizes profit and is therefore the optimal allocation[1]. To apply this allocation theory to actual advertising effort, the decision maker must, in effect, establish the conditions under which it is possible to measure marginal cost and marginal revenue. If you

---

[1] Joel Dean, *Managerial Economics* (Englewood Cliffs, N.J.: Prentice-Hall, 1951), pp. 363 ff.

reflect on the requirements for this measurement, you will see that the necessary conditions, while not impossible to create, are extraordinarily restrictive. In all likelihood, a new product (not carrying an established product line, family, or company brand) will have to be both advertised and sold only through direct mail. Under these restrictive conditions, and within a range of marginal ad preparation costs (say, printing lot size) and marginal distribution costs (say, mailing lot size), an advertiser can match the marginal cost of advertising with the marginal returns (sales) from that advertising. Here the advertiser simply increases advertising allocation until the theoretical optimum is reached, or until $MC = MR$.

At this juncture, it is not uncommon to find that advertising readers are discouraged over the whole business of advertising budget allocation. Clearly, the methods actually used are sloppy. In contrast, the theoretically correct method gains precision at the expense of restrictions and wide-ranging unsuitability. What is the prudent advertiser to do?

HOW ADVERTISERS MIGHT IMPROVE ADVERTISING ALLOCATION DECISIONS

Several possibilities exist for improving actual allocation practices by combining some aspects of advertising allocation theory with decision theory used in other business areas and with quantitative methods that estimate or isolate advertising's costs and contribution over time.

These improvements have a cost—most noticeable is the increase in the resources devoted to decision making. It is our judgment that the extra time, difficulty, and expense required to improve advertising appropriation methods are likely to improve the efficiency of advertising for most advertisers.

Empirical Approaches

One way to avoid both arbitrariness and unrealistic restrictions is to try a variety of advertising allocation levels and then attempt to isolate and compare the benefits that each level produces. There are several ways to do this. Keep in mind that most empirical approaches produce data that are mathematically evaluated. Our discussion here is largely limited to the "results" of these methods.

Experiments

One way to let the facts speak for themselves is to conduct an experiment to find out whether one level of allocation produces significantly better results than another. Figure 4–4 summarizes such an experiment. Two

FIGURE 4–4   Advertising Allocation Experiment

	Percent of National Population	Test Sales during Month ($000)	Sales Advertising Ratio
Allocation level A:			
$100,000 per city			
Wichita, Kansas	.5%	$509	5.09
San Antonio, Texas	.6	660	6.60
Richmond, Virginia	.5	494	4.94
Des Moines, Iowa	.5	501	5.01
	Total: 2.1%	Average: $541	Average: 5.41
Allocation level B:			
$120,000 per city			
Louisville, Kentucky	.6%	$804	6.70
Tulsa, Oklahoma	.5	828	6.90
Norfolk, Virginia	.6	707	5.87
Jacksonville, Florida	.5	710	5.92
	Total: 2.2%	Average: $762	Average: 6.35

ANOVA Summary

	Sum of Squares	df	Mean Square	F Ratio
Between groups	1.757	1	1.757	3.85*
Within groups	2.740	6	.457	

* $p < .10$

per-city levels of advertising ($100,000 and $120,000) are compared on the basis of the sales-to-advertising ratio for two groups of cities of roughly equivalent population. By simply inspecting the sales-to-advertising ratios, an advertiser could conclude that the larger appropriation produced a higher mean ratio (6.35 compared with 5.41). Use of one-way analysis of variance (ANOVA) permits the inference that the difference in these mean ratios is significant at a relatively high level of confidence. Thus, the higher per-city expenditure seems to be warranted by benefits that are larger than proportional to the increased expenditure.

Correlation Methods

Often it is possible to examine historical data and, by correlating two or more such measures, reach conclusions about the presence of trends. This analysis is called regression. In one famous regression, Palda found that in combination with other measures, the historical relationships between advertising allocations and sales for a patent medicine were positive but nonlinear.[2] That is, larger advertising allocations were associated with

---

[2] K. Palda, *The Measurement of Cumulative Advertising Effects* (Englewood Cliffs, N.J.: Prentice-Hall, 1964), pp. 67 ff.

FIGURE 4–5   Secondary Data Sources Commonly Used in Advertising Budgeting

Data Sources	Percent of Firms Using
Internal company records	93
Nielsen	70
SMRB (Simmons Market Research Bureau)	50
Media Records	45
BAR (Broadcast Advertisers Reports)	42
LNA (Leading National Advertisers)	40
SRDS (Standard Rate and Data Service)	35
SAMI (Selling Areas Marketing Inc.)	35
PIB (Publishers Information Bureau)	33
ARBITRON (American Research Bureau)	28
MRI (Mediamark Research Inc.)	22
RADAR	13
RER (Radio Expenditure Report)	8
Others	33

SOURCE: Kent Lancaster and Judith Stern, "Computer-Based Advertising Budgeting Practices of Leading U.S. Consumer Advertisers," *Journal of Advertising* 12, no. 4 (1983), p. 7.

greater sales but at a diminishing rate of efficiency. In this situation, whether advertising allocations earn their keep by generating sales depends on the level of advertising. Using actual data (from 1950), advertising expenditures were associated with a sales figure "due to advertising" about 3½ times as large.[3]

Another method that combines empirical data with the substance of correlation procedures is based on the use of good secondary data. Here, the approach is empirical in that it is not based on guesstimates, judgments, or simulations but on real numbers for actual variables. Lancaster and Stern found that a majority of the firms they surveyed had relied on one or more secondary data sources in preparing advertising budgets. Figure 4–5 shows the data sources such firms used in budget preparation in addition to internal corporate records.

In this same general methodology, important work by the Strategic Planning Institute has developed a data base of corporate histories of over 1,000 companies. This archive, called Profit Impact of Market Strategy, or PIMS, contains a minimum of four years of data for each firm. Based on the combined experience of a sample of about 600 of PIMS firms, a set of "rules" or guidelines for ad budgeting in the capital goods and industrial marketing firms was distilled. These guides are shown in Figure 4–6.

---

[3] As reported in J. Simon, *The Management of Advertising* (Englewood Cliffs, N.J.: Prentice-Hall, 1971), p. 107.

FIGURE 4-6   Factors Associated with Higher Advertising Expenditures

---

1.   Higher market share.
2.   Higher new product introduction rates.
3.   Faster growing markets.
4.   Lower utilization rates for plant capacity.
5.   Lower unit price.
6.   Products that represent a low portion of customers' purchases.
7.   High (or premium) and low (or discount) product prices.
8.   Higher quality products.
9.   Broad product lines.
10. Standard (as contrasted with "custom" or "special ordered") products.

SOURCE: V. Kijewski, "Advertising and Promotion, How Much Should You Spend?" The Strategic Planning Institute, 1983.

ADVERTISING CARRYOVER EFFECTS

One area of study that has proven particularly difficult to quantify is the effect of advertising over time. It is widely recognized that the result of a particular ad or campaign is not seen immediately. Good advertising, comprised of themes and placements that are memorable and effective, can be recalled by consumers long after the campaign is over. Unfortunately, bad advertising produces long-lived effects too.

Measured in almost any possible way, advertising's effects at any time are a result of the advertising at that time and advertising done in previous time periods. The effects of past advertising are less potent than current advertising because of factors such as forgetting and the clamor of competing ad claims. Nevertheless, the effect of past advertising has not entirely evaporated since it persists and operates in conjunction with current advertising. Sometimes the effect is called the decay function of advertising—similar to the "decay" in radioactivity that is the basis for carbon-dating procedures. It is also known as the residual effect of advertising.

Residual advertising effects operate as a lagged or delayed influence on present advertising. They also exhibit a nonlinear influence with a shape and size unique to each product situation. Residual effects are important in advertising budgets for several reasons. They account for much of the difference between market share and share of voice. When positive, they amplify the results of current advertising. And they are an important reason to consider advertising as the producer of "capital goods" and to evaluate advertising expenditures within the framework of capital budgeting.

Combinations of Traditional Methods

Most advertisers recognize that any single method for setting the advertising allocation has theoretical and/or practical difficulties. So far, our suggestions for empirical approaches have assumed a facility with quantitative analysis, which some decision makers don't have (or choose not to acquire). For such decision makers, improvements in budget allocations seem to be found in combining more than one traditional method. They hope to offset the disadvantages of one approach with the strengths of another. Unfortunately such "improvements" often prove to be a mirage; combining frequently produces a proliferation of problems.

Two such combinations are frequently used. The first of these combinations is often called the market share theorem; in it, sales, which are expressed as percentage share of a market, are highly correlated with percentage expenditures on promotional activity in that market. This seems like a correlation method. In addition, empirical evidence supporting the theorem is available, though it is highly concentrated in the performance of mature products in competitive markets. However, two problems plague the theorem approach. First, total expenditure figures for future periods are difficult to acquire. Second, the passive assumptions of other parity methods are present here too.

The second combination, recommended recently by Wademan, combines objective and task with break-even-analysis.[4] This effort can be commended for moving in the proper direction, but breakeven analysis (which fails to account for the time value of money) is inferior to the capital budgeting approach, which is discussed below.

Capital Budgeting

Capital budgeting is the budgeting approach relevant to the management of long-lived assets. Specifically, capital budgeting reflects the time value of money and applies this concept to assets that will produce a stream of benefits or returns for more than the current period.

Remember that advertising allocations create "assets" in the form of favorable attitudes, competitive advantages, and, especially, decisions to purchase, which produce a stream of future benefits for the advertiser. Thus, the concept of capital budgeting seems appropriate to advertising budget decisions.

---

[4] V. Wademan, "How to Set Your Advertising Budget," *Public Relations Quarterly,* Winter 1975, pp. 21–24.

Applying Capital Budgeting to Advertising

How can capital budgeting be applied to advertising allocation? Its advertising applications are quite similar to those for other capital budgeting problems and processes.

Step 1. Regardless of application, the first step in capital budgeting is to measure the cost of capital for a project. To do this, the decision maker must not only discover the cost of a particular source of funds but must also know the availability of funds from this source. And when more than one source of funds is used for a project, financial managers often weigh the aftertax proportion from each source in order to compute the effective overall cost of capital for the project.

Advertisers should recognize that using funds generated internally (i.e., by past sales) is not costless, since these same dollars can be applied elsewhere. They should also recognize that funding for capital projects can come from external sources. The two major sources of external funds are debt and equity, or borrowing and the sale of additional shares of stock.

In case of debt, the cost of capital is the effective interest rate charged on the borrowed funds.

Step 2. The second step in capital budgeting is to calculate the time-discounted rate of return expected from the project. To do this, the dollar benefits expected in each future period, or cash flows, are discounted by a factor reflecting the time interval that elapses until they are received.

Step 3. To calculate the discount factor, we use the formula for the present value (PV) of a dollar, received n periods in the future, when the effective interest rate (or cost of capital) is r.

$$PV = \frac{1}{(1+r)^n}$$

Step 4. By inserting values into the PV formula, you can see that the effect of having to wait a long time for a dollar ($n = $ large number) is to reduce the present value of this future payment. Likewise, the present value of a future payment is reduced as the cost of capital is increased. To convert a future payment to its present value, simply multiply the size of the payment in dollars by the PV value (or discount factor).

Figure 4–7 gives a highly simplified example for an advertising campaign producing benefits over several years. Here, the calculations are based on a constant cost of capital of 9 percent and a stream of sales over the campaign period and three additional years. For a given dollar amount of total benefits, if either the cost of capital or the waiting

FIGURE 4-7 Net Present Value of a Campaign Lasting One Year and Producing Sales over Four Years

Year	Sales* Due to Campaign in t = 1	Cost of Capital	Discount Factor †	Present Value
Same as campaign (t = 1)	$100,000	9%	.917	$ 91,700
Next year (t = 2)	60,000	9	.842	50,520
Third year (t = 3)	30,000	9	.772	23,160
Final year (t = 4)	10,000	9	.708	7,080
			Net present value =	$172,460

Note:

At $t = 1$, $PV_1 = \dfrac{1}{(1.09)^1} = .917$

At $t = 2$, $PV_2 = \dfrac{1}{(1.09)^2} = .842$

At $t = 3$, $PV_3 = \dfrac{1}{(1.09)^3} = .772$

At $t = 4$, $PV_4 = \dfrac{1}{(1.09)^4} = .708$

* A simplifying assumption was made that sales for each year were received at year-end. Since sales are likely to occur during each year, and thus become available earlier than assumed, the present values for each year and in total are conservatively understated.

† Obtained from the present value formula, $PV = \dfrac{1}{(1+r)^n}$

interval for receiving benefits increases, the present value declines. Conversely, reductions in the cost of capital or the waiting interval produce an increase in present value. This is another way of saying that it is preferable to use low-cost capital and to produce quick returns. Converting the net present value of a capital project to an annualized percentage return on investment gives the discounted rate to return. An example of this calculation is presented in Figure 4-8.

In this method, the rate selected must set the sum of all time-discounted cash flows to zero. So the rate lies between 54 percent and 55 percent and is approximately 54.2 percent. This rate may seem high compared to rates of return on other capital projects. In truth, the use of typical (or ordinary) values for cash flows produced by advertising and the capital budgeting method highlight how productive advertising expenditures can be.

The third stage in capital budgeting is to choose capital projects. Obviously prudent decision makers will not select projects whose cost of capital is greater than the discounted rate of return. For the remaining projects, where returns exceed costs, the decision maker usually chooses

FIGURE 4–8 Rate of Return on an Advertising Campaign Lasting One Year and Producing Sales over Four Years

		Present Value Factor and Net Present Value if Effective Interest Rate Is:					
Period	Cash Flow*	50 Percent		54 Percent		55 Percent	
0	−$100,000	(1)	−$100,000	(1)	−$100,000	(1)	−$100,000
1	100,000	(.667)	66,700	(.649)	64,900	(.645)	64,500
2	60,000	(.444)	26,650	(.422)	25,320	(.416)	24,960
3	30,000	(.296)	8,880	(.274)	8,220	(.269)	8,070
4	10,000	(.198)	1,980	(.178)	1,780	(.173)	1,730
		+$	4,200	+$	220	−$	740

NOTE: By interpolation, the effective rate that lies between 54 percent and 55 percent is about 54.2 percent.

* Assumes that the ad campaign expenses, which total $100,000, are all expended at the beginning of the first year and that the sales results flow in the same way as in Figure 4–7.

projects with the highest rates of return, up to the amount of available capital. Again, recall that available capital is not restricted to surplus funds generated internally. By available capital we mean funds from either external or internal sources which can be obtained at a cost less than the projected rate of return. In the example in Figure 4–8, and using plausible figures for cash flow, we see that the campaign has an exceptionally high rate of return. We feel that the application of capital budgeting procedures to advertising allocations will produce high expected rates of return in many organizations. Further, financial managers will become better informed about the attractiveness of advertising campaigns relative to other, often competing, capital projects. Then if external funds are required, creditors are usually more willing to extend funds for a project that has been scrutinized in the capital budgeting process than for one whose costs have been arbitrarily set and whose returns are only generally surmised.

A garden variety of capital budgeting, called payback , is sometimes used for advertising budgeting. Here, we compute the time required to "pay back" the investment. If competing investments are being considered, the project with the shortest payback period is thought to have the least risk and, other things equal, is selected. Actually, other things are not often equal, and relying on payback analysis fails to provide the decision maker with information about the relevant time-discounted cash flows.

Advertisers who use this method usually call it the payout method. They use it not so much to rank competing projects as to decide whether to introduce a new product. In this application, decision makers combine advertising investment and projected profits to get an estimate of overall investment. Then they estimate the number of periods (months, quarters, or year) required to recover this investment. Finally, they apply some rule of thumb to decide whether the payout interval is short enough to warrant introducing the product. While payout is a budgeting method that uses proper notions, it is less complete than the capital budgeting methods and should probably be replaced by the complete capital budgeting process.

Three final comments conclude our discussion of capital budgeting. First, some empirical approaches to budgeting can be combined productively with capital budgeting. For example, it is possible to use estimates of the residual effects of advertising to forecast the future cash flows that will be produced by present-day campaigns. These flows, of course, are an important ingredient in calculating rate of return. Second, the trade press has been stressing the undesirable tax consequences of amortizing (or timing out) the benefits of advertising. From a pure tax perspective, it is always better to "expense" a cost, thereby realizing the entire expenditure as a business expense in the period when it occurs. Nevertheless, advertising campaigns meet the test of capital goods in that they produce benefits over a longer time interval. It is both unrealistic and an impediment to careful financial planning to continue to treat advertising as an ephemeral cost, here today and gone before the next planning period. Further, this historical treatment of the advertising function deprives business planners of many of the advantages that flow from a rational treatment of advertising, such as the chance for advertising to compete for funds with any other capital projects. Finally, while capital budgeting has been discussed only within the context of decisions on total advertising allocation, it can be correctly applied to subsequent budgeting decisions for allocation to specific media. Traditionally, decisions on how to allocate total advertising funds to vehicles and to media have been made on the basis of costs per "exposure." If applied to this problem, capital budgeting offers the prospect of highlighting differences in the time that benefits are realized, but it also requires that defensible measures of return be developed.

TASKS PERFORMED BY ADVERTISING FUNDS

After the total advertising allocation has been determined, the allocation is broken down into specific expenditures of the advertising campaign. A first step in this process is to determine the legitimate charges against the advertising allocation. One of the most quoted lists of such charges appeared in *Printers' Ink* and is reprinted in Figure 4–9. This list gives some indication of the items the industry considers reasonable charges against the advertising budget (white area), those that are doubtful (light

---

FIGURE 4–9 **Ad Department Charges in Descending Order**

Space and time costs in regular media
Advertising consultants
Ad-pretesting services
Institutional advertising
Industry directory listings
Readership or audience research
Media costs for consumer contests, premium,
   and sampling promotions
Ad department travel and entertainment
   expenses
Ad department salaries
Advertising association dues
Local cooperative advertising
Direct mail to consumers
Subscriptions to periodicals and services for
   ad department
Storage of advertising materials

Catalogs for consumers
Classified telephone directories
Space in irregular publications
Advertising aids for salesmen
Financial advertising
Dealer-help literature
Contributions to industry ad funds
Direct mail to dealers and jobbers
Office supplies

Point-of-sale materials
Window display installation costs
Charges for services performed by other
   departments
Catalogs for dealers
Test-marketing programs
Sample requests generated by advertising
Costs of exhibits except personnel
Ad department share of overhead
House organs for customers and dealers
Cost of cash value or sampling coupons
Cost of contest entry blanks
Cross-advertising enclosures
Contest judging and handling fees
Depreciation of ad department equipment
Mobile exhibits
Employee fringe benefits
Catalogs for salespeople
Packaging consultants
Consumer contest awards

FIGURE 4–9 *(concluded)*

Premium handling charges
House-to-house sample distribution
Packaging charges for premium promotions
Cost of merchandise for tie-in promotions
Product tags
Showrooms
Testing new labels and packages
Package design and artwork
Cost of non-self-liquidating premiums
Consumer education programs
Product publicity
Factory signs
House organs for salespeople
Signs on company-owned vehicles
Instruction enclosures
Press clipping services
Market research (outside produced)
Samples of middlemen
Recruitment advertising
Price sheets
Public relations consultants
Coupon redemption costs
Corporate publicity
Market research (company produced)
Exhibit personnel
Gifts of company products
Cost of deal merchandise
Share of corporate salaries
Cost of guarantee refunds
Share of legal expenses
Cost of detail or missionary men
Sponsoring recreational activities
Product research
House organs for employees
Entertaining customers and prospects
Scholarships
Plant tours
Annual reports
Outright charity donations

---

gray), and those the majority of firms would not classify as advertising expenses (darkest area). The gray areas are not illegal, however; they are simply not advertising.

Common Budget Areas

After the advertiser decides what general areas will be funded from the advertising budget, the next step is to budget against specific tasks in the current advertising campaign. While each campaign has some unique features, there are common areas that most campaign budgets must consider.

Space and Time.   At least half of most campaign budgets is expended for media space and time costs. Television is often the most costly medium for a national campaign, although most of the major media are competitive on a cost per thousand (cpm) basis. The advertiser must exercise care in space and time purchases since any unnecessary purchase of media can be a tremendous waste of money, especially at the national level. Chapter 5 discusses in detail the considerations to be incorporated into media buying.

An important development in budgeting any advertising activity is the concept of inflation accounting. At its core, inflation accounting attempts to distinguish between increases in expenditure produced by the purchase of greater volume or higher quality and increases created by price inflation in the goods being purchased.

When purchasing space and time in advertising media, the advertiser clearly buys a commodity whose current prices are partly the result of price inflation. Figure 4–10 shows price rises in major media groups for a recent period. Obviously a 10 percent per year increase in media purchases for a medium displaying a 15 percent per year inflation rate represents, in real terms, a shrinking volume purchased from that medium.

A second accounting concept that finds growing application in the area of budgeting media purchases is "zero-based" budgeting. This notion, which prohibits the carryover of past spending levels to the future being budgeted, is as much or more a management control practice than an accounting practice. Zero-based budgets usually require the calculation and justification of the entire amounts planned, rather than concentrating on percentage changes from historical levels of spending. Thus, an expenditure of $1 million in network television last year is not budgeted this year on the basis of a 10 percent increase in network television purchases. Rather, the entire $1 million must be justified.

Like almost every popular business concept, zero-based budgeting is often misunderstood and misapplied. Without doubt, it requires more analytical work than traditional percentage increases on a historical base figure. The principal advantage of the zero-base method is that it prevents past inefficiencies from becoming honored traditions. It also encourages decision makers to rethink the relative merits of expenditures for each budgeting period.

Mechanical Work and Artwork.   The second largest area of budget expenditures is the actual preparation of advertising. The agency commission normally covers a minimum of advertising preparation; the advertiser usually assumes a large portion of production costs, for television commercials.

FIGURE 4-10 Inflation in Advertising Media Prices

Broadcast cost index/January

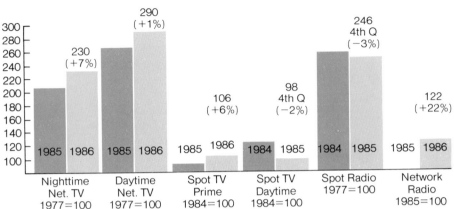

Print cost index/January

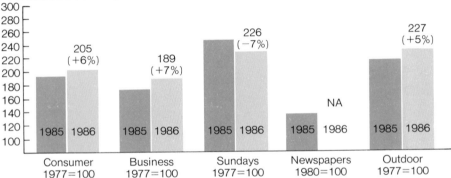

Nighttime Network TV—Cost per average 30-second spot, 7:30-11 P.M. Monday-Saturday and 7-11 P.M. Sunday from Broadcast Advertisers Reports' (BAR) Network TV Service.

Daytime Network TV—Cost per average 30-second spot, 10 A.M.-4:30 P.M. Monday-Friday from BAR's Network TV Service.

Network Radio—Cost per average 30-second radio announcement from BAR's Network Radio Service.

Consumer Magazines estimate based on reported SRDS cost of a page, four-color in 40 national consumer magazines, as reported by Magazine Publishers Assn.

National Sunday Mags estimate based on published (rate cards) costs of a page, four-color in the national entries.

Daily Newspapers estimate based on Newspaper Advertising Bureau report of SRDS costs per agate line of a sample of 788 newspapers weighted to represent the universe.

Business Publications estimate based on reported SRDS cost of a page, four-color in 48 publications representing 42 business and professional classifications.

Outdoor Posters based on estimate prepared by Institute of Outdoor Advertising.

Spot Radio index represents cost of a 60-second spot in the top 100 markets from data supplied to Radio Expenditure Reports by major radio representatives.

How to read: Media Cost Index reflects latest available costs compared with base year. Percent change shows rate of change from the same month in previous year.

SOURCE: "Economic Eye," *Marketing and Media Decisions*, May 1986, p. 146.

Some advertisers deal with their agencies on a fee basis; for example, they pay the agency on a project or hourly basis for work performed. As this fee relationship becomes more prevalent, advertisers will assume a larger share of production costs, and the proportion of the advertising budget allocated to the creative area will increase.

The so-called noncommissionable media comprise another creative area covered by the advertising budget. This area usually involves brochures, direct-mail pieces, annual reports, and other collateral materials prepared by an agency for an advertiser. Such materials are charged against the advertising budget.

Noncommisionable materials are sometimes categorized as billable services—services the agency doesn't cover but charges to the client. Nonbillable services, on the other hand, are the services an agency normally provides to earn its commission. To avoid problems, the contractual agreement between the agency and the client should spell out all nonbillable services.

Research. The costs of the research necessary to gather primary and secondary data for the advertising campaign are included in the advertising budget. The extent of billable research activities and the preliminary research performed "free" by an agency as part of its nonbillable service must be considered in budgeting for research.

The research budget is determined by many diverse factors. Among the major ones are the newness of the product, anticipation of a dramatically different creative approach, or a movement into previously unused media. The cost and value of usual information, as discussed in Chapter 2, are critical here. The type of research methodology needed also affects the budget. For instance personal interviews, in-depth or motivation tests, or research requiring sophisticated equipment (such as eye cameras) increase the research budget.

Administrative and Miscellaneous. The advertising budget may also include items such as travel, salaries, advertising department overhead, and other expenses connected with the advertising function. Normally, these administrative and miscellaneous costs are not figured as part of the campaign budget.

BUDGETARY CONTROL

After the advertising allocation is determined and the specific budgetary areas covered, plans must be made to control the expenditure of funds. To control the advertising budget, managers must know all current and future commitments, and they must provide contingencies.

Current Commitments

Current commitments are invoices due during the current billing period. To exercise control in this area, managers must make sure all the services billed were actually performed and performed properly. The major problem they face is determining if media bills for space and time reflect advertisements and commericals that actually ran in the media. The print media routinely provide agencies with tear sheets (copies of the ads or the entire publication). Syndicated services such as the Advertising Checking Bureau perform a similar service for advertisers. The broadcast media are much more difficult to check. Stations occasionally bill for spots that didn't run or ran in cheaper positions than those billed. In any case, the advertiser and the agency have a major financial responsibility for determining that they pay only for services satisfactorily rendered.

Future Commitments

In any campaign, financial commitments must be made well in advance. These commitments must be anticipated and considered in all budget planning. How much of the budget is committed to future obligations is primarily determined by (1) the type of media mix used and (2) the sophistication of the creative message. Network television, in particular, demands long-range commitments in order to guarantee availabilities during premium time periods. Newspaper media schedules, conversely, allow a much wider flexibility in budgeting.

Contingencies

Most of the advertising budget is committed to specific areas prior to initiation of the campaign. However, an ongoing review of the campaign in progress is mandatory to make sure that the campaign is progressing as expected. Managers normally set aside some budgetary reserve to correct weak areas in the campaign. If changes in the campaign are necessary, the advertising planner needs complete knowledge of both current and future financial commitments.

Two basic approaches to measuring an advertising campaign's effectiveness are sales and communication success. Budgetary review during the campaign often centers on one of these criteria. Sales criteria are normally measured by such techniques as store audits. These techniques may also be used to determine the geographic distribution of sales and the types of retail outlets in which sales are made. Communication success is measured by various types of recall and recognition studies conducted among listeners to and readers of the media.

The budgetary process is not a matter of allocating funds prior to the start of the campaign and then forgetting about them. Instead, the budgetary process of planning, expenditure, and control is an integral part of the campaign and one that must continue throughout its duration.

REVIEW QUESTIONS

1. What is a budget?
2. Discuss four major managerial benefits of budgets.
3. What is the difference between a cash budget and a capital budget?
4. Describe the probable personality of a decision maker who prefers to use parity methods to develop the advertising budget.
5. In economic theory, what is the optimum level of advertising expenditure?
6. Explain to a beginning advertising student the PIMS findings, and how they apply to advertising budgets.
7. Using the formula for present value,

$$PV = \frac{1}{(1 + r)^n}$$

calculate the net present value for a four-period cash flow as follows:

Period	Cash Flow
1	$50,000
2	20,000
3	15,000
4	10,000

The effective cost of capital is 13 percent.

8. What is the difference between a flexible budget and an appropriations budget?
9. Name and describe three methods an advertiser might use to improve budgeting decisions.
10. List and describe the tasks performed by advertising funds.
11. List the advantages and disadvantages of using capital budgeting to plan for advertising expenditures.
12. Using the data in Figure 4–3, identify the periods in which ad expenditures are an annual maximum for:
     Television
     Newspapers
     Radio
     Magazines
     When are these at an annual minimum?

SUGGESTED ADDITIONAL READING

AAKER, DAVID A., and JOHN G. MYERS. "The Budget Decision." In *Advertising Management*. Englewood Cliffs, N.J.: Prentice-Hall, 1975, pp. 51–84.

"Advertising Budgeting," White Paper Series no. 4. New York: B/PAA, 1982.

"Advertising-to-Sales Ratios, 1985 (by industry)." *Advertising Age,* September 13, 1986.

BARNES, JIMMY D.; BRENDA J. MOSCOVE; and JAVAD RASSOULI. "An Objective and Task Media Selection Decision Model and Advertising Cost Formula to Determine International Advertising Budgets." *Journal of Advertising* 11, no. 4 (1982), pp. 68–76.

DHALLA, NARIMAN K. "Assessing the Long-Term Value of Advertising." *Harvard Business Review*, January/February 1978, pp. 87–95.

DICKINSON, ROGER A., and ANTHONY F. HERBST. "Understand Deficiencies of Capital-Budgeting Techniques before Applying Them to Planning." *Marketing News*, March 16, 1984, p. 10.

JOY, D. MAURICE. "Risk Concepts" and "Capital Budgeting Techniques." In *Introduction to Financial Management*. Rev. ed. Homewood, Ill.: Richard D. Irwin, 1980.

KIJEWSKI, VALERIE. *Advertising and Promotion: How Much Should You Spend?* The Strategic Planning Institute, 1983.

LANCASTER, KENT M., and JUDITH A. STERN. "Computer-Based Advertising Budgeting Practices of Leading U.S. Consumer Advertisers." *Journal of Advertising* 12, no. 4 (1983), pp. 4–9.

LARIC, MICHAEL L., and RONALD STIFF. "Advertising Decisions." In *Lotus 1-2-3 for Marketing and Sales*. Englewood Cliffs, N.J.: Prentice-Hall, 1986.

LECKENBY, JOHN D., and NUGENT WEDDING. "Management of the Advertising Budget." In *Advertising Management: Criteria, Analysis and Decision Making*. Columbus, Ohio: Grid, 1982.

PATTI, CHARLES H., and VINCENT BLASKO. "Budgeting Practices of Big Advertisers." *Journal of Advertising Research* 21, no. 6 (1981), pp. 23–29.

PATTI, CHARLES H., and JOHN MCDONALD. "Corporate Advertising: Process, Practices, and Perspectives (1970–1989)." *Journal of Advertising* 14, no. 1 (1985), pp. 42–49.

The Advertising Media-Buying Process

*Advertisers should become more involved with the media
and creative process. Independent analysis—then joint
decision—make for more effective and efficient use of
advertising dollars.**

> Christopher Wackman,
> *Subaru of America*

*Work hard, be open-minded, be focused and creatively
take no prisoners!†*

> Patrick Fallon,
> *President of Fallon McElligott Rice*

An inherent danger exists in writing a separate chapter on the advertising media-buying process. Compartmentalizing media from the other marketing and advertising functions can be a dangerous course. Media selection is basically the identification and delivery of people in the most efficient manner possible. Consequently, the media-buying function must consider identifying prospects (market segmentation), appropriating allocated funds (budgeting), developing a proper communication environment (creative), and fulfilling ultimate business goals (profits).

For advertising to do its job, well-conceived messages must reach potential prospects at the proper time and place. Media planners and creative personnel should regard their functions as complementary rather than competitive. Some advertising practitioners take the shortsighted view that they are working on either a creative or media project rather than a *marketing* problem. In accomplishing general marketing

---

* "Strategy, Creative Shaping Ad Budgets" *Advertising Age,* January 20, 1986, p. 28.
† "Strategy, Creative Shaping Ad Budgets" *Advertising Age,* January 20, 1986, p. 28.

goals, the creative aspects of a campaign are sometimes planned first or given priority over the media function. Other projects may demand more of a media orientation. In a successful campaign, creative, media, and research personnel cooperate in the best interests of their clients. Petty, provincial interests have no place in successful advertising.

In the following discussion, we assume that the media planner clearly understands the client's marketing strategy and that the basic creative strategy and problems have been discussed with creative people working with the product. With this "homework" completed, the media planner is ready to assemble a media buy. The media buy must complement the overall advertising and marketing strategy (see Chapter 1). It details the specific manner in which the media process will carry its weight in achieving overall goals.

STEPS IN THE MEDIA-BUYING PROCESS

There are five important steps in the media-buying process:

1. Prospect identification.
2. Basic media strategy.
3. Media tactics and competition.
4. Media evaluation.
5. The media schedule.

The first step is really dictated by the marketing requirement to know the consumer; the remaining steps are required to reach the customer with an advertising message.

Step 1: Prospect Identification

The media process must begin with an appropriate identification of the consumer. There are many ways to describe a potential prospect for a product, just as there are many ways to describe the characteristics of a person. The media planner or researcher usually has less flexibility in identifying prospects than does his creative counterpart. The media buyer must have data compatible with similar information about the media to be bought. For instance, a media buyer who categorizes prospects as being between 20 and 30 years old will have trouble matching this information with media that designate their audiences as 18–24 and 25–34. A company that identifies its customers as "hypochondriacs" can use this information to design creative messages, but it will have trouble finding media that identify the percentage of hypochondriacs in their audiences.

Advertising has four major means of identifying, or segmenting, subgroups within the general population: geographic, demographic, product-user, and inner-directed consumer indentification.

Geographic Identification. The oldest form of segmentation is geographic. By the late 19th century, merchants recognized variance in sales by territories. Today marketers increasingly use local and regional rather than national advertising strategies. (For instance, certain types of GM trucks are primarily advertised in the Southeast and West.) Media planners find they need regional and market-by-market data as well as national information to buy time and space in local broadcast stations, newspapers, regional magazines, and outdoor media.

Most geographic information for advertising purposes is presented in one of two ways: by broad regional breakdowns or by local markets, usually in order of population.

Regional Identification. The four U.S. Census regions—North East, North Central, South, and West—are too broad for most purposes so advertisers usually use a more traditional regional breakdown—New England, Middle Atlantic, East Central, West Central, South East, South West, and Pacific.

Market Identification. The most common way to identify markets is by the Metropolitan Statistical Area (MSA). Basically, an MSA includes a city of 50,000 population or a city of 25,000 with a contiguous area population of 50,000. Markets are also designated by county size, as defined by the A. C. Nielsen Company. These are: **A—counties** in the top 25 metropolitan areas; **B—counties** with over 150,000 population and not in Class A; **C—counties** with over 35,000 population not included in A or B; **D**—all other **counties.**[1]

A major problem for media buyers is that neither media distribution nor product distribution follows these artificial boundaries. Therefore, the media planner has the continuing problem of attempting to be as efficient as possible when dealing with noncompatible data.

Figure 5–1 presents a hypothetical situation media planners often face. Our fictional media planner has market information on the population of a specific MSA, but his primary sales area includes Seneca, Cayuga, Graham, Coolidge, and Cooper counties. The sales and media areas do not follow the MSA boundaries, and they include territory for which there is no information. Adding to this problem is a mismatch between the sales territory and the media coverage area.

---

[1] *Sales and Marketing Management,* July 23, 1979, p. A–43.

FIGURE 5-1 Coverage Area Problems of Media Planners

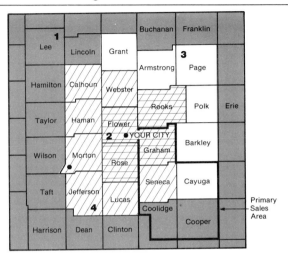

1. The map shows the survey area(s) included in a market definition and for which audience estimates are reported. Areas in grey are not included in a market definition (unless it is a part of an ADI to be reported for that particular market) and will have no audience estimates included in the Report.

2. The Metro Survey Area (MSA) of the reported market is shown by horizontal hatching.

3. The Total Survey Area (TSA) of the reported market is shown in white.

4. The Areas of Dominant Influence (ADI) of the reported market, if applicable, is shown by diagonal hatching.

SOURCE: "Description of Methodology," Arbitron Radio Market Reports, 1984, p. 20. Reprinted with permission—Arbitron Ratings Company.

Demographic Identification. The most common method of identifying prospects is by demographic characteristics. Marketing studies usually cover such categories as sex, education, age, and income. However, other media buys require information about marital status, number of children, type of living quarters, or even ethnic origin. Only rarely will one variable provide adequate information; therefore, several variables are sometimes combined into a single number or index. One of the most used is the Buying Power Index (BPI) developed by *Sales & Marketing Management.* The BPI is a weighted index that converts three basic elements—population, effective buying income, and retail sales—into a measure of a market's ability to buy, and expresses it as a percentage of the U.S./Canada potential. BPI is calculated by giving a weight of 5 to the market's percentage of U.S./Canada effective buying income, 3 to its percentage of U.S./Canada retail sales, and 2 to its percentage of U.S./Canada population. The total of those weighted percentages is then divided by 10 to arrive at the BPI.

Media Selection and Demographic Matching. Identifying prospects by demographics involves two complementary steps. First, media planners must determine a product's prime prospects from the mass audience. Second, they need to gather demographic information on the various media available to the media planner. If they find that the major and/or potential users of their product are black adults, the logical media choices would be black-oriented magazines, television, and radio shows, and possibly certain sections of selected newspapers. Although they have narrowed the number of media choices, there is still a large number from which to choose.

Media planners normally gather information from syndicated services and media-provided sources to determine the relative popularity of the various media among black adult prospects. Figure 5–2 from Simmons Market Research Bureau, Inc., illustrates the procedure of demographic matching.

To use the SMRB report in Figure 5–2, assume we are interested in finding the most appropriate magazines to reach black adults. The SMRB report gives several types of information.

1. Total U.S. Adult Population: This column tells us there are 164,927,000 adults in the United States. As we go down this column, we see how many adults read each of the magazines listed (e.g., *Barron's* has 958,000 adult readers, *Essence* has 2,908,000 adult readers, and so on).

2. Column A—Black: This column lists the total number of black adult readers of the various magazines. Of the 2,908,000 adult readers of *Essence,* 2,745,000 are black.

3. As media buyers, we are interested in the audience coverage— the percentage of our target a media vehicle reaches. Again, looking at *Essence* magazine, we find:

$$\text{Column B coverage} = \frac{\text{Black adults who read } Essence}{\text{Black adults in U.S.}}$$

$$= \frac{2,745,000}{17,832,000} \quad = .1539 \quad = 15.4\%$$

4. Column C—Black: In addition to audience coverge, we are interested in composition, or audience makeup, of the media we are considering. Composition is the percentage of readers within any particular demographic or product category. In our *Essence* magazine example, column C—Black is computed as follows:

$$\text{Column C composition} = \frac{\text{Black adults who read } Essence}{\text{All adult readers of } Essence}$$

$$= \frac{2,745,000}{2,908,000} \quad = .9439 \quad = 94.4\%$$

5. Column D—Black: The index in column D is a means of comparing the composition of each magazine against the national population. For instance, 94.4 percent of adult readers of *Essence* magazine are blacks, whereas blacks make up only 10.8 percent of the total U.S. adult population.

$$\text{Index} = \frac{94.4}{10.8} \times 100 = 873$$

Demographic Matching: A Caution. The media planner must remember that demographic matching deals with groups rather than individuals. A demographic category, no matter how carefully selected, only indicates that, on average, more prospects will be found in this group than in some other. However, within any group there will be nonbuyers, just as in unlikely demographic groups (based on purchases of the product) there will probably be buyers. Dealing with groups rather than individuals can be dangerous to media planners who rely too heavily on this technique.

Look again at Figure 5–2 and consider a hypothetical situation concerning *Essence* magazine. As we have indicated, we can reach 15.4 percent of black adults with this vehicle. Now assume that 15.4 percent of all adult blacks use our product. The question facing the media planner is "How many of the 2,745,000 adult blacks in the vehicle's audience are the same as the 2,745,000 adult blacks who use our product?" The answer is unknown, given the available information, but there is some chance that only a small portion of users are also "readers" of *Essence*. Because of the uncertainty created by using a single demographic variable, the media planner normally uses at least two or three variables to reduce the risk of making an improper media buy.

Product-User Identification. Although demographic matching is the most commonly used technique for media buying, advertisers are increasingly turning to product-user matching. Product-user techniques are different from demographic matching because they are concerned with individuals rather than groups, and the variable they employ is product usage rather than some personal, demographic characteristic.

In theory, the product-user technique is very simple. The media planner determines the heavy, medium, and light users of the product from among the audiences of the various media. Then, considering the media cost, the planner builds a media schedule around vehicles with the highest concentration of "heavy" users.

One approach to product-user identification begins with syndicated services reports or media-supplied data. Figure 5–3 shows a portion of the SMRB report for media consumption by female users of toothpaste. Use is categorized as heavy, medium, and light. In this report, heavy users accounted for 51.8 percent of total consumption of toothpaste. You can see

FIGURE 5–2   Demographic Matching Example from SMRB Report (race, adults)

	Total U.S. 000	White				Black				Other				Spanish-Speaking			
		A 000	B % Down	C Across %	D Index	A 000	B % Down	C Across %	D Index	A 000	B % Down	C Across %	D Index	A 000	B % Down	C Across %	D Index
Total adults	164,927	143,976	100.0	87.3	100	17,832	100.0	10.8	100	3,119	100.0	1.9	100	11,306	100.0	6.9	100
Barron's	958	887	0.6	92.6	106	48†	0.3	5.0	46	23†	0.7	2.4	127	36†	0.3	3.8	55
Better Homes & Gardens	20,826	18,580	12.9	89.2	102	1,956	11.0	9.4	87	291*	9.3	1.4	74	945	8.4	4.5	66
Bon Appetit	3,263	3,088	2.1	94.6	108	148*	0.8	4.5	42	27†	0.9	0.8	44	216*	1.9	6.6	97
Business Week	4,444	3,956	2.7	89.0	102	397	2.2	8.9	83	91†	2.9	2.0	108	233*	2.1	5.2	76
Car and Driver	2,722	2,364	1.6	86.8	99	245	1.4	9.0	83	113†	3.6	4.2	220	210*	1.9	7.7	113
CBS Magazine Network (gross)	8,735	7,596	5.3	87.0	100	812	4.6	9.3	86	327*	10.5	3.7	198	478	4.2	5.5	80
Changing Times	2,655	2,419	1.7	91.1	104	207*	1.2	7.8	72	29†	0.9	1.1	58	45†	0.4	1.7	25
Colonial Homes	1,945	1,797	1.2	92.4	106	149†	0.8	7.7	71	0†	0.0	0.0	0	52†	0.5	2.7	39
Conde Nast Mag. Pkg. (gross)	17,524	14,840	10.3	84.7	97	2,359	13.2	13.5	125	326*	10.5	1.9	98	1,619	14.3	9.2	135
Consumers Digest	2,569	2,322	1.6	90.4	104	213	1.2	8.3	77	33†	1.1	1.3	68	78†	0.7	3.0	44
Cosmopolitan	9,637	8,468	5.9	87.9	101	932	5.2	9.7	89	237†	7.6	2.5	130	1,036	9.2	10.8	157
Country Living	2,685	2,564	1.8	95.5	109	107†	0.6	4.0	37	15†	0.5	0.6	30	68†	0.6	2.5	37
Cuisine	2,228	2,035	1.4	91.3	105	167*	0.9	7.5	69	26†	0.8	1.2	62	104†	0.9	4.7	68
Cycle World	1,705	1,536	1.1	90.1	103	125†	0.7	7.3	68	44†	1.4	2.6	136	66†	0.6	3.9	56
Decorating & Craft Ideas	2,754	2,404	1.7	87.3	100	331	1.9	12.0	111	19†	0.6	0.7	36	105*	0.9	3.8	56

	Total Audience					Men					Women					Adults 18–34				
Dec Crft ID/South Liv(gross)	8,487	7,633	5.3	89.9	103	789	4.4	9.3	86	66†	2.1	0.8	41	294	2.6	3.5	51
Discover	2,217	1,905	1.3	85.9	98	243	1.4	11.0	101	69†	2.2	3.1	165	89†	0.8	4.0	59
Ebony	7,141	522	0.4	7.3	8	6,601	37.0	92.4	855	18†	0.6	0.3	13	400	3.5	5.6	82
Esquire	2,062	1,543	1.1	74.8	86	468	2.6	22.7	210	52†	1.7	2.5	133	124*	1.1	6.0	88
Essence	2,908	155*	0.1	5.3	6	2,745	15.4	94.4	873	9†	0.3	0.3	16	168†	1.5	5.8	84
Family Circle	18,898	17,568	12.2	93.0	106	1,196	6.7	6.3	59	134†	4.3	0.7	37	666	5.9	3.5	51
The Family Handy-Man	3,367	3,167	2.2	94.1	108	166*	0.9	4.9	46	33†	1.1	1.0	52	238*	2.1	7.1	103
Family Weekly	24,856	23,247	16.1	93.5	107	1,404	7.9	5.6	52	204*	6.5	0.8	43	1123	9.9	4.5	66
Field & Stream	9,179	8,589	6.0	93.6	107	537	3.0	5.9	54	54†	1.7	0.6	31	385	3.4	4.2	61
Food & Wine	976	835	0.6	85.6	98	137†	0.8	14.0	130	4†	0.1	0.4	22	27†	0.2	2.8	40
Forbes	2,641	2,459	1.7	93.1	107	89*	0.5	3.4	31	93†	3.0	3.5	186	99†	0.9	3.7	55
Fortune	2,757	2,533	1.8	91.9	105	151	0.8	5.5	51	73†	2.3	2.6	140	126†	1.1	4.6	67
Gentlemen's Quarterly	2,764	1,720	1.2	62.2	71	878	4.9	31.8	294	166†	5.3	6.0	318	228*	2.0	8.2	120
Glamour	6,147	5,297	3.7	86.2	99	774	4.3	12.6	116	77†	2.5	1.3	66	542	4.8	8.8	129
Golf Digest	2,508	2,393	1.7	95.4	109	70†	0.4	2.8	26	45†	1.4	1.8	95	86†	0.8	3.4	50
Golf Digest/Tennis (gross)	3,941	3,582	2.5	90.9	104	258	1.4	6.5	61	101†	3.2	2.6	136	123†	1.1	3.1	46
Golf Magazine	1,695	1,583	1.1	93.4	107	87†	0.5	5.1	47	24†	0.8	1.4	75	40†	0.4	2.4	34
Golf Magazine/Ski (gross)	3,219	3,038	2.1	94.4	108	116*	0.7	3.6	33	66†	2.1	2.1	108	100*	0.9	3.1	45
Good House-keeping	19,754	17,874	12.4	90.5	104	1,665	9.3	8.4	78	215*	6.9	1.1	58	792	7.0	4.0	58
Grit	2,431	2,261	1.6	93.0	107	168*	0.9	6.9	64	3†	0.1	0.1	7	29†	0.3	1.2	17

* Projections relatively unstable because of sample base—use caution.

† Number of cases too small for reliability. Shown for consistency only.

SOURCE: Simmons Market Research Bureau, Inc.: *1983 Study of Media and Markets*, p. 76.

FIGURE 5-3 Product-User Example from SMRB Report (toothpaste usage on average day, females)

		All Users				Heavy Users				Medium Users				Light Users			
	Total U.S. 000	A 000	B % Down	C Across %	D Index	A 000	B % Down	C Across %	D Index	A 000	B % Down	C Across %	D Index	A 000	B % Down	C Across %	D Index
Total females	86,771	81,935	100.0	94.4	100	25,641	100.0	29.6	100	39,439	100.0	45.5	100	16,856	100.0	19.4	100
Barron's	251*	251*	0.3	100.0	106	129†	0.5	51.4	174	116*	0.3	46.2	102	7†	0.0	2.8	14
Better Homes & Gardens	16,703	16,066	19.6	96.2	102	5,041	19.7	30.2	102	7,822	19.8	46.8	103	3,203	19.0	19.2	99
Bon Appetit	2,289	2,203	2.7	96.2	102	776	3.0	33.9	115	1,022	2.6	44.6	98	406	2.4	17.7	91
Business Week	1,380	1,341	1.6	97.2	103	395	1.5	28.6	97	832	2.1	60.3	133	114*	0.7	8.3	43
Car and Driver	386	377	0.5	97.7	103	118†	0.5	30.6	103	181*	0.5	46.9	103	78†	0.5	20.2	104
CBS Magazine Network (gross)	2,805	2,711	3.3	96.6	102	992	3.9	35.4	120	1328	3.4	47.3	104	391	2.3	13.9	72
Changing Times	1,173	1,132	1.4	96.5	102	335	1.3	28.6	97	612	1.6	52.2	115	184*	1.1	15.7	81
Colonial Homes	1,268	1,248	1.5	98.4	104	300	1.2	23.7	80	862	2.2	68.0	150	86†	0.5	6.8	35
Conde Nast Mag. Pkg. (gross)	16,044	15,760	19.2	98.2	104	6,186	24.1	38.6	130	7,886	20.0	49.2	108	1,689	10.0	10.5	54
Consumers Digest	1,203	1,130	1.4	93.9	99	396	1.5	32.9	111	490	1.2	40.7	90	244*	1.4	20.3	104
Cosmopolitan	8,253	8,046	9.8	97.5	103	3,083	12.0	37.4	126	3,820	9.7	46.3	102	1,143	6.8	13.8	71
Country Living	1,975	1,901	2.3	96.3	102	698	2.7	35.3	120	978	2.5	49.5	109	225*	1.3	11.4	59
Cuisine	1,457	1,401	1.7	96.2	102	408	1.6	28.0	95	789	2.0	54.2	119	204†	1.2	14.0	72
Cycle World	258*	258*	0.3	100.0	106	124†	0.5	48.1	163	81†	0.2	31.4	69	53†	0.3	20.5	106
Decorating & Craft Ideas	2,348	2,289	2.8	97.5	103	709	2.8	30.2	102	1,129	2.9	48.1	106	451	2.7	19.2	99

Dec Crft ID/South																
Liv (gross)	6,379	6,175	7.5	96.8	103	2,227	8.7	34.9	118	2,959	7.5	46.4	102	988	5.9	15.5	80
Discover	910	884	1.1	97.1	103	254	1.0	27.9	94	461	1.2	50.7	111	169*	1.0	18.6	96
Ebony	4,306	4,169	5.1	96.8	103	1,468	5.7	34.1	115	2,256	5.7	52.4	115	446	2.6	10.4	53
Esquire	792	749	0.9	94.6	100	286	1.1	36.1	122	356	0.9	44.9	99	108†	0.6	13.6	70
Essence	2,145	2,052	2.5	95.7	101	732	2.9	34.1	115	1,151	2.9	53.7	118	170*	1.0	7.9	41
Family Circle	16,613	15,752	19.2	94.8	100	4,935	19.2	29.7	101	7,513	19.0	45.2	99	3,305	19.6	19.9	102
The Family Handy-Man	1,048	971	1.2	92.7	98	211*	0.8	20.1	68	491	1.2	46.9	103	270†	1.6	25.8	133
Family Weekly	13,140	12,379	15.1	94.2	100	3,806	14.8	29.0	98	5,959	15.1	45.4	100	2,614	15.5	19.9	102
Field & Stream	1,936	1,880	2.3	97.1	103	560	2.2	28.9	98	937	2.4	48.4	106	383	2.3	19.8	102
Food & Wine	607	575	0.7	94.7	100	211*	0.8	34.8	118	323	0.8	53.2	117	42†	0.2	6.9	36
Forbes	946	943	1.2	99.7	106	335	1.3	35.4	120	522	1.3	55.2	121	87†	0.5	9.2	47
Fortune	897	885	1.1	98.7	104	352	1.4	39.2	133	433	1.1	48.3	106	100†	0.6	11.1	57
Gentlemen's Quarterly	931	916	1.1	98.4	104	375	1.5	40.3	136	419	1.1	45.0	99	122†	0.7	13.1	67
Glamour	5,784	5,713	7.0	98.8	105	2,345	9.1	40.5	137	2,728	6.9	47.2	104	640	3.8	11.1	57
Golf Digest	634	617	0.8	97.3	103	113*	0.4	17.8	60	398	1.0	62.8	138	106†	0.6	16.7	86
Golf Digest/Tennis (gross)	1,246	1,217	1.5	97.7	103	371	1.4	29.8	101	674	1.7	54.1	119	172*	1.0	13.8	71
Golf Magazine	422	389	0.5	92.2	98	108†	0.4	25.6	87	230*	0.6	54.5	120	50†	0.3	11.8	61
Golf Magazine/Ski (gross)	953	912	1.1	95.7	101	329	1.3	34.5	117	488	1.2	51.2	113	96†	0.6	10.1	52
Good House-keeping	17,340	16,566	20.2	95.5	101	5,348	20.9	30.8	104	8,038	20.4	46.4	102	3,180	18.9	18.3	94
Grit	1,541	1,427	1.7	92.6	98	390	1.5	25.3	86	702	1.8	45.6	100	334	2.0	21.7	112

* Projections relatively unstable because of sample base—use caution.

† Number of cases too small for reliability. Shown for consistency only.

SOURCE: Simmons Market Research Bureau, Inc.: 1983 Study of Media and Markets, p. 388.

that certain of the magazines listed have "heavy users" indexes either much greater or much lower than the national average. For example, the heavy user index for *Glamour* magazine is 137; for *Colonial House,* it is 80. Of course, this report does not contain information on the *prospects* for future heavy use.

Inner-Directed Consumer Identification. In recent years, techniques from psychology and small-group sociology have been increasingly applied to marketing problems. These methods are called lifestyle, psychographic, and benefit segmentation. Despite differences among them, they all help determine *why* some consumer behavior happened. Media planners find it difficult to get valid information of this type from the media, and, therefore, its use in media planning is limited.

Step 2: Basic Media Strategy

Once the media planner has thoroughly researched the prospective market and understands the marketing, advertising, and creative objectives, it is time to begin studying the principles that apply to the media schedule.

Reach versus Frequency: The Great Compromise. A major dilemma for media planners is deciding what people to reach and how many times to reach them. Step 1, Prospect Identification, should give the answer to the first question, but the problem of how often to reach these people is even more difficult.

Few products can be sold with only a single audience exposure. Likewise, it is wasteful to continue delivering advertising messages to an audience that is not interested in the product. The media planner must decide where the schedule should fall on a frequency continuum between one exposure and some point of diminishing return. The planner must also remember that each additional exposure to one group precludes reaching some other group.

The reach versus frequency problem comprises five related factors; the media planner who, through study and experience, can cope with these five factors is well on the way to the "ideal" media buy.

Factor 1: Reach. The media planner must first decide what prospects (including primary and secondary prospects) to contact.

Factor 2: Frequency. Next, it must be decided how many times to reach each prospect. When determining frequency, the media planner often has to work intuitively. However, factors such as price, frequency of product purchase, level of competitive advertising, and stage in the product life cycle give some indication of proper frequency levels.

FIGURE 5–4 The Learning Theory Concept of Advertising Frequency

---

Marginal product information learned

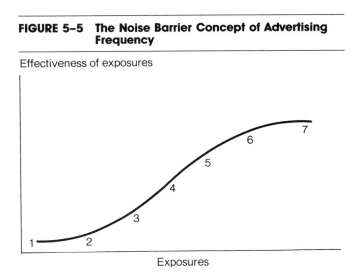

Exposures

Another major factor in determining frequency is the theoretical conception advocated by the individual media planner. There are basically three ways of viewing the purchase of frequency in an advertising campaign (see Figures 5-4, 5-5, and 5-6).

First, the learning theory concept of frequency takes the view that each impression of an advertising message results in an additional increment of learning for the prospect. At some point (after the seventh insertion in Figure 5-4), the prospect has full knowledge of the adver-

---

FIGURE 5–5 The Noise Barrier Concept of Advertising Frequency

---

Effectiveness of exposures

Exposures

FIGURE 5-6 The Need-Perception Concept of Advertising Frequency

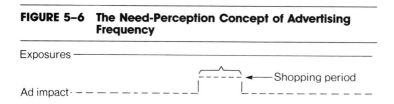

tiser's message; additional repetitions will result in no further learning and, consequently, diminishing returns on the advertising dollar.

Second, Figure 5-5 is a version of the learning theory concept that might be called the noise barrier concept. Here the assumption is that the first few exposures do little good since people must be made aware of the message through multiple exposure. Advertising must break through the barrier of competing advertising. Note in Figure 5-5 that the most effective exposures are in a middle range after the advertising has gained the prospect's attention but before the inevitable wearing-out period begins.

Third, the need-perception concept of frequency (Figure 5-6) is based on advertising impact as a function of need. For instance, assume that Figure 5-6 represents a washing machine owner who is satisfied with his present washer. Although the consumer comes into contact with numerous washer ads, they make no particular impression. However, when the consumer's old machine breaks and he needs a new one, his perception of the ads and the ads' impact increase dramatically.

After the consumer buys a new washer, his perception of washer ads drops to its former low level. The need-perception concept of frequency says that the greater the frequency of advertising, the greater the chance that an advertising message will be available when a prospect's need for an interest in a product peaks.

Factor 3: Continuity. A third factor related to the reach versus frequency compromise is the advertising campaign's **continuity** (the period of time an advertising schedule will run). The length of the campaign determines the number of people who can be reached and the number of times they can be exposed to the message. A media planner dealing with a six-week introductory or special offer campaign has more opportunity to extend both reach and frequency than if the same budget has to be allocated over an entire year. Regardless of the continuity, media planners must still determine reach and frequency goals. However, they have more flexibility as the length of the campaign decreases.

Factor 4: Length and Size of Advertisements. The frequency of ad insertions is affected by the length of the commercial or the size of the print advertisement the media planner chooses. Normally, the cheapest ads (i.e., smaller ads) are the most cost-efficient. However, the most cost-efficient advertisement may not carry out the campaign's advertising and marketing goals.

Normal advertisements usually run 30 seconds in television, 30 or 60 seconds in radio, a full page in magazines, and a wide range of sizes in newspapers. The smaller the ad, the greater the number of insertion opportunities and the greater the opportunities for added reach and frequency impact. Media planners must coordinate budget considerations with the considerations of their creative counterparts to determine the size of an advertisement—one more reason why the actual purchase of time and space is usually one of the final steps in a campaign.

Factor 5: Budget. The size of the advertising budget devoted to the media function permeates all media considerations. In essence, it is the budget that dictates compromises among the various elements of media strategy.

Step 3: Media Tactics and Competition

The competitive environment of advertising was discussed in Chapter 1. Nowhere is the analysis of competition more important than in the media function. Ideally, the media planner should begin by determining the media that best reach prospects without regard for competitors and their advertising strategy. However, it would be foolhardy to construct a media plan without considering what advertisers of similar products are doing. If you build a media plan that meets your needs, but it is totally unlike those of your competitors, consider the following possibilities:

> You found something your competitors overlooked that will give you a "noncompetitive" media schedule and should be of tremendous value to your client.
> You overlooked something about your schedule that your competition is aware of and that will result in a costly mistake for you and your client.

Under normal circumstances, competing advertisers use closely re-lated media. As you flip through a magazine or watch an evening of television, notice how many competitive products use the same general media outlets for their advertising. Since advertisers tend to make sim-ilar media buys, smaller advertisers have great difficulty gaining a competitive advantage over companies with larger budgets. The follow-ing techniques can help smaller advertisers extend their advertising budgets and compete effectively against larger budgets.

Technique 1: The Wave Theory. A technique used to some degree by almost every advertiser is the so-called wave theory (often called "**flight-**

FIGURE 5-7 The Wave Theory

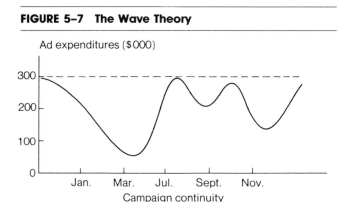

ing" or "pulsing"). In Figure 5–7, an advertiser starts a campaign with a high level of expenditure (relative to the total budget). After this initial wave or flight of advertising, the expenditure is reduced so that by March it is at the lowest level of the campaign. August marks the culmination of another flight with a smaller trough in August, followed by yet another flight in early September.

The rationale of the wave theory is that advertising recall occurs without continuous advertising. If the message has high initial impact, the prospect can remember the product without constant reminders. This consumer recall is called **continuity of impression** and is represented by the dashed line in Figure 5–7. Continuity of impression refers to the fact that product awareness is continuous although advertising expenditures are not.

Several precautions are in order before you develop a "flighting" campaign. The media schedule should take the following into account.

1. Quality of the Advertising Message.   To have continuity of impression, you must achieve high initial impact. This impact is also a function of the length of time you can afford to advertise at some peak level. Many advertisers make the mistake of cutting back on their advertising just when the audience is becoming aware of it.

2. Interval between Flights.   Perhaps the two most important considerations in determining the maximum time between flights are the level of competitive advertising and your own budget. It is important to analyze what competitive advertising activity will take place when you cut back. Obviously, the more competitive the advertising situation, the greater the chance that the consumer will forget your advertising message. In addition, remember that what is a wave to you might be only a

FIGURE 5-8   The Wave Theory and Competition

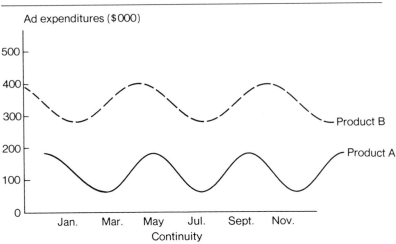

"ripple" to the competition. Figure 5–8 demonstrates the importance of considering competitive activity in planning the wave theory. Product A is probably wasting its efforts on the wave theory since its maximum expenditure does not even reach the lowest levels of product B. In such a situation, some alternative strategy must be found if product A wants to be competitive in the promotional area.

3. The Media Mix.   The types of media selected for the campaign may play a major role in the advisability of using the wave theory. If television is to be the major medium in the campaign, flighting is difficult to use effectively. The problems are discounts and availabilities. As we discuss later, television rates and discounts are designed with the large, continuous advertiser in mind. An advertiser who continually gets in and out of the medium loses substantial bulk and continuity discounts.

More important to the media planner considering the wave theory is the problem of availability. The broadcast media, as contrasted to the print media, deal in relatively fixed units of advertising time. Note the differences in the size of the pre-Christmas issues of popular magazines and the issues appearing shortly after Christmas. There may be a difference of 100 pages in some cases as advertisers pull out after the Christmas rush. Television does not have this flexibility. Consequently, stations and networks give favorable treatment to advertisers who are willing to sign long-term contracts and agree to advertise in slack periods as well as peak seasons. Advertisers using the wave theory often find that prime availabilities are not open to them on either the network or local

FIGURE 5-9   Media Dominance

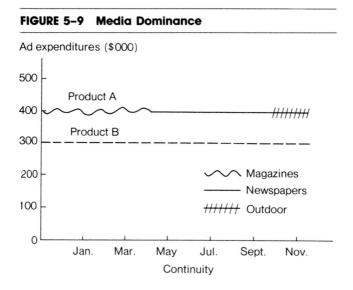

Ad expenditures ($000)

station level. In effect, by losing most discounts and having a low priority for choosing advertising spots, wave theory advertisers pay a premium price for secondary availabilities.

Technique 2: Media Dominance.   Media dominance is a media-buying technique sometimes used by advertisers who find themselves in the type of relative financial disadvantage shown in Figure 5-8. Advertiser A realizes that a traditional media mix cannot achieve any particular advertising impact in the face of a much larger competitor. However, some impact might be achieved by placing all or a significant proportion of the available advertising dollars in a single medium. This avoids the mistake of spreading the advertising budget across several media and making no impression in any. On the other hand, many small advertisers have a diversified market that cannot be reached adequately by a single medium. Media dominance is essentially an attempt to achieve a compromise between these two problems.

A media dominance plan uses several media over a period of time, but it uses them sequentially. This way, the advertiser is dominant, or at least competitive, with larger competitors in a single medium. However, the product is competitive with only a narrow segment of the total audience. Figure 5-9 demonstrates how this might change the competitive situation shown in Figure 5-8.

Now product A is more than competitive with product B. However, like most concepts of buying media, media dominance is a far from perfect solution to product A's problems. First, while competitive in one medium,

FIGURE 5-10 **Media Concentration** (one medium)

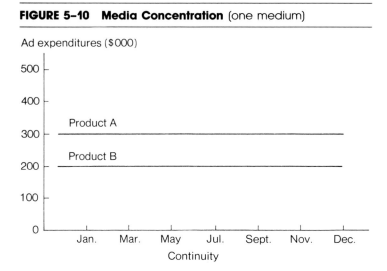

advertiser A is delivering no messages to prospective consumers who use other media. Second, advertiser A must take care not to use too many media and spread too thin horizontally. In determining how many media to use, and for how long, advertiser A needs to consider many of the same factors involved in determining the duration of waves. Likewise, television is normally not an ideal alternative for media dominance plans for the same reasons as those discussed in connection with the wave theory.

Technique 3: Media Concentration. A final media-buying technique for a small advertiser attempting to achieve parity with larger competition is media concentration. Basically, media concentration means that an advertiser chooses one medium that will best reach prospects and advertises exclusively in that medium for an indefinite period of time.

Advertisers choose media concentration over media dominance for several reasons. First, advocates of media concentration think the type of coverage offered by media dominance is too risky. They feel that to be effective advertising must be offered on a relatively continuous basis to the same audience. Another budgetary reason for using media concentration is that it allows advertisers to take advantage of media discounts and to compete for broadcast availabilities.

Figure 5-10 demonstrates a typical media concentration plan, again using products A and B from our earlier examples.

To consider media concentration, the media planner must be satisfied that a significant number of prospects can be reached by a single medium. Media concentration often means a lower share of market for the product. But above all, in the one medium used, dominance must be achieved. It is important to remember that few advertisers (especially advertisers of consumer goods) choose either media dominance or media concentration, given an alternative. However, small advertisers rarely have any option other than being overwhelmed by larger advertisers if they choose a more traditional multimedia approach.

A final consideration in developing a media plan is the qualitative versus the quantitative decisions. Media is a "by-the-numbers" enterprise. However, the numbers are usually estimates, and in any case, they cannot substitute for common sense and experienced judgment. The creative media planner must consider the quality of the media environment and its effect on the advertising message.

Bernie Orvett, creative group head at J. Walter Thompson, states:

> When I look at media, I worry about environment more than audience. The same women may read *Ladies' Home Journal, Woman's Day,* and *Vogue*—but they go to *Vogue* in a different frame of mind.
>
> I used to have terrible arguments with our media department about Mink International. They kept pointing to the cpms we could get in books like *Woman's Day* and *Family Circle.* I said we couldn't sell mink in those books. I wanted *Vogue* or *Harper's.* If we had to go to a service environment, I insisted we at least go into *Ladies' Home Journal*—which has more of a fashion environment.
>
> I'm convinced that cpms can sometimes put clients into unsympathetic environments.[2]

Step 4: Media Evaluation

To this point, the steps in the media plan have dealt with overall marketing and advertising concepts—the strategy of the plan. Now we must begin to develop the media schedule. The **media schedule** designates the media (e.g., magazines, television), the specific vehicles (e.g., *Time*, "60 Minutes"), and the insertion dates of the advertising. Chapters 6 through 11 analyze each of the media in light of specific advertising requirements.

The media planner has many other sources of information. Among the most valuable are the general media guides published by most large advertising agencies and many media organizations. These guides are not rate cards, but they can be used to estimate audience size, demographics, and basic costs for classes of media. They can save the media planner valuable time by indicating if the media plan being developed is consistent with previously determined objectives. Many of the guides also offer rules for determining reach or frequency, given other media schedule data. See Figures 5–11 and 5–12 for examples of such guides.

---

2 "Look Past the Numbers," *Media Decisions,* July 1977, p. 66.

FIGURE 5–11 How the Media Rate in Terms of Quantitative Media Factors

	TV	Radio	Magazines	Newspapers
Total population reach (Adults plus children)......	Very strong	Good	Fair	Good
Selective upscale adult reach	Fair	Good	Very strong	Good
Upscale adult selectivity (per ad exposure)	Poor	Fair	Very strong	Good
Young adult selectivity (per ad exposure)	Fair	Very strong	Very strong	Fair
Cost per 1,000 ratios	Fair-good	Very strong	Strong	Good
National media availabilities and uniform coverage ..	Very strong	Poor	Good	Poor
Local market selectivity	Good	Good	Poor	Very strong
Ability to control frequency	Fair	Good	Good	Very strong
Ability to pile frequency upon reach base	Very strong	Very strong	Good	Fair
Ability to exploit time-of-day factors (in scheduling)	Fair	Very strong	Poor	Poor
Ability to exploit day-of-week factors (in scheduling)	Fair	Very strong	Poor	Very strong
Seasonal audience stability	Poor	Very strong	Good	Good
Predictability of audience levels	Fair-poor	Good	Good	Very good
Depth of demographics in audience surveys	Poor	Poor	Very strong	Fair-good
Reliability and consistency of audience surveys	Fair-good	Good	Fair-good	Good
Ability to monitor schedules	Good	Poor	Very strong	Very strong
Ability to negotiate rates	Good	Fair	Poor	Poor
Fast closing and air dates	Fair	Good	Poor	Very strong

Step 5: The Media Schedule

The worst mistake a media planner can make is to begin media buying before completing the marketing and research steps outlined in the previous sections. The media schedule is the culmination of extensive examination of the total advertising problem, and if that examination has been done properly, the schedule based on it should fall into place naturally.

The media schedule serves two purposes: (1) It gives the client and other advertising decision makers a clear idea of the media function as part of the total marketing/advertising program, and (2) it is a working plan for carrying out the mechanics of purchasing time and space. The media schedule can take an indefinite number of different formats, but it must be unambiguous so that anyone in the media department can purchase the time and space specified in the schedule. After the planning

FIGURE 5–12 Audience Composition for TV Show Types

| | Adult Viewer Profiles for TV Show Types (average ¼-hour audiences) | | | | | |
| | Men | | | Women | | |
	18–34	35–49	50+	18–34	35–49	50+
M-F daytime						
"Good Morning America"/						
"Today Show".	22%	29%	49%	27%	29%	44%
Situation comedies	27	23	50	46	28	26
Game shows.	22	19	59	31	16	53
Serials	33	17	50	41	19	40
M-F early evening						
Game shows.	22	20	58	23	18	59
Newscasts	21	22	57	21	20	59
Situation comedies	48	23	29	47	23	30
Police/detective/						
action/adventure	38	24	38	39	21	40
Prime time						
Movies	36	26	38	35	25	40
Situation comedies	36	24	40	35	25	40
Serialized dramas	36	18	46	31	21	48
Detective/police dramas .	35	29	36	35	25	40
Adventure/sci. fi. shows . . .	40	27	33	44	26	30
News magazine shows . . .	28	23	49	21	23	56
Late evening						
Newscasts	32	27	42	30	26	44
"Tonight Show".	43	24	33	30	21	49
Movies	44	28	28	38	28	36
Situation comedies	47	25	28	46	24	30
Detective/police dramas .	45	21	34	38	26	36
Comedy/variety shows . . .	55	25	20	57	26	17
(Men/women pop.)	(43)	(24)	(33)	(40)	(23)	(37)

SOURCE: *Adweek's Marketer's Guide to Media* 10, no. 1 (1987), p. 20.

and selection processes for media are complete, time and space are pur-chased.

THE FINANCES OF MEDIA BUYING

Advertising is a $110 billion a year business, most of which is devoted to space and time costs. As with any other business of that size, many complex relationships exist, which all parties must understand. This section discusses the three types of firms most concerned with the adver-tising media process: the advertising agency, the independent media buyer, and the media representative.

The Advertising Agency

Most national advertising is placed by advertising agencies. These agencies are usually independent, but some advertisers establish in-house advertising departments to carry out a portion of the advertising function. Since media expenses make up a major portion of most advertising budgets for consumer goods, media plays a crucial role in an agency-client relationship.

Normally a full-service agency's media responsibilities include the following:

1. Make basic recommendations to the client about general media strategy.
2. Enter into contracts (which set time and space prices) with the media and submit **insertion orders.**
3. Engage in research, usually based on syndicated data, for major media decisions.
4. Ensure that all advertising runs on schedule and that production quality meets minimum standards.

These functions are normally part of the basic agency function. If the agency operates on the traditional 15 percent media commission system, these functions are called **nonbillable services.** That is, they are included in the basic services covered by the commission. Services such as primary research, which is rarely conducted by an agency, or other specialized client services cost extra and are called **billable services.**

One of the major components of the client-agency relationship is determining the method of compensation. Four systems of compensation are used.

Basic Media Commission. In the most traditional method of agency compensation, the agency bills the client at the current media rates and in turn pays the media at the same rates, less 15 percent. In addition, media may offer a 2 percent discount for prompt payment. The agency generally returns this **cash discount** to the client, assuming that it pays the media in time to qualify for the discount.

For noncommissionable media, such as direct mail, the agency usually marks up its cost by 17.65 percent. This markup provides the agency with the equivalent of 15 percent of the gross bill (see Figure 5–13). The 17.65 percent markup is also used to compute billing, printing, and other production charges as well as other media rate calculations. For instance, some newspapers are now offering identical rates for national and local advertisers. However, if the national advertiser uses an agency, the newspaper marks up the cost 17.65 percent to cover the agency discount.

FIGURE 5–13 The 17.65 Percent Markup: An Example

	Full Page— Local Rate	Full Page— National Rate
Undifferentiated local/national rate..........................	$1,000	$1,000
National rate with agency placement..................	$1,000 + 17.65% = $1,176.50	
Net to newspaper after agency commission is paid..........	$1,176.50 − 15% = $1,000	

Media Commission Method as a Draw against a Minimum Fee. This simply means that the client agrees to pay the agency a minimum fee (usually on a monthly basis). Any media commissions or other agency fees are deducted from this fee.

Retainer or Fee Method. Here the client contracts with an agency for specific services at a set fee. Usually this method is used where the agency-client relationship is a long-standing one. For instance, a brochure or a consumer research project is often paid on a per-job basis. A full-service agency generally doesn't deal with clients on this basis.

Incentive Fee Method or Shared Profit Fee Method. This method guarantees the agency some minimum net profit on gross billings of the account. It can be computed either before or after taxes. A common application of the method guarantees the agency 1.5 percent profit on gross billings. If profits fall within a 1.5 to 2.5 percent range, there is no adjustment; if agency profits exceed 2.5 percent, the agency returns some contracted proportion of the surplus to the client. This is advantageous to the advertiser only when advertising investment is heavy.

The conversation with Al Achenbaum, reprinted in Figure 5–14, covers the demise of the rigid 15 percent commission "rule" and the growing practice of more flexible agency compensation plans.

Regardless of the basic compensation method, it is crucial that a detailed letter of agreement between the client and the advertising agency be completed *before* any work is done. This agreement specifies which charges for production, talent, and services will be included in commissions and which will not. It may also specify research charges and, occasionally, the people or the levels of personnel that will handle the account. Finally, the agreement includes a statement of the client's liability to the media. Some advertisers pay their agencies only to find the agencies aren't paying third parties. The courts have generally held that advertisers are not liable for work contracted by an agency. A few media require dual-liability contracts, and some advertisers ask their

FIGURE 5–14 How Are Agencies Really Compensated?

A CONVERSATION WITH AL ACHENBAUM*

Michael Mella

Q. *Why do you say the 15 percent commission really doesn't exist?*
A. The traditional 15 percent commission is dead. Very few companies in the country and very few agencies basically adhere to it. Everybody negotiates something. It was originally put into effect by print media over 100 years ago for brokers to write copy and get paid for selling space. Today, the advertising agency is the agent of the client not the media. So advertisers must negotiate and decide what is fair.

Q. *What hurt the 15 percent system?*
A. Media inflation, which began about 1976, was a big reason. Advertising rates grew rapidly. There was a 25 percent rise in television rates. All of the other media followed suit. As long as agencies were getting a commission they were getting more money for less work. Meanwhile, general inflation, salaries, rents were going up more slowly than media rates.

Q. *Many people still defend the traditional 15 percent commission as though it is alive and well. Is it?*
A. First of all it's a simple, easy number to calculate. Secondly, from the agency point of view it is very, very profitable. You make a heck of a lot of money on the 15 percent commission if you have a large advertiser. So for the agencies—and there's nothing inherently wrong with the commission system—it makes the most sense.

Q. *What basic points should be considered when negotiating compensation with an agency?*
A. I don't believe one should look for the best deal. By that I mean paying the least amount of money. Try for equity on both sides. The agency must make a fair and reasonable profit and the client must get what it pays for. Understand the amount and distribution of people assigned to the accounts, the salaries and other expenses besides direct salary. If you know these numbers you should be able to structure an equitable arrangement.

Q. *What lies ahead?*
A. Basically, the movement is toward the variable or sliding scale commission system. That's the best direction to go.

* Alvin A. Achenbaum is chairman of Canter Achenbaum Associates Inc., a New York marketing counseling firm.

SOURCE: "Agency Compensation: Fees vs. Commission," *Marketing and Media Decisions*, Special Issue, Fall 1984, p. 110.

agencies to take out insurance or a bond to protect them from having to pay twice. A simple way of handling this is for the client to ask the agency for copies of paid invoices and copies of any ads placed.

Agency of Record

In cases where a multiline company has several advertising agencies servicing its brands, some coordination of the media function is necessary. Corporations often qualify for media discounts higher than the total discounts for which their individual brands qualify (see Figure 5–15). Large advertisers often appoint one of their agencies as the "agency of record" to coordinate the media discounts the firm qualifies for. The agency of record normally negotiates time and space contracts, and the firm's other agencies submit insertion orders based on these contracts.

The agency of record receives a percentage of the commissions of the other agencies. Usually this extra fee is 15 percent of the 15 percent agency commission, or 2.25 percent. Consequently, the "other" agencies receive only 12.75 percent instead of the normal 15 percent commission for media placement.

The Independent Media Buyer

In contrast to the full-service agency, which plans an entire campaign, independent media-buying organizations deal strictly in the purchase of media. Independent media buyers usually work for agencies, which use them as the media department for some or all of their clients, or directly for clients who handle their own creative activities.

Most of the media purchases made by the independent media organizations are in broadcast. Fees are often set on the basis of how much the client saves compared to the prices originally quoted by the media. Since broadcast time charges are more negotiable than print charges, experienced buyers can realize major savings. Print media generally sell space on a fixed basis, with fewer opportunities for negotiated buys.

Independent media-buying services compete with, and are often disparaged by, the full-service agencies. Full-service agencies contend that their own media buyers are as qualified as those employed by independents and that independents effect savings by making "inferior" buys. The independents naturally dispute this charge, claiming that since they are media specialists, they can do the media-buying job better than a full-service agency, which must deal with a whole range of nonmedia functions.

Both the full-service agency and the independents are probably correct. As discussed earlier, the buying of GRPs rather than individual spots makes precise evaluation of media buys difficult. Occasionally,

---

FIGURE 5–15 Computing Media Discounts for Companies versus Brands

---

PDQ Gadget Company

Brand	Number of Standard Advertising Units (SAUs) Bought	Discount
A	2,000	3%
B	1,800	3
C	3,000	5
D	2,000	3
E	2,400	3

Total = 11,200 Average discount = 3.4%

**Oblivion City *Clarion*
Rate Card**

Annual SAU Purchase	Annual Discount
3,000	3%
5,000	6
8,000	10
10,000	14

Notes: A Standard Advertising Unit is 1 column (2¹⁄₁₆ inches) wide and 1 inch deep. While the average brand discount earned was only 3.4 percent, the PDQ Company earned an annual discount of 14 percent.

---

large clients "test" their agencies by giving identical media assignments to the agency and one or more independent media buyers. This may keep the agency on its toes; however, it does little to further good agency-client relationships.

The Media Representative

The media **representative (rep)** works for media enterprises rather than advertisers. Historically, media reps functioned as media sales personnel in major markets and were paid commission for the time and space they sold. This meant that newspapers and broadcast stations could compete for national dollars without incurring the expense of having their own sales force in New York, Chicago, Los Angeles, and other major markets. Media reps still perform this basic sales function, but they have added more sophisticated services. For example, the major reps—such as Blair, Eastman, McGavren-Guild, Katz, and Torbet Radio—developed buying combines for radio, called *nonwired networks* (see Chapter 7). They now use interactive computer systems to obtain immediate information on time availabilities. Blair recently experimented with the satellite transmission of television spots to local stations.

In addition to functioning as time and space sales organizations, media reps have become an integral part of the total advertising media process. Media reps are excellent sources of local market information, and they increase local media revenues by bringing national dollars to many previously overlooked broadcasters and publishers. Finally, media reps provide an orderly flow of advertising from nationally oriented accounts to local media.

More and more media groups have been forming their own rep subsidiaries. These companies function similarly to the independent reps, but they restrict their clients to company-owned or otherwise related media. Gannett Newspaper Advertising Sales and NBC Spot Sales are examples of these group-oriented reps.

SUMMARY

This chapter has outlined the basic functions and terminology of media buying. At this point, you should have a basic idea of how buyers and sellers of advertising media function. It is important to understand the broad system by which advertisements and commercials progress from the initial concepts of copywriters to the mass media and ultimately to the consumers of advertisers' products.

In Chapters 6 through 11, we analyze various media and their specific options and limitations for the advertisers who use them. As we discuss each of the media, keep the general concepts of this chapter in mind. Remember that advertising media buying is not done in a vacuum. Rather, every media-buying decision is also a decision *not* to buy various media alternatives. Only by viewing the media as an interrelated communication system can you grasp the complexities of managing the media function.

REVIEW QUESTIONS

1. What are the five areas of the media-buying function?
2. Briefly describe four methods of audience segmentation. Give an example of each.
3. What is the major problem with using lifestyle or psychographic data in media planning?
4. Describe "flighting" and some considerations in using the technique.

5. Discuss the use of television in media dominance and media concentration.

6. Discuss three concepts of frequency.

7. Discuss at least two alternatives to the agency commission system of payment.

8. In a recent four-week period, the "CNN Evening News" had the following audience in Metropolis (6,000 TV households):

Week	Number of Households Viewing	Unduplicated Audience
1	2,500	2,500
2	2,700	1,000
3	2,300	700
4	2,500	400

   a. What was the reach during this period?
   b. What was the frequency?
   c. Assuming that a 30-second spot costs $150, what was the cpm/household during the first week?
   d. What was the rating during the third week?
   e. If the average audience in the base year was 2,100, what would the audience index be for the second week?
   f. If the HUT during the fourth week was 65 percent, what was the program's share?
   g. What GRP level was achieved during this period?

9. Using the data in Figure 5-3, identify the "best" magazine for reaching females who are heavy users of toothpaste. Restrict your choice to a magazine that is read by at least 1 percent of the female heavy users of toothpaste.

10. Should there be any uncertainty about this conclusion (in 9 above) about whether this magazine is really "best"?

SUGGESTED ADDITIONAL READING

BARWISE, T. P. "Repeat-Viewing of Prime-Time TV Series." *Journal of Advertising Research* 26, no. 4 (1986), pp. 9–14.

"Bates Rates CPM Performance." *Marketing and Media Decisions,* August 1986, pp. 45–50.

CANNON, HUGH M. "A Method for Estimating Target Market Ratings in Television Media Selection." *Journal of Advertising* 15, no. 2 (1986), pp. 21–26.

"47 Steps to the Upfront Buy." *Marketing and Media Decisions,* March 1985, p. 46.

GAY, VERNE. "Animated Children's Show Ratings on the Skids." *American Demographics,* September 1986, pp. 38 + .

LASTOVICKA, JOHN L. "Convergent and Discriminant Validity of Television Commercial Rating Scales." *Journal of Advertising* 12, no. 2 (1983), pp. 14–23, 52.

LINDEN, FABIAN. "Spending Boom and Bust," (Index of 1985 Consumer Spending by Age and Product Category). *American Demographics,* October 1986, pp. 4+.

LUMPKIN, JAMES R., and WILLIAM R. DARDEN. "Relating Television Preference Viewing to Shopping Orientations, Life Styles and Demographics." *Journal of Advertising* 11, no. 4 (1982), pp. 56–67.

PFAFF, FRED. "Enter the Rate Disk." *Marketing and Media Decisions,* November 1986, pp. 67–70.

ROONEY, JOHN F. "The Pigskin Cult and Other Sunbelt Sports." *American Demographics,* September 1986, pp. 38+.

RUST, ROLAND T.; ROBERT P. LEONE; and MARY R. ZIMMER. "Estimating the Duplicated Audience of Media Vehicles in National Advertising Schedules." *Journal of Advertising* 15, no. 3 (1986), pp. 30–37.

SWARTZ, TERESA A., and LUANNE MEYER. "News versus Entertainment TV Viewers." *Journal of Advertising Research* 25, no. 6 (December 1985/January 1986), pp. 9–17.

WEILBACHER, WILLIAM M. "The 15% Media Commission Is on the Way Toward Becoming a Relic in Ad Agency Compensation Plans." *Marketing News,* June 10, 1983, p. 9.

ZAHRADNIK, RICH. "Media's Micro Age." *Marketing and Media Decisions,* November 1986, pp. 67–70.

ZELTNER, HERBERT. "Strategy, Creative Shaping Ad Budgets." *Advertising Age,* January 20, 1986, pp. 3+.

CHAPTER SIX

Television

Television's detractors argue that it is a boob tube, that it requires a minimum of intelligence to use . . . . Actually, television is a very demanding mode of communication. Television's information is ephemeral; there is no way for the viewer to go back over the material, in the way a newspaper reader or book reader can glance back over the page.*

E. Diamond

After having his house wired for cable he found himself addicted to ESPN's round-the-clock sports programming, sitting up past midnight watching sports he never knew existed. Finally, his wife said it was her or ESPN. He went with ESPN.†

"The Nature of Cable"

In three manic weeks of July the TV networks sold a record $2 billion of commercials for the 1983–84 season, late September to late April. On one memorable day ABC did over $170 million of business. Salespeople stumbled out of ABC's New York offices at 4 A.M., eyes glazed and fingers cramped from writing orders. But all this glorious selling obscured the real news: the networks were unable to raise prices as they once had, and a continuing rise in programming costs threatens to pinch the free-spending industry.‡

Steven Flax

---

* *The Tin Kazoo* (Cambridge: MIT Press, 1975), p. 64.

† Editorial, *The Wall Street Journal,* June 5, 1986, p. 26.

‡ "Squeeze on the Networks," *Fortune,* September 5, 1983, p. 84.

America has had an uninterruped love/hate relationship with television since 1950. Television is more than a medium of advertising and communications; it is an institution in the United States and throughout much of the world. It is criticized and praised with equal fervor by special-interest groups, legislative bodies, and organizations across the political and social spectrum.

TELEVISION INDUSTRY OVERVIEW

Currently, the U.S. television industry is composed of about 1,500 television stations, of which approximately 1,170 are commercial. Of these, the ratio of very high frequency to **ultra high frequency** (or VHF to UHF) stations is about 7:5. By 1990, it is projected that there will be 300 **independent stations,** unaffiliated with any network—up from 200 in 1985.[1] In addition, there are about 9,700 cable television systems in the United States. These stations and cable systems offer a wide variety of viewing choices. Counting both cable-furnished and over-the-air frequencies, 84 percent of U.S. households can receive 9 or more channels, and 19 percent of these households can receive 30 or more channels.

In 1980, the combined gross advertising revenues of ABC, CBS, and NBC totaled $4.7 billion. By 1986, network ad revenues had grown to $8.3 billion.[2] In 1984, total television advertising revenues were $19.9 billion.[3] That year, KLTA, an independent television station in Los Angeles, was sold for an estimated price of $245 billion.[4] Cable television industry revenues, including advertising revenues and all other sources, are projected to be over $20 billion by 1990.[5]

In April 1985, the Federal Communications Commission changed its rules on ownership of television stations. Formerly, the FCC permitted a corporation or individual to own up to seven television stations; no more than five of these could operate in the VHF frequency range. The change permits an entity to own 12 television stations, subject to the provision that these stations operate in markets that together contain no more than 25 percent of the nation's television households. Of special importance are the stations owned and operated by the three television net-

---

[1] "How to Cash in on Television Reruns," *Fortune,* March 18, 1985, p. 176.

[2] "Future Shock Rattles the TV Networks," *Fortune,* April 14, 1986, p. 24.

[3] *Statistical Abstract of the United States, 1986* (Washington, D.C.: U.S. Government Printing Office, 1986), p. 552.

[4] "Why Television Stations Are Such Hot Properties," *Business Week,* June 20, 1983, p. 159.

[5] "Cable's Effects below the Surface," *Marketing and Media Decisions,* September 1983, p. 50.

works. These **O&O** stations are important because they are located in major population centers and are extremely profitable. In addition, they serve as benchmarks against which networks measure the success of certain syndicated programs, local news formats, and local market ratings.

Television viewership statistics are as impressive as television revenues. Over 98 percent (85.9 million) American households have at least one TV set. In 1985, 57 percent had two or more sets, and 93 percent (79.9 million) had a color set. According to A. C. Nielsen Company, cable penetration among U.S. households in 1985 was slightly over 45 percent. By 1986, 33 percent of U.S. households owned video cassette recorders (VCRs).

Television is the leading advertising medium among national advertisers by a wide margin. In 1984, the top 10 national advertisers spent $1.88 billion on network television advertising and an additional $881 million on spot television advertising. This combined sum of $2.77 billion represented 74 percent of total advertising expenditures for the 10 top advertisers. In the previous year, the top 100 advertisers devoted 76 percent of their combined budgets to television advertising; the ratio of dollars spent on network versus spot (or "by station") advertising was 2:1.

Television revenues are concentrated in a relatively few product categories, and one or two large corporations tend to dominate each category. Figure 6–1 shows this concentration for the largest TV advertisers.

The absolute cost of using television can be tremendous. Television CPM values compare favorably with those of other mass media. However, the real costs and message perishability, which demands high frequency levels, prevent most small and medium-sized advertisers from using television as their primary medium. Television is a complex medium with many quantitative and qualitative forces restricting advertising flexibility. This chapter deals primarily with television as an advertising medium. However, we also show the medium in the perspective of a leisure-time activity, which is used over seven hours per day in the average American home.

TELEVISION AS AN ADVERTISING MEDIUM

Unlike most advertising media, television is a multipurpose advertising vehicle. It appeals to different audiences and advertisers at different times. The various segments of television must be examined from a marketing perspective almost as if they were different media. Figure 6–2 outlines the relationships and marketing strategies of television's several faces.

FIGURE 6–1 Media Buying for the Top 200 Advertised Brands

Product Category	n	Magazines	Supps	Newspapers	TV Net	TV Spot	Radio Net	Radio Spot	Outdoor	Total, $ Millions
Retail chains	5	5%	*	77%	8%	5%	1%	4%	*	$1,389
Automobiles	20	17	*	14	35	25	*	8	1%	1,232
Cigarettes	16	35	6%	42	*	*	*	*	17	653
Beers	9	2	*	1	54	21	1	20	1	333
Medicines	10	7	1	*	81	8	2	1	*	255
Cereals	3	4	*	2	71	21	1	1	*	151
Coffees	5	6	1	3	63	20	4	3	*	125
Dog foods	3	10	*	1	75	14	*	*	*	95
Soft drinks	8	4	*	3	42	41	1	7	2	231
Candy/gum	2	4	*	2	72	18	*	4	*	64
Miscellaneous food	17	14	11	3	47	21	2	2	2	492
Fast food	7	*	*	*	38	57	1	2	2	321
Airlines	5	7	*	48	7	22	*	14	*	214
Oil/gas	6	17	2	10	34	26	4	7	*	153
Toys/games	3	5	*	4	55	36	*	*	*	88
Entertainment	7	3	*	2	58	31	*	6	*	186
Media	4	41	*	30	*	24	5	*	*	112
Soap/cleansers	5	5	*	1	82	12	*	*	*	112
Personal care	18	18	1	2	66	10	1	2	*	458
Cameras	4	23	*	4	61	10	1	1	*	156
Insurance	2	6	*	1	73	9	*	11	*	36
Apparel	3	11	*	2	68	11	2	6	*	66
Appliances	5	25	3	15	43	10	2	2	*	187
Computers	2	34	1	11	44	4	3	3	*	61
Miscellaneous	31	22	3	5	41	22	2	4	1	794

* Indicates expenditures of less than 1 percent.

SOURCE: "Big Advertisers' Budget Splits." Marketing and Media Decisions. Fall 1982 Special Issue, pp. 131–39.

FIGURE 6–2   Various Programming Segments of Television

Television Segment	Primary Audience	1987 Household CPM	Typical Products
Late fringe time	Young adults, 18–24	$5.80	Records, movies
Daytime	Women, 35+	3.25	Soaps and detergents
Prime time (8–11 P.M.)	Adults (children and some teens until 9 P.M.)	8.70	Consumer goods, depends on program
Children, Saturday and afternoons	Children, 2–11	4.00	Cereals, toys
News (including "Today Show," "Good Morning America," "CBS Morning News")	Upscale adults, more women in morning and early news shows	5.75	Utilities
Sports	Men, 18–35	7.75	Automobiles, beer
Prime time access (7–8 P.M.)	Adults, 35+	5.00	Consumer goods

Television Dayparts[6]

Television is divided into several segments (or dayparts) during each broadcast day. As shown in Figure 6–2, each of these dayparts has its own primary audience, programming, and advertising. A brief discussion of each of the major dayparts and its strengths follows.

Prime time.   **Prime time** is the glamour segment of the medium. The stars, the major advertisers, the blockbuster shows, and, not coincidentally, 60 percent of all households are part of the prime time television audience. The networks schedule all the programming that is shown on their **affiliates** during this period.

In the prime-time segment, the networks compete for rating points and advertising dollars with a fierceness unknown in any other medium. Costs for 30-second commercials on popular shows exceed $250,000, and program production costs are well over $1 million per 30 minutes. Made-for-TV movies (e.g., *Thorn Birds*) cost about $1.5 million per hour to make. With so many complaints about the quality of television programming, including an excess of sex and violence, many people wonder how television can continue to command these high prime-time commercial fees.

To understand this, you must first understand the economics of television and the psychology of the television viewer.

---

[6] All references are to Eastern time. A network program broadcast at 8 P.M. in New York would be broadcast at 8 P.M. in the Pacific time zone and at 7 P.M. in the Central and Mountain time zones.

Television rates are set by market forces, that is, by supply and demand. Advertisers will buy television advertising as long as it delivers their message in a way and at a cost that cannot be equaled by other advertising media. Even at annual price increases of 5 to 7 percent for commercial time, the demand for prime-time advertising remains strong because the supply of commercial time is fixed.

The demand for television commercial time is derived from, and is only as strong as, the public's demand for television programming. Each year such groups as the National Citizens Committee for Broadcasting and Action for Children's Television (ACT) publish their lists of the most violent shows. Each year these shows include some of the most popular programs. Without defending or condoning network prime-time programming, a realistic appraisal of the situation indicates that the networks and the public at least share the responsibility for current television fare. Regardless of the program content or criticism, every show that stays on the air is watched by millions of people.

Daytime. **Daytime** television is either a local or network-dominated segment, depending on the time. Networks generally provide programming from 10 to 4 P.M. The percentage of stations accepting network programs (designated as percent of clearance) varies; many stations preempt noon programs for local news. The formula for network daytime is soap operas, 70 percent; game shows, 8 to 10 percent; and network reruns, 5 to 7 percent.

Only a few seasons ago, the percentage of game shows and soap operas was almost equal. Networks prefer to broadcast game shows since these are less expensive to produce than soap operas. However, game shows generally suffered when placed opposite dramas, and the networks usually program the highest rated format.

The period from 9 to 10 A.M. is filled with syndicated talk shows, off-network reruns, and a few locally produced news and information programs. These shows are directed to a primarily female audience. Early morning daytime is controlled by the networks with their news programs. Independent stations counterprogram the period with inexpensive reruns of "The Three Stooges," "The Lone Ranger," and cartoons.

Fringe Time. **Fringe time** is the period preceding and following prime time. Early fringe time starts with afternoon reruns devoted to children, and it becomes more family- and adult-oriented as prime time approaches. In recent years, the 5 to 6 P.M. period has been hotly contested among local stations seeking strong lead-ins to their lucrative local news shows.

Late fringe is programmed primarily for young adults, and it has become much more competitive than it was only a few years ago when

FIGURE 6–3 Network, spot, and local television advertising revenues
($ millions)

	1968		1977		1986	
	Amount	Percent	Amount	Percent	Amount	Percent
Network	$1,428.5	48.9%	$3,248.1	47.4%	$ 8,923	42.9%
Spot	1,000.1	34.6	1,967.3	28.8	6,004	28.9
Local	482.0	16.5	1,630.9	23.8	5,844	28.1
	$2,910.6	100.0%	$6,846.3	100.0%	$20,771	99.9%

SOURCE: *Television/Radio Age,* June 4, 1979, p. 38; the 1986 figures are a composite developed from various trade press sources.

Johnny Carson dominated the period. Both ABC and CBS have programmed network reruns of crime/adventure shows against Carson with some success. Independent stations and a number of network affiliates choose to run movies during the period.

On a typical autumn day, 25 million households are still watching television at midnight. This number steadily declines until 5:30 A.M., but an incredibly large number of households (about 4 million) are still watching even at this hour. Late-night spots were typically used for advertising used cars, appliance stores, and gadgets. However, big-league national advertisers such as Time, American Express, and Avon are now purchasing late-night spots. In place of historical ad practices such as "per inquiry" pricing of late-night spots (i.e., advertisers paid the station a negotiated fee for each inquiry the ad produced), sophisticated marketing programs now use 800 toll-free phone numbers.

National and Local Television Advertising

Although primarily a mass medium, television can reach different audiences and provides various methods of buying time. Television advertising is divided into three categories: network, national spot, and local. National spot is the advertising purchased on individual local stations by national advertisers. That is, they "spot" their advertising instead of purchasing network time. Throughout most of the modern broadcast era, network television advertising has been the major recipient of advertising revenue, with **spot advertising** a distant second, and local advertising representing a small percentage of total revenues (see Figure 6–3). However, in recent years local television advertising has become a significant factor, and most observers predict that it will exceed spot revenues in the next several years.

The growing influx of local advertisers has had an effect on the medium. The demand for television time from such traditional newspaper advertisers as banks, car dealers, and grocery stores has further squeezed already tight inventories and driven up both local and national spot costs. More important than these advertising cost increases, which have generally been more moderate in local television than in network costs, the local advertiser is making spot-buying strategy more difficult by decreasing available time. National advertisers find that they commit themselves to longer schedules to guarantee availabilities. These long-term commitments decrease flexibility, a major reason why many national advertisers use spot television in the first place.

A large measure of the increase in local television advertising must also be credited to local stations. When independent television began to grow nationally, it appealed primarily to local advertisers. Largely ignored by national advertisers, independents' rates were low enough for local retailers to experiment with television advertising. Spot advertisers are increasingly considering independent stations, and many local advertisers brought to the medium are not only remaining but expanding their television buys to local network affiliates.

Currently, cable systems have continued the practices of the independent stations by encouraging local businesses to try TV advertising. Even small cable companies have some capability to produce commercials for retailers and others who traditionally relied on newspapers and radio. The resulting ads are often inept, sometimes laughably so. Nevertheless, these attempts increase both the number and expenditures of local television advertisers.

National advertisers find problems in both network and spot buys. Network advertising offers lower CPMs and broad coverage with minimal administrative costs, and it often gains the prestige of being associated with network programs. On the other hand, network advertising does not allow for market-by-market variance. Many advertisers prefer to alter copy or even substitute brands in certain markets.

One approach currently being used to offer the advertiser the convenience of network with the flexibility of spot is the **cut-in.** This permits the advertiser to substitute another commercial for the network commercial in certain markets. Currently all three networks offer the service primarily to very large advertisers. The cut-in can be used either to account for local market variances or to test some portion of the advertising or marketing program.

A growing problem has arisen between networks and their affiliates over cut-ins. Many affiliates see any growth in network cut-ins as a danger to national spot revenues. While networks pay a fee to stations when cut-ins are used, some stations think they should receive more from the networks, and others simply bill the advertiser directly for cut-ins. Advertisers are generally willing to pay an additional fee for a cut-in, but they want the networks and their affiliates to work out a standard fee system satisfactory to all parties.

Types of Sponsorship

Advertisers have a wide choice of advertising relationships with the networks and stations. This section outlines some of the basic ways in which advertisers can gain access to television.

Participating Sponsorships. The most common prime-time relationship between the advertiser and the networks is participating sponsorship. The networks decide on the shows they will air during the coming season and then offer advertising time on these shows. Advertisers provide little or no input into the development of the shows; they "participate" only by buying one or more commercials. In many ways this is how advertisers buy most other media. When an advertiser purchases a page in *Time* magazine, no one considers that the advertiser has sponsored any particular section of the publication. For this reason, participating television sponsorship is sometimes known as the "magazine concept."

Sole Sponsorship. Sole sponsorship usually refers to programs that are supplied, owned, and controlled by advertisers. Since 1965 this concept has been largely confined to daytime television, where mammoth advertisers such as Procter & Gamble own their own shows. In prime time, most of the advertiser-controlled shows are specials and a few made-for-television movies.

It is important to emphasize that an advertiser-owned show must meet network standards before it will be accepted. The network must consider the effect a show will have on adjacent programs and the alternative programming that could fill the same slot. The high cost of program production works against an advertiser considering this type of investment. Advertisers generally refrain from spending such a large sum on one show, preferring instead to spread their budget over several shows to increase audience reach.

The appeal of sole sponsorship is the control and identification it gives the advertiser. Advertisers producing their own programming can develop projects that they think complement their marketing strategy to a greater degree than network-provided programs. In addition, sole sponsorship of a successful program offers tremendous sponsor identification. The average person would be hard pressed to recall a single sponsor from a currently top-ranked show. Yet the same person might easily identify Dinah Shore with Chevrolet and Milton Berle with Texaco two decades after these shows went off the air.

Barter. **Barter** is defined as the exchange of goods without money. In advertising, barter takes two basic forms. In the more common form, an advertiser exchanges goods for advertising time or space. Traditionally, this has been done at the local market level among small advertisers, but it is not restricted to small players. Some barter merchants have annual sales volumes in excess of $50 million.

A more formal (and expensive) form of barter is barter syndication. The idea of barter syndication is a simple one. Advertisers supply a show to television stations at no cost. This show usually carries two minutes of commercial time for the advertiser who provided the show and three to four minutes to sell to national or local advertisers. Thus, the advertiser has a property that he controls and that fulfills his program requirements, and the station has a free program, plus the money it earns from nonbartered spots.

At one time, bartered shows were stigmatized as those that couldn't be sold. However, in recent years, some of television's most popular syndicated shows (e.g., "Entertainment Tonight") have been fully or partly bartered.

Estimates vary on the extent of barter syndication. In 1985, networks estimated that it amounted to no more than $400 million. Syndicators, on the other hand, claimed to have reached the $700 million level. Barter syndication has enjoyed a growing popularity among major national advertisers. For example, an *Advertising Age* story estimated that General Foods spent $43.7 million on national barter in 1985, compared with $108.4 million for spot TV, and $163.6 million for network advertising.[7] Further, the story asserts that much of the growth in barter syndication has occurred at the expense of spot TV budgets.

Syndication

Only a few years ago, television **syndication** was a simple process. (Syndication is broadcast programming sold to stations on a market-by-market basis.) Network shows ran their course, and when their prime-time ratings started to fall, they were relegated to the minor leagues of afternoon reruns. Local stations were provided with inexpensive afternoon fillers, and networks made some extra profit in addition to what the shows had brought in during their first run.

The economics of syndicated programming changed dramatically with the 1970 Federal Communications Commission regulation known as the "Prime Time Access Rule." Actually the rule contains three important restrictions on syndication activity. First, it denies off-network reruns to network affiliates in the top 50 markets (which contain over two thirds of total U.S. TV households) in the 7 to 8 P.M. slot formerly programmed by networks. Exceptions are made for the network news shows and for Sunday evening programming. Independent stations re-

---

7 "GF Rebuts ABC Study on Barter," *Advertising Age*, October 7, 1985, p. 70.

sponded by airing very popular off-network reruns, obtained from syn-dicators, against the "dross-and-drivel" programming fare then available from non-network sources. During this same period, advertisers demand-ing additional commercial time began to buy independents. In addition, the "superstation," which is an independent carried by satellite to cable systems around the country, brought network nonaffiliates or indepen-dents high advertising revenues that could then be used to buy popular programs.

The second and third provisions of the FCC rule prohibit television networks from selling the programs they show and from having any ownership in programming produced by someone else. Thus, beyond the right to "rent" a program (actually the right to air the program twice), networks are prevented from integrating backward toward a partnership in program production, or forward, toward participation in syndication. During 1983, the second and third restrictions came under attack from the federal administration (Departments of Commerce and Justice, par-ticularly). Not surprisingly, networks saw their interests as parallel to the deregulation forces and jumped into the melee. At present, the rule stands, but syndicators and independent program producers would be foolish not to expect continued, well-financed assaults on the rule that protects them from network competition in the syndication arena.

In the last 15 years, stations in the largest markets have paid dra-matically increased prices for syndicated network reruns. In 1970, the per-episode price for reruns of "Petticoat Junction" in these large mar-kets was $6,500. By 1978, the price per episode of the "Mary Tyler Moore Show" was $38,000 and that of "Laverne and Shirley" was more than $60,000. In 1985, "Magnum, P.I." had been sold to KTLA, Los Angeles, for $115,000 per one-hour episode and "The Bill Cosby Show" for over $300,000 in several major markets. These prices usually give stations the right to up to 14 repeats over a period of from five to seven years.

The continued popularity of the best syndicated programs is astonish-ing as well as lucrative. Viacom Enterprises obtained syndication rights to 179 episodes of "I Love Lucy" in 1971 and has since sold the "Lucy" package to stations in 94 markets that cover 75 percent of the U.S. market. In addition, the show airs in 27 foreign markets as diverse as Australia, Great Britain, Bermuda, Bangladesh, Mexico, Greece, Saudi Arabia, and Singapore. Successful syndication can produce revenues of $100 to $200 million or more for program producers.

The increase in syndication prices has not only altered the economics of reruns and their advertising rates, but has also changed the basic relationship between networks and the producers who supply the major-ity of television series. As the profitability of reruns increases, the net-works can justify paying producers lower rates per show. According to program producers, this is actually happening. In recent years, major producers have claimed that network fees are less than production costs. To fully assess this claim, however, you should understand that a substantial portion of program production costs goes for the high salaries paid to "star" performers who, in turn, often own a part of the independent production company and who also stand to profit from syndication and other residual revenues.

A series usually needs three to five years (75–120 shows) of network production before enough episodes are available for effective syndication. Consequently, the producer has less of a bargaining position with the networks as the length of the series run (and potential syndication profitability) increases.

Added to what is fundamentally an internal broadcast industry problem is the lack of quality (popular) series reruns. The ideal syndicated series runs one-half hour, is a comedy, and appeals to a family audience. Only a small number of network series meets these criteria and has 100 or more episodes on tape. Existing demand, coupled with a scarcity of shows, will continue to drive up the costs of syndication to stations and advertising rates to sponsors. This is particularly true as more stations "strip" their syndicated programs by running a show five days a week.

FACTORS TO CONSIDER IN BUYING TELEVISION

Advertisers, considering television as an advertising medium, are told that it combines sight, sound, and motion with a broad potential reach. Television provides immediacy, prestige, and instant brand recognition. All of these features are potential benefits and worthy of examination by a prospective advertiser. However, from a marketing and managerial perspective, other, less discussed issues should also be considered.

Inflation

In the view of many advertisers, television costs got completely out of hand in the 1970s. While audience size showed minimal increases, overall costs and CPMs for network advertising doubled. Since 1977, network rates for a 30-second commercial have grown at an annual rate of 10 percent, and spot prices for this length ad have increased 12 percent per year. Current predictions are for less significant increases of 5 percent annually in the cost of network time. With supplies of commercial time relatively stable, the quadrennial election cycle and Olympics only serve to drive prices up more sharply with new or infrequent advertisers vying for time. A top-rated program like "The Bill Cosby Show" or the Super Bowl can command over $400,000 for a 30-second commercial.

FIGURE 6-4 **Prices for 30-Second Advertisements during Selected Sporting Event Broadcasts**

Sport (Network)	1985 Price ($)
College football (CBS)	35,000–40,000
College football (ABC)	45,000
Baseball's champion series (NBC)	50,000 (prime time)
	85,000–90,000 (weekends)
	35,000–40,000 (weekdays)
World Series (ABC)	250,000
NFL "Monday Night Football"	175,000 (with guarantees)
NFL regular season (CBS)	160,000
NFL regular season (NBC)	145,000
AFC playoffs (NBC)	200,000
NFC playoffs (CBS)	215,000
AFC championship game (NBC)	250,000
NFC championship game (CBS)	250,000
Super Bowl (NBC)	550,000

SOURCE: Reprinted with permission *Advertising Age,* July 8, 1985, p. 64. Copyright Crain Communications, Inc.

Historically, the networks have been insulated from the financial shocks of macroeconomic events such as recession. In the economic recessions of 1974 and 1980, network prices and revenues were relatively unscathed. However, by the recession of 1982, there were signs that networks would share in some of the general economic pain. By 1983, the ever-present grumbling about network price levels and price increases had grown to a crescendo. More important, alternatives to network television had proliferated to the point where even the networks had to admit to a declining share of the television audience and a generalized softening in demand. Figure 6-4 shows price levels that prevailed for network advertising during broadcasts of sports events in 1985.

In addition to these problems, new categories of advertisers have come into the medium, further sharpening demand. The effects of local advertisers on national spot advertising were discussed earlier. But fast-food chains, video equipment, and national retailers have become major television advertisers in recent years. Today, both Sears and McDonald's are among the top 20 network advertisers.

The basic cause of the continuing inflation in television prices is that advertisers think television sells products better than alternatives. During most dayparts, television delivers audiences at a CPM significantly less than that of magazines, the major alternative for most national advertisers. As long as advertisers successfully sell their products through television, demand for time and commercial costs will remain high.

Clutter

Advertisers are concerned not only about the high cost of advertising but also about the number of television commercials. The "clutter" problem is a three-sided dispute between advertisers, station affiliates, and the networks. Stations charge that networks have expanded their commercial time and reduced the number of local prime-time spots, thereby depriving local stations of millions of dollars in revenues. A study by the Station Representative Association charged that the networks carried 638 more commercial minutes in the second quarter of 1978 than were permitted under existing standards. CBS vehemently denied this charge.[8]

The problem of advertising clutter is partly one of definition. The National Association of Broadcasters (NAB) had set the maximum time for nonprogram material at 9½ minutes per hour during prime time. Nonprogram material includes commercials, program promotions, billboards, and program credits. A question has arisen as to whether some of these announcements, for instance public service announcements, should be counted against the 9½-minute limit.

Added to the confusion were announcements by the NAB and the Justice Department concerning clutter. Starting January 1, 1980, the NAB's TV Code Board increased the "nonprogram material" limit to 10 minutes. The NAB claimed that clearer definitions of nonprogram material would reduce clutter by counting material that formerly was not included in the category. However, many advertisers remained skeptical that this increase would alleviate the clutter problem.

In June 1979, the U.S. Department of Justice filed a civil antitrust suit against the NAB seeking to overturn the association's 9½-minute limit. The department contended that this limit on supply keeps television advertising rates much higher than they would be if competition were freer.

In July 1982, NAB and Justice settled the matter by signing a consent decree, which said, in effect, that the NAB code was anticompetitive and would be dropped. The legal effect was to permit networks to sell as much advertising time as they cared to; the practical effect was to increase advertising during prime time to 10½ minutes per hour. But adding more commercial time to an already crowded environment hardly seems the solution to most advertisers.

Finally, advertisers themselves are partly responsible for the clutter problem. What started as multiple-product or "piggyback" advertising, where an advertiser divided a 30-second commercial into two, 15-second

---

[8] "Are the TV Networks Selling Too Many Ads?" *Business Week*, September 18, 1978, p. 26.

advertisements for two of the advertiser's brands, has now become a practice of buying and selling freestanding commercial intervals of 15 seconds. The 15-second intervals are used by a rapidly growing number of advertisers who "save money" by paying from 60 to 75 percent of the 30-second price. In the process, the number of ads is also rapidly increased. And, in case the clutter problem isn't aggravated enough by the sale of 15-second intervals, a growing number of advertisers, such as Swissair and Federal Express, are beginning the systematic use of 10-second commercials. While the artistic, creative, and communicative merits of 15- or 10-second commercials is still a topic for debate and empirical research, the use of shorter-interval advertisements exacerbates the problem of clutter.

The Fragmented Audience

In the past, television advertisers had two alternatives for their advertising schedule. At the national level, the three networks provided the only television coverage. In all but the largest markets, advertisers could choose only among the three affiliated stations. Even in the few major markets where independent television stations existed, national advertisers largely ignored these alternatives.

In the 1980s, several factors combined to increase the options and complexities of buying television advertising. These changes included:

1. *New technology.* Advertisers found that a number of innovations made the system of networks and affiliates only one of a number of options. Independent stations and "superstations" are examples of such expansion. However, predictions of the demise of the network/affiliate relationship are premature at best.
2. *Greater demand for commercial time.* The relatively fixed inventory of television commercial minutes and increasing demand for this time forced advertisers to look for nontelevision advertising alternatives. Some advertisers moved into other media; others looked to forms of television that they had formerly ignored or underutilized.
3. *Aggressive selling by independents and cable.* Taking advantage of the increased demand for television time, independent stations and a few cable operators began to compete aggressively for advertising dollars.
4. *Changing emphasis in marketing strategy.* National advertisers began to examine the value and desirability of audience segmentation. They found that in some cases nontraditional broadcast outlets offered specialized programming (particularly sports) more suited to their needs and often at a lower CPM than network or affiliate buys.

For decades, marketing theory has stressed the advantages of developing more specialized media. The implication was that an increasingly fragmented audience would naturally divide into sections that met the tests for target market segments. Buzzwords like "narrowcasting" popped up overnight, saturated conversations among professionals and the trade press, and were relegated to a well-deserved obscurity. Programming would be more specifically directed to individual rather than mass tastes. The fragmented audience would offer the communication industry more opportunities for entry, thereby creating an expanded information and entertainment industry. Finally, advertisers would benefit by decreasing the waste circulation found in current mass media outlets.

At present, the industry realizes that even in television, there are no "free lunches," and that audience fragmentation carries with it risks and costs that will require future adjustments. For instance, the historical rule of thumb for measuring the success of a network show was that it should attain a 30 share of audience. Under normal circumstances, anything less than a 27 share placed the show's existence in jeopardy.

The 30-share guideline is no longer the standard. While the network share of noncable households remains approximately 90 percent in noncable homes, it may be eroding dramatically in cable households. A study by the A. C. Nielsen Company in Tulsa, Oklahoma, estimated that in "12-channel" cable homes, network share of prime-time viewing was only 74 percent; in "36-channel" cable homes, the network share declined to 56 percent. Remember that cable is available in almost half the homes in the United States, and continued growth is the only realistic prediction.

Since each program source has to cover certain overhead expenses regardless of audience size, we will not see a drop in advertising rates proportionate to the decrease in per-channel audience. Fragmentation of what has been an audience divided "into thirds" means that CPMs will increase significantly (see Figure 6–5). Part of this increase in CPM will be offset by lower waste circulation. Thus, the advertiser will have a more favorable CPM per prospect. However, even with this more favorable targeting of prospects, advertisers must expect higher real costs in the future.

As the hypothetical case in Figure 6–5 demonstrates, advertisers are faced with increasing CPM. In addition, more astute media planning will be required to reach the fragmented audience of the 1980s. Figure 6–5 points up another problem, which is potentially more ominous than higher advertising costs. As we have noted, 3 of the 10 viewing alternatives are noncommercial. The introduction of video cassette recorders (VCRs) allows viewers to record programs for viewing at their preference (time-shift viewing), and some VCRs can delete commercials from the programming.

FIGURE 6–5   Effects of Audience Fragmentation on TV Costs in a Local Market

	Average Prime-time Audience	Share of Audience	Cost per 30 Seconds	CPM per Household
1975: Three-station market (market population = 100,000 TV households)				
ABC affiliate	22,000	38.6	$150	$ 6.82
NBC affiliate	15,000	26.3	90	6.00
CBS affiliate	20,000	35.1	130	6.50
Average HUT	57,000 (57%)			
1985: Four-station market with cable (market population = 120,000 TV households)				
ABC affiliate	18,000	22.7	180	10.00
ABC affiliate*	11,000	13.8	100	9.09
NBC affiliate	16,000	20.0	130	8.13
CBS affiliate*	17,000	21.4	170	10.00
CBS affiliate	10,500	13.2	120	11.43
Home Box Office—pay TV†	3,500	4.4	—	—
Cable news network	1,200	1.5	50	41.67
Cable system channels	1,150	1.4	40	34.78
Video cassette recorder	300	.3	—	—
Educational station	800	1.0	—	—
Average HUT	79,450 (66.2%)			

* A second network affiliate brought in by cable.
† Noncommercial.

This practice, which is known as "zapping," can be done with the "fast forward" control on a VCR (to speed by the commercials when viewing a previously recorded program) or with the remote control device (by selecting an alternate channel when a commercial break in the program occurs). Zapping uses electronics to avoid exposure to television advertising. However accomplished, zapping gives the television advertiser a smaller audience and different audience than the one selected on the basis of the *program* audience estimates. One expert, Ronald Kaatz, estimates that by 1990, half of all television viewers will tune out commercials. One solution advertisers are testing is a commercial so "interesting" that it is zap proof. This approach generally sends creative and production costs through the roof. One deodorant advertiser shot 13,000 feet of film, with a running time of 150 minutes, in order to create a 68-foot, 45-second commercial.[9] Another response is based on a "join 'em" philosophy in which companies like Red Lobster are placing ad messages

[9] "In Search of Zap-Proof Commercials," *Fortune,* January 21, 1985, p. 68.

FIGURE 6-6 Major Cable Networks, Subscribers, and Cost Data

Network	Subscriber Households, May 1985 (millions)	Estimated Household CPM ($/000)
ESPN	36.5	$ 4.50
WTBS	34.8	2.25–2.75
CNN	34.8	4.00
USA	30.6	2.00–2.30
CBN	29.7	1.50–2.00
MTV	28.0	5.00–6.50
LIFETIME	23.8	1.35–5.25
Nickelodeon	25.5	5.00
FNN	16.1	10.40
The Weather Channel	18.7	3.50
Nashville Network	23.8	1.50–3.00

SOURCE: Paul Kagan Associates, Inc., as reported in *Marketing and Media Decisions,* Fall 1985 Special Edition, p. 44.

on prerecorded video cassettes. Recognizing that no commercial is truly zap proof, *Ski* magazine produced a "How to Ski" tape that contained ad messages from Head Skis, Subaru, Molson's Ale, and Ray Ban. Other advertisers using this tactic include Reebok, *Esquire*, Kodak, Mr. Boston, and American Health, Inc.[10]

In truth, such tactics don't really solve the problem of television ad zapping. Rather, they substitute another medium, prerecorded tapes, for over-the-air television programs. The immediate effect of television zapping is higher CPMs and different-than-planned audience composition. The long-run solution is probably going to be found in a combination of better creative quality, reduced clutter, additional program production and sponsorship, and more effective use of the new technology.

THE NEW TECHNOLOGY

Let's take a look at the new technology that is having, or will have, an impact on television.

Cable Television

Cable, the oldest of the "new" technology, has changed from a technique for transmitting weak television signals to remote areas to a major segment of the broadcasting industry. Currently, 9,700 cable systems, covering almost 39 million households, are in operation. By 1993, cable

---

[10] "Zap-Proof," *Marketing and Media Decisions,* May, 1986, pp. 49–56.

FIGURE 6–7   Major Cable Advertisers (000s)

	1983	1984	Percent Change
Procter & Gamble	$15,172.2	$24,182.2	59.4%
Anheuser-Busch	15,760.9	15,477.8	−1.8
General Foods	11,290.3	13,169.1	16.6
General Mills	10,258.8	11,339.3	10.5
Time Inc.	5,517.7	7,191.5	30.3
Ford Motor Co.	5,087.0	6,892.1	35.5
Bristol-Myers	6,505.5	6,242.2	−4.0
Toyota	5,247.6	5,390.7	2.7
Thompson Medical	1,016.2	4,456.0	338.5
AT&T	2,789.3	3,456.6	23.9
Total/Avg.	$78,645.5	$97,797.5	16.7%

SOURCE: BAR, as reported in *Marketing and Media Decisions*, Fall 1985 Special Edition, p. 45.

TV will have 60 million household subscribers. These subscribers will pay an average monthly subscription fee of $30 to $35 and will have access to almost three times the number of subscription services available 10 years earlier.

In addition to cable systems, the technology has allowed the "cable network" to emerge. These sources of programming are also sellers of advertising. This ad time has two properties that make it especially attractive to some advertisers: selective, homogeneous audiences and lower-than-network CPMs. Major cable networks, subscriber bases, and CPM data are presented in Figure 6–6; major cable advertisers are shown in Figure 6–7. One of the areas in which cable has proven itself is financial news reporting. Across cable networks, household CPM figures range from less than $5 ("WSJ Weekend Memo") to $10.37 ("Wall Street Final II"). This compares favorably with CPM/primary circulation figures for the five leading financial magazines whose values ranged from $29 to $52.70.[11]

The cable television industry has become one of the most innovative, exciting, efficient segments of broadcasting. Not only have advertisers been provided new opportunities to reach consumers with ad messages, but programming alternatives have blossomed. In many respects, cable enterprises have acccomplished what proponents of the Prime Time Access Rule envisioned—more program diversity, better coverage of local news and events, less expensive access to program production and distribution, and better coverage of the arts and cultural events.

The distribution of distant signals as well as the expansion of types of

---

[11] "Financial Cable Nets Mean Business," *Marketing and Media Decisions*, April 1985, pp. 64–66.

television service will offer greater diversity to the public and new problems for media planners. The expansion of satellite transmission has created opportunities for networklike systems such as the superstations. These independent stations, such as WGN in Chicago and WTBS in Atlanta, have gained national coverage through cable systems.

The cable television industry is not without its warts and blemishes, however, and considerable improvement is needed before the industry can be satisfied with its public image. One set of practices in need of major improvement is the marketing programs used by local cable companies. The business press has a surplus of stories about the uninformed "marketing rep" from the cable company who uses telephone solications without knowing much more than the prices of the offerings. Equally detrimental is the common practice of using installers who have inappropriate dress, manners, and speech.

These and other practices are all too common among monopolists. In fact, cable companies have, almost without exception, enjoyed local monopolies. Customer complaints evoke the response, "Take it or leave it," and in order to obtain cable television programming, the customer has been compelled to accept whatever treatment the cable company chooses to offer. But such monopolies are under serious legal attack, and they probably won't survive. In place of local monopolies, the courts are moving toward the position that municipal utility poles (or other delivery systems) are "rentable" to two or more competing cable systems. Such competition will go a long way toward giving cable systems incentive to practice the marketing concept. Curiously, the removal of local monopoly status will have a healthy influence on the industry, too. Instead of municipalities holding cable franchises "hostage" for all sorts of non-business contributions (5 percent of gross revenues to the city treasury and 20,000 trees planted on public property are two actual examples), competing systems would simply rent "access" to homes via the city's utility system. The top 50 cable markets are shown in Figure 6–8; some indication of the international success of cable can be inferred from the cable data for Europe shown in Figure 6–9.

Other Forms of New Television Technology

In addition to ordinary cable television, a number of other communications and entertainment variations on television have been developed, or are in intermediate stages of development. These include pay television, two-way cable, and equipment used in-home to acquire and process information and for entertainment. Of the different forms available, the most popular kind of pay television is pay cable. In this system, programming without commercial interruption is furnished to cable subscribers at

FIGURE 6–8   Top 50 Designated Market Areas Ranked by Percent of Cable Penetration (Nielsen Station Index Estimates, July 1986)

Rank	Designated Market Area	Percent Penetration, July 1986	Rank	Designated Market Area	Percent Penetration, July 1986
1	San Angelo	88.2	27	Clarksburg-Weston	66.8
2	Palm Springs	85.3	27	Cheyenne-Scottsblf-	
3	Santa Barbara-			Sterling	66.8
	SanMar-SanLuO	84.9	29	West Palm Beach,	
4	Laredo	79.0		Ft. Pierce	66.6
5	Parkersburg	76.6	29	Honolulu	66.6
6	Marquette	73.6	31	Bakersfield	66.3
7	Victoria	73.0	32	Amarillo	66.0
8	Ft. Myers-Naples	72.7	33	Wichita Falls & Lawton	65.4
8	Yuma-El Centro	72.7	34	Binghamton	65.1
10	Utica	72.2	35	Greenwood-	
11	Monterey-Salinas	71.9		Greenville	65.0
12	Biloxi-Gulfport	71.8	36	Helena, MT	64.9
13	Odessa-Midland-		37	Presque Isle	64.4
	Monahans	71.6	38	Bend, OR	64.0
14	Johnstown-Altoona	71.1	39	Wichita-Hutchinson	
15	Eureka	69.9		Plus	63.5
16	Lima	69.5	40	Eugene	63.4
16	Abilene-Sweetwater	69.5	41	Salisbury	63.3
18	Elmira	69.2	42	Glendive	63.0
19	Zanesville	69.0	43	Topeka	62.9
19	Casper-Riverton	69.0	43	Champaign &	
21	Springfield-Holyoke	68.8		Springfield-Decatur	62.9
22	Wilkes Barre-Scranton	68.6	45	Charleston-Huntington	62.7
23	Roswell	68.1	46	Erie	62.6
24	Hartford & New Haven	67.8	46	Waco-Temple	62.6
25	San Diego	67.7	48	Pittsburgh	61.7
26	Beckley-Bluefield-		48	Reno	61.7
	Oak Hill	67.6	50	Wheeling-Steubenville	61.6

SOURCE: A. C. Nielsen Company.

additional cost. Of course ads and cable system promos are placed *between* programs.

Home information techonology, based on personal computers, has grown beyond the stage of games, and both hardware and software are marketed in highly competitive ways. Of particular interest to advertisers are the prospects for developing an ad message medium as data sources for this technology are developed (e.g., The Source and Dow-Jones News Retrieval). Other forms of home information technology, such as videotext systems, have proven a bitter disappointment to their developers; after taking fearsome financial lickings, companies like Knight-Ridder are leaving rather than entering this sector. Although videotext technology is potentially attractive to both consumers and advertisers,

FIGURE 6–9 Overview of the European Cable Television Industry

	Households Cabled (Percent)	Ownership	Allow Advertising	Allow Pay TV	Cable Operators Allowed to Produce Programs	Allow Satellite Delivery	Cable Network Must Carry National Broadcast Channels
Britain	5	Private	Yes	Yes	Yes	Yes	Yes
France	2	Public	Yes	Yes	No[1]	Yes[7]	Yes
West Germany	4.5	Public	Yes	Yes	Yes	Yes	Yes
Belgium	83	Mixed	No[2]	Yes[4]	No[5]	Yes	Yes
Luxembourg	83	Mixed	Yes	Yes	No	Yes	Yes
Netherlands	60	Mixed	No[3]	Yes	Yes[6]	Yes	Yes
Sweden	5	Mixed	No[8]	No	No[5]	Yes	Yes
Norway	14	Mixed	No	No	Yes	Yes	Yes
Finland	8	Mixed	Yes	Yes	Yes[5]	Yes	Yes
Denmark	7	Mixed	No[9]	Yes	No[5]	No[10]	Yes
Austria	8	Private	Yes	No	No	No[11]	Yes
Switzerland	48	Mixed	Yes[12]	Yes	No[5]	Yes	Yes
Ireland	29	Mixed	Yes	Yes	No[5]	No[1]	Yes

[1] New legislation expected soon.

[2] The ban on Belgian syndicated TV advertising is due to be lifted. Advertising has been allowed on imported broadcast channels.

[3] Advertising is not allowed on pay-TV. Advertising is allowed on imported channels (providing it is not targeted at Dutch market) and on teletext.

[4] Only one pay-TV license issued so far to RTBF.

[5] Except local and/or experimental projects.

[6] Under license.

[7] Hotel Meridien and Biarritz network on experimental basis only.

[8] Apart from imported broadcast (mainly German) and satellite channels.

[9] The ban on Danish-originated TV advertising is expected to be lifted soon. Advertising is allowed on imported satellite and broadcast channels.

[10] Apart from Sky Channel at Hotel Scandinavia in Copenhagen.

[11] Apart from trial of Sky Channel on Viennese network.

[12] Except local TV.

SOURCE: Reprinted with permission *Advertising Age*, July 11, 1985, p. 26. Copyright Crain Communications, Inc.

the intriguing promise of this particular technology has not yet been effectively marketed.

BUYING TELEVISION

When the media planner has considered all the dayparts, formats, and programs offered by television, the job of buying time has only begun. The buying of television advertising time is divided into several categories, depending on the nature of the buy:

1. Prime-time network buys.
2. National spot buys.
3. Local buys.

Prime-time Network Buys

At the television network level, media planners deal with experienced experts in buying and selling time. Corporate advertising directors, agency media executives, and network salespeople must consistently prove that their selling and negotiating skills and judgment are better than those of their competitors. The major buying period for network advertising is in the early spring. Figure 6–10 examines a hypothetical network and advertiser as the firm makes its network buys for the following season.

National Spot Buys

In some ways, planning television spot buys in major markets requires even more skill than buying network advertising. Instead of buying three networks, the media planner is faced with more than 700 station coverage areas and audiences in approximately 200 major television markets.

These areas are usually referred to as **areas of dominant influence** (ADIs), a term used by the **Arbitron** Syndicated Research Service to designate a unique group of counties served by a particular market's stations. An ADI includes all counties in which the central market's stations receive the major viewership. There are currently 209 ADIs. They are reevaluated annually, and counties are added or deleted as station coverage patterns change.

ADIs are normally determined by the concentration of population. Large metro areas include as few as three or four counties in their ADIs, although the Salt Lake City ADI covers all of Utah and parts of Idaho, Nevada, and Wyoming. The ADI may be used not only to buy television but also to designate general market areas for local advertising buys in all media. Thus, a national advertiser may plan regional magazine buys to conform as closely as possible to spot television bought on the basis of ADIs. The A. C. Nielsen Company has a similar technique to measure coverage areas known as the designated market area (DMA).

Astute media planners generally use the services of a station representative when buying spot television. The job of the television representative has expanded from simply selling time to advising local television stations on a host of topics, including rate setting, programming, and overall station sales policies. The primary task of the rep remains selling, and recent developments in computer-based research and inventory control have been directed toward facilitating this function.

Television reps are paid a commission of from 5 to 15 percent by the stations they represent. The average commission is about 10 percent. A rep in a major market may earn $75,000 to $150,000; $45,000 is the average annual earnings of reps in medium-sized markets. The two largest reps, both in revenues and in stations represented, are Blair and Katz.

FIGURE 6–10 The Network Negotiation Game

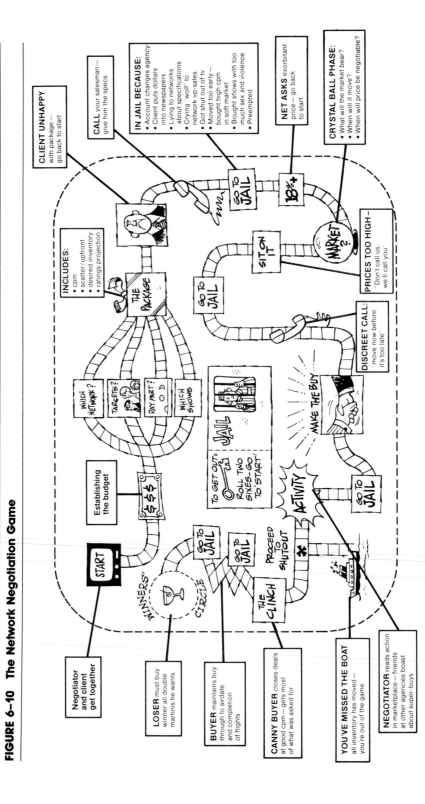

CLIENT UNHAPPY with package — go back to start

CALL your salesman — give him the specs

IN JAIL BECAUSE:
• Account changes agency
• Client puts dollars into newspapers
• Lying to networks about specifications
• Crying "wolf" to network vp-sales
• Got shut out of tv
• Moved too early — bought high cpm in soft market
• Bought shows with too much sex and violence
• Preempted

NET ASKS exorbitant price — go back to start

CRYSTAL BALL PHASE:
• What will the market bear?
• When will it move?
• When will price be negotiable?

PRICES TOO HIGH — "Don't call us, we'll call you"

DISCREET CALL: "move now before it's too late"

INCLUDES:
• cpm
• scatter/upfront
• desired inventory
• ratings projection

Establishing the budget

Negotiator and client get together

LOSER must buy winner all double martinis he wants

BUYER maintains buy through to airdate and completion of flights

CANNY BUYER closes deals at good cpm — gets most of what was asked for

YOU'VE MISSED THE BOAT all inventory has moved — you're out of the game

NEGOTIATOR reads action in marketplace — friends at other agencies boast about super-buys

source: *Marketing and Media Decisions*, February 1981.

Local Buys

Normally, local television sales are handled by a station's own sales force. A station in a "top 20" market may have as many as 20 salespeople, while a station in a small market may have only 2 or 3.

In small markets the station sales department is responsible for local advertising. In large markets, local salespeople may approach national spot advertisers as well as local concerns. Since the station's rep may attempt to sell the same company, disagreements sometimes arise between the rep and the station over who actually sold the time.

To prevent this problem, reps may agree not to approach certain advertisers. In rare instances, the station may turn over its entire sales operation to a rep organization. When problems arise between a station's sales force and its rep, it is important not to involve the advertiser. Advertisers are not interested in internal station sales problems, and rather than become involved, they may take their business elsewhere.

Television Rate Structure

Regardless of the level at which television time is bought, the same basic rate structure applies. Throughout television, the fixed rate is disappearing, if not gone. Rates are computed on length of continuity requested, demand from other advertisers, and volume of annual business. However, most television time is purchased by negotiation and in **packages** of several commercials rather than single spots. A package plan offers the advertiser a lower rate for buying a group of broadcast commercials. Normally, neither an advertiser nor the station/network can (or will) quote a price for a single spot. The **cost per rating point** (CPP) or the average cost per spot can be computed, but not the single commercial price. As discussed in Chapter 3, the weight of a schedule is measured in gross rating points (GRPs), and various estimating guides are used to give the buyer a preliminary idea of broadcast costs.

When rate cards or directory listings (such as *Spot Television SRDS*) exist, they are usually intended as a general guide. Because of the negotiated nature of television buys, price lists (called grids) are often coded so that some or all prices are not given for specific spots. There are three types of grid cards: full disclosure cards, nondisclosure cards, and partial disclosure cards (which give rates for only a portion of the schedule). Within these grids, prices are also quoted for fixed (guaranteed) rates and preemptible rates (when another advertiser agrees to pay a higher rate than the fixed rate). See Figure 6–11.

Because of the complex nature of television rates, the rep can be valuable to the spot advertiser. Since the rep's firm is aware of the rate structure of the client stations, the rep can save media buyers the time they would spend either contacting stations or making wrong estimates.

FIGURE 6–11   Examples of Grids in Television Pricing

Full-disclosure grid: Prime time, 30 seconds				Nondisclosure grid: 30 seconds		
	Fixed	*I*	*II*	*Code‡*		
"60 Minutes"............100*		†	†	1 100	6	55
"Archie's Place"......... 90	80	60		2 90	7	50
"The Jeffersons"......... 90	75	55		3 80	8	45
"Alice" 80	60	50		4 70	9	40
				5 60	10	35

---

* Units in dollars.

† No preemptible rate available.

‡ Average rates for estimating: Early morning (9/10); daytime (4/8); fringe time (5/7); prime time (1/4).

Television Discounts and Special Features

Three types of television discounts are offered. (For a discussion of the broadcast discounts most applicable to radio, see Chapter 7.) These are:

1. **Bulk discount**—offered for purchasing a certain number of spots, usually within a month or year.
2. **Volume discount**—based on dollars spent during a set period.
3. **Continuity discount**—given for consecutive advertising over a set number of weeks.

In addition, two other features are often associated with television prices:

1. *Product protection.*   Many stations attempt to keep a 10-minute separation between competing products. However, most stations do not offer rebates unless competing commercials are back-to-back.
2. *News and special features.*   Stations may have different rates for news and other special features. The media buyer should check the rate card carefully or contact the station when considering such purchases.

TELEVISION RATINGS

Television, more than any other medium, lives and dies by the rating numbers. As we have mentioned earlier, a shift of only one rating point can mean a difference of millions of dollars annually to a network. Ratings are no less important to the revenues of a local station. Currently television ratings are dominated by two firms: Arbitron and Nielsen.

Arbitron is stronger in the local station ratings, while Nielsen dominates the national ratings. Although there are some differences in the methodology and the reports of the two services, they are basically quite similar. The following primary Nielsen services will give an overview of the basic rating services.

Nielsen Television Index (NTI)

The NTI, based on a national sample, is one of the two major reporting systems offered by the A. C. Nielsen Company. The foundation of the NTI System is the Storage Instantaneous Audimeter (SIA, or simply Audimeter). The **Audimeter** is a device that is mechanically and electrically fixed to the television receiver. It automatically records the time of day and the date, whether the receiver is turned on and when, and the electronic frequency of the station being received. The Audimeter is supplemented with a viewer diary called an **Audilog.**

The national Nielsen service uses two samples of national household ratings. The NTI provides household ratings based on 1,700 metered households. The National Audience Composition (NAC) sample of 3,200 reports individual diary data. The major NTI and NTI/NAC reports include:

1. *NTI National Nielsen TV Ratings.* This is the most familiar report, often referred to as the "pocket piece" because of its size. Issued biweekly, it reports ratings for all network programs 48 weeks during the year.

2. *NTI Multi-Network Area Ratings (Fast MNA).* The Fast MNA reports the weekly network audience for the largest 70 markets with full network service.

3. *NTI Market Section Audiences.* The MSA report, issued 9 times annually, describes the households tuned to network programs on 10 variables, including household income, education of head of household, and household size.

4. *NTI Brand Cumulative Audience Report.* The BCA Report measures how advertising for individual brands performs against competition. It is issued three times a year.

5. *NTI/NAC Audience Demographics (NAD).* The NAD is the basic demographic report of the Nielsen service. Issued 15 times a year, it provides estimates of individual viewing of network programs. In addition to the basic NTI/NAC Service, four supplementary reports are issued.

Many of the NTI and NSI services are available at extra cost on a "day-after" basis through computer terminals. In addition to the services discussed here, both Nielsen and Arbitron provide specially designed studies for individual clients. Some of these services utilize the **coincidental telephone** method, a data-gathering technique in which interviews are conducted at the same time the program is being broadcast. Here phone surveys are conducted while a program is being broadcast.

Both major rating services, as well as smaller competitors, now employ a "people meter," a device for recording information about the viewers of a particular television viewing. Developed to overcome some of the recording problems associated with diary data, the people meter is actually a keyboard, similar to that on a pocket calculator. Viewers in a particular household are each assigned a number; they (are supposed to) push their code into the system as they start to watch and again when they finish watching TV. A. C. Nielsen also measures the extent of zapping for a sample of TV viewers.

Nielsen Station Index (NSI)

Diaries and meters are combined to gather data for the NSI reports. However, Nielsen's basic local market reports utilize primarily the Audilog diary. NSI issues three principal reports:

1. NSI metered services reports are issued for New York, Los Angeles, Chicago, and San Francisco. These markets include approximately 20 percent of U.S. TV households.
2. All television markets are measured three times a year—November, February, and May. These are the "sweep" periods, and the *Viewer in Profile* report provides the results of these ratings. Since the ratings are conducted so infrequently, they are extremely important to local station spot sales and local advertising. A continuing controversy surrounds the artificial inflation of ratings by networks and local stations that schedule extraordinary programming during these periods.
3. Five times a year, NSI issues a key markets rating to supplement the regular *Viewer in Profile* report.

Figure 6–12 compares Nielsen and Arbitron rating features in local television measurement.

Other Television Research

Most of the familiar television rating services measure households and/or people's viewing habits. Other less well-known services measure the degree of audience involvement or popularity for a brand, program, or individual performer. Two of the major firms doing this type of research are Burke International Research Corporation and Marketing Evaluations, Inc., which produces the TVQ report.

Burke offers a host of specialized client services for advertisers. However, the best known of Burke's research studies is the **day-after-recall** technique (recall measured the day after exposure) for measuring effectiveness, exposure, memorability, and content retention. This research is conducted for either pretesting or posttesting of commercials or both on a before and an after basis.

TVQ publishes two reports. The most common is the annual "Performer Popularity Poll," which measures the popularity of individual performers. In addition, the television-program TVQ, issued seven times a year, measures program popularity. In both cases the research does not measure the number of people watching a show, but how well liked the program (or performer) is among those people who do watch. The report gives two scores for a program or performer—the percent of familiarity (FAM score) and the percent of likability (Q score). The Q number is found by dividing the percentage of people saying the program or performer is "one of my favorites" by the percentage familiar with the program or performer.

$$Q = \frac{FAV}{FAM}$$

Advertisers use the TVQ score in casting celebrities in commercials as well as an aid in choosing popular program formats. Examples of celebrities with long-standing levels of high Q scores include Alan Alda, Carol Burnett, Bob Hope, and Bill Cosby. Those with low recognition but high appeal include Jane Curtin and Gilda Radner. Turn-off Q scores have been measured for Howard Cosell, Barbara Walters, and Muhammed Ali.

THE OUTLOOK

Any attempt to predict the future of television is risky, and 50 percent accuracy would be a high score. While we have no crystal ball, we can point out several areas of television in which change is inevitable during the next decade.

1. *Inflation.* The cost of television advertising during the 1980s will be discussed, criticized, and reviewed. None of the rhetoric, however, will alter the continuing upward spiral of commercial pricing. Both real costs and CPMs will increase by about 10 percent annually until at least 1990. The fact is that most advertisers, particularly at the national level, view television advertising as more effective than available alternatives. If this attitude and the accompanying advertiser demand continue, there is no

FIGURE 6–12   Local TV

	Nielsen Station Index (NSI)	Arbitron Ratings Co.
Media covered	All local TV markets (219) in 50 states	213 local TV markets
Audience definition	Household and individual audience per station/program	Household and individual audience per station/program
Methodology Sample size-derivation	• Participants randomly selected by possession of phone • Sample size varies by market • Each national sweep—100,000 avg.—in tab households	• Participants randomly selected by possession of phone • Sample size varies by market • 350 to 500 households metered per market
Interviewing technique	• Viewing data collected via diaries—one per TV • Meters used in top 15 markets to measure household usage	• One household diary per set for individual viewing • Meter in eleven (11) major markets to measure household usage
Quality control	Spot checks by editors and/or computers	Manual and computer edit on selected basis
Data supplied Time breaks	Average quarter-hour household and individual viewing for individual stations	• Four-week household totals and program averages, average quarter-hour household and audience dayparts totals • Share trend, daily and weekly
Demographics	Standard age and sex breaks with combinations	Standard age and sex breaks with combinations, working women
Geographics	• Household audience for metro areas and 209* DMA's • Individual audience for DMA, also DMA plus surrounding areas, all United States.	• Metro, home county. 213 ADI(s). total survey areas • Custom via database

Cumulative	Household cumulative audience reported by daypart—weekly and four-week	Household cumulative audience reported by daypart—weekly and four-week
Interduplication	Available within medium by special analysis	Via database within medium
Format Frequency	• Each DMA measured four to seven times per year depending on size • Primary and supplementary detailed reports • In metered markets, daily and weekly reports optional	• At least four sweeps yearly • Weekly meter in New York, Los Angeles, Chicago, San Francisco, Philadelphia, Boston, Detroit, Dallas-Ft. Worth, Washington, D.C., Houston, Miami • In metered markets, daily and weekly household reports are available
Reported on	Hard copy, tape, special runs available, database	Hard copy, tapes, database, special runs
Subscriber universe	TV stations, advertising agencies, advertisers, station representatives, producers/syndicators	3,350—advertisers, agencies, TV stations
Terms of sale	Single reports or subscription	One + year subscription, also single reports
Special features, services	• NSI Plus (Client Designs Report) • Cable, Pay Cable & VCR penetrations • ClusterPlus & PRIZM—Special area data (e.g., Zips, county-by-county) • Micro Services—Audience Analysts Spot Buyer	• CLUSTERPLUS/PRIZM • Direct access to database (ADI) • County-by-county report • TARGET ADI • ARBITRENDS II • SCANAMERICA
Contact	JoAnn LaVerde-Curcio, Press Relations Manager, New York 212-708-7548 Terri V. Lake, Promotion Manager, Northbrook, IL 312-498-6300 Larry Frerk, Director of Media Advertising and Public Relations, Northbrook, IL 312-498-6300	Thom Mocarsky, director of communications. New York 212-887-1314 Kenneth Wollenberg, vp-sales and marketing, advertisers/agencies, New York 212-887-1328

* July Reports on 207 DMA's—Honolulu & Fairbanks are excluded.
SOURCE: Reprinted with permission—Arbitron Ratings Company.

way the television pricing structure will significantly change in the foreseeable future.

2. *Government deregulation.* It is unclear exactly what form future deregulation of the broadcast industry will take. However, the government has made a decision to return broadcasting to the free market as it interprets that concept. Radio may experience the most dramatic short-term effects. However, recent decisions on importation of cable signals, increase in FCC licensing of earth station satellite receivers, and liberal court interpretation of potential copyright infringement by private citizens may have greater impact on broadcasting in the long run.

3. *Broadcast diversity and advertising.* Some of the technology, such as satellite receivers and electronic newspapers, is probably still years away from extensive use at the household level. However, in the next decade we will see greater utilization of these scientific developments at the broadcaster level. Most of the work will concentrate on narrowcasting—identifying and reaching small, better-defined market segments. Of course, these audiences will be reached at a premium cost to advertisers.

The 1980s will establish which of the diverse outlets will survive. By 1990, we may have only one or two pay cable (or subscription) television networks, one sports network, and a superstation or two. There is only so much household time and advertiser money, and ultimate decisions about where to allocate these resources will have to be made. We may look back on the 1980s as a period in which broadcast technology developed beyond the public's ability to fully utilize it.

REVIEW QUESTIONS

1. What are O and Os, and why are they so important?
2. Describe the sources of television revenues, including dayparts, types of advertisers, and any changes in revenues during the last decade.
3. What is barter? Barter syndication?
4. How did the prime-time access rule change the economics and content of syndication?
5. Discuss the concept of the fragmented audience and some technologies that are bringing it about.
6. Discuss "sweep weeks" ratings and how they differ from national ratings.
7. Discuss the "package" concept of television commercial buys.
8. View several hours of television programming during other than prime time. Record the number of commercial minutes aired each hour. Make a list of the products and brands that are advertised, and from this list attempt to

characterize the audience. Check your characterization for accuracy against SMRB research data.

9. Discuss the options available to television advertisers to alleviate the problem of clutter. Select the best of these and explain why you consider it to be the best.

10. Discuss the options available to television advertisers to alleviate the problem of "zapping." Pick the best option, in your opinion, and defend this choice.

SUGGESTED ADDITIONAL READING

"AGB Expands Its TV Ratings Market." *Marketing News,* October 25, 1985, p. 14.

"AGB Happy with PeopleMeter." *Marketing News,* September 13, 1985, p. 14.

CANNON, HUGH M. "Media-Market Matching versus 'Random Walk' in Television Media Selection." *Journal of Advertising Research* 26, no. 2 (April/May 1986), pp. 37–52.

"Complex Productions Proving Costly to Advertisers." *Marketing News,* December 6, 1985, pp. 7, 13.

Description of Methodology, Arbitron Ratings Company, Television Market Reports, October 1983.

GATES, FLIECE. "Further Comments on the Miscomprehension of Televised Advertisements." *Journal of Advertising* 15, no. 1 (1986), pp. 4–9.

HARVEY, MICHAEL G., and JAMES T. ROTHE. "Video Cassette Recorders: Their Impact on Viewers and Advertisers." *Journal of Advertising Research* 26, no. 6 (December 1985/January 1986), pp. 19–28.

KRUGMAN, DEAN M. "Evaluating the Audiences of the New Media." *Journal of Advertising* 14, no. 4 (1985), pp. 21–27.

KRUGMAN, HERBERT E. "Low Recall and High Recognition of Advertising." *Journal of Advertising Research* 26, no. 1 (February/March 1986), pp. 79–88.

"Mixed Spot Lengths Increase Effect of the Longer." *Marketing News,* April 26, 1985, p. 6.

"Service Measures Cable TV Audience." *Marketing News,* September 13, 1985, pp. 44, 47.

STEPHENS, NANCY, and MARY ANN STUTTS. "Preschoolers' Ability to Distinguish between Television Programming and Commercials." *Journal of Advertising* 11, no. 2 (1982), pp. 16–26.

STERN, BRUCE L., and ROBERT R. HARMON. "The Incidence and Characteristics of Disclaimers in Children's Television Advertising." *Journal of Advertising* 13, no. 2 (1984), pp. 12–16.

TVQ Performer Ratings, Marketing Evaluations, New York, 1986.

"Viewer Loyalty Major Factor in TV Ratings." *Marketing News,* August 2, 1985, p. 5.

CHAPTER SEVEN

Radio

The radio business has never been in better shape. Radio has found its niche through narrowly defined formats that appeal to specific demographics. Radio is in everybody's lives to a greater degree.*

Norman Pattiz,
President-Chair, Westwood One

Few industries could have successfully survived the boom-bust cycle experienced by radio in the last six decades. On November 15, 1926, the NBC radio network made its inaugural broadcast, a four-hour show from the Grand Ballroom of the Waldorf-Astoria Hotel. This broadcast cost $50,000, featured remote pickups of Will Rogers from Independence, Kansas, and opera soprano Mary Garden from Chicago, and required 100 engineers and 5,000 miles of telephone cable. The broadcast was carried by 24 affiliated stations and was heard by an audience of 12 million. By 1942, over 70 percent of the public cited radio as its principal source of news. In the late 1940s, radio accounted for 15 percent of all advertising dollars; by 1960, radio's share had declined to only 6 percent. In 1960, a third of the nation's commercial radio stations were losing money, and network affiliation for AM stations had dropped from a high of 95 percent (1945) to 33 percent.[1]

By 1985, a redefined radio enjoyed a revitalized role as a communications medium, and radio advertising revenues reached $6.7 billion.[2]

---

* As reported in *Advertising Age,* August 29, 1985, p. 19.

[1] *Advertising Age,* Special Report, Network Radio, April 14, 1986, pp. S1–S5.

[2] *Advertising Age,* Special Report, Radio, August 28, 1986, p. 15.

GENERAL CHARACTERISTICS OF RADIO

Radio's major dimensions as an advertising medium are a result of its being an individual medium and its specialized formats. Each member of a radio audience typically listens to his or her "own" receiver. This pattern is different from past generations, when radio listening was a family or group activity. In addition, a listener chooses a radio frequency (station) on the basis of format—the station's characteristic style of programming. This pattern is different from television, where a viewer chooses a station based on a particular program. So TV audiences view particular programs; radio audiences listen to stations that broadcast preferred formats.

In the United States, the average person owns more than two radios; the typical household owns almost six. During a normal week, about 94 percent of adult women, 96 percent of adult men, and virtually every person between the ages of 12 and 17 listen to some radio. Average daily listening time exceeds three hours. There are about 126 million out-of-home radio receivers, e.g., automobile radios, in the United States.[3]

AM Radio

Amplitude modulation (AM) radio is the oldest and most popular form of transmitting broadcast signals. Currently there are four major categories of AM radio among the approximately 4,938 commercial AM stations:[4]

1. *Class I: Clear channel stations.* These normally operate on the maximum power assigned AM stations (50,000 watts). There are currently 25 Class I stations in the country, and many of them (such as WLS—Chicago, WSB—Atlanta, WHO—Des Moines, and WJR—Detroit) can be heard for several hundred miles at night. In 1979, the FCC cut back the power of the Class I stations drastically to open up access to 120 to 700 new local stations.
2. *Class II: Secondary clear channel stations.* These stations are designed to serve a population center and a surrounding rural area. They do not interfere with the Class I clear channel stations and operate with 250 to 50,000 watts of power.
3. *Class III: Regional stations.* A regional station operates on a maximum of 5,000 watts and shares a channel with several other stations located far enough away to eliminate signal interference.

---

[3] *Broadcasting/Cablecasting Yearbook, 1986,* p. G16.

[4] For a full discussion, see *Broadcasting/Cablecasting Yearbook, 1986,* p. F111.

FIGURE 7-1   Leaders in Radio Advertising

Radio's Top 10 National Spot Advertisers, 1984 (thousands)		Radio's Top 10 Network Advertisers, 1984 (thousands)	
Anheuser-Busch	$38,287.6	AT&T	$16,343.9
AT&T	33,316.3	Cotter & Co.	10,201.3
GM	30,835.9	Jeffrey Martin	9,349.1
Van Munching & Co.	30,650.9	Sears Roebuck & Co.	8,630.3
Pepsico	25,025.3	Warner-Lambert Co.	8,143.0
Miller Brewing	20,855.7	GM	6,745.6
Delta Airlines	19,321.0	Purex Indus.	6,715.0
Coors Brewing	18,926.9	Dow Jones & Company	6,430.5
Chrysler Corp	18,776.6	Anheuser-Busch.	6,231.4
Political advertising	14,317.1	Triangle Publications	5,227.7

SOURCE: As reported in *Marketing and Media Decisions*, Fall 1985, Special, p. 52.

4. *Class IV: Local stations.*   Local stations operate on a maximum of 1,000 watts and often are on the air only during daylight hours.

FM Radio

Frequency modulation radio was developed as a practical means of communication shortly before World War II. However, not until the early 1960s did the FCC take steps to position FM as a vital part of radio. In 1963, the FCC assigned commercial FM channels to states and communities and ruled that FM programming could not duplicate more than half of AM programming among jointly owned stations in markets with more than 100,000 population. In the long term, the trend is probably toward separate ownership of AM and FM stations.

Currently FM stations are allocated according to national zones and classes (assigned by power among these zones). Figure 7-2 summarizes these assignments.

Once many of the technological and administrative problems of FM were solved, it began a dramatic growth period. About 5,500 FM stations operate in the United States today.[5] FM radio's image of classical music; few commercials; and a small, commercially insignificant audience is gone forever. Today FM stations rank among the top stations in nearly every top 50 market.

FORMATS

Radio formats, or station formats as they are sometimes called, are descriptive titles for the kind of music or other programming the station

---

[5] *Broadcasting/Cablecasting Yearbook, 1986*, p. F11.

FIGURE 7-2 Classification of FM Stations

Zone I: 18 Northeastern states and Washington, D.C.

Zone I-A: Southern California

Zone II: The rest of the country

Class A: Low-power, maximum 3 kilowatts; located in all zones

Class B: Maximum 50 kilowatts; located in Zones I and I-A

Class C: Most powerful, up to 100 kilowatts; located in Zone II.

---

broadcasts. The format names are straightforward. Country music stations play country music, talk stations broadcast talk programs, and religious stations broadcast programming of a religious nature. As radio stations become more competitive, their format descriptions are sometimes broadened to appeal to a larger number of advertisers. Two general categories, Adult Contemporary and Middle of the Road, are less precise. The former is programming generally addressed to adults between 20 and 39 years. The latter, almost any nonspecific, noncontroversial programming, may be the source for the claim that (some) radio is as unobtrusive as "musical wallpaper." Figure 7-3 shows the distribution of U.S. radio stations by region and format.

NETWORKS

Wired Networks

The major radio networks, once a prestige medium, almost went out of existence during the late 1960s. The only regular network programming was short newscasts. Total network revenues, which reached a high of $133 million in 1948, fell to $35 million by 1960.[6] However, in the years since 1975, network revenues have grown at an annual rate of 15 to 28 percent. Despite this growth, network radio accounts for only about 6 percent of total radio revenues.

During the last several years, much of the publicity surrounding network radio has concerned the return of radio drama. The "CBS Radio Mystery Theater" is credited with providing the push for more recent programming, such as the "Sears Radio Theater," begun in January 1979, and National Public Radio's "Masterpiece Radio Theater."

In 1985, Mutual Broadcasting System emphasized the drawing power of key personalities. Its programming included Dick Clark's National Music Survey, Lee Arnold's Country Road, the Larry King Show, a baseball show hosted by Tommy Lasorda, a football show hosted by Pat Summerall, and an entertainment program with gossip columnist Rona Barrett.

---

6 "Radio Billings, 1935-1977," *Broadcasting Yearbook, 1979,* p. C342.

FIGURE 7–3 **Distribution of Radio Stations in the United States** (by region and format)

Category	North East	Mid-Atlantic	East Central	West Central	South	South West	Mountain	Pacific	U.S. Total
AMs	389	302	828	492	1,594	520	288	525	4,938
FMs	529	362	1,128	659	1,268	607	348	621	5,522
Total	918	664	1,956	1,151	2,862	1,127	636	1,146	10,460
Adult Contemporary	197	143	386	220	452	175	143	232	1,948
Agricultural	1	4	35	95	35	19	8	4	201
Beautiful Music	44	39	97	43	99	40	29	65	456
Big Band	28	14	28	3	38	10	6	28	155
Black	13	14	31	11	159	7	2	7	244
Classical	37	21	76	52	70	26	17	44	273
C & W	77	81	425	321	910	361	139	185	2,499
Talk	56	34	87	44	76	31	13	47	388
French	—	—	—	—	1	—	—	—	1
German	—	—	1	—	—	—	—	—	1
Italian	—	—	—	—	—	—	—	—	
Urban	11	11	25	7	67	14	3	6	144
Progressive	109	67	107	52	86	45	30	78	574
Top 40	89	75	188	113	—	91	61	121	738
Other	5	6	18	7	14	1	—	9	60
Ethnic	4	—	3	—	—	—	1	—	8
Indian	—	—	1	1	—	5	1	1	9
Education	39	16	86	36	67	22	17	29	312
Oldies	39	39	64	31	100	32	11	34	350
Jazz	30	18	49	45	63	24	8	33	270
MOR	147	90	273	158	259	90	84	112	1,213
News	46	18	47	36	55	31	16	38	287
Polish	—	—	—	—	1	—	—	—	1
Religious	28	57	132	74	318	76	28	83	796
Spanish	7	8	10	—	14	79	6	47	171
Variety	91	51	135	79	121	41	35	84	637

SOURCE: Reprinted with permission from *Broadcasting/Cablecasting Yearbook, 1986*, p. F111.

However, for all the attention given these shows, network programs remain mostly five-minute newscasts and occasional short fillers. Special events such as major sports contests, news conferences, and miscellaneous programs make up a minute portion of network programming.

Structure of Wired Networks

Soon after commercial radio began, radio networks were created as a means of reaching national audiences and spreading program costs among several local stations. The network era began in 1926 when the National Broadcasting Company was formed by its parent company, the Radio Corporation of America (RCA).

Currently there are five major radio networks. The networks and the approximate number of affiliates in each are shown in Figure 7–4. The Mutual Broadcasting System (MBS) is the largest single network, while the American Broadcasting System (ABC) has the largest number of affiliates under its four-network system.

Advertising costs and ratings for network radio are low compared to television. The cost of a typical drive-time, one-minute network commercial averages around $4,000. (**Drive time** is the period during morning and evening weekdays when automobile radio usage is at its highest.) The low cost and the ability to reach specific audience segments with certain types of programs (news, sports, features) make network radio attractive to many advertisers. Some advertisers consider radio a supplemental medium (General Motors Corporation), while others see it as a major medium in their overall advertising strategy (Blue Nun wine). Figure 7–5 lists typical network and format radio coverage.

Major Problems of Network Radio

Program Clearance. Chapter 6 discussed network television clearances. It was noted that most network programs are carried by 98 to 99 percent of affiliates. A top-10 market television affiliate that fails to carry a program presents a serious problem to network programmers. In radio, unlike television, stations depend on local programming for their audiences. Most stations regard network programs as secondary to their own programming.

Consequently, radio networks have different relations with their affiliates than television networks do. Radio networks expect to have a far lower percentage of stations carrying their programs (known as percent of **clearance**).

Radio networks may even present different formats of the same

---

FIGURE 7–4   Wired Networks and Their Affiliates

Network	Approximate Number of Affiliates
National Broadcasting Company (NBC)	260
Mutual Broadcasting System (MBS)	950
Columbia Broadcasting System (CBS)	276
National Black Network (NBN)	90
American Broadcasting Company (ABC)	1,565
ABC Contemporary	400
ABC Entertainment	475
ABC Information	500
ABC FM	190

FIGURE 7-5 Summary of Adult Radio Audiences (by format and network)

	U.S. Total	Average Daily (M-F) Cume	Rating	Turnover Rate	Total Adults Weekday Radio (6 A.M.-Midnight) Reach and Frequency (in thousands) — Reach					Frequency Distribution				
					1 Day	2 Day	3 Day	4 Day	5 Day	1 of 5	2 of 5	3 of 5	4 of 5	5 of 5
Total 6 A.M.–midnight	167,727	127,571	76.1	.144	127,571	145,887	153,000	156,731	159,009	11,394	14,515	19,320	29,430	84,351
Formats:														
Adult Contemporary	167,727	34,009	20.3	.456	34,009	49,533	59,146	65,942	71,120	25,889	16,185	11,984	9,479	7,583
All News	167,727	6,062	3.6	.520	6,062	9,211	11,325	12,910	14,176	6,328	3,196	2,087	1,493	1,071
AOR/Progressive	167,727	11,884	7.1	.512	11,884	17,966	22,000	24,996	27,369	11,866	6,231	4,142	2,988	2,143
Beautiful Music	167,727	11,180	6.7	.574	11,180	17,594	22,035	25,406	28,111	13,525	6,666	4,024	2,511	1,385
Black	167,727	4,538	2.7	.563	4,538	7,092	8,861	10,210	11,299	5,445	2,605	1,591	1,034	625
Classical	167,727	3,857	2.3	.571	3,857	6,059	7,593	8,768	9,719	4,753	2,244	1,352	863	507
CHR/Rock	167,727	21,946	13.1	.515	21,946	33,238	40,638	46,059	50,297	21,190	11,834	7,946	5,604	3,723
Country	167,727	27,262	16.3	.499	27,262	40,855	49,595	55,913	60,800	24,436	14,309	9,913	7,193	4,949
Golden Oldies	167,727	3,339	2.0	.572	3,339	5,251	6,585	7,608	8,436	4,142	1,946	1,169	745	436
MOR/Nostalgia	167,727	10,346	6.2	.571	10,346	16,253	20,338	23,440	25,931	12,451	6,121	3,710	2,336	1,312
News/Talk	167,727	8,929	5.3	.459	8,929	13,024	15,656	17,586	19,106	7,600	4,104	2,912	2,350	2,140
Religious	167,727	5,488	3.3	.575	5,488	8,645	10,846	12,532	13,894	6,811	3,231	1,936	1,220	696
Soft Rock	167,727	1,232	0.7	.599	1,232	1,970	2,496	2,905	3,238	1,669	748	428	257	136
Urban Contemporary	167,727	3,184	1.9	.573	3,184	5,009	6,285	7,263	8,055	3,963	1,858	1,114	708	413
Wired networks:														
ABC Contemporary	167,727	6,911	4.1	.537	6,911	10,625	13,146	15,046	16,567	7,605	3,791	2,414	1,658	1,099
ABC Direction	167,727	5,212	3.1	.533	5,212	7,989	9,872	11,291	12,428	5,687	2,822	1,806	1,257	857
ABC Entertainment	167,727	10,385	6.2	.511	10,385	15,691	19,214	21,835	23,914	10,397	5,418	3,599	2,607	1,893
ABC FM	167,727	4,762	2.8	.589	4,762	7,568	9,547	11,072	12,309	6,187	2,871	1,677	1,022	552
ABC Information	167,727	11,339	6.8	.561	11,339	17,704	22,072	25,373	28,014	13,205	6,600	4,068	2,618	1,523
ABC Rock	167,727	4,878	2.9	.529	4,878	7,458	9,203	10,518	11,570	5,264	2,618	1,685	1,183	822
CBS	167,727	10,709	6.4	.484	10,709	15,890	19,267	21,758	23,724	9,829	5,249	3,618	2,773	2,254
Mutual	167,727	10,251	6.1	.506	10,251	15,436	18,868	21,417	23,438	10,105	5,285	3,535	2,590	1,923
NBC	167,727	12,243	7.3	.455	12,243	17,809	21,364	23,958	25,993	10,175	5,596	4,006	3,250	2,966
Radioradio	167,727	4,606	2.7	.692	4,606	7,796	10,224	12,179	13,811	8,159	3,224	1,514	682	231
RKO One	167,727	5,148	3.1	.575	5,148	8,106	10,170	11,750	13,027	6,386	3,025	1,814	1,145	657
RKO TWO	167,727	7,313	4.4	.580	7,313	11,556	14,520	16,787	18,618	9,154	4,367	2,598	1,610	889
The Source	167,727	5,981	3.6	.544	5,981	9,234	11,453	13,132	14,479	6,734	3,318	2,091	1,417	919
Nonwired networks:														
Blair	167,727	19,330	11.5	.480	19,330	28,611	34,582	38,932	42,328	16,982	9,533	6,678	5,109	4,025
Internet	167,727	27,139	16.2	.491	27,139	40,461	48,988	55,142	59,898	23,783	13,966	9,773	7,221	5,155
Katz Radio Group	167,727	36,319	21.7	.441	36,319	52,323	62,101	68,962	74,163	26,008	16,594	12,572	10,267	8,722
Supernet	167,727	22,362	13.3	.495	22,362	33,429	40,585	45,796	49,855	20,299	11,508	7,945	5,860	4,243

SOURCE: Simmons Market Research Bureau, Inc.: 1984 Study of Media and Markets.

programs to different affiliates. CBS "World News Tonight" is a 15-minute evening broadcast, but many stations carry only the first 5 to 7 minutes. The format of the program provides a break that allows local stations to cut in. Moreover, stations are permitted to move network programs to other time slots more often in radio than in television.

Credibility.   Network radio, like FM radio, faces the intangible problem of lack of credibility. Many advertisers think of radio only in terms of local AM stations. Often they don't even consider network advertising when building a media schedule. Yet network radio is usually available at a lower CPM than the same stations individually.

Quality of Affiliates.   Unlike television, where network programming determines the strength of the affiliates, in radio local stations decide how strong the network is. Consequently, audience demographics differ from one station to another within a network's lineup. In signing new stations, networks are beginning to pay more attention to the quality of a station's audience and to its compatibility with the audiences of other network affiliates. However, advertisers still regard network buys as difficult because of inconsistency in audience profiles.

Nonwired Networks

In the last decade, a second type of "network" has been formed. Unlike the wired network, which places the signal, programming, and commercials under the control of a single company, a nonwired network connects a group of what would otherwise be spot buys to form an interconnected system. What interconnects the system is a single rep who sells the participating stations' advertising time in a single transaction.

The nonwired networks do not sell programs or even simultaneous advertising, as do the wired networks. Instead, the rep, through a network of clients, allows an advertiser to purchase all stations, or a sizable number of them, with one invoice. The time is usually placed within a particular daypart (e.g., drive time).

Currently there are four major radio reps with nonwired networks: Blair, Internet, Katz, and Supernet. In addition, there are several smaller groups. The major advantage promoted by the nonwired networks is that they combine the flexibility of market-by-market spot advertising with the convenience of network. However, critics of the nonwired concept charge that when dealing with a rep, the client really has only one station to choose from in each market. Consequently, much of the flexibility of the nonwired network is an illusion. Figure 7–6 lists the major advantages and disadvantages of wired and nonwired networks.

FIGURE 7–6   Claims and Counterclaims of Wired versus Nonwired Radio Networks

Advantages claimed by all networks

Easy to buy; permit larger margin of profit for the agency than market-by-market spot.

One order and one invoice.

One affidavit.

Pre- and postbuy analyses at no extra cost to advertiser.

Promotion and merchandising from station at no extra charge to advertiser.

Both competitive with market-by-market spot buys.

Advantages claimed for wired networks

The CPM for a wired network is half or less than half that for a nonwired network.

The wired networks offer a wide spectrum of audience profiles collectively: ABC via its contemporary (C), entertainment (E), information (I), and FM networks; MBS via its general marketing and black networks; CBS via its news and information and drama networks.

NBC through its National News and Information Service network expects to achieve a maximum of station clearance for commercials, since the affiliated stations will get six commercial minutes to sell against each NNIS-oriented program (three in the program, and three following).

The CBS, NBC, ABC, MBS network names provide the national advertiser with familiar prestigiousness that he can capitalize on in dealing with brokers, distributors, and retailers.

Advantages claimed for nonwired networks

Greater flexibility in implementing a national marketing plan.

Better control over station clearances. Can deliver larger percentage of stations and commercial clearances than wired networks.

Stations are more inclined to cooperate with nonwired networks since stations' share of nonwired network revenue is greater.

The advertiser can vary his weight of schedules and impressions per market and select the daypart and programming adjacent to his commercial and compatible with his product's local or regional requirements. Starting dates of schedule per market can also be varied.

Nonwired networks combine the best features of both wired and market-by-market spot, adding reach to the wired network's frequency.

Nonwired network stations generally cooperate better on promotion and merchandising than do wired network affiliates.

Rep network salesmen are more likely to take the advertiser's marketing objective into account. Therefore, presumably, if a market-by-market spot campaign seems more appropriate, he would recommend spot. The premise here: the rep network is not pitching against spot but rather against wired networks.

If an advertiser's target is so many gross rating points per market, he can use a wired network as a base and fill in the holes or heavy-up as needed with a nonwired network.

Duplicates of taped commercials are made and distributed to stations on nonwired network without added expense to the advertiser.

SOURCE: *Media Decisions,* April 1975, p. 67.

RADIO AS AN ADVERTISING MEDIUM

Strengths

Selectivity and Audience Segmentation. Radio is a medium of selective tastes. Through the wide range of formats radio offers, an advertiser can reach practically every demographic audience with a minimum of waste circulation. The *Spot Radio SRDS* lists more than 160 radio station formats, from Adult Contemporary to Young and Beautiful. Many stations use as many as four format descriptions to describe various parts of their programming.

Figure 7–5 presents some of the major formats. Since these format designations are made largely by the stations themselves, advertisers must use some judgment in selecting a specific station.

Out-of-Home Audience. One of radio's major strengths is its ability to effectively reach the out-of-home audience. However, in recent years, the stereotype of drive time (approximately 7 to 9 A.M. and 5 to 7 P.M.) as a mostly male, automobile audience has been challenged by radio audience research. One such study by RADAR (Radio All-Dimension Audience Research) showed that the in-car share of the drive-time audience was only 21.2 percent. This study also indicated that women made up a sizable portion of the drive-time audience.[7]

These data have implications for FM radio. Many advertisers assume that most drive-time radio listeners are away from home. However, if these figures are correct (see Figure 7–7), then most listeners are at home during all dayparts. This does not mean that drive-time, out-of-home listeners are not an important target segment for many advertisers. It does mean that drive-time buys should be made on the basis of available research, not traditional wisdom.

Low Unit Cost. As we have noted, all media advertising rates have risen dramatically in the last two decades. However, radio has had the smallest overall increase in CPM. This increase has been far below the overall rate of inflation and only about 70 percent of the comparable increases in television and newspapers (see Figure 7–8).

Radio's relatively low cost allows advertisers to utilize the medium to gain supplemental reach (new audience) or to generate heavy frequency by buying multiple spots on a few stations. Heavy frequency also permits advertisers to qualify for various discounts, making the cost of radio even lower.

---

[7] "Who's Listening in Drive Time?" *Media Decisions,* November 1977, p. 126.

FIGURE 7–7 **Drive-Time Radio Audiences—How Listening by Men and Women Differs by Time of Day**

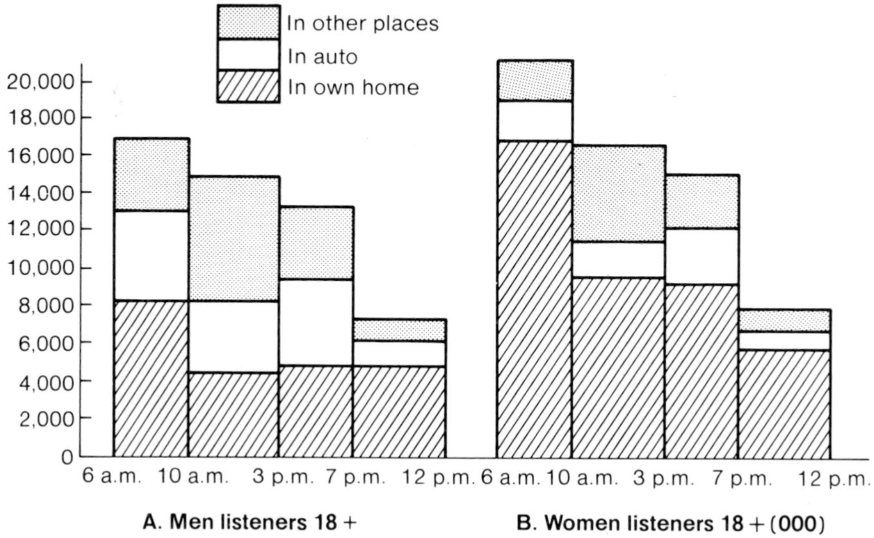

A. Men listeners 18 +   B. Women listeners 18 + (000)

SOURCE: Radar, fall 1978, spring 1977, average quarter hour.   Courtesy of *Media Decisions.*

Inexpensive Copy Opportunities. The costs of television and print production are rising, but radio production remains relatively inexpensive. Radio's low (often negligible) production costs in turn allow quick copy changes and short scheduling deadlines. Radio can take advantage of short-term changes in the marketplace without junking expensive advertisements prepared before these changes occurred.

Cooperative Advertising. Cooperative advertising is the national manufacturers' and retailers' sharing of local advertising costs. Radio has become more aggressive in pursuing the co-op dollar in recent years. While co-op is used predominantly in newspapers (discussed more fully in Chapter 8), events have made co-op more of a multimedia enterprise:

> Because of media cost inflation, advertisers have been looking for ways to save money, and co-op has become a consideration in all media.
>
> The Radio Advertising Bureau (RAB) has led industry-wide efforts to encourage advertisers to consider radio co-op. Co-op plans allowing the use of radio (and prepared by RAB) have almost tripled in number (1,200 to 3,300) between 1978 and 1983.[8]

---

[8] "Co-op Is Tempting," *Advertising Age*, March 7, 1983, p. M–11.

FIGURE 7–8 Radio's Twenty-Year Cost per Thousand Increase

McCann-Erickson Media Price Indexes
(base year 1976)

Year	News-papers	Maga-zines	Net TV	Spot TV	Net Radio	Spot Radio	Out-Door	Direct Mail	Composite *	Composite †	Consumer Price Index
1967	100	100	100	100	100	100	100	100	100	100	100
1968	104	101	101	104	96	100	103	125	107	102	104
1969	109	105	109	106	96	101	106	132	112	107	110
1970	115	106	108	99	96	102	117	132	114	107	116
1971	118	112	96	95	88	97	119	143	115	104	121
1972	122	112	105	104	96	102	130	167	124	110	125
1973	126	109	114	109	95	106	136	174	129	114	133
1974	135	113	120	112	94	108	142	212	141	119	148
1975	154	120	126	119	98	114	151	219	153	127	161
1976	169	125	149	147	111	122	161	272	176	144	171
1977	183	133	177	152	133	131	174	268	186	159	182
1978	195	145	197	167	147	140	187	282	199	174	195
1979	213	158	219	183	161	149	202	244	206	190	217
1980	235	173	238	201	178	164	111	235	218	206	247
1981	263	188	261	223	202	182	242	263	244	230	272
1982	288	205	292	248	220	195	262	286	268	254	289
1983	314	221	318	268	244	207	286	290	287	275	298
1984	342	239	359	294	259	226	309	283	307	303	311
1985(e)	366	258	388	312	279	240	331	302	329	325	322
1986(e)	392	273	415	329	293	250	346	314	349	347	335

(e) Estimate.

Note: The McCann-Erickson annual advertising expenditure reports are a main source for the indexes. Yearly change in expenditures is a function of change in price and change in the unit volume. Synthesis of such data is necessary because actual prices are often not publicly known.

* Based on national and local budgets in all eight media

† Based on national budgets in seven media excluding direct mail

SOURCE: Reprinted with permission Advertising Age, November 21, 1985, p. 15. Copyright Crain Communications, Inc.

Greater emphasis is being placed on local market strategies. Major manufacturers realize that local retailers know the customer best and are giving them more flexibility in spending co-op dollars.

Better controls of co-op have been developed. Radio stations are routinely required to sign affidavits attesting to performance in co-op advertising.

Weaknesses

Low Attention Levels. Perhaps radio's greatest drawback is that it can easily be ignored. Because radio lacks the visibility of other media, listeners use it as background while they engage in other activities. As more and more products are "presold," radio's inability to provide package identification is a major problem for certain classes of advertisers, such as advertisers of detergents and packaged/prepared foods.

Frequency Expensive. Because the average quarter-hour audience of any radio station is relatively low, radio advertising schedules must have extremely high frequency to obtain broad reach. Radio audiences are smaller than television audiences, they are spread over more stations, and they pay less attention to the medium.

RATE STRUCTURE IN LOCAL RADIO

Media buyers often regard radio time sales as complex. In some cases, television buyers are often assigned to buy radio "on the side." Since they may be unfamiliar with the medium, they naturally find radio more difficult to buy than the medium they work with regularly. In addition, radio exaggerates the buying problem by using an unstandardized system of rate cards, including fixed rates, grid rates, and a number of different combination or package discount rates. Most of the grid rates are similar to those discussed in Chapter 6 in connection with television. However, most radio grid cards offer fewer options than the similar system in television.

Nevertheless, radio time sales are similar in many ways to those of television since prices are set largely by demand and ratings. However, radio rates are less subject to negotiation. The media buyer needs to confirm rates (largely through contracts agreed on previously) and availabilities. Since most radio time is bought during dayparts rather than within a participating program, as in television, there is a greater flexibility for the station to place commercials.

The potential radio advertiser considers several factors in buying a station: format, coverage area ratings, daypart, and commercial time.

Format

Most stations are bought primarily on the basis of format. Local advertisers, of course, know the general program format of stations in the community. National advertisers must depend primarily on descriptions provided by stations. Most stations provide program descriptions under their listings in the *Spot Radio SRDS*. A few stations also have a system that permits advertisers to hear recorded program segments by telephone. An actual comparison of formats for the Los Angeles market is shown in Figure 7–9.

Coverage Area Ratings

Stations are bought on the basis of ratings over a specific geographic area.

> The **Metro Survey Area (MSA)** conforms to a Standard Metropolitan Statistical Area (SMSA) as defined by the U.S. Department of Commerce.
> The **Total Survey Area (TSA)** includes the Metro Survey Area plus certain adjoining counties. The number of counties included in a TSA is determined by the number of stations that achieve minimum coverage in these counties.
> The **Area of Dominant Influence (ADI),** discussed in Chapter 6, is primarily a television term. However, national advertisers sometimes define markets in terms of ADIs and buy other media, including magazines and newspapers, to conform to these areas.

The advertiser is not interested in the coverage area of a station per se, but in the audience the station reaches in its coverage area. Radio advertising is normally bought in one of two ways or a combination of both.

Gross Rating Points. This strategy of buying broadcast time has already been discussed in Chapter 6. Compared to television, any particular level of GRPs in radio usually requires a greater number of spots since the average rating per spot is lower.

Cume. Short for accumulated audience, cume is simply radio terminology for reach. However, radio audience surveys commonly report the number of different households (or individuals in certain age categories).

FIGURE 7-9 Top Radio Performers of 1985 by Arbitron Rating in Los Angeles Metro Market

Call Letters and Affiliation†		Owner	Format†	Arbitron 1985* Spring	Summer	Spot Cost	Highest Rated Programming	Promos and Advertising	Rating Service
KIIS-fm	IND	Gannett	CHR	11.5	11.8	$2,000	Rick Dees, a.m. drive	$50,000 giveaway; outdoor/transit	Arbitron, Birch, Scarborough
KABC	ABC	Cap Cities/ABC	Talk	7.5	8.8	N/A	Ken & Bob Co., a.m. drive	Celebration 25, cash giveaways, games; all media	Arbitron, Birch, Scarborough
KFWB	NBC	Westinghouse	News	5.2	4.5	N/A	A.M. drive	TV, newspapers, outdoor	Arbitron, Scarborough
KNX	CBS	CBS Inc.	News	4.8	4.9	N/A	A.M. drive	Anniversary promo, outdoor, tv, print, direct mail, radio	Arbitron
KJOI-fm	IND	Noble Brdcstng**	EZL	4.0	3.7	N/A	Fred Missman, midday	Giveaways: cars, fur coats, Paul Anka concert	Arbitron
KBIG-fm	IND	Bonneville	EZL	3.8	3.7	N/A	Harry Johnson, midday	Four major trip giveaways; all major media	Arbitron
KMPC	IND	Golden West	B/BND	3.7	4.7	$500	Jim Healey, a.m. drive	Cash giveaways, major media	Arbitron
KROQ-fm	IND	Mandeville	AOR/CHR	3.4	3.3	$250 avg	Richard Blade, a.m. drive	Safe Ride Program, concerts, outdoor, major media	Arbitron
KOST-fm	IND	KFI Inc.††	A/C	3.1	2.9	N/A	M.G. Kelley, a.m. drive	Cash/car giveaways, tv, radio	Arbitron
KKHR-fm	CBS	CBS Inc.	CHR	3.0	3.0	N/A	P.M. drive	Nissan cars, cash, trip giveaways; tv, outdoor	Arbitron, Scarborough, SMP
KMET-fm	IND	Metromedia	AOR	2.8	2.5	$350 avg	P.M. drive	All media	Arbitron
KLOS-fm	ABC	Cap Cities/ABC	AOR	2.6	3.9	N/A	Geno Mitchellini, p.m. drive	Porche giveaway; transit ads	Arbitron
KMGG-fm	IND	Emmis Brdcstng	A/C	2.6	2.7	N/A	N/A	N/A	N/A
KFI	ABC	KFI Inc.††	A/C	2.6	2.9	N/A	Lohman & Barkley a.m. drive	Car giveaways, traffic helicopter	Arbitron
KRTH-fm	US2	RKO General	Gold	2.5	2.8	N/A	Pat Evans, midday	Giveaways, other media	Arbitron
KTNQ	IND	K-LOVE Radio	Span	2.4	3.0	$95	Humberto Luna, a.m. drive	On-air spots only	None
KZLA-fm	IND	Cap Cities/ABC***	C/W	2.3	2.6	$300 avg	P.M. drive	"Artist Arbitron of the Day" promo w/$100 prizes	Arbitron
KHTZ-fm	IND	Greater Media	A/C	2.2	1.6	N/A	Charlie Tuna, a.m. drive	N/A	Arbitron, Scarborough
KUTE-fm	IND	Inner City****	C/JM	2.1	1.7	$130 avg	Lawrence Tanter, p.m. drive	Trip giveaways, transit, outdoor	Arbitron

KJLH-fm	IND	Taxi Prod.	B/U	2.0	3.1	N/A	A.M. drive	N/A	Arbitron
KRLA	IND	Greater Media	Gold	2.0	1.9	N/A	Multi-personality format	Giveaways, other media	Arbitron, Scarborough
KDAY	NBN	Rollins Brdcstng	B/U	1.6	1.2	N/A	N/A	$25,000 scholarship; weekend trips; $30,000 giveaway	N/A
KLAC	ABC	Cap Cities/ABC***	C/W	1.5	2.2	$300 avg	Scott Carpenter, a.m. drive	Giveaways, tv & other media	Arbitron
KWKW	IND	Lotus ComCorp	Span	1.5	1.0	N/A	A.M. drive	On-air promos, contests	None
KNOB-fm	IND	Pennino Music	BM/EZL	1.4	1.1	N/A	N/A	N/A	N/A
KACE	APR	All Pro Best	B/U	N/A	1.9	$100 avg	Pam Robinson, p.m. drive	London bus promo, concerts, trip giveaways	Arbitron
KSKQ-fm	IND	SBSC	Span	1.3	1.7	N/A	P.M. drive	Car giveaways, Mexican Holiday promos	None
KKGO-fm	APR	Mt. Wilson FM	Jazz	1.2	1.3	N/A	P.M. drive	N/A	N/A
KIQQ-fm	IND	Outlet Comm.†††	A/C	1.2	1.2	$125 avg	Midday	TV promos, trips	Arbitron
KFAC	IND	KFAC Inc.††††	CL	1.0	1.2	$200 avg	N/A	Tie-ins w/cultural events, all media	Arbitron
KLVE-fm	IND	K-LOVE Radio	Span	0.9	1.4	$95	Willie Chavez, a.m. drive	On-radio spots	None
KALI	IND	TBC	Span	0.9	1.1	N/A	A.M. drive	N/A	N/A

* Ratings based on ARB Spring and Summer books; 6-10 a.m. morning drive times for am stations, 3-7 p.m. afternoon/evening drive times for fm stations, corresponding to the highest rated programing, but where average is noted, rate is average of the four dayparts; N/A indicates station may be on flexible grid system, declines to publish spot rates and will supply rates to advertisers and media buyers on request.

** Sold to Regency Broadcasting effective Feb. 1986

*** Sold to Malrite effective Jan. 1986

**** Sold to Golden West Broadcasters effective Dec. 1986

† Formats & abbreviations: A/C, Adult Contemporary; AOR, Album Oriented Rock; BM, Beautiful Music; CHR, Contemporary Hit Radio; C/W, Country/Western; C/J, Contemporary Jazz; CL, Classical; EZL, Easy Listening; B/BND, Big Band; B/U, Black Urban; Span, Spanish/Mexican; Gold, Golden Oldies; News, All news; Talk, News/talk; ABC, American Broadcasting Co.; CBS, Columbia Broadcasting Co.; NBN, National Black Network; APR, Associated Press Radio Network; NBN, National Black Network; SBSC, Spanish Broadcasting System of Cal.; TBC, Tele Broadcasters of Cal.; (United Broadcasting Group); US2, United Stations Radio Networks Inc. 2.

†† Owned by Cox Communications

††† A subsidiary of the Rockefeller Group

†††† Owned by ASI Communications

SOURCE: Reprinted with permission Advertising Age, November 21, 1986, p. 42. Copyright Crain Communications, Inc.

The advertiser using cumes buys a specified number of different households. GRPs only provide a specified level of exposure; they don't indicate the extent of duplication.

Daypart

While station format and coverage area ratings are perhaps the two most important factors in choosing a station, the advertiser must also schedule the commercial in the most advantageous daypart. Stations vary greatly in the daypart segments they make available to advertisers. Most stations offer a minimum of two dayparts, however, and a few have more than four. Dayparts are usually designated by letters, with AAA often being the highest-priced period. There is no consistency to these designations, and the media planner must designate times rather than letters when giving instructions to buyers. Figure 7–10 shows how two stations use different letter designations for the same time.

Commercial Time

Next a decision must be made as to the length of the commercial messages to be purchased. Normally radio commercials are one minute long, although stations do permit 30-second spots. Most stations also allow 10- and 20-second spots, but such spots are rarely used in radio. Before considering a spot of less than one minute, advertisers should examine the cost differential. Stations often charge up to 80 percent of the one-minute price for commercials of less than one minute. For most advertisers, this saving is not worth the loss of commercial time. Also, fewer commercials create a less cluttered environment for the advertiser.

Discounts. Radio stations typically offer a wide range of discounts to regular advertisers. While discounts vary from station to station, they generally fall into one of two categories.

FIGURE 7–10 Daypart Letter Designations for Two Stations

WADO (New York City)	WWOK (Miami)
AAA Monday–Saturday 6:00–10:00 A.M.	AAA Monday–Saturday 6:00–10:00 A.M. and 3:00–7:00 P.M.
AA Monday–Sunday 10:00 A.M.–3:00 P.M.	AA Monday–Saturday 10:00 A.M.–3:00 P.M. Sunday 6:00 A.M.–7:00 P.M.
A Monday–Sunday 3:00–7:00 P.M.	A Monday–Sunday 7:00 P.M.–midnight
B Monday–Saturday 7:00 P.M.–midnight Sunday 7:00–8:00 P.M.	
C Tuesday–Sunday midnight–6:00 A.M.	

Bulk Discounts. Advertisers get a *bulk* or **frequency discount** for buying a certain number of spots during a specific time period (normally one month or one year). When the discount is based on money spent rather than commercials purchased, it is called a *volume discount.* Volume discounts are more common in television than radio.

Package Discounts. Radio stations offer a wide array of discounts based on the purchase of certain dayparts or on the use of some pattern in scheduling commercials. The following are some of the most common discounts.

Annual discount: The annual discount (sometimes referred to as a continuity discount) requires an advertiser to purchase a 52-week schedule with a minimum number of spots per week.

Consecutive week discount (CWD): A CWD is similar to the annual discount, but it usually requires only 13 weeks to qualify.

Rotations (also called *Orbits*): Rotations are offered on either a horizontal or vertical basis. A horizontal rotation places a spot at the same time on different days. A vertical rotation moves a spot through dayparts.

Run of Station (ROS): An ROS buy allows the station to place the advertiser's spots at its discretion. Although it is the cheapest buy, many advertisers think they need more control over their advertising. Stations often list ROS as Best Times Available (BTA) in their rate cards.

Total Audience Plan (TAP): The TAP discount permits the advertiser to buy several spots in each of the dayparts. The price for these spots is determined by the proportions of the spots scheduled for each of the dayparts. A typical listing for a TAP plan would be: 1/3 AAA, 1/3 AA, 1/3 A. In this case, one third of the spots would be run in each of the three time periods.

Other Discounts. Other discounts include combination rates and preemptible rates. Often, when the same company owns more than one station, an advertiser can buy the stations in combination at a reduced price. In radio, **combination rates** are most common where AM/FM stations are held by the same company in a specific market. In smaller markets, the advertiser may have no choice if the FM station is simulcast (i.e., carries most of the same programs broadcast by its AM sister station). Other combination buys are available through regional agreements under which stations allow themselves to be sold with other stations.

An advertiser may save money by paying less than the maximum price for a **preemptible spot** with the understanding that the commercial may be preempted, or bumped, by an advertiser paying a higher price for the same spot. This system is known as fixed and preemptible rates, and it is usually indicated on a rate card in this way:

	I	II	III
AAA	100	90	80
AA	70	65	60
A	50	40	30

The letters indicate the daypart (e.g., AAA might be 7 to 9 A.M. daily), and the Roman numerals give the prices the station charges for this time. In the example above, I-AAA is called fixed time. An advertiser who buys this time is guaranteed the time indefinitely. On the other hand, an advertiser who buys III-AAA is taking a chance that no other advertiser will pay more than $80 and thus preempt the time. Levels II and III differ in length of notice an advertiser will be given by the station before being preempted. For instance, II might mean two weeks' notice, while III might be only 24 hours' notice.

Sometimes stations do not offer their most valuable time on a preemptible basis. The lack of preemptible rates for certain time periods usually indicates that demand is great enough so the station can always sell this time at the fixed rates. A typical rate card might indicate this as follows:

	I	II	III
AAA	100	*	*
AA	70	65	60
A	50	40	30

* Preemptible rates not available.

In addition to buying at these discounts, advertisers sometimes want to buy spots at certain times. *Fixed position* means a station guarantees to run a spot at a specific time. Fixed positions can cost the advertiser 10 to 25 percent extra, and not all stations carry fixed positions.

Two final comments should be made about radio rates. In the station listings in the *Spot Radio SRDS,* under the heading "Time Rates," some stations say "National and local rates same." If this statement does not appear, it is assumed that the quoted rates are for national advertisers. Also, radio stations usually do not give the 2 percent discount for cash.

SOURCES OF RATES AND AUDIENCE DATA

Buying radio is often the most difficult and time-consuming task for the media buyer. With so many stations, formats, and pricing structures, the radio media buyer has a difficult time making and justifying radio buys. In this section, we will discuss the major information sources available to the radio media buyer.

Spot Radio Standard Rate and Data Service

The SRDS is the general information book for the media buyer. In addition to rates, the SRDS listing for a station gives information concerning station policies, reps, network affiliation, and power. However, SRDS is viewed as a guide rather than the definitive word on rates. Broadcast rates are usually negotiable, and buyers normally contact the station before making a final decision.

Estimator Books

Advertising agencies and other organizations often publish media data that include rate estimates. These and more elaborate references are also available from reps, broadcast industry associations, and most major agencies. Such "estimating books" are not used for final advertising pricing, but they can be useful to get an idea of costs. They can also be helpful in giving the media buyer a starting point for negotiation. Figure 7–11 presents a section from a typical estimating guide.

The rep is a valuable source of information. Although advertisers should evaluate rep information as coming from a salesperson, reps know that future sales depend on how accurate and candid they are with media buyers. Media reps are in an advantageous position to know local markets and special factors that don't show up in general audience information sources.

Syndicated Audience Services

For local radio audience ratings, there are two major reports: *Arbitron Radio* and the *Birch Report*. Both reports include average quarter-hour ad cume listening estimates for men and women reported by various age groups. An Arbitron example shows how these data are reported by metro and total survey areas (see Figure 7–12). Both services are described in greater detail in Chapter 15.

Arbitron Radio uses the diary method of gathering data. This method enables Arbitron to report not only listening levels but also the demo-

FIGURE 7–11 Radio Cost Data

	Daypart Rates Cost per 30-Second Commercial†			
	6–10 A.M.	10 A.M.–3 P.M.	3–7 P.M.	7 P.M.–Midnight
ABC Contemporary		$2,900 R.O.S.		
ABC Direction		1,500 R.O.S.		
ABC Entertainment		2,500 R.O.S.		
ABC FM		2,400 R.O.S.		
ABC Information		2,700 R.O.S.		
ABC Rock		2,100 R.O.S.		
ABC Talk		600 R.O.S.		
CBS Radio Talk		2,600 R.O.S.		
CBS RADIORADIO		2,000 R.O.S.		
CMN		750 R.O.S.		
CNN		1,500 R.O.S.*		
MBS		2,700 R.O.S.		
NBC	2,500	1,500	1,800	650
NBC "The Source"		3,500 R.O.S.		
NBC Talknet		750 R.O.S.		
Satellite		1,600 R.O.S.		
Sheridan Broadcasting		1,200 R.O.S.		
Transtar		1,500 R.O.S.*		
United Stations One		3,000 R.O.S.		
United Stations Two		2,500 R.O.S.		
United Sts. Programming		2,000–8,000		
Wall Street Journal Report		4,250 R.O.S.[1]		

	Cost Per Metro Rating Point, Fall 1986 (60-second units)					
	Men			Women		
ADI Markets	18+	18–34	25–54	18+	18–34	25–54
Top 10	$1,844	$1,114	$1,955	$1,942	$1,302	$1,896
Top 20	2,840	1,702	2,873	2,883	1,887	2,825
Top 30	3,482	2,044	3,495	3,555	2,340	3,451
Top 40	4,067	2,379	4,097	4,068	2,634	3,933
Top 50	4,587	2,620	4,596	4,580	2,874	4,363
Top 60	4,982	2,815	4,955	4,980	3,185	4,722
Top 70	5,299	2,986	5,267	5,283	3,385	4,985
Top 80	5,559	3,184	5,517	5,518	3,538	5,237
Top 90	5,761	3,428	5,726	5,697	3,710	5,446
Top 100	5,965	3,608	5,934	5,870	3,858	5,580

[1] 60-second unit; 30s are 75% of 60s.

NOTE: These are general rates, subject to specific negotiation and package buys.

† Weekdays

* CNN and Transtar sold as one unit

SOURCE: *Adweek's Marketer's Guide to Media* 10, no. 1 (1987), pp. 95 and 98.

graphics of the audience. Recently Arbitron has taken steps to more adequately report ethnic audiences (primarily black and Spanish listeners). Since diaries are placed in telephone households, Arbitron has also developed a computer random dial system (called Expanded Sample Frame) to reach unlisted numbers. Arbitron reports are available from one to four times a year, depending on the size of the market. The April/May survey is conducted in every Arbitron market and is the radio equivalent of the sweep periods in television.

While the basic rating mathematics of radio are similar to those used in television, some differences should be noted. Radio ratings are almost always based on age/sex rather than on households. Television uses a four-week period for analysis of reach and frequency levels, but radio commonly uses both one- and four-week periods.

Local radio ratings encounter the same "sweep weeks" hypoing problem that was discussed in Chapter 6. If anything, the problem of ratings inflation is even more serious in radio than in television. Since most radio markets are rated only once or twice a year, any ratings problem means that an advertiser will buy from the wrong numbers for up to a year. To address the problem, Arbitron carries a list of the stations that engaged in promotional activities during the rating period. It is important to remember that Arbitron does not regulate broadcast practices, and consequently its ability to prevent hypoing is limited.

Some agencies don't buy stations that call attention to rating diaries or engage in extraordinary promotions during a rating period. From a practical standpoint, this position is effective only if a few stations, which your client didn't need in the first place, engage in the practice. To emphasize the seriousness of hypoing, Arbitron carries the following statement in its rating books:

> The FTC Guidelines Regarding Deceptive Claims of Broadcast Audience Coverage contain language which points out that RADIO STATIONS . . . "should not engage in activities calculated to DISTORT or INFLATE such data—for example, by conducting a SPECIAL CONTEST, or otherwise varying . . . usual programming or instituting UNUSUAL ADVERTISING or other promotional efforts, DESIGNED TO INCREASE AUDIENCES ONLY DURING THE SURVEY PERIOD. Such variation from normal practices is known as 'HYPOING.'"

> It is the opinion of Arbitron that while many radio stations that engage in promotional activities during a survey period are not attempting to hypo audiences, many other stations conduct their promotional activity for the specific purpose of increasing audiences artificially during the rating period.

> This activity could distort the behavior of the listening audience by making the estimates higher than they would have been if no promotional activity had been conducted during the survey period.

> The purpose of this notice is to call attention to the text of the FTC Guidelines and to call attention to report users where there is a possibility

FIGURE 7–12 Average Quarter-Hour and Cume Listening Estimates—Woman 18+

| | Mon-Fri 6:00 AM-Mid | | | | | | Mon-Fri 6:00 AM-7:00 PM | | | | | | |
| | Total Area | | Metro Survey Area | | | | Total Area | | Metro Survey Area | | | | |
Station Call Letters	Avg. Pers. (00)	Cume Pers. (00)	Avg. Pers. (00)	Cume Pers. (00)	Avg. Pers. Rtg.	Avg. Pers. Shr.	Avg. Pers. (00)	Cume Pers. (00)	Avg. Pers. (00)	Cume Pers. (00)	Avg. Pers. Rtg.	Avg. Pers. Shr.	Station Call Letters
KCAS	*3	*28	*3	*26	*.4	*1.9	*3	*28	*3	*26	*.4	*1.6	KCAS
KEND	7	115	7	104	.9	4.5	9	111	8	100	1.0	4.2	KEND
KFMX	9	114	4	71	.5	2.5	11	114	6	71	.7	3.2	KFMX
KFYO	17	221	7	97	.9	4.5	20	217	8	93	1.0	4.2	KFYO
KJAK	3	72	3	58	.4	1.9	5	68	4	54	.5	2.1	KJAK
KKAM	2	53	2	43	.2	1.3	3	53	3	43	.4	1.6	KKAM
KLFB	12	68	12	66	1.5	7.6	13	61	13	59	1.6	6.8	KLFB
KLLL	43	385	32	251	3.9	20.4	54	368	37	247	4.5	19.5	KLLL
KRLB	*7	*69	*6	*63	*.7	*3.8	*7	*69	*6	*63	*.7	*3.2	KRLB
KRLB FM	31	215	28	183	3.4	17.8	38	209	36	178	4.4	18.9	KRLB FM
KRUX	24	210	12	108	1.5	7.6	30	200	16	103	2.0	8.4	KRUX
KSEL	17	244	9	135	1.1	5.7	23	236	12	135	1.5	6.3	KSEL
KSEL FM	9	151	5	84	.6	3.2	11	136	5	81	.6	2.6	KSEL FM
KTEZ	30	260	19	162	2.3	12.1	35	246	24	151	2.9	12.6	KTEZ
KWAZ	*4	*85	*3	*65	*.4	*1.9	*4	*85	*3	*65	*.4	*1.6	KWAZ
Metro Totals	157			772		19.2	190			770		23.2	Metro Totals

Mon-Fri 6-10 AM + 3-7 PM / Weekend 6:00 AM-Mid

Station Call Letters	Total Area Avg. Pers. (00)	Total Area Cume Pers. (00)	Metro Survey Area Avg. Pers. (00)	Metro Survey Area Cume Pers. (00)	Metro Survey Area Avg. Pers. Rtg.	Metro Survey Area Avg. Pers. Shr.	Total Area Avg. Pers. (00)	Total Area Cume Pers. (00)	Metro Survey Area Avg. Pers. (00)	Metro Survey Area Cume Pers. (00)	Metro Survey Area Avg. Pers. Rtg.	Metro Survey Area Avg. Pers. Shr.	Station Call Letters
KCAS	* 3	* 28	* 3	* 26	* .4	* 1.5		* 16		* 16			KCAS
KEND	11	111	10	100	1.2	5.1	5	64	4	53	.5	3.6	KEND
KFMX	10	108	6	64	.7	3.0	8	78	6	48	.7	5.5	KFMX
KFYO	23	192	10	83	1.2	5.1	20	156	9	90	1.1	8.2	KFYO
KJAK	5	68	4	54	.5	2.0	6	40	3	26	.4	2.7	KJAK
KKAM	4	50	4	40	.5	2.0	1	41	1	41	.1	.9	KKAM
KLFB	14	61	14	59	1.7	7.1	13	65	13	58	1.6	11.8	KLFB
KLLL	59	355	43	233	5.3	21.7	30	240	22	174	2.7	20.0	KLLL
KRLB	*11	* 62	* 9	* 56	*1.1	* 4.5	* 1	* 15	* 1	* 15	* .1	* .9	KRLB
KRLB FM	32	200	29	169	3.5	14.6	14	137	11	118	1.3	10.0	KRLB FM
KRUX	26	193	13	100	1.6	6.6	19	162	9	75	1.1	8.2	KRUX
KSEL	25	212	14	128	1.7	7.1	10	120	6	83	.7	5.5	KSEL
KSEL FM	10	104	6	74	.7	3.0	6	86	4	59	.5	3.6	KSEL FM
KTEZ	29	211	21	132	2.6	10.6	20	159	14	97	1.7	12.7	KTEZ
KWAZ	* 6	* 76	* 5	* 56	* .6	* 2.5	* 3	* 49	* 2	* 37	* .2	* 1.8	KWAZ
Metro Totals			198	758	24.2			Metro Totals	110	650	13.4		

* Audience estimates adjusted for actual broadcast schedule.

SOURCE: The Arbitron Company, Arbitron Ratings Radio Lubbock, Fall 1982, p. 24. Reprinted with permission–Arbitron Rating Company.

that some kind of hypoing might have been conducted during the survey period by one or more stations in the market.

Network radio audience ratings are measured primarily by RADAR. RADAR uses the telephone coincidental technique with a sample of approximately 6,000.

Intermedia Approaches to Buying Radio

As we discussed earlier in this chapter, radio is seldom used alone or as the primary medium in a campaign. Radio is a complement to other media, and most advertisers buy radio time on the basis of how it fits into their overall schedule. For some time, the RAB and other industry groups have promoted radio as part of an intermedia schedule.

One of the most widely known studies of radio and other media is the RAB's All-Radio Marketing Study (ARMS II). The details of this comprehensive study show how radio fits into schedules using different levels of television and newspaper advertising (see Figure 7–13).

THE OUTLOOK

Radio's future as an advertising medium appears solid. Radio is becoming aggressive and innovative in its competition for audiences and advertising dollars. One of the most obvious areas of change in radio has been the return to programming at both the local and network levels. As discussed

---

FIGURE 7–13 Example from ARMS II Report

Product: Shampoo
Target: Females, 12–34
Weekly budget: $9,250

			Cumulative Frequency Distribution			
Schedule	Net Reach	Average Fre- quency	One or More Times/ Week	Two or More Times/ Week	Three or More Times/ Week	Four or More Times/ Week
100% spot TV . .	29.9%	1.4%	29.9%	8.0%	3.4%	1.4%
⅔ TV, ⅓ radio	40.2	1.8	40.2	19.0	8.5	2.7
⅓ TV, ⅔ radio	48.9	2.3	48.9	27.8	16.3	10.1
100% spot radio	51.7	3.1	51.7	34.5	23.9	17.8

SOURCE: Radio Advertising Bureau.

earlier, several network-produced programs have met with success. However, the largest number of new programs are offered by syndication.

Radio syndication includes both reruns of well-known programs of the 1930s and 40s, such as "The Lone Ranger" and "The Shadow," and first runs of new programs such as "Alien Worlds," released in mid-1979. However, the bulk of syndicated programs are short subjects, from 90 seconds to 5 minutes in length, on a host of entertainment and public affairs issues. Shows such as "Home Handyman" can charge premium advertising rates because of higher ratings and because listeners pay more attention to "talk" programs than to a steady diet of music.

Cost increases for television advertising are helping radio immeasurably. With 30-second commercials on major prime-time series costing $100,000 to $250,000 or more, advertisers look to alternatives to stretch limited budgets. Traditionally, magazines have been the major supplement to television. However, radio has been getting a larger share of the advertising dollar. Since neither radio's popularity nor television's costs show any signs of abating, radio's future as an alternative to television looks bright.

Implications of Radio Deregulation

The process of deregulating radio broadcasting began in earnest with the Communications Act of 1978. Radio deregulation is too complex to cover here, but some implications for the future of radio should be mentioned. The deregulation process is supposed to create diversity through increased competition. Let's look at four of the proposed deregulation provisions and their implications for advertising.

Deletion of the "Public Interest" Section of the Communications Act of 1934.[9] Will this lead stations to forgo news and public affairs programming? Will candidates be denied access to broadcast facilities for political advertising if the Fairness Doctrine is abolished? Will stations expand commercial minutes per hour since they will not have to answer to a public interest criterion for license renewal?

Station Log Requirements. Before 1984, the FCC required broadcasters to maintain a log of each broadcast day. Included in the station log were not only records of programs broadcast, but also all commercials

---

[9] "Public interest means that a station is serving the needs of the community. Licensees are required to ascertain these needs and program accordingly. The FCC does not prescribe a standard format.

that had been aired. These records figured in the public hearings held to renew a broadcast license. They also provided a means of verifying commercials to advertisers. Since mid-1984, FCC regulations no longer require stations to maintain broadcast logs. However, advertising industry groups (AAAA, AAF, ANA) have strongly urged stations to continue past logging practices, especially because of the need for advertising authentication.

Station Ownership Limits. Under rules adopted in 1985, single entities may now own 12 AM and 12 FM radio stations, an increase from the earlier restriction to 7 of each type. By 1987, no entity was at the new limit, but broadcasters were openly discussing the prospects for regional "networks" of stations and also the possibilities of owning more than one major station in a particular market.

The Question of Diversity. At the heart of the argument over deregulation is the question of whether diversity would really result. Cyril Penn, director of media, Shaller Rubin Associates, sees just the opposite effect:

> The new commission would be denied authority over all intrastate cable systems, and the role in communications of the antitrust division of the Department of Justice would specifically be curtailed.
>
> In my opinion, this may not lead to diversity through competition in the free marketplace. In 1956, Bell Telephone came to an agreement with the Department of Justice, in the face of pending antitrust action, to refrain from going into other unregulated businesses, which could interface with its existing services.
>
> Bell has now applied for permission to establish cable telecommunications systems. If cable transmission of radio and other origination of programming becomes unregulated, Bell's monopolistic power may not, in fact, lead to development of alternative technologies and services. Under the new act, there would be no regulation of competitive rates by common carriers.
>
> Deregulation of the communications industry will not necessarily promote the kind of desirable diversity that radio as an advertising medium can benefit by. Further market segmentation in radio would please many advertisers, but the public could soon find that its only means of obtaining quality programming, even of a mass entertainment nature, would be by direct subscription.[10]

The final decision on deregulation is yet to be made. However, radio will probably gain some freedom from current regulation. Advertisers will have to be aware of and adjust to these changes over the next several years.

---

[10] Cyril Penn, "The Future of Radio—Will It Be Diversity or Monopoly?" *Advertising Age,* June 25, 1979, p. 66.

FIGURE 7–14 **Comparative Ranks of Advertising Research and Advertising Revenue Dollars**

Ad Research Dollars	Ad Revenues
1. Television	1. Newspapers
2. Magazines	2. Television
3. Newspapers	3. Radio
4. Radio	4. Magazines

Research

While radio's future looks bright, audience research remains a major problem for the industry. The primary problem is the nature of the medium itself. Radio has a sizable out-of-home audience, which is virtually impossible to measure accurately. In addition, the number of stations in the major markets and the lack of programming lead to confusion among respondents reporting their listening behavior. Finally, a lack of money to tackle these problems puts radio research far behind television in the development of audience measurement techniques.

However, remember that no particular relationship exists between the advertising research problem to be solved and the money available to solve it. Figure 7–14 shows the comparative ranks of advertising research dollars spent and advertising revenues among the various media.

Note that advertising research dollars roughly follow advertising expenditures by national advertisers. Television and magazines, which rank first and second among national advertisers, are the subject of the most research. On the other hand, newspapers, the leader by a wide margin in total advertising revenue, rank a poor third in research dollars. Radio, with the smallest percentage of national advertising dollars, is last in research expenditures.

REVIEW QUESTIONS

1. Describe some of the major changes in radio revenues and radio stations during the last decade.
2. How is a nonwired network organized? What is its purpose?
3. How does radio differ from television as an advertising medium?
4. Discuss radio as an out-of-home medium.
5. Discuss MSA and TSA as they relate to radio ratings.
6. Discuss some of the implications of radio deregulation for advertising.
7. What steps have been taken to discourage hypoing in radio ratings?
8. Why do you think that radio stations have evolved toward a distinctive "format" but TV stations have not?

9. Using a current SRDS *Spot Radio Rates and Data,* find the air date, the programming description, the one-minute time rate for fixed, AAA time, and the broadcast transmitter power for KORN, Mitchell, South Dakota.

10. Repeat this exercise (9 above) for WSB, Atlanta, Georgia, and KNX, Los Angeles, California.

11. Using a current SRDS *Spot Radio Rates and Data,* make a listing of all the radio stations:

    a. In Texas that regularly schedule black-oriented programs.
    b. In Wisconsin that regularly schedule farm programs.
    c. In Ohio that regularly schedule Spanish-language programs.
    d. In the United States that regularly schedule programming in the Croatian language.
    e. In the United States that regularly schedule programming in Navajo or Pueblo languages.

SUGGESTED ADDITIONAL READING

"AM Radio Talking to Older Audience." *Marketing News,* August 16, 1985, p. 16.

BARTOS, RENA. "Archibald Crossley: Father of Broadcast Ratings." *Journal of Advertising Research* 26, no. 1 (February/March, 1986), pp. 47–49.

DUNCAN, CALVIN P., and JAMES NELSON. "Effects of Humor in a Radio Advertising Experiment." *Journal of Advertising* 14, no. 2 (1985), pp. 33–40, 64.

GELB, BETSY D., and GEORGE M. ZINKHAN. "Humor and Advertising Effectiveness after Repeated Exposures to a Radio Commercial." *Journal of Advertising* 15, no. 2 (1986), pp. 15–20, 34.

HEDGES, MICHAEL. "Radio's LifeStyles." *American Demographics,* February 1986, pp. 32–35.

"Kids and Collegians Targeted by New Networks." *Marketing News,* April 12, 1985, p. 14.

LALLANDE, ANN. "The FCC's Sweeping Broadcast Changes." *Marketing and Media Decisions,* May 1986, pp. 150+.

McCORMICK, MOIRA. "Format for Change." *Marketing and Media Decisions,* April 1986, pp. 85–92.

McGUIRE, DENNIS P. "Buying Radio: A Primer." *Marketing and Media Decisions,* January 1986, pp. 92–93.

"Network Radio." *Advertising Age Special Report,* April 14, 1986, pp. S1–S21.

"Radio Special Report." *Marketing and Media Decisions,* April 1985, pp. 83–108.

"San Diego Radio Stations Adopt Target Marketing." *Marketing News,* April 12, 1985, p. 3.

Understanding and Using Radio Audience Estimates: A Quick Reference Guide, Arbitron Ratings, 1982 (or current issue).

CHAPTER EIGHT

Newspapers

*Newspapers sell access. This process works in two
complementary ways. Advertisers buy access to potential
purchasers of their products, providing newspapers with 70%–
80% of their revenues. Readers pay for access to news,
information, advertising and entertainment arranged in a
convenient, predictable, and cheap package.**

Patrick O'Donnell

GENERAL CHARACTERISTICS OF NEWSPAPERS

Despite the advent of the new media during the last several decades,
newspapers continue to occupy a predominant position among advertisers. There are about 1,740 daily newspapers in the United States with
a combined circulation of over 63 million readers. In addition, some 7,700
weeklies serve rural and metropolitan suburban readers throughout the
country. Advertisers searching for more selective newspaper readership
may look to the ethnic and specialty press that includes black, hispanic,
and religious newspapers. Traditionally, the evening daily newspaper
has accounted for the majority of total newspaper circulation, but recently this has changed. At present, evening paper circulation comprises
only 42 percent of daily circulation (26 million readers).

To some extent, both the Sunday and Saturday morning editions
differ as advertising media from their daily counterparts. The almost 800
Sunday newspapers are often used by national advertisers as introductory vehicles and by retailers for announcements of sales during the next
week. The Saturday newspaper has changed to a feature and human-
interest emphasis from a strict news orientation, and it is an excellent
outlet for youth and young adult markets. Entertainment guides and

---

* "The Business of Newspapers: An Essay for Investors," E. F. Hutton, February 12,
1982, p. 1.

similar features of many Saturday newspapers offer excellent opportunities for record, movie, and restaurant advertisements. Food and household product categories continue to make the Wednesday or Thursday newspaper the major weekday revenue producers.

If asked, the average person would probably name television as the dominant advertising medium in terms of advertising revenues. However, newspapers are by far the leading advertising medium (over $25 billion in 1985), with a 27 percent share of total advertising expenditures compared to television's 21 to 22 percent. While television's share of advertising dollars has increased steadily over the last two decades, newspaper's share has declined slightly. Nevertheless, newspaper enterprises remain profitable as a group. In particular, the well-managed newspaper chains and certain industry leaders like *The Wall Street Journal* remain exceptionally prosperous.

NEWSPAPERS AS AN ADVERTISING MEDIUM

Categories of Newspaper Advertising

Local. Local advertising is the economic foundation of newspapers. Nearly all local businesses use newspaper advertising to some extent. Local advertising accounts for more than $22 billion, or 85 percent, of total newspaper advertising revenues. As discussed later in this chapter, the use of cooperative advertising makes this figure somewhat misleading in terms of the sources of these funds. However, it is significant that one quarter of total U.S. advertising is placed in newspapers by local advertisers.

All local businesses, including local chain outlets, generally qualify for **local rates,** which run 25 to 50 percent less than national rates. Newspaper circulation is sometimes divided into three geographic categories: **city zone, retail trading zone,** and other. Normally the "other" category is inconsequential, although a newspaper such as the *New York Times* has a significant number of out-of-city readers. Local rate information is usually obtained from individual rate cards provided by the newspapers (see Figure 8–1).

National. The national advertising category accounts for approximately $3 billion. The national rate normally provides for the 15 percent agency commission as well as a 10 to 20 percent commission for the media representative (for a full discussion of the media rep's role, see Chapter 5). National rate information can be obtained from the newspaper edition of Standard Rate and Data Service. A version of this service is also available for a limited number of weekly newspapers.

FIGURE 8–1 Portions of Newspaper Rate Card (*Rocky Mountain News*, July 1, 1986)

3. COMMISSION AND TERMS OF PAYMENT
    a. Agency Commission 15% to recognized agencies.
    b. No cash discount allowed.
    c. Commissions apply to this rate card only.

4. GENERAL RATE POLICY
    a. Publisher reserves the right to revise advertising rates at any time. All orders and contracts are accepted subject to this reservation. Publisher may cancel contracts on which space has not been used within sixty days of initiation of contract. Publisher reserves right to reject or cancel any ad at any time.
    b. The advertiser and/or agency shall designate the SAU size by width in columns and depth in inches in which case the newspaper agrees to bill the advertisement in exact space ordered.

5A. GENERAL ROP RATES
Open and Discount Contract Rates—B/W newsplan

Tab Pages— # of Inches	Less than Tab Page (per inch rate)		Tab Page or Larger (per inch rate)	
	Daily	Sunday	Daily	Sunday
Open	79.50	91.25	74.25	85.25
1–70	77.25	88.50	71.75	82.50
2–140	76.50	87.25	71.00	81.25
4–280	75.75	86.50	70.25	80.50
6–420	75.00	85.75	69.50	79.75
8–560	74.25	85.00	68.75	79.00
13–910	73.50	83.75	68.00	77.75
20–1,400	72.50	83.00	67.25	77.00
26–1,820	71.75	82.25	66.50	76.25
39–2,730	71.00	81.25	65.75	75.25
52–3,640	70.25	80.50	65.00	74.50
65–4,550	69.50	80.00	64.25	73.75
78–5,460	68.75	79.00	63.50	73.00
91–6,370	68.00	78.00	62.75	72.25
104–7,280	67.25	77.25	62.00	71.50
156–10,920	66.50	76.50	61.25	70.75
208–14,560	65.75	75.75	60.50	70.00

5B. PREPRINTED INSERTS
(Wednesday & Sunday)

Insert Sizes	Cost per Thousand
Free standing to 6 tab pages	$36.00
8 to 12 tab pages	$38.00
14 to 36 tab pages	$43.00

Rates based on 280,000 minimum order. Total delivery daily 365,000: Sunday 415,000. For rate quotes on inserts of greater than 36 pages or less than 280,000 distribution contact: Paul Campbell (303)892-5304. CMC Program available.

ANNUAL INSERT CONTRACT DISCOUNTS

6–12 inserts or up to 2,730 ROP inches	Less 6%
13–19 inserts or 2,730-inch ROP contract	Less 8%
20–25 inserts or 3,640-inch ROP contract	Less 10%
26–32 inserts or 5,460-inch ROP contract	Less 12%
33–39 inserts	Less 14%
40–45 inserts	Less 16%
46–52 inserts	Less 18%

Inserts should be shipped prepaid to the Rocky Mountain News, delivered to 1350 Rio Court, arriving in Denver 10 days prior to date of issue, on skids in cuts of at least 100 on powdered stock not to exceed 2,000 pounds per skid. Deliveries accepted Monday through Friday between the hours of 8 A.M. and 4 P.M.

FIGURE 8-1 *(continued)*

5C. GENERAL TV DIAL RATES
Sold in units (10 per page). Note Category 15c.

Units

1	$295
2	$380
3	$520
4	$650
5 (Horizontal Half Page)	$750
6	$875
10 (Full Page)	$1,350
20 (Center Spread)	$2,700

4 unit horizontal ads not accepted.

Frequency Contract Discounts
Six weeks within one year (any size) .... 5% discount
Thirteen weeks within one year (any size) .... 10% discount
Twenty-six weeks within one year (any size) .... 15% discount
Fifty-two weeks within one year (any size) .... 20% discount
For mechanical specifications see section 15C of rate card.

6. GROUP COMBINATION RATES
Not applicable

7A. ROP COLOR RATES
a. Black and one, two or three colors available daily and Sunday subject to prior orders. Advertisers to furnish veloxes.
b. Daily and Sunday ROP, 5 column x 14 inch. 70-inch page. Full tabloid page unit required for color.
1. ANPA standard color, black & white rate, plus $750
2. ANPA standard colors, black & white rate, plus $1,000
3. ANPA standard colors, black & white rate, plus $1,250
Colors other than ANPA process red, yellow, blue or bright red charged an additional $200. Tabloid page production material for black plus two or three colors may not exceed 10⅜" in width.

7B. FOOD FARE COLOR RATES
a. Broadsheet section published Wednesday. Black plus one, two or three colors available subject to mechanical limitations.

	33–70 SAU inches	71–132 SAU inches
1. ANPA standard color, black & white rate, plus	$750	$925
2. ANPA standard colors, black & white rate, plus	$1,000	$1,250
3. ANPA standard colors, black & white rate, plus	$1,250	$1,475

Colors other than ANPA process red, yellow, blue or bright red charged an additional $200.00.

7C. TV DIAL COLOR RATES
a. Published Sunday, see section 15c for ad unit size and page size mechanical information. Minimum ½ page.
b. Black plus one, two or three colors available subject to prior orders.
1. ANPA standard color, black & white rate, plus $365
2. ANPA standard colors, black & white rate, plus $550
3. ANPA standard colors, black & white rate, plus $735
Colors other than ANPA process red, yellow, blue or bright red charged an additional $100.00.

8. SPECIAL ROP UNITS
a. Strip ads available in selected topical sections.

FIGURE 8–1 *(concluded)*

---

9. SPLIT RUN
    a. Split run daily or Sunday's b/w or b/w 1c. $225.00 makeover charge (non-commissionable). Minimum ad size: Black & White, 20 inches; Color, Food Fare 33", ROP color 70".
10. SPECIAL SERVICES
    a. The Rocky Mountain News' Research Department maintains extensive comparative, demographic and psychographic information pertinent to the market place. Available on request.
    b. The Rockey Mountain News' Art Department is available to provide creative layout services and resizing of advertising materials on request. Allow additional lead time for proper handling of your request.
11. SPECIAL DAYS/PAGES/FEATURES
    a. MONDAY "SPORTS PLUS"
        1. Tabloid section publishing every Monday.
        2. Regular rates apply.
        3. Section contains wrap-up of weekend events—Pro, College, and High School; outdoors and many special features.
    b. TUESDAY "BUSINESS"
        1. Tabloid section publishing every Tuesday.
        2. Regular rates apply.
        3. Section contains local, regional, national and international news on business, finance, energy and people. Also complete Monday closings on N.Y., American, over-the-counter tables. Commodities, money markets, precious metals and other pertinent information.
    c. WEDNESDAY "FOOD FARE"
        1. Broadsheet section published Wednesday.
        2. Regular rates apply.
        3. Section devoted to food, couponing and homemaker hints.
    d. THURSDAY "STYLE"
        1. Tabloid section publishing every Thursday.
        2. Regular rates apply.
        3. Section includes fashion styles for the West covering both men's and women's styles. This section also contains "LIFESTYLES" with stories on travel, health, home-maker hints and other women's features.

SOURCE: As reprinted by permission of *Rocky Mountain News*, Denver, Colorado.

National advertisers use newspapers for a variety of reasons. In order, the four largest categories of national newspaper advertisers are cigarettes, automobiles, airlines, and liquor. Since liquor has never had access to the broadcast media to any extent and cigarette ads have been banned since 1971, it is natural that these industries would use the print media on a large scale. In this era of deregulation, airlines compete on a price basis, which sometimes escalates to a "fare war." Price competition must be done for airfares on a market-by-market basis. Most airline advertising uses localized copy and gives details on fares and schedules, thus dictating heavy expenditures in newspapers. Finally, auto makers supplement their general, national appeals with hard-sell advertising at the local level. The newspaper advertising of each national advertiser has its own specific objectives. The opportunity for couponing, introductory messages to a broad audience, and supplemental advertising to markets inadequately covered by national advertising schedules are other reasons why national advertisers choose newspapers. Figure 8–2 shows the top 100 national newspaper advertisers for 1985.

Despite substantial increases in national advertisers' use of newspapers, some newspaper media planners remain unsophisticated. There are two mistakes frequently made by media planners. First, they often ignore duplicated coverage by two dailies; that is, by totaling the morning and evening readership, they may grossly inflate actual reach (see Figure 8–3). For example, a media planner using data from the *Morning Sun* and the *Evening Herald* may overestimate coverage by figuring on 86 percent reach when the actual unduplicated coverage is 57 percent.

A second major error made by newspaper media planners is using metro area coverage as the basis for media planning. In many large markets, metro area coverage ignores the growing, affluent suburbs. Often one or more suburban daily or weekly newspaper, in combination with a daily newspaper, gives better coverage of the *total* market than the traditional morning/evening metropolitan newspaper. However, few national media planners give adequate consideration to the suburban press.

National Advertising and the Newspaper Advertising Bureau.[1] Since the late 1970s, newspapers have become aggressive in their efforts to increase national advertising. The Newspaper Advertising Bureau, a nonprofit sales and research organization, has been active in promoting newspapers to national advertisers. Among its major services are the one-order/one-bill placement service; Newsplan, a national advertising newspaper discount and research plan; and NCN, a newspaper co-op network. (Cooperative or co-op advertising is more fully described in the next section.) The major services of the Newspaper Advertising Bureau are given below.

NAB Placement Service. The NAB placement service makes it possible for national advertisers to place **inserts** (advertisements usually prepared by the advertiser) in most U.S. daily newspapers. The combined circulation of participating dailies is over 59 million; for Sunday papers, the circulation figure is 56 million. Over half of the participating Sunday papers can distribute an insert in less than full-run quantities, and about three quarters of these will accept an insert with an attached product sample. The service handles all paperwork, makes reservations, issues insertion orders, provides proof-of-performance tear sheets, forwards payment to each newspaper in the schedule and furnishes the advertiser

---

[1] The information included in this section was provided by the Newspaper Advertising Bureau.

FIGURE 8–2 Top 100 National Newspaper Advertisers, 1985

Rank		1985 Investments	1984 Investments
1.	General Motors Corp.	$140,979,000	$109,359,000
2.	Philip Morris Cos.	78,031,000	69,023,000
3.	Ford Motor Co.	77,295,000	62,063,000
4.	R. J. Reynolds Industries	73,321,000	101,990,000
5.	American Telephone & Telegraph Co.	57,210,000	58,200,000
6.	Chrysler Corp.	42,000,000	34,962,000
7.	International Business Machines	30,610,000	36,036,000
8.	People Express Airlines, Inc.	29,212,000	8,953,000
9.	B.A.T. Industries (Batus Inc.)	28,425,000	25,317,000
10.	Eastern Air Lines, Inc.	24,838,000	18,654,000
11.	Pan-American World Airways, Inc.	21,218,000	11,395,000
12.	CBS Inc.	20,936,000	21,519,000
13.	Trans World Airlines, Inc.	20,870,000	21,436,000
14.	Toyota Motor Sales, U.S.A., Inc.	20,761,000	14,913,000
15.	United Airlines, Inc.	19,987,000	6,112,000
16.	RCA Corp.	19,537,000	36,962,000
17.	American Airlines, Inc. (AMR Corp.)	19,534,000	13,496,000
18.	Capital Cities/ABC Inc.	18,168,000	16,155,000
19.	Mercedes-Benz of North America	18,008,000	6,545,000
20.	Delta Air Lines, Inc.	17,116,000	26,331,000
21.	Northwest Orient Airlines	16,851,000	10,265,000
22.	Nissan Motor Co.	16,504,000	13,170,000
23.	U.S. Government	15,826,000	16,797,000
24.	NYNEX Corp.	15,133,000	11,781,000
25.	Texas Air Corp.	15,075,000	17,636,000
26.	American Express Co.	14,864,000	11,481,000
27.	Loews Corp.	13,815,000	17,095,000
28.	GTE Corp.	13,665,000	11,631,000
29.	Time, Inc.	13,592,000	13,319,000
30.	Norwegian Caribbean Lines	11,948,000	11,112,000
31.	Xerox Corp.	11,351,000	8,595,000
32.	Volkswagenwerk AG	10,966,000	11,051,000
33.	Liberty Travel, Inc.	10,902,000	7,880,000
34.	Ameritech	10,829,000	11,110,000
35.	General Electric Co.	10,332,000	14,984,000
36.	Honda Motor Co.	10,331,000	9,001,000
37.	American Motors Corp.	9,902,000	7,572,000
38.	Peugeot Motors of America	9,799,000	3,140,000
39.	Volvo North American Corp.	8,970,000	5,599,000
40.	Jaguar Cars Inc.	8,810,000	6,353,000
41.	United Technologies Corp.	8,807,000	7,283,000
42.	Cunard Line Ltd.	8,791,000	9,839,000
43.	Beatrice Companies, Inc.	8,773,000	12,340,000
44.	Republic Airlines, Inc.	8,352,000	9,165,000
45.	Brown-Forman Inc.	8,187,000	4,791,000
46.	Apple Computer, Inc.	8,139,000	8,026,000
47.	MCI Communication Corp.	7,782,000	3,491,000
48.	Pacific Telesis Group	7,706,000	5,142,000
49.	Mobile Corp.	7,668,000	6,757,000
50.	B.M.W. of North America Inc.	7,594,000	6,109,000

FIGURE 8-2 *(concluded)*

51.	Procter & Gamble Co.	7,345,000	6,547,000
52.	Southwestern Bell Corp.	7,286,000	5,798,000
53.	Abernathy & Closter Ltd.	7,229,000	2,070,000
54.	Grandmet USA, Inc.	7,101,000	12,842,000
55.	Seagram Company Ltd.	7,054,000	9,426,000
56.	Franklin Mint Corp.	6,960,000	6,654,000
57.	Coca-Cola Co.	6,941,000	6,747,000
58.	Pleasant Hawaiian Holidays	6,901,000	6,101,000
59.	Bell South Corp.	6,820,000	7,260,000
60.	Piedmont Aviation, Inc.	6,813,000	5,686,000
61.	Royal Caribbean Cruise Line	6,591,000	6,860,000
62.	Carnival Cruise Lines	6,506,000	5,129,000
63.	USAIR Group, Inc.	6,471,000	6,349,000
64.	Dart & Kraft, Inc.	6,433,000	6,919,000
65.	Princess Cruises	6,198,000	6,639,000
66.	Hyatt Corp.	5,990,000	11,762,000
67.	Epson America, Inc.	5,975,000	9,761,000
68.	Southwest Airlines Co.	5,953,000	4,109,000
69.	PepsiCo, Inc.	5,926,000	5,036,000
70.	Club Med, Inc.	5,865,000	5,208,000
71.	U.S. West, Inc.	5,722,000	4,981,000
72.	Hattori Corp. of America	5,638,000	5,181,000
73.	Anheuser-Busch Cos.	5,611,000	6,868,000
74.	May Department Stores Co.	5,609,000	3,480,000
75.	NEC Electronics Inc.	5,551,000	3,952,000
76.	Midway Airlines, Inc.	5,529,000	5,365,000
77.	Hearst Corp.	5,446,000	3,335,000
78.	Mitsubishi International	5,362,000	3,217,000
79.	Sitmar Cruises	5,158,000	9,731,000
80.	Carlson Companies, Inc.	5,123,000	1,650,000
81.	Mazda Motors of America (Central)	5,036,000	3,018,000
82.	Frost Co.	4,962,000	3,838,000
83.	Saab-Scania of America, Inc.	4,950,000	4,239,000
84.	Blue Shield of California	4,792,000	3,053,000
85.	Intl. Thomson Organization Ltd.	4,634,000	4,440,000
86.	Sundance Cruises	4,621,000	1,468,000
87.	Maytag Co.	4,481,000	3,565,000
88.	World Airways, Inc.	4,471,000	4,507,000
89.	Holland America Line-Westours	4,425,000	6,276,000
90.	Carter Hawley Hale Stores, Inc.	4,420,000	2,728,000
91.	Bell Atlantic Corp.	4,369,000	6,402,000
92.	Doubleday & Company, Inc.	4,342,000	5,263,000
93.	Subaru of America, Inc.	4,321,000	4,557,000
94.	Armstrong World Industries	4,218,000	1,537,000
95.	Alamo Rent A Car	4,195,000	1,175,000
96.	Rapid-American Corp.	4,183,000	3,615,000
97.	American Brands, Inc.	4,050,000	4,994,000
98.	Matsushita Electric Co.	4,046,000	3,217,000
99.	Transamerica Corp.	4,040,000	4,014,000
100.	Estee Lauder, Inc.	3,447,000	3,301,000
	Total top 100 newspaper advertisers		$1,384,425,908

SOURCE: *Marketing and Media Decisions*, June 1986. p. 56.

FIGURE 8–3   Newspaper Coverage and Duplication

	Total Circulation	Metro Circulation	Percent Metro Coverage	Unduplicated Coverage
Morning Sun	25,000	20,000	40%	40%
Evening Herald	30,000	23,000	46	17

with a single invoice. In addition, the service can be used by advertisers to plan insert programs by providing estimates of costs, specifications for the insert, and newspaper availabilities. Similar services are furnished to advertisers who wish to use multinewspaper **run of paper** (ROP) color ads (advertising placed at the discretion of the publisher).

NAB Newsplan. Newsplan is a cooperative agreement between NAB and over 1,000 newspapers (with 82 percent of total U.S. circulation) to allow national advertisers to earn annual discounts. In addition, Newsplan permits advertisers to use the expanded Standard Advertising Unit (SAU) system by allowing a single finished advertisement to be placed in up to 1,600 newspapers with a circulation equal to 98 percent of the U.S. total. Finally, Newsplan, through its CAN DO (Computer Analysed Newspaper Data On-Line) program furnishes a variety of research reports.

Advertising planned on an annual basis can accumulate space discounts. Space can be accumulated on the basis of column inches or modular units (e.g., half page, full page, etc.). At present, over 1,000 newspapers offer discounts of 10 to 30 percent, at cumulative volumes of 6, 13, 26, and 52 pages.

One of the most promising incentives for national advertisers to increase their level of newspaper advertising has been the adoption, in mid-1984, of a uniform method of selling ad space. Before the SAU system was put in place, newspapers sold space on an **agate-line** basis. An agate line is defined as a space $\frac{1}{14}$ inch deep by one column wide. Because wide variation existed in the number of columns printed on a page, the careful national or regional newspaper advertiser was forced to convert the agate-line costs to page (or part page) costs for each newspaper in the schedule.

Since the advent of the SAU system, advertisers now have a standard sizing system for all of the participating newspapers. See Figure 8–4 for a chart showing the present SAU ad sizes. The system accommodates both standardized (broadsheet) as well as tabloid-sized newspapers.

NAB provides a series of reports of net reach and frequency (CAN DO Reports) for virtually any newspaper schedule and/or geographic area,

FIGURE 8-4

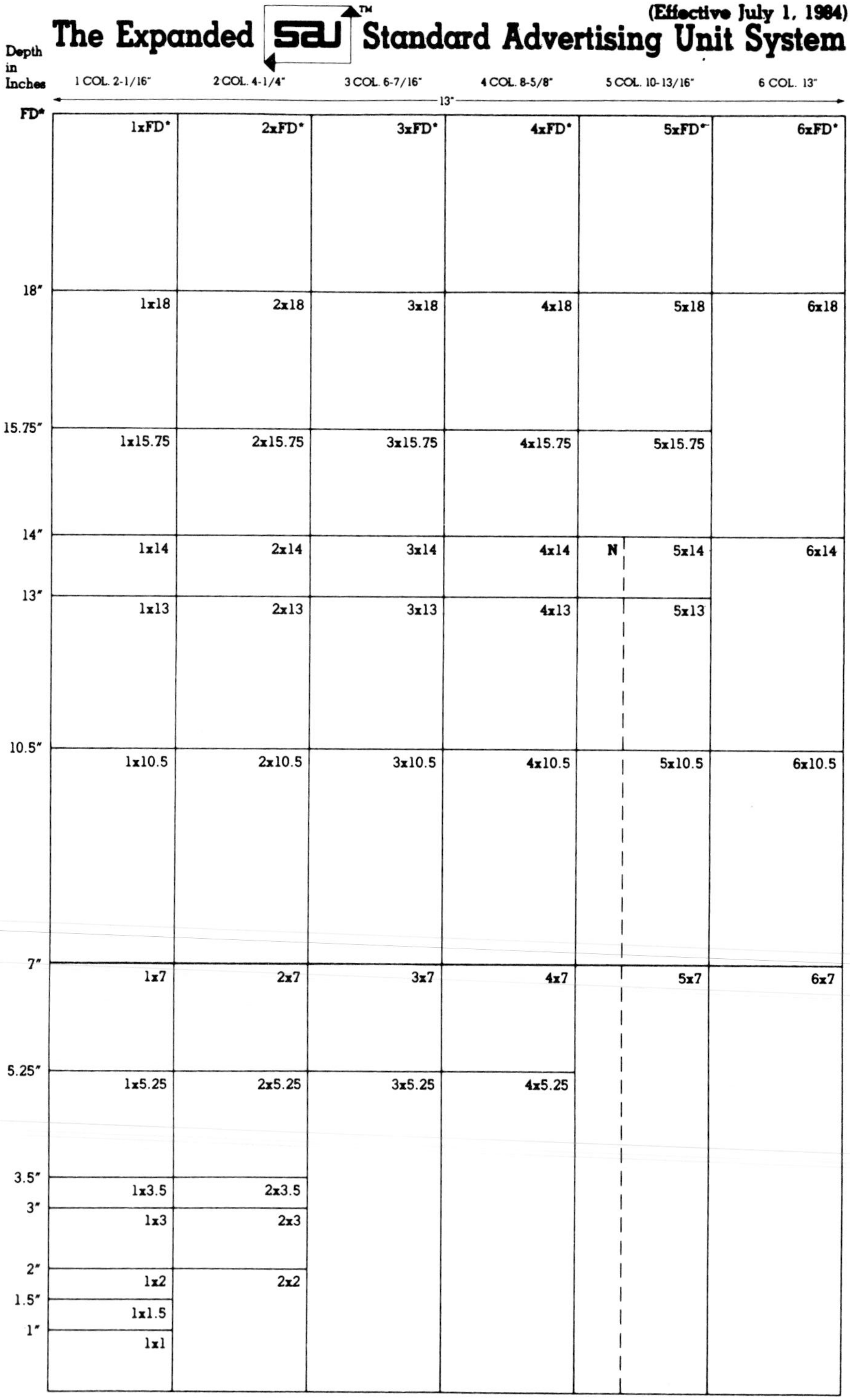

The Expanded **sau**™ Standard Advertising Unit System (Effective July 1, 1984)

Depth in Inches	1 COL. 2-1/16"	2 COL. 4-1/4"	3 COL. 6-7/16"	4 COL. 8-5/8"	5 COL. 10-13/16"	6 COL. 13"
FD*	1xFD*	2xFD*	3xFD*	4xFD*	5xFD*	6xFD*
18"	1x18	2x18	3x18	4x18	5x18	6x18
15.75"	1x15.75	2x15.75	3x15.75	4x15.75	5x15.75	
14"	1x14	2x14	3x14	4x14 N	5x14	6x14
13"	1x13	2x13	3x13	4x13	5x13	
10.5"	1x10.5	2x10.5	3x10.5	4x10.5	5x10.5	6x10.5
7"	1x7	2x7	3x7	4x7	5x7	6x7
5.25"	1x5.25	2x5.25	3x5.25	4x5.25		
3.5"	1x3.5	2x3.5				
3"	1x3	2x3				
2"	1x2	2x2				
1.5"	1x1.5					
1"	1x1					

13"

down to the county level. Audience figures can be furnished by age, sex, household income, or household size. The reports can be obtained from NAB at cost and can be routed through the advertiser's own computer terminal. In addition, these reports can furnish **cost-per-thousand** information for a particular newspaper audience.

In addition to the CAN DO reports, NAB offers a variety of annual reports prepared by its Economic and Media Analysis unit. A complete listing of these reports can be obtained from NAB.

Advertisers and advertising agencies can place dealer listing co-op ads through NAB for any number of markets. Benefits from the NCN placement include all those of any co-op program, plus improved capability to use co-op in test marketing, product inventory management, and the one-order/one-bill features of Newsplan.

Cooperative Advertising. Another advertising category, a hybrid with aspects of both local and national advertising, is *cooperative advertising,* or simply "co-op." Co-op expenditures are currently estimated at more than $10 billion, and about 70 percent of this is spent on newspaper advertising.[2]

The concept of co-op advertising is simple. National advertisers pay a percentage of retailer scheduled advertising, usually 50 percent or more. Co-op has obvious advantages for participating retailers. It helps to pay the retailer's advertising bill, and it often furnishes advertising aids that include professionally prepared advertising layouts. Less obvious but no less real are the advantages to national advertisers:

1. Financial savings. The national advertiser is able to stretch the media budget by splitting the cost of local advertising with a retailer and placing the advertising at local rates.
2. Localization of promotion. Co-op advertising allows the national advertiser to provide a local tie-in with each market. This market-by-market approach enables consumers to identify not only with the national brand but also with the local distributor. In addition, it permits more price advertising and the advertising of unique services, which are provided by dealers in one area but are not available throughout the country.
3. Strengthening local distribution. Done properly, a co-op program allows the national advertiser to demonstrate support to its retailers. It may also be used to develop coordinated merchandising programs for sales and special promotions between national and local advertising.

A major problem of co-op advertising is that national advertisers

---

[2] "Co-op's Quiet Revolution," *Marketing and Media Decisions,* November 1983, p. 148.

must control expenditures. The national advertisers must make certain that co-op dollars are spent properly, that the ads actually ran, and that the rate fairly reflects the retailer's cost.

One form of co-op fraud is called **double billing.** Double billing occurs when retailers request an advertising allowance from the national advertiser greater than what the retailer actually paid for the advertising. The term *double billing* is used because such retailers send national advertisers dummy (or double) bills showing an amount greater than the retailer actually paid. The national advertiser then reimburses the local advertiser based on this fraudulent bill. The retailer thus obtains a reduced price (or even free) advertisement plus extra cash. Although double billing is uncommon, national advertisers should take steps to ensure that they are not victimized by this practice. The usual procedure is to have the newspaper send a copy of the advertisement (called a **tearsheet**) to ensure its publication and some type of rate verification.

All forms of co-op fraud are estimated to have an annual value of one half of 1 percent (0.5 percent) of co-op expenditures. At the current annual rate of $10 billion, the estimated level of fraudulent co-op practices is still $50 million.

Large co-op advertisers often hire an independent firm to audit the expenditure of co-op dollars. The largest and oldest of these, **Advertising Checking Bureau, Inc.,** was founded in 1963 (see Figure 8–5). Of the 10,000 or so co-op advertising programs in the United States, about 1,400 are audited externally.

The national advertiser engaging in co-op must comply with Federal Trade Commission regulations, which require that expenditures for co-op advertising be distributed to retailers on a basis proportionate to the volume of the goods they purchase. Despite the problems that national advertisers encounter in utilizing co-op advertising, it is an alternative worth considering, especially when newspaper advertising is expected to be a major feature of a national campaign.

In recent years, the number of co-op offers and the number of companies offering co-op arrangements have grown tremendously. To make retailers aware of co-op opportunities, several reference books have been compiled to outline the sources and types of available co-op plans. Local media space and time salespeople also find that these catalogs of co-op plans can be invaluable in gaining additional advertising from retailers. Figure 8–6 shows a typical listing from one of the standard co-op guides.

Figure 8–7 shows the form suggested by the Newspaper Advertising Bureau to aid retailers in obtaining reimbursement of advertising dollars. It is important to emphasize the term *cooperative* in this type of advertising. Cooperative advertising can be beneficial to media, national advertisers, and retailers. However, to carry out its mission effectively, it must be planned with the same types of marketing objectives and advertising strategy that are supplied to other forms of advertising.

FIGURE 8–5   The Advertising Checking Bureau

If your Co-op program's a circle of frustration, let ACB run it – and make more money for you!

Problems with Billings? Rate verification? Paying? Conformance? Hours and hours of time spent by too many people trying to make your Co-op work better? And those hidden costs on top of it all—how much do *they* run?

Let ACB take over and change frustration into success! ACB will do *all* the nitty-gritty work for you—the planning, checking, auditing, paying and reporting.

And ACB will give you complete Co-op control for far less than doing it yourself.

You see, we're the largest, most experienced Co-op audit, payment and verification service in the country, handling more than 600 plans, processing more than one million claims every year.

So break the circle of Co-op frustration and let your Co-op make money for you. Call your nearest ACB representative. Or, if you'd like more information first, send for our comprehensive Co-op Booklet 500.

You can't beat experience.

 The ADVERTISING CHECKING BUREAU, INC.

Call your nearest ACB office.
NEW YORK: 2 Park Avenue, 10016; Phone 212/685-7300
CHICAGO: 434 South Wabash Avenue, 60605; Phone 312/922-2841
COLUMBUS, OHIO: 941 North High Street, 43201; Phone 614/294-4761
MEMPHIS: 52 South Second Street, 38103; Phone 901/526-3281
SAN FRANCISCO: 1453 Mission Street, 94103; Phone 415/626-6546
ORLANDO: 1010 Executive Center Drive, 32803; Phone 305/898-7680

SOURCE: Advertising Checking Bureau

FIGURE 8–6 Example Listings from a Co-op Guide

The Manhattan Shirt Company—John Henry
1271 Avenue of the Americas
New York NY 10020

Contact
Katherine Klinke; Bruce P. Fogwell, Vice President Advertising and Public Relations
(212) 265-3700

Retailer Co-op Plan

Products
Sportswear for men; dress shirts.

Trademarks
"John Henry".

Eligible media
Radio; TV; newspaper; weekly newspaper; Christmas catalog.
Other media require prior approval.

Timing
Program: Calendar year
Accrual: Previous calendar year
Claim: Within 30 days of ad run

Accrual
2½% of net purchases.

Participation
50-50.
Lowest earned rate.

Alberto-Culver Company
2525 Armitage Avenue
Melrose Park IL 60160

Contact
Sales Manager
(312) 450-3000

Retailer Co-op Plan

Products
Health and beauty aids.

Trademarks
VO5 Hairdressing; VO5 Hair Spray; VO5 Shampoo; VO5 Hot Oil; VO5 Hot Protein Pac; Get Set Setting Lotion; FDS; Command Hair Spray; New Dawn; For Brunettes Only Haircoloring.

Eligible media
Radio; TV; newspaper; weekly newspaper.
Other media require prior approval.

Timing
Accrual: Calendar year quarters
Advertising: Each calendar year quarter

Accrual
Varies from promotion to promotion. See sales rep for exact details.

Participation
100%.

Royal Insurance
Corporate Communications Dept.
150 William St.
New York NY 10038

Contact
Marianne Hughes
(212) 553-4075

Agent Co-op Plan
Complete Application/Media Plan and Agreement & submit to mktg. rep.

Products
Insurance.

Trademarks
Royal Insurance.

Eligible media
Radio; newspaper; magazine; direct mail; outdoor; printed sales aids; special promotional items.

Timing
Program: Calendar year
Accrual: Calendar year
Advertising: Calendar year
Claim: Within 45 days of ad run

Accrual
$1,000.00 per agent.

Advertising specifications
Trademark name must be prominent.
Broadcast ads must mention tradename at least twice.

Media requirements
Newspaper: Paid circulation; audited circulation.
Weekly newspaper: Paid circulation; audited circulation.
Catalog: Christmas catalog paid at fixed rate.

Reimbursement method
Check.

Claim documentation
Radio: Debit memo or invoice from advertiser; station affidavit; script.
TV: Debit memo or invoice from advertiser; station affidavit; script.
Newspaper: Debit memo or invoice from advertiser; full page tearsheet.
Weekly newspaper: Debit memo or invoice from advertiser; full page tearsheet.
Catalog: Debit memo or invoice from advertiser; complete copy of piece.

Claim address
"John Henry" Design Collections
c/o The Advertising Checking Bureau
P.O. Box 330
New York NY 10001

Advertising specifications
Minimum size: 2 col. inch.
Only advertising material supplied by manufacturer may be used.

Media requirements
Radio: Prior approval required.
TV: Prior approval required.

Advertising aids
Print elements.

Reimbursement method
Check.

Claim documentation
Radio: Paid media invoice; station affidavit; script.
TV: Paid media invoice; station affidavit; script.
Newspaper: Paid media invoice; full page tearsheet.
Weekly newspaper: Paid media invoice; full page tearsheet.

Claim address
Send claim to manufacturer's local representative.

Participation
50-50.
Lowest earned rate.
May include: space or time only.

Advertising specifications
Prior approval required for advertising material not supplied by manufacturer.

Media requirements
Radio: Serving retailer's primary trading area.
Newspaper: Serving retailer's primary trading area.
Magazine: Prior approval required.
Outdoor: Prior approval required.

Advertising aids
Print elements; special promotional items.

Reimbursement method
Check
Minimum reimbursement $50.00.

Claim documentation
Radio: Paid media invoice; manufacturer's claim form; ANA/RAB—electronic tearsheet.
Newspaper: Full page tearsheet; manufacturer's claim form.
Weekly newspaper: Full page tearsheet; manufacturer's claim form.

Claim address
Attn: Marianne Hughes
Royal Insurance
Corporate Communications Dept.
150 William St.
New York 4, NY 10038

SOURCE: SRDS Co-op Source Directory, no. 2 (Winter 1984–1985).

FIGURE 8–7   Cooperative Advertising Claim

Collect co-op money using a form like this

Cooperative
Advertising Claim

To:
Co-op Auditing Dept.
Nordstrom Manufacturing Co.
1435 Sanders St.
Bell City, Ohio 06512

From:
Frank's Appliance Store
185 Madison St.
Lebanon, Missouri
61202

We submit the following cooperative advertising claim in accordance with the terms of your cooperative advertising program. Proof of advertising is enclosed in the form of duplicate bills and newspaper tear sheets.

Your prompt issuance of a credit or a check covering payment of this claim is expected and will enable us to continue and extend use of your cooperative advertising program.

Newspaper	Date of Advertisement	Space Used	Net Rate	Total Cost	Vendor's Co-op Cost
Lebanon Daily Record	April 15, 1980	80 inches	$5.00 per inch	$400.00	$400.00

I certify that the above is billed at my exact LOWEST NET RATE, computed after all normally earned discounts and expected rebates—and that the amount billed does not include (1) production costs, (2) special or preferred position premiums. If any further discounts, or rebates, other than those already computed, are earned by us for space used, your share will be promptly refunded.

Date   May 3, 1980

Signature   Frank W. Wilson

SOURCE: Newspaper Advertising Bureau, *Newspaper Advertising Planbook*, 1980, p. 14.

Classified Advertising.   A final category of newspaper advertising is classified advertising. While everyone is familiar with the "want ad" section of the newspaper, few realize its importance. It is estimated that for a daily newspaper with 75,000 in paid circulation, classified advertising provides almost 20 percent of total revenue, or about $3.6 million per year. This figure is not quite half (43 percent) of the paper's retail advertising revenues and over three times the amount it receives in national advertising. Further, classified ad revenues are earned at lower cost than national advertising. The three major types of classified advertisers are *help wanted, real estate,* and *automotive;* together these three produce about 90 percent of newspapers' classified revenues. In most papers, advertisers have the option of planning all-text notices or display ads within the classified section.

Major Advertising Considerations for Newspapers

As we have pointed out, the newspaper is an extremely adaptable medium for advertisers. The advertising community's respect for the medium is reflected not only in the billions of dollars that advertisers spend in newspapers but also in the number and diversity of the advertisers that regularly use newspapers as a primary or secondary advertising vehicle. Nevertheless, before investing in the medium, advertisers need to consider certain major characteristics of newspapers.

Pro-Newspaper.   As an advertising medium, newspapers have a number of advantages.

Audience Coverage.   Newspaper penetration covers all strata of society with the exception of the very young and the very poor. In some major markets, newspapers cover as many as 70 percent of all households. The typical daily newspaper reader spends an average of 44 minutes a day reading one or more newspapers. Newspapers provide an excellent vehicle of high-intensity coverage for product introductions and sales.

Flexibility.   As advertisers increasingly develop localized market plans, the newspaper offers the ability to reach customers on a market-by-market basis with messages designed specifically for local conditions. Because of its short production closing deadlines, the newspaper can be used to tie in advertising messages with changing market conditions and current news and sports events.

Editorial Association.   Advertisers can associate their products with a section of the newspaper designed for a particular audience. By placing ads in various sections (financial, entertainment, sports, travel, food etc.), advertisers increase the chances of directing their messages to prospects.

Long Copy. Newspapers allow advertisers to provide in-depth product information at prices impossible in most other media. Broadcasting and outdoor advertising restrict copy length, while magazines are not a practical advertising alternative for many advertisers.

Disadvantages. Newspapers also have a number of disadvantages.

Lack of Audience Selectivity. A few major newspapers have made progress in audience segmentation by offering advertisers some simple circulation breakouts. Most of these attempts have involved only geographic buys rather than the demographic segmentation many advertisers need. Many newspaper executives think that greater utilization of the computer and the natural advantage newspapers have in controlling their own distribution will lead to audience segmentation of circulation in the future. However, today the newspaper is not a totally acceptable medium for advertisers that need to reach specific audiences.

Clutter. The term *clutter* is usually associated with television. However, while television normally schedules 15 to 25 percent of its time for nonprogram content, advertising space takes up more than 60 percent of the average daily newspaper. In recent years, studies have indicated that the adult reader usually spends less than 45 minutes with the newspaper, so a newspaper advertisement must compete with many other messages during a relatively short time.

Lack of Quality Color Reproduction. In the years since the advent of offset printing, newspapers have made strides in improving color reproduction. However, the quality of color advertising is still uneven from newspaper to newspaper. Lack of guaranteed color quality reduces the use of newspapers by some major national advertisers and causes others to use preprinted supplements and inserts as alternatives to advertising within the newspaper itself. Advertisers that need both local coverage and high-quality color have used other media, such as outdoor, direct-mail, and regional editions of magazines.

Buying Difficulties. In spite of recent industry efforts to improve efficiency, national advertisers still experience difficulty in purchasing newspaper advertising. Programs such as those of NAB and attempts to standardize rate cards have only met with limited success. More work remains to be done before national advertisers can utilize this medium with the facility available from other media. Until then, newspapers will remain a medium used primarily by local advertisers.

NEWSPAPER RATE STRUCTURE

National Rates versus Local Rates

Most newspapers have a different rate structure than that used by the majority of other advertising media. Newspapers normally charge national advertisers significantly higher rates compared to local advertisers. The amount of the local-national rate difference varies from as little as 10 percent to as much as double the **local rate.** Regardless of the amount, the practice is prevalent; less than 100 daily newspapers (approximately 5 percent) offer a single rate schedule for national and local advertisers.

While some national advertisers are vocal in their opposition to the national-local rate differentiation, newspapers give several reasons for the practice. Most national advertising is placed through advertising agencies, which qualify for an agency discount, usually 15 percent (see Chapter 5 for a discussion of media discounts to agencies). In addition, a major portion of national advertising is solicited by media reps, who are normally paid a percentage of the space costs. Finally, newspapers argue that the national advertiser normally obtains full advantage of the entire circulation of a newspaper, while a local business may serve only a portion of a market. There is also the intangible factor that newspapers have long regarded local merchants as "their" customers, while they have seen national advertisers as outsiders—a perception that the national-local differentiation reinforces.

National advertisers have criticized the **rate differential** on the basis that they often receive fewer services from the newspaper than the local retailer who pays a reduced rate. Many critics of the higher national rate claim that it is self-defeating and has kept some national advertisers out of newspapers. In addition, many of the abuses of co-op advertising stem primarily from these higher costs to national advertisers. Finally, there is evidence that the gap between national and local rates is widening rather than narrowing.

Units of Purchase

The basic unit of purchase for newspaper space is the column-inch. This uniformity did not exist prior to the widespread adoption of the Standard Advertising Unit system in 1984. Before that time, agate-line units were typical, and buyers of newspaper advertising space needed to be aware of the differences between papers in number of columns per page as well as in number of lines per column in order to calculate prices and estimate price comparisons. With SAU, every participating broadsheet newspaper has six *advertising* columns per page, and tabloid-sized papers have four. Thus, a column inch in any paper is identical in size to the column inch in any other paper, and each of the 57 different SAU sizes have uniform dimensions across all participating newspapers.

Open Rate versus Flat Rate

Newspaper rate schedules fall into one of two categories: open rate (also called sliding scale) or flat rate. An open-rate newspaper offers bulk discounts based on the amount of space purchased or the number of continuous weeks a product is advertised. Most metropolitan dailies offer some form of discount to their advertisers. A **flat-rate** paper charges the same price per column inch, regardless of the amount of space bought. The flat rate is most prevalent among weeklies and smaller daily newspapers. The newspaper whose rates are shown in Figure 8–8 charges a flat rate for display advertising. A flat-rate newspaper may use a local-national rate differentiation but give no discounts to either type of advertiser. It may also use either flat or open rates for its classified ad space.

Figure 8–8 also shows classified rates for a newspaper pricing this advertising space on an open-rate basis. Note that even after the advent of SAU sizing for display advertising, the agate line continues to be used at many newspapers for sizing and pricing classified ad space.

There is a legal question whether newspapers that use open-rate schedules are bound by the price-discrimination provision of the Robinson-Patman Act. Taking the position that they were, the Federal Trade Commission in 1977 brought suit against the *Los Angeles Times* for price differences contained in the *Times* rate schedule. In July 1982, under a different set of FTC commissioners, the commission officially dropped the matter.

It is premature to relegate this legal question to a dusty shelf for historical footnotes. Administrations, FTC appointees, and fashions in the interpretation of federal antitrust law come and go. The Robinson-Patman Act requires, among other things, that interstate sellers charge uniform prices to all buyers except when the *seller* can show that different prices are justified by proportionally different costs or when different prices represent a "good-faith" effort to meet competition. A story in *Advertising Age*[3] called the application of the Act to newspapers the worst scare to free-market newspaper ad pricing in years.

---

[3] "FTC Bows Out of Ad Rate Foray in 'Times' Case," *Advertising Age,* July 12, 1982, p. 2.

Flat Rate for Display Advertising	Open Rate for Classified Advertising

Chattanooga

Hamilton County—Map Location H-5
See SRDS Consumer market map and data at beginning of the state.

NEWS-FREE PRESS
TIMES

P.O. Box 1447, 400 E. 11th St., Chattanooga, TN 37401-1447.
Phone 615-756-6900, Telecopier, 615-756-2436.

Media Code 1 144 1025 1.00   **Mid 017391-000**
News-Free Press—EVENING AND SUNDAY.
Times—MORNING (ex. Sunday).
Member: INAME; NAB, INC.

1. PERSONNEL
Publisher—Roy McDonald (News-Free Press).
President—Frank McDonald (News-Free Press).
President—A. William Holmberg (Times).
Advertising Director—Frank McDonald.
National Representative—Lola Robinson.

2. REPRESENTATIVES and/or BRANCH OFFICES
Landon Associates, Inc.

3. COMMISSION AND CASH DISCOUNT
15% to agencies; 2% 15th following month.

4. POLICY-ALL CLASSIFICATIONS
30-day notice given of any rate revision.
Alcoholic beverage advertising accepted mornings (Times) only. Not in evening or Sunday editions.
ADVERTISING RATES
Effective October 1, 1985.
Received September 6, 1985.

5. BLACK/WHITE RATES

	Morn.	Eve.	M&E or Sun
SAU flat, per inch	12.60	15.40	21.36

Inches charged full depth: col. 21.25; pg. 127.5; dbl truck 276.25.

7. COLOR RATES AND DATA
Use b/w rate plus the following applicable costs:

	b/w 1 c	b/w 2 c	b/w 3 c
Morn. or Eve, extra	300.00	432.00	564.00
M&E Comb., extra	540.00	780.00	1,020.00
Sunday, extra	540.00	780.00	1,020.00

Closing dates: 7 days in advance for reservations. Printing material 2 days in advance daily; 4 days in advance Sunday.

11. SPECIAL DAYS/PAGES/FEATURES
Best Food Days: Wednesday Eve.-Thursday Morn. Travel Resort pages, Garden Pages, Book page Sunday/Saturday morning.

12. R.O.P. DEPTH REQUIREMENTS
Ads over 20 inches deep will be charged as a full column.

13. CONTRACT AND COPY REGULATIONS
See Contents page for location of regulations—items 1, 10 thru 14, 16, 18, 21, thru 25, 27, 31 thru 35.

14. CLOSING TIMES
Order and material 2 working days before publication date.

15. MECHANICAL MEASUREMENTS
For complete, detailed production information, see SRDS Print Media Production Data.
PRINTING PROCESS: Photo Composition Direct Letterpress.
6/13/18—6 cols/ea 13 picas/18 pts betw col.
Inches charged full depth: col. 21.25; pg. 127.5; dbl truck 276.25.

Dallas Times Herald

1101 Pacific Ave., Dallas, TX 75202.

Media Code 1 145 2600 7.00   **Mid 017440-000**
ALL DAY, SATURDAY MORNING AND SUNDAY.
Member: INAME; NAB, Inc.: ABC Coupon Distribution Verification Service.

1. PERSONNEL
Pub & Chief Ex. Officer—Arthur E. Wible.
Vice-Pres. Adv.—Robert A. Sproat.
National Adv. Director—Joe Allen.

2. REPRESENTATIVES and/or BRANCH OFFICES
Times Mirror National Marketing.
Towmar—Mexico.

3. COMMISSION AND CASH DISCOUNT
15% to agencies; no cash discount.

4. POLICY-ALL CLASSIFICATIONS
30-day notice given of any rate revision.
Alcoholic beverage advertising accepted daily and Sunday.
ADVERTISING RATES
Effective January 1, 1986.
Received November 8, 1985.

5. BLACK/WHITE RATES

	Daily	Sun.
SAU open, per inch	89.50	93.00

Inches charged full depth: col. 21; pg. 126.
FREQUENCY CONTRACT RATES
All ads must be 10 inches or greater within 1 year.

	Daily	Sun.
5 times	88.00	91.50
10 times	87.50	91.00
20 times	86.50	89.50
30 times	85.50	88.50
40 times	84.50	87.50
50 times	83.00	86.50
75 times	81.00	84.00
100 times	79.50	82.00
150 times	75.50	80.00

BULK INCH CONTRACT
Ads must be 10 inches or greater within 1 year.

	Daily	Sun.
135"	88.50	92.00
270"	88.00	91.00
405"	87.50	89.50
540"	87.00	88.50
1,000"	85.50	87.50
1,300"	84.00	86.50
1,750"	83.00	85.50
2,350"	82.00	84.50
3,125"	81.00	83.00
4,150"	75.50	78.50
5,500"	70.00	73.00
7,325"	69.00	72.00
9,750"	68.00	71.00
13,000"	67.00	70.00

To be eligible for Frequency Contract Rates or Bulk Contract Inch Rates, advertisers must be on contract and any contract revisions must cover same period as original contract. Frequency Contract Rates and Bulk Contract Inch Rates are not interchangeable.
NEWSPLAN—SAU

Pages	Daily	Sun.	Inches
6	85.00	87.50	756
13	82.00	85.50	1,638
26	68.50	72.50	3,276
52	68.00	70.50	6,552
65	67.50	69.50	8,190
78	67.00	69.00	9,828
91	66.50	68.50	11,466
104	66.00	68.00	13,104
130	65.00	67.00	16,380
156	64.00	66.00	19,656

See Newsplan Contract and Copy Regulations—items 1, 2, 3, 4, 5, 6, 7, 9, 10, 11, 13, 14, 18, 19, 21, 22, 23, 24, 30, 31.

5a. ZONE EDITIONS

	Extra per inch
Plano/Allen	15.30
Richardson	20.00
Northwest	14.70
North	17.65
East	17.65
Northeast	15.90
Southeast	14.70

SOURCE: Standard Rate and Data Service.

Short Rate versus Rebate

Normally newspaper advertising contracts are price-setting devices based on the anticipated advertising of a firm in a particular newspaper. In a flat-rate newspaper, this is no problem since each column inch of advertising is purchased at the same rate. In an open-rate newspaper, the newspaper and the advertiser agree on a rate to be paid for some period, usually a year, then make necessary adjustments at the end of the contract period. Figure 8–9 demonstrates typical short-rate and rebate situations.

In example 1, advertiser A originally agreed to pay the maximum column-inch rate of $23. However, at the end of the contract period, that advertiser had qualified for the lower $19.55 rate, and the newspaper

---

FIGURE 8–9   Short Rate and Rebate: Newspaper XYZ, Open-Rate Pricing

Number of Column Inches Purchased in One Year	Cost per Column Inch	Percent Discount
0–755	$23.00	0
756–1,637 (6+ pages)	21.85	5
1,638–3,275 (13+ pages)	20.70	10
3,276–6,551 (26+ pages)	19.55	15
6,552–13,104 (52–104 pages)	17.71	23

Example 1: Rebate
Advertiser A contracts for maximum rate and uses 26 pages:

3,276	Column inches used
× $23.00	Estimated contract cost
$75,348.00	Amount paid
3,276	Column inches used
× $19.55	Actual cost
$64,045.80	Amount owed
$75,348.00	
− 64,045.80	
$11,302.20	Rebate

Example 2: Short Rate
Advertiser B contracts for minimum rate and uses 26 pages:

3,276	Column inches used
× $17.71	Estimated contract cost
$58,017.96	Amount paid
3,276	Column inches used
× $19.55	Actual cost
$64,045.80	Amount owed
$64,045.80	
− 58,017.96	
$ 6,027.84	Short rate

owed the advertiser a rebate of $11,302.20. In example 2, advertiser B failed to qualify for the rate ($17.71/column inch) agreed on at the beginning of the contract period. At the end of the period, advertiser B had to make up the difference between what should have been paid and what was actually paid. This difference, a **short rate,** was $6,027.84.

Run-of-Paper and Special Rates

Most newspaper space is bought on a ROP basis. ROP simply means that the newspaper may place the advertisement wherever it wishes. Advertisers often request a particular position, and when possible, the newspaper will try to accommodate them. Remember that it is to the newspaper's advantage to give an advertiser the best possible position to make the advertising effective.

In addition to ROP, many newspapers charge special rates for placing advertising in certain sections or on especially visible portions of a page. Advertisers may have to pay a premium to guarantee space in, say, the sports section. Or newspapers may charge extra for guaranteeing placement at the top of a column next to a news story (generally known as full position). The types of premium rates vary with individual newspapers, and the advertiser must check rate cards or inquire as to the availability of such special rates.

Combination Rates

As the number of major cities with jointly owned morning and evening newspapers increases, advertisers find that they are often able (or required) to purchase space in a combination of these newspapers. Generally the space must be bought in consecutive editions and the same space and copy must be used. For the advertiser, the combination rate usually offers significant savings over buying space in the two newspapers individually.

AUDITING THE NEWSPAPER AUDIENCE

Since newspapers set their rates largely according to circulation, it is important for advertisers to know that newspaper circulation figures are correct. Beginning in 1914, the Audit Bureau of Circulations (ABC) has provided verified circulation figures for major newspapers and consumer magazines. The ABC report provides information not only concerning paid circulation, but also the circulation in city, trade, and other zones as well as the number of subscribers who received the newspaper at a discount and the newspapers sold at the newsstand versus subscription.

ABC issues two major reports. The Publisher's Statement is issued twice a year and covers the periods ending March 31 and September 30. The ABC Audit Report is issued annually after an on-premise audit of the publisher's circulation data. In addition, ABC also provides custom-order information on circulation, population, household, and demographic data for almost 2,000 magazines and newspapers through it *Circulation Data Bank Report.*

THE OUTLOOK

Move to the Suburbs

The movement to the suburbs during the last two decades has had profound effects on American culture. Education, housing, and transportation are only a few of the areas that have been changed by the transition from an urban to a suburban society. The traditional metropolitan daily newspaper has also been forced to adapt to this movement away from the inner city.

Long after the pattern of suburban living was established, the metropolitan daily continued to ignore the suburban population as a distinct audience. Local news coverage concentrated on city-wide issues, and the specific concerns of the suburbs were usually covered by small weeklies or not at all. This neglect was largely a result of financial considerations. National and large local advertisers, such as department stores, largely ignored the suburban press, and consequently, the metro newspapers saw no need to spend time and effort cultivating or competing for a market that advertisers felt the metro dailies were already reaching adequately.

In the last several years, however, the suburban market, and the suburban press serving it, have become increasingly difficult to ignore. Suburban readers are beginning to view themselves as part of a community distinct from the metropolitan area. They have problems unique to the suburbs, and they are turning to suburban newspapers as a supplementary source of information. From an advertising viewpoint, the market is simply too lucrative to overlook. As national advertisers turn their attention to local market strategies, they will treat the suburban audience as an audience separate from the larger metropolitan population.

Several large metropolitan newspapers are meeting the competition of the suburban press with zoned editions or local supplements for outlying areas. A combination of 30 weekly newspapers, called the Suburban Newspapers of Greater St. Louis, claims 93 percent coverage of the metropolitan market. In the future, the competition for the suburban audience will intensify as it becomes apparent that appealing to this group is the only way to maintain or increase newspaper circulation (and advertising revenues).

In the short term, the suburban press will remain a local, retailer-oriented medium. The daily metropolitan press will continue to increase the zoned distribution approach to keep national advertisers and bring small retailers into the fold. The suburban press will entice national advertisers with incentives such as an upscale audience, greater selectivity, and easier national buys through such representative organizations as the U.S. Suburban Press, Inc., which services suburban newspapers through a nationwide network (see Figure 8–10). USSPI represents 1,055 newspapers in 45 suburban market areas. Each of the participating suburban newspapers is audited, and all use the SAU system.

Local Market Research

Despite advertisers' massive investment in newspapers, the medium's research expenditure has been meager. In the past, newspapers often assumed that they were the only practical retail advertising vehicle and that there was therefore no reason to spend funds proving what to them was obvious. In recent years, however, other media—regional editions of national magazines, radio, and television—have started to compete for advertising dollars once conceded to newspapers.

As a result, newspapers have had to demonstrate their value compared to other media. When William Simmons' Three Sigma company contracted with 26 media clients, including eight newspapers in the New York area, for a local market comparison of the audiences of these media, many advertisers hoped that this would be the beginning of general syndicated research on a market-by-market basis.[4] In the future, advertisers will expect newspapers to provide comparable audience data similar to the data that have long been demanded of other media.

Unsuccessful efforts to develop a newspaper data bank indicate that the availability of broadly based newspaper audience data may be further from reality than advertisers would like. Despite efforts by the Audit Bureau of Circulations and other interested parties, collection of newspaper data remains a largely individualized enterprise, with some newspapers providing extensive audience and market data and others virtually none.

The Newspaper as a Delivery System

When discussing the newspaper as an advertising medium, we often overlook that fact that in addition to providing space for advertisements, the newspaper is also used as a delivery vehicle for separate material.

---

[4] "Media Research: The Trend Is to Local Multi-Media Studies," *Media Decisions*, February 1977, p. 68.

FIGURE 8–10   Rate Card of U.S. Suburban Press, Inc.

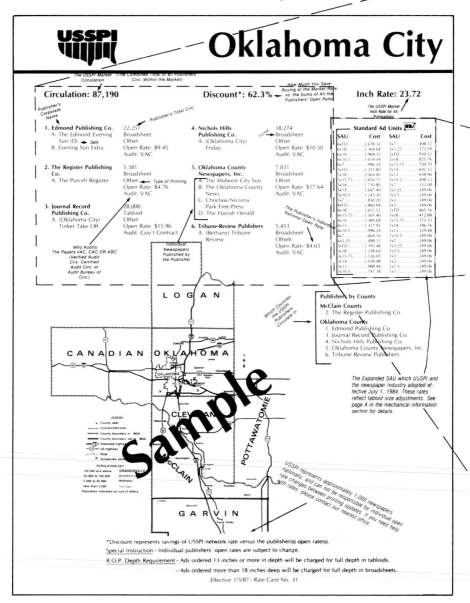

*Discount represents savings of USSPI network rate versus the publisher(s) open rate(s).

Special Instruction – Individual publishers' open rates are subject to change.

R.O.P. Depth Requirement – Ads ordered 13 inches or more in depth will be charged for full depth in tabloids.

— Ads ordered more than 18 inches deep will be charged for full depth in broadsheets.

Effective 1/5/87 – Rate Card No. 31

SOURCE: U.S. Suburban Press, Inc. (USSPI), Schaumberg, Illinois.

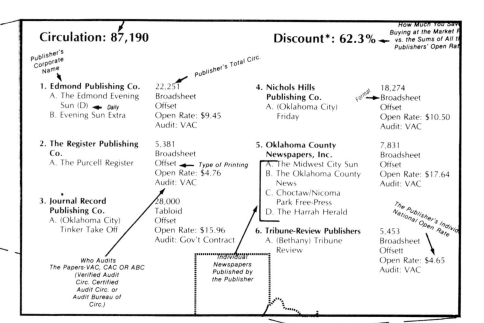

Circulation: 87,190

Discount*: 62.3% ← How Much You Save Buying at the Market Rate vs. the Sums of All the Publishers' Open Rates

Publisher's Corporate Name

Publisher's Total Circ.

1. Edmond Publishing Co.
  A. The Edmond Evening Sun (D) ← *Daily*
  B. Evening Sun Extra

22,251
Broadsheet
Offset
Open Rate: $9.45
Audit: VAC

2. The Register Publishing Co.
  A. The Purcell Register

5,381
Broadsheet
Offset ← *Type of Printing*
Open Rate: $4.76
Audit: VAC

3. Journal Record Publishing Co.
  A. (Oklahoma City) Tinker Take Off

28,000
Tabloid
Offset
Open Rate: $15.96
Audit: Gov't Contract

Who Audits
The Papers-VAC, CAC OR ABC
(Verified Audit
Circ. Certified
Audit Circ. or
Audit Bureau of
Circ.)

Individual
Newspapers
Published by
the Publisher

4. Nichols Hills Publishing Co. *Format*
  A. (Oklahoma City) Friday

18,274
→ Broadsheet
Offset
Open Rate: $10.50
Audit: VAC

5. Oklahoma County Newspapers, Inc.
  A. The Midwest City Sun
  B. The Oklahoma County News
  C. Choctaw/Nicoma Park Free-Press
  D. The Harrah Herald

7,831
Broadsheet
Offset
Open Rate: $17.64
Audit: VAC

6. Tribune-Review Publishers
  A. (Bethany) Tribune Review

The Publisher's Individual
National Open Rate

5,453
Broadsheet
Offsett
Open Rate: $4.65
Audit: VAC

Standard Ad Units 🆂🅰🆄

SAU	Cost	SAU	Cost
6xFD	2,678.32	3x7	498.12
6x18	2,364.64	3x5.25	373.59
6x14	1,964.32	2xFD	930.32
6x10.5	1,614.04	2x18	825.76
6x7	996.24	2x15.75	750.70
5xFD	2,325.80	2x14	692.32
5x18	2,064.40	2x13	658.96
5x15.75	1,876.75	2x10.5	498.12
5x14	1,730.80	2x7	332.08
5x13	1,647.40	2x5.25	249.06
5x10.5	1,245.30	2x3.5	249.06
5x7	830.20	2x3	249.06
4xFD	1,860.64	2x2	249.06
4x18	1,651.52	1xFD	465.16
4x15.75	1,501.40	1x18	412.88
4x14	1,384.64	1x15.75	375.35
4x13	1,317.92	1x14	346.16
4x10.5	996.24	1x13	329.48
4x7	664.16	1x10.5	249.06
4x5.25	498.12	1x7	249.06
3xFD	1,395.48	1x5.25	249.06
3x18	1,238.64	1x3.5	249.06
3x15.75	1,126.05	1x3	249.06
3x14	1,038.48	1x2	249.06
3x13	988.44	1x1.5	249.06
3x10.5	747.18	1x1	249.06

National advertisers can use preprinted inserts by providing either rolls of newsprint with their advertisement on one side or freestanding or loose inserts, which may vary from a single sheet to a 96-page booklet. In both cases, the insert has several advantages for the advertiser:

1. The advertiser can control the printing quality from newspaper to newspaper—a factor that may be very important when using color.
2. A national advertising supplement may be localized with the name of the individual retailer.
3. The space and production costs of inserts printed in bulk can be significantly lower compared to the costs of purchasing the same space in individual newspapers.
4. Inserts can provide coupons and long copy, which would be impractical or expensive if run as a regular advertisement.

Some newspapers offer zoning of insert distribution. This regionalization of circulation allows smaller retailers as well as national firms the opportunity to use inserts. Some newspapers are experimenting with the delivery of advertising material to nonsubscribing households. Since the newspapers already have distributors who pass each household, they can increase their profits by operating as a delivery agent to all households, not just subscribing households. This system also provides 100 percent household coverage for the advertiser, regardless of newspaper penetration. In the future, newspapers will provide means of delivering supplemental material that will give them an even greater advantage over their local media competitors.

Clouding this bright picture is the possibility that the courts may rule that newspapers are not eligible for favorable second-class postal rates when used to deliver products or samples. At the same time, newspapers are locked in a lively struggle with direct mailers over how much the latter should pay under third-class postal rates.

The Shopper

In the late 1960s the free delivery, all-advertising **shopper** was aggressively promoted in many markets. The early shoppers were either delivered to each household in a market or were available free through retail outlets, most of which were also advertisers. The initial reaction of newspapers was to ignore the shopper and hope it would go away. However, favorable public response as well as more sophisticated marketing by these publications has made them a viable competitor to newspapers in many markets.

In some instances, newspapers have started their own shoppers or have bought out competitors' publications in order to serve advertisers in both types of outlets. Harte-Hanks Communications, Inc., a major communication corporation with newspapers and broadcast stations throughout the country, has found shoppers (or "pennysavers" as it calls them) to be among its most profitable enterprises.

Shoppers promise extensive coverage at a very low cost to advertisers. They are unaudited, and so there are no circulation guarantees comparable to those of other media. As a matter of policy, many advertisers, particularly national firms, will not advertise in unaudited publications. Consequently, the shopper tends to be a local advertising vehicle whose success depends on the ability of the advertising sales force and the value of the local newspaper.

In recent years, the trend has been for shoppers to accompany the advertising with a limited amount of editorial material. Usually the material is more filler than meaningful information. However, some shoppers have actually evolved into regular weekly newspapers with a full news staff. One popular shopper format is the local television schedule. This gives the consumer a reason to pick up the shopper in the first place and increases the average life of the publication.

The Youth Market

One of the most discussed topics of the last several years has been how to get and keep the young adult reader. The ability to solve this problem successfully may determine the future of newspapers as a communications and advertising medium. Newspapers face two crucial problems in their quest for the youth market. First, young adults aged 18 to 34 represent a prime target for many advertisers. Second, the person who is not a regular newspaper reader by the age of 20 is probably not going to become one in later years. Newspapers have devoted considerable research to the problem of appealing to younger readers. Studies have indicated that features, how-to-do-it articles, and personality pieces (in addition to hard news) appeal to these readers. Despite efforts to alter content and format, newspaper readership among 18- to 34-year-olds declined by 10 percentage points between 1973 and 1985, from 67 percent to 57 percent.[5]

Economic Forces

The typical daily newspaper requires substantial amounts of both labor and capital. It is thus subject to economic forces in both categories of input. Newspapers employ over 450,000 people, many of whom are mem-

---

[5] Debbie Solomon, "Trends in Newspaper Readership," *Marketing and Media Decisions,* April 1986, p. 104.

bers of highly skilled trades and occupations. (This figure does not include the more than 1 million newspaper carriers who are considered contract workers.) And rapidly changing technology is creating obsolescence in much of the industry's plant and equipment. Together these factors place newspapers under especially strong cost pressures. At the same time, the major raw material used in newspaper publishing, newsprint, increased in price by 250 percent in the period from 1970 to 1981. While this steep rate of increase has moderated considerably since 1981, the accumulated price increases apply further pressure on newspaper profitability. Among the major media, only television time costs have increased at a greater rate than costs of newspaper advertising since 1970.

A final factor in this industry is a growing level of economic concentration. Group-owned daily newspapers increased in number by 17 percent from 1984 to 1985. This bought the total number of group-owned dailies in the United States to 1,186, representing 71 percent of U.S. daily newspaper circulation.[6]

The Electronic Newspaper

With the development of electronic editing, much of the production process has been moved from the back shop to the newsroom. Some newspaper executives foresee a day when newspapers will be delivered electronically to readers who use a video display terminal (VDT). Readers will then order only the portions they want to keep for future reference in the form of "hard copy."

Some people in the newspaper industry are also predicting the advent of more national newspapers with a basic national edition sent by satellite to many markets where local news and features can be added. *The Wall Street Journal* and *USA Today* are already doing this.

Such an electronic revolution has major implications for newspaper advertising. While the practical possibilities are many, let's look at one potential tie-in between advertising and the "electronic newspaper."

All of us are familiar with the coded symbols on most common consumer items. This Universal Product Code (UPC) was originally intended to facilitate inventory control and reduce labor costs at the retail level. However, the UPC may one day become the center of a marketing information system among retailers, distributors, manufacturers, advertising agencies, and the media. Figure 8–11 demonstrates a projected use of the UPC in such a network.

Here the UPC, in combination with other facilities, could go far beyond simple inventory control. Data reflecting a retailer's current

---

[6] American Newspaper Publishers Association, *'86 Facts about Newspapers*, p. 21.

FIGURE 8-11 Advertising and the Electronic Newspaper

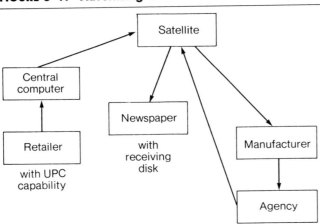

stock could constantly be coded into a central computer and printouts then transmitted to the manufacturer by either satellite or ordinary telephone lines. The manufacturer in consultation with its advertising agency could then adjust inventories and promotion to the current local market situation. The advertising agency could prepare advertisements and transmit them by satellite to a newspaper or other local medium equipped with a receiving disk. Advertisements in tomorrow's newspapers could be based on today's sales activity.

Extensive utilization of the UPC for implementing marketing strategy is still some years away. However, in certain test cities, marketing research is using the UPC as part of a realistic advertising measurement technique. One system provides a consumer panel with supermarket credit cards. The supermarkets are equipped with UPC scanners so that a continuing measurement of sales can be made. The system also allows matched subgroups of panelists to be reached with different television commercials through cut-ins and newspaper **split runs.** A split run is the placement of two versions of an ad in alternating copies of a single edition.

One variation on the theme of electronic newspapers is Videotext,[7] a system that supplied subscribing homes and businesses with news, electronic mail, personal banking, access to data banks, and a variety of other services. Some hailed the concept as one that would kill off traditional newspapers. Perhaps not surprisingly, several prominent newspaper publishers quickly adopted the concept and began to market videotext

---

[7] Also spelled Videotex.

systems. By early 1986, however, the Times Mirror Company folded its $15 million service, and the industry videotext leader, Knight Ridder Newspapers, wrote off its service because of poor financial performance despite a $52 million investment. In both instances, a combination of too-few customers using the system too infrequently produced operating losses too large for company management to accept.

The variations of electronic technology used for this and other purposes are limitless. However, both newspapers and advertisers must adjust to the era of electronic communication as the traditional boundaries between print and electronic media continue to disappear.

Despite the growing competition faced by newspapers and the many problems yet to be solved, the newspaper's future seems bright. The newspaper will maintain its predominant position as an advertising medium for some time to come.

REVIEW QUESTIONS

1. Briefly describe the advantage of newspapers as an advertising medium.
2. Discuss the major categories of newspaper advertising.
3. What is the Newspaper Advertising Bureau, and what are some of its services?
4. Discuss the role of cooperative advertising in newspapers.
5. How much would a 6-column, 14-inch ad cost at $10 SAU, per inch?
6. Briefly define the following:
   a. Flat rate.
   b. Short rate.
   c. SAU.
   d. ROP.
   e. ABC.
   f. ACB.
7. Discuss the national/local rate differentiation of newspapers from the perspective of newspaper publishers and from the point of view of national advertisers.
8. What are the implications of the Universal Product Code for newspaper advertising research?
9. How many of your classmates read a newspaper every day? Do you? If you do, what are the most important reasons for doing so? If you do not, what are the major reasons?
10. In spite of the efforts of NAB and others, national advertisers represent a small fraction of newspaper advertising revenues. Construct a list of the changes that the newspaper industry could make that would increase reve-

nue from national advertisers and explain how/why each change would be effective.

SUGGESTED ADDITIONAL READING

ALSOP, RONALD. "To Some Papers, Readership Is Not As Elementary As ABC." *The Wall Street Journal*, January 16, 1986, p. 27.

"The Art of Newspapers." *Marketing and Media Decisions*, December 1985, pp. 20–21.

BELTRAMINI, RICHARD F., and VINCENT J. BLASKO. "An Analysis of Advertising Headlines." *Journal of Advertising Research* 26, no. 2 (April/May 1986), pp. 48–53.

"Business Information Is Profit Leader among Media." *Marketing News*, April 12, 1985, p. 12.

Facts About Newspapers '86, American Newspaper Publishers Association, April 1986.

"Gannett's Four-Color Newspaper Network." *Marketing and Media Decisions,* March 1985, p. 18.

GLOEDE, WILLIAM F. "'USA Today' Up, 'Journal' Down in Study." *Advertising Age,* July 28, 1986, pp. 6, 63.

Guide to Quality Newspaper Reproduction, Newspaper Advertising Bureau and American Newspaper Publishers Association, 1986.

"Key Facts about Newspapers and Advertising." Newspaper Readership Project, Newspaper Advertising Bureau, Inc., April 1986.

KURZBARD, GARY, and LAWRENCE C. SOLEY. "Estimating Newspaper Cumulative Audiences." *Journal of Advertising* 14, no. 2 (1985), pp. 57–61.

LOUIS, ARTHUR M. "Does Gannett Pay Too Much?" *Fortune,* September 15, 1986, pp. 59–64.

"Neuharth's Last Scoop." *The Economists,* May 31, 1986, pp. 70, 73.

"Print's New Priorities: The Experts' View." *Marketing and Media Decisions,* September 1985, pp. 44–69.

"Publisher Fights *LA Times* over Freestanding Insert," *Marketing News,* December 6, 1985, pp. 1, 14.

SOLOMON, DEBBIE. "Trends in Newspaper Readership." *Marketing and Media Decisions,* March 1985, p. 18.

TAYLOR, ROBERT L. "The Last Stronghold of Child Labor." *The Wall Street Journal,* November 10, 1986.

CHAPTER NINE

Magazines

*Nearly 100 years ago, Edward Bok, then editor-in-chief
of* Ladies' Home Journal, *decided to have some fun and write a
column for his readers called "Side Talks for Girls" under
the pseudonym of "Ruth Ashmore." Chatty and intimate in
tone, these columns were full of advice on men, dating, and
sex—written in a one-on-one style, answering questions you
wouldn't ask your mother. After the first column, Bok was
deluged with letters from readers confiding their
secrets . . . [T]he column continued for years, one of the most
popular features of the magazine.**

Carol Sonenklar

The magazine medium is commonly divided into several distinct media—consumer, business, and farm publications. However, each of these categories can easily be divided into several subcategories.

Although similarities exist, there are enough distinctions for the three categories to be treated separately in the present discussion. We present first the most familiar one—consumer magazines.

CONSUMER MAGAZINES

Consumer magazines are intended for the ultimate customers of most retail goods and services; these magazines have experienced recent prosperity after several years of adapting to changing forces in the marketplace. In 1984, magazines had advertising revenues of more than $4.9 billion. Although this represented an annual growth rate of about 8 percent, it also signaled a change in the fortunes of this industry. From 1979 to 1983, annual growth in advertising revenues had averaged 15 percent. For 1986, Robert Coen predicted a 5 percent increase in maga-

---

* "Women and Their Magazines," *American Demographics*, June 1986.

zine advertising.[1] Although annual growth rates have moderated, most observers see a bright future for magazines, especially among national advertisers who must contend with increasing costs and high demand for television time.

It is only a minor simplification to say that the modern magazine's opportunities and problems are created by two factors: the changing pattern of costs and revenues and selectivity.

Cost and Revenue Patterns

The current optimism of magazine publishers is tempered by an awareness of cost pressures and evolving revenue patterns. The primary costs associated with magazine publishing are paper, printing, and distribution. While paper and printing cost increases have moderated in recent years, distribution cost increases have not. On the revenue side, a different mix of advertisers are now found in magazines than in previous years. For example, in 1984, tobacco advertising declined by 15 percent. Computer and liquor advertising declined by lesser amounts. Offsetting these losses were increases in food, soft drink, and entertainment advertising. And circulation revenue sources have changed, too. Single-copy sales declined for many magazines in 1984 when, for example, some personal computing magazines posted 30 percent losses in single-copy circulation. Some of these losses were caused by publishers' successes at marketing subscriptions, which for many readers represented a cheaper way to buy magazines. Also, a portion of the decline is attributed to restrictions in the number and type of titles stocked by newsstands. Another part of the problem is that an increasing number of titles creates added competition for readers' time and money.

Solutions to Cost Pressures. Most publishers see distribution cost increases, especially in postal rates, as a serious long-term problem, even more pressing than increased costs for paper and printing. The creation of the quasi-independent U.S. Postal Service (USPS), with its mandate to operate at break-even prices, produced dramatic increases in second-class postal costs. In managing these cost increases, publishers have three options:

Lobby Congress for USPS Rate Relief. The Magazine Publishers Association (MPA) has done this almost from the inception of the USPS. Any success publishers have had in keeping mailing costs down has been largely one of delaying rather than preventing programmed increases.

---

[1] "Coen Sees U.S. Ad Spending Slowdown," *Advertising Age,* June 30, 1986, p. 6.

Open Additional Outlets for Newsstand Sales. Both the number of magazine outlets and the number of titles carried by retailers have increased markedly during the last several years. However, it is rare for a supermarket or convenience store to carry more than 50 of the over 11,000 magazines. Consequently, while a few large magazines benefit from the new distribution outlets, most magazines do not. In addition, the retailer's commission (up to 35 percent) offsets much of the savings gained by not mailing.

Use Alternative Delivery Systems. Approximately 1.2 million magazines are home-delivered monthly by private companies. To date, only major publishers have experimented with such a system and then only in large markets. Generally the problems of the home-delivery systems— not being able to distribute nationally with any single private carrier, not being able to use mailboxes (due to government prohibition), and inconsistent delivery quality from market to market—have outweighed the advantages. However, as postal costs continue to increase and more experience is gained in private delivery, it may become a viable alternative to the USPS.

Coincidentally, this option is being pursued by newspaper publishers, especially national papers, who are also burdened by rising second-class postal rates. If successful, this tactic may arrest a portion of the decline in single-copy sales.

Selectivity

What is "new" in the marketing of magazines is really the completion of a cycle that began in the 19th century. The magazines of the mid-1800s were characterized by high cost to readers, little or no advertising, and literary or political content intended for the educational and financial elite. The magazine of the 1980s, while anything but devoid of advertising, will be much more expensive to the reader and will generally be intended for a selective audience.

The magazine of 1850 was selective by necessity rather than design. The magazines of that day, such as *North American Review, Harper's Weekly, Century,* and the *Knickerbocker,* catered to an upscale portion of the population who were literate and interested in current affairs and the arts. Not until the decade of the 1890s did the mass circulation magazine come into its own. At this time, companies began to distribute their products nationally, and editors such as Frank Munsey (*Munsey's* magazine), S. S. McClure (*McClure's* magazine), and Edward Bok (*Ladies' Home Journal*) saw an opportunity for magazine advertising. Utilizing the formula that newspapers had adopted a half century earlier, magazines cut their prices to readers, popularized their content, and aggressively promoted their advantages as an advertising medium.

By 1900, the *Ladies' Home Journal* had a circulation of over 1 million, and the era of the mass circulation magazine had begun. The advent of radio, two world wars, and a great depression did little to alter magazines' place as the major medium for national advertisers.

In 1947, television arrived on the scene, and magazines were totally unprepared to cope with this new competitor for the national advertising dollar. Magazines had largely ignored any sales criteria except circulation—the magazine that sold the most copies was automatically the best. Magazines panicked when faced with television, which could deliver more people at a cheaper cost per thousand. Instead of selling the unique qualities of their medium (color, long life, selective editorial content, and audience flexibility), they chose to meet television head-on and play the "numbers game."

THE NUMBERS GAME

Simply put, the numbers game meant that magazines sold readership (circulation multiplied by readers per copy) without regard to the quality of the audience. Unfortunately for magazines, even these inflated audience figures could not keep up with television audiences and their lower CPM figures. By 1965, the situation was desperate for magazines. Many national advertisers either ignored the mass circulation magazines or used them only as an occasional supplement to television. Some of the oldest and most prestigious publications (*Life, Look, Saturday Evening Post, Collier's,* and *Woman's Home Companion*) had either died or were in imminent danger of doing so. Clearly something had to be done.

The answer to the magazine crisis had already been discovered by a few specialized publications founded in the 1950s. These publications— *Sports Illustrated, Hot Rod,* and *Playboy*—all succeeded, while their more famous, well-established contemporaries failed. Today, the formula for magazine success is to deliver an acceptable editorial format to an audience segment that is important to some group of advertisers. With the exception of a few general-circulation magazines (notably *Reader's Digest*), virtually every consumer magazine is now targeted to a limited audience.

Types of Specialization.   Magazines are specialized in two ways. The most obvious way is represented by the relatively low circulation and specialized editorial matter of a publication such as *Gourmet*. A second approach to selectivity is to divide a magazine's circulation into regional and/or **demographic editions.** Magazines such as *Business Week,* which already reach a specialized audience, usually limit themselves to **regional editions,** which are distributed to a single area. The general-circulation magazines, such as *Time* or *Newsweek,* offer advertisers both

---

FIGURE 9-1   Newsweek Demographic Editions

Newsweek's Top Thirty-Three Edition

Rate Base: 1,856,000   B&W Page Rate: $37,115

All of the thirty-three Metro Markets in a convenient single buy.

Newsweek's Top Twenty Edition

Rate Base: 1,550,000   B&W Page Rate: $32,155

A single group of the top twenty business and industrial areas comprising an affluent network of Metro Markets: Atlanta, Baltimore, Boston, Chicago, Cleveland, Dallas/Ft. Worth, Denver, Detroit, Houston, Los Angeles, Miami, Minneapolis/St. Paul, New York, Philadelphia, Phoenix, Pittsburgh, St. Louis, San Francisco, Seattle, Washington, D.C.

Newsweek's Top Ten Edition

Rate Base: 1,150,000   B&W Page Rate: $24,605

A single group of the top ten business and industrial areas comprising an affluent network of Metro Markets: Atlanta, Boston, Chicago, Detroit, Houston, Los Angeles, New York, Philadelphia, San Francisco, Washington, D.C.

State Marketing Plan

A highly flexible option that enables an advertiser to buy any of the 50 states individually or in combination.

Newsweek Canada

Estimated Circulation: 85,000
B&W Page Rate: $1,925 (U.S. dollars)

This regional advertising edition was created in response to demand for Newsweek by Canadian readers and advertisers. It is an efficient and effective vehicle to reach a select audience of upscale Canadian adult readers.

---

regional and demographic editions (see Figure 9-1). These regional and demographic editions account for approximately 15 percent of all magazine advertising revenues. Most magazines have repositioned themselves as a segmented audience (or specific target) medium, not a mass medium in the television sense.

The Media Imperatives.   Recently, industry-wide promotions by organizations such as the MPA have attempted to show that there are certain people national advertisers miss if they don't include magazines in the media schedule. Since magazines and television have their own special audiences, both media must be used to reach the total audience—hence, the term *Media Imperatives.* The individual segments are named after the medium they consume heavily, e.g., "Television Imperatives" or "Magazine Imperatives" (see Figure 9-2).

The index numbers in Figure 9-2 tend to substantiate claims that consumers who are heavy readers of magazines but light viewers of television are also younger, better educated, more likely to be employed

---

FIGURE 9–1 *(concluded)*

Demographic Flexibility

Newsweek Gold

Rate Base: 600,000   B&W Page Rate: $21,460

With subscribers qualified by *both* income and occupation, this is the most selective newsweekly demographic edition available to advertisers. To receive this edition, a subscriber must have an annual personal income of at least $25,000 as well as a professional or managerial title. Since it is the only edition individually qualified by income, it is a most effective vehicle to target a select, affluent, consumer market. Average personal income: $78,000.*

Newsweek Executive Plus

Rate Base: 950,000   B&W Page Rate: $26,425

Circulation is concentrated exclusively among executives across the entire spectrum of corporate management. Each subscriber is individually qualified by professional or managerial job title, through completed questionnaires verified by ABC. A highly effective way to reach a broad base of key business customers. Average personal income: $64,000.*

Newsweek Woman

Rate Base: 600,000   B&W Page Rate: $10,800

No other newsweekly offers a demographic edition targeted exclusively to women. An ideal choice for advertisers who need to reach affluent, educated, mostly working women, in a prestigious editorial setting.

Newsweek On Campus

Rate Base: 1,100,000   B&W Page Rate: $21,475

The first and only full-color college publication produced by the editorial staff of a major news magazine, Newsweek On Campus rates highest in "awareness" and "readership" among all college publications.

---

* Newsweek update of 1981 Subscriber Study based on data from Bureau of the Census Current Population Reports.

SOURCE: Standard Rate and Data Service, February 27, 1985.

---

in professional/managerial/technical occupations, and more affluent than the U.S. average.

We should mention that there is some controversy, especially in television circles, as to the validity of the research technique involved. Without debating this issue here, the Media Imperatives concept is important in that it shows the radically different approach that magazines have adopted in their competition with television since the black days of the 1960s.

A final point should be made about magazine selectivity. While selectivity offers most magazines their best chance to compete effectively for national advertising, it does not guarantee the success or survival of any particular magazine. In the late 1970s, *Viva, New Times, Muse,* and *Your Place* all failed despite being aimed at narrow markets.

FIGURE 9-2   Media Profiles

Demography	Magazines	TV	Newspapers	Radio
Age				
18–24	120	97	90	115
25–34	111	90	90	111
35–44	104	88	106	102
45–54	96	95	113	99
55–64	91	113	110	90
65 and older	62	124	90	74
Education				
Attended/ graduated college	128	86	118	102
Graduated high school	98	103	100	106
Did not graduate high school	64	114	74	89
Employment				
Professional/ manager	125	77	123	101
Technical/ clerical/sales	122	84	110	112
Precision/craft	84	80	94	120
Other employed	91	91	87	108
Unemployed	85	124	90	87
Household Income				
$50,000 and over	138	81	139	97
$40,000–49,999	115	82	119	100
$30,000–39,999	111	86	114	107
$25,000–29,999	103	96	93	102
$20,000–24,999	93	100	103	105
$15,000–19,999	102	101	94	102
$10,000–14,999	82	110	81	100
Under $10,000	73	125	68	90
Household Members				
1 person	80	109	87	96
2 people	91	104	100	92
3 or 4 people	107	95	103	104
5 or more people	109	97	97	107

Index of 100 = U.S. Average

SOURCE: As reported in *The Magazine Magazine,* Magazine Publishers Association, 1985.

Overall, however, the selective approach to magazine marketing has been successful. Magazines offer advertisers a narrowly targeted, usually upscale audience, selective editorial material for good association between advertiser and reader interest, and a cost per *prospect* competitive with television.

Yet the fact remains that while industry averages have been booming, individual magazines continue to fail. Why do some magazines succeed, while others, similar in content, fail? Successful magazines must appeal to both readers and advertisers. Magazines that appeal to a sizable number of readers can still fail if they lack advertising support.

WHY ADVERTISERS BUY MAGAZINES

As discussed earlier in this chapter, advertisers normally buy magazine space to reach a particular market segment. In addition, advertisers choose magazines for several other reasons. Let's examine the major advantages and disadvantages that must be considered when making a magazine buy.

Strengths

Audience Characteristics. Of all the attractive characteristics of magazine audiences, the major factor is selectivity. It is by no means the only one. According to MPA, magazines reach 94 percent of all U.S. adults, who read an average of 9.9 different magazine issues each month.[2] The typical issue is read a total of 4.2 hours by adults. Forty-nine percent of adult readers have shopped for products after reading magazine ads, 47 percent have tried ideas from magazine ads, 48 percent have decided to buy advertised products, and 64 percent of women readers have clipped or used coupons from magazine ads. Seventy-eight percent of magazine reading takes place in the reader's own home.

Selective Editorial Content that Complements the Advertiser's Message. Advertisers must choose magazines on the basis of qualitative judgment as well as quantitative audience information. Some advertisers demand compatibility between their customers' attitudes and preferences and an advertising medium's editorial emphasis. Sometimes this is obvious, such as when a golf club manufacturer advertises in *Golf Digest*. Other associations are subtler. For instance, Kraft Foods does not advertise in fashion magazines because management believes that a

---

[2] Magazine Publishers Association, *The Magazine Magazine,* 1985, p. 4.

woman thinking of fashion will not be in the proper frame of mind to read recipes.[3]

Excellent Color Reproduction.   Although magazines no longer have color as a unique selling feature, it remains a major strength of the medium. Products that seek label identification and food products find magazines an excellent advertising medium.

Long Issue Life.   Magazines are the only medium that regularly acquires repeat exposures. It is not uncommon for many types of magazines (home service, hobby and special interest, and business) to be kept for long periods and referred to often. Seventy percent of magazine readers re-read articles and save issues for future reference.

Weaknesses

Lack of Geographic Flexibility Offered by Other Media.   While a few large-circulation magazines offer metropolitan editions, most magazines offer only broad areas if less than national circulation is available.

One-Dimensional.   Magazines find that their major problem in competing with television is that they lack the sound and movement desired by so many national advertisers. Television proponents claim that television, with sight, sound, color, and movement, is at a disadvantage with magazines only in the area of message perishability.

Lack of Audience Reach.   If reach (or the accumulation of new audience) is an advertising objective, then magazines may not perform well. Magazines tend to reach the same audience over long periods of time. Consequently, in a selected magazine schedule, frequency levels are acquired at the sacrifice of reach with a given budget.

Buying by the Numbers

Despite all the discussion of audience selectivity and other strengths and weaknesses, magazines, like other media, are still bought "by the numbers." Advertisers divide magazine vehicles into acceptable and nonacceptable categories, but the final buy is usually made from those with the highest audience figures (and the lowest CPM).

What is an audience? This seems like a silly question, but magazines,

---

[3] "The Courtice Recipe," *Marketing and Media Decisions*, November 1979, p. 136.

by accident or design, have made it complex. There are really three ways to answer the question:

1. *Paid circulation.* The number of people who subscribe to or buy a magazine at the newsstand is normally called circulation or primary readership. **Primary readers** are generally considered more valuable than pass-along readers, since primary readers are more interested in a magazine and, we assume, in the advertising it carries.
2. *Readership.* Another method of defining magazine audiences is to compute the sum of the primary readers and the pass-along readers or the product of the total copies circulated and the readers per copy. This is usually called either readership or total audience.
3. *Prospects.* Advertisers consider only the prospects for their product in the total audience. This is probably the fairest method of comparing one magazine with another, and it usually combines both prospects and cost of advertising to figure the CPM/ prospects.

SOURCES OF MAGAZINE CIRCULATION DATA

Regardless of the particular "audience" an advertiser is using, circulation figures should be readily available for advertising decisions. Several major sources are used by advertisers to obtain accurate audience information.

Independent Auditing Companies

Most major magazine circulations are audited or checked by an independent company. Among the best known of these are the Audit Bureau of Circulations (ABC), the Business Publications Audit of Circulations, Inc. (BPA), and the Verified Audit Circulation Corporation (VAC). The reports of these organizations are normally carried in other rate and circulation directories, such as those of the Standard Rate and Data Service (SRDS). The rate cards of individual magazines will also note that the circulation has been audited (see Figure 9–3).

Rate Cards

Individual rate cards must be used if a magazine is not audited. Rate cards must often be used to obtain circulation of regional and/or demographic editions since only a limited number are carried in SRDS.

FIGURE 9-3 ABC Magazine Audit Report

PROTOTYPE

New York, New York

CLASS, INDUSTRY OR FIELD SERVED: A sports fan's guide to the major sports with emphasis on the season's winners and losers, picks, predictions, and profiles.

1. AVERAGE PAID CIRCULATION FOR 12 MONTHS ENDED DECEMBER 31, (YEAR):

Subscriptions:		774,713
Single Copy Sales:		136,136
AVERAGE TOTAL PAID CIRCULATION		910,849
Advertising Rate Base during Audit Period. . . . . to 3-1-(YEAR)	900,000	
	since 3-1-(YEAR)	930,000
Average Total Non-Paid Distribution		21,211

1a. AVERAGE PAID CIRCULATION of Regional, Metro and Demographic Editions:

Edition & number of issues		Edition & number of issues		Edition & number of issues	
East (12)	281,723	South (6)	167,629	South/Southwest (6)	277,129
Midwest (6)	257,248	West (6)	161,007	Midwest/West (6)	311,244

2. PAID CIRCULATION BY ISSUES:

Issue (YEAR)	Subscriptions	Single Copy Sales	Total Paid	Issue (YEAR)	Subscriptions	Single Copy Sales	Total Paid
Jan.	746,213	166,279	912,492	July	769,026	129,926	898,952
Feb.	759,079	157,498	916,577	Aug.	753,182	166,782	919,964
Mar.	779,103	133,030	912,133	Sept.	783,202	112,432	895,634
Apr.	772,726	140,146	912,872	Oct.	794,596	137,811	932,407
May	777,457	129,471	906,928	Nov.	793,784	113,524	907,308
June	778,045	121,557	899,602	Dec.	790,143	125,176	915,319

AVERAGE PAID CIRCULATION BY QUARTERS for the previous three years and period covered by this report:

Calendar Quarter Ended	(YEAR)	(YEAR)	(YEAR)	(YEAR)
March 31	1,202,696	915,447	899,337	913,734
June 30	1,163,946	881,716	976,093	906,467
September 30	1,053,932	878,935	954,846	904,850
December 31	941,786	882,249	900,095	918,345

AUDIT STATEMENT

The difference shown in average total paid circulation, in comparing this report with Publisher's Statements for the period audited, amounting to an average of 17,855 copies per issue, is accounted for by deductions made for additional newsdealer returns, publisher having underestimated returns in filing statements with the Bureau, 13,141 copies per issue; additional copies served on credit subscriptions cancelled for nonpayment, 2,427 copies per issue; copies served on special reduced price subscriptions not qualifying as paid in accordance with the Bureau's Rules, 1,331 copies per issue; clerical errors in the circulation records, 956 copies per issue.

The records maintained by this publication pertaining to circulation data and other data as reported for the period covered have been examined in accordance with the Bureau's bylaws, rules and auditing standards. Tests of the accounting records and other auditing procedures considered necessary were included. Based on ABC's examination, the data shown in this report present fairly the circulation data and other data as verified by Bureau auditors.

January, (YEAR).   **Audit Bureau of Circulations**
(04-1140-0 - #141590 - WJC - KL)   900 N. Meacham Road, Schaumburg, IL 60173-4968

Syndicated Research Services

Audits and circulation figures tell only part of the story. Most of this information is confined to readers and their territorial distribution (see Figure 9-4). However, the figures give no information about the demographics of magazine audiences (occasionally magazines will provide limited information in promotional pieces, as exemplified by the ad for *Money* in Figure 9-5) or about purchase behavior. Most advertisers use one of the major syndicated services to obtain such information.

The Syndicated Magazine Services

In recent years the measuring of magazine readership has been one of the most controversial areas of media research. Currently the two major services are Magazine Research, Inc. (MRI), and Simmons Market Research Bureau (SMRB). While space does not permit a full explanation of the various concerns of subscribers to these services, the major characteristics are highlighted below.

Methodologies. Although MRI and SMRB are similar in approach, their methods are dissimilar in some major ways. Briefly the two services operate as illustrated in Figure 9-6.

Measurement of Total Readership Only. The services measure only readership, not primary circulation. Some advertisers think it a mistake to give equal weight to paid circulation and pass-along readers. A pilot study of primary readers was recently completed by Starch INRA Hooper, but high cost makes it problematic whether this service will gain wide acceptance.

Respondent Fatigue. With the number of magazines to be measured and the additional buying behavior collected by the services, there is a concern about wearing out the respondent. Some observers think a larger sample with shorter interviews is the answer, but this would significantly increase the cost of the studies.

Number of Magazines Surveyed. Fewer than 300 magazines are included in these reports. The lower circulation, specialized magazines, so important to many advertisers, are excluded. This not only leaves advertisers with no consumer information regarding the excluded magazines, but can prevent these magazines from attracting additional advertising revenue. Some advertisers buy space only in magazines that are included in a readership service.

FIGURE 9-4 Rate Card, *Money*

PUBLISHER'S EDITORIAL PROFILE
MONEY is America's magazine of personal finance.
Each issue tackles subjects that concern affluent men
and women most today: gaining maximum return on investments, increasing earning power, saving wisely,
obtaining quality and values in key purchases. Rec'd 11/
23/82.

1. PERSONNEL
Publisher—William M. Kelly.
Managing Editor—Lanny Jones.
Advertising Sales Director—Charles Rubens II.
Production Manager—Rosemary Lowther.

2. REPRESENTATIVES and/or BRANCH OFFICES
New York 10020—Nancy Van Leight, Mgr.; Winslow
Lewis Jr., Assoc. New York Mgr., Rockefeller Center.
Phone 212-586-1212.
Chicago 60611—Thomas Huber, Mgr., 312-329-7241;
Todd Ford, 312-329-7859; James E. Nugent, 312-329-
7858, 303 E. Ohio St. Phone 312-329-7858.
Detroit 48202—Alan C. Wiber, Mgr., 1510 Fisher Bldg.
Phone 313-875-1212.
Los Angeles 90024—Cathie H. Kanuit, Mgr.; John Buck-
ingham, 10880 Wilshire Blvd., Suite 1700. Phone 213-
824-7200.
San Francisco 94104—Alison Embree, Mgr., 100 Bush St.
Phone 415-982-5000.
Atlanta 30305—Michael McFadden, Mgr.; Karen
Schmeichel, 10 Piedmont Center, Suite 500. Phone
404-233-3847.
Boston 02116—Betsy Martin, New England Mgr.; 399
Boylston St. Phone 617-267-9500.
Clearwater, FL—Russell Johns Associates, Ltd. (Classi-
fied only).

3. COMMISSION AND CASH DISCOUNT
15% to recognized agencies; 2% of net allowed for
payment on or before due date. Bills rendered on 10th of
month of insertion and are due within 10 days from invoice date.

4. GENERAL RATE POLICY
Announcement of any change in rates at least 7 weeks in
advance of issue date of 1st issue to which such rates will
be applicable.

ADVERTISING RATES
Rates effective January 1, 1986.
Rates received October 31, 1985.

5. BLACK/WHITE RATES

	1 ti	6 ti	12 ti	18 ti	24 ti
1 page	32,325.	31,030.	30,385.	29,740.	29,095.
2 columns	24,570.	23,585.	23,095.	22,605.	22,115.
*1/2 page	19,405.	18,630.	18,240.	17,855.	17,465.
1 column	12,920.	12,405.	12,145.	11,885.	11,630.
1/2 column	6,470.	6,210.	6,080.	5,950.	5,825.
	36 ti	48 ti	54 ti	60 ti	
1 page	28,445.	27,800.	27,475.	27,155.	
2 columns	21,620.	21,130.	20,885.	20,640.	
*1/2 page	17,075.	16,690.	16,495.	16,300.	
1 column	11,370.	11,110.	10,980.	10,855.	
1/2 column	5,695.	5,565.	5,500.	5,435.	

(*) Units available on a limited basis.

FREQUENCY DISCOUNT
Ads must be inserted within 1 year of 1st insertion to earn
a frequency discount. Advertising schedules composed of
mixed space units are entitled to earn frequency discounts except when use of the least expensive unit
lowers the total cost of the campaign below the amount
which the other units reached at their earned rate.

CONSECUTIVE PAGE DISCOUNTS
Consecutive pages will earn discounts based on the following schedule:

3-7 pages	5%	12-15 pages	15%
8-11 pages	10%	16 or more	20%

Each page of a multiple page ad will be considered a
separate insertion towards earning a frequency discount.

SPACE RENEWAL CREDIT PROGRAM:
An advertiser who runs a minimum of 3 National
Equivalent Pages in the prior year (calendar 1985) and
then renews at the same level the following year earns
space credit. Renewed and increased pages generate a
2,000.00 per page credit which may be applied to additional space. Space credits are earned by advertisers on
a corporate basis; they are earned in addition to and
combined with Money's frequency discount.

TWO YEAR COMMITMENT PROGRAM:
An advertiser who commits, in each of the next two contract years, to a minimum increase of 3 National
Equivalent Pages over a base contract year will earn pre-
established discounts based on the committed level of
growth.
Advertisers may either select the higher of the past two
consecutive years or average the two to determine their
National Equivalent Pages (NEP) base year. The maximum base year shall not exceed 48 pages. Two year
commitment program discounts are offered in addition to,
and combined with, Money's frequency discounts. Participants are not entitled to Space Renewal Credit. Discounts are as follows:

Growth Over Base Yr. (NEP'S)	Highest	Average
+ 3.00-5.99	3%	2%
+ 6.00-11.99	5%	4%
+12.00-17.99	7%	6%
+18.00-23.99	8%	7%
+24.00+ over	9%	8%

6. COLOR RATES
2 color:

	1 ti	6 ti	12 ti	18 ti	24 ti
1 page	40,460.	38,840.	38,030.	37,225.	36,415.
2 columns	30,755.	29,525.	28,910.	28,295.	27,680.

	1 ti	6 ti	12 ti	18 ti	24 ti
*1/2 page	24,270.	23,300.	22,815.	22,330.	21,845.
1 column	16,185.	15,540.	15,215.	14,890.	14,565.
1/2 column	8,085.	7,760.	7,600.	7,440.	7,275.
	36 ti	48 ti	54 ti	60 ti	
1 page	35,605.	34,795.	34,390.	33,985.	
2 columns	27,065.	26,450.	26,140.	25,835.	
*1/2 page	21,360.	20,870.	20,630.	20,385.	
1 column	14,245.	13,920.	13,755.	13,595.	
1/2 column	7,115.	6,955.	6,870.	6,790.	

4 color:

	1 ti	6 ti	12 ti	18 ti	24 ti
1 page	50,575.	48,550.	47,540.	46,530.	45,520.
2 columns	40,460.	38,840.	38,030.	37,225.	36,415.
*1/2 page	32,870.	31,555.	30,900.	30,240.	29,585.
1 column	21,745.	20,875.	20,440.	20,005.	19,570.
	36 ti	48 ti	54 ti	60 ti	
1 page	44,505.	43,495.	42,990.	42,485.	
2 columns	35,605.	34,795.	34,390.	33,985.	
*1/2 page	28,925.	28,270.	27,940.	27,610.	
1 column	19,135.	18,700.	18,485.	18,265.	

(*) Units available on a limited basis.

7. COVERS

	1 ti	6 ti	12 ti	18 ti	24 ti
4th cover (4 color)	63,725.	61,175.	59,900.	58,625.	57,355.
	36 ti	48 ti	54 ti	60 ti	
4th cover (4 color)	56,080.	54,805.	54,165.	53,530.	

8. INSERTS
Gatefold Units: front cover, single and double gatefold
units available.
Insert Cards: standard size 6″ x 4-1/4″; maximum size 7″
x 6″ available. A 5% margin must be allowed in delivery
of insert cards.
Supplied Inserts: specially designed inserts such as
gatefolds, die cuts, etc. available.

9. BLEED
Full page, double column and vertical single
column, extra 15%
No charge for bleed across gutter for facing space units.

13a. GEOGRAPHIC and/or DEMOGRAPHIC EDITIONS

NEW YORK EDITION
Sectional centers: 06400-21, 066, 068-9, 070-9, 088-9,
100, 103-19.
BLACK AND WHITE RATES:

	1 ti	6 ti	12 ti	18 ti	24 ti	36 ti
1 page	4,980.	4,780.	4,681.	4,580.	4,480.	4,380.
	48 ti	54 ti	60 ti			
1 page	4,285.	4,235.	4,185.			

COLOR RATES:
2 color:

	1 ti	6 ti	12 ti	18 ti	24 ti	36 ti
1 page	6,230.	5,980.	5,855.	5,730.	5,605.	5,480.
	48 ti	54 ti	60 ti			
1 page	5,360.	5,295.	5,235.			

4 color:

	1 ti	6 ti	12 ti	18 ti	24 ti	36 ti
1 page	7,775.	7,465.	7,310.	7,155.	7,000.	6,840.
	48 ti	54 ti	60 ti			
1 page	6,685.	6,610.	6,530.			

CIRCULATION:
A.B.C. 12-31-85—164,268
Rate Base: 160,000.

CHICAGO EDITION
Sectional centers: 463-4, 600-6.
BLACK AND WHITE RATES:

	1 ti	6 ti	12 ti	18 ti	24 ti	36 ti
1 page	1,865.	1,790.	1,755.	1,715.	1,680.	1,640.
	48 ti	54 ti	60 ti			
1 page	1,605.	1,585.	1,565.			

COLOR RATES:
2 color:

	1 ti	6 ti	12 ti	18 ti	24 ti	36 ti
1 page	2,335.	2,240.	2,195.	2,150.	2,100.	2,055.
	48 ti	54 ti	60 ti			
1 page	2,010.	1,985.	1,960.			

4 color:

	1 ti	6 ti	12 ti	18 ti	24 ti	36 ti
1 page	2,915.	2,800.	2,740.	2,680.	2,625.	2,565.
	48 ti	54 ti	60 ti			
1 page	2,505.	2,480.	2,450.			

CIRCULATION:
A.B.C. 12-31-85—61,724
Rate Base: 60,000.

CALIFORNIA EDITION
BLACK AND WHITE RATES:

	1 ti	6 ti	12 ti	18 ti	24 ti	36 ti
1 page	6,230.	5,980.	5,855.	5,730.	5,605.	5,480.
	48 ti	54 ti	60 ti			
1 page	5,360.	5,295.	5,235.			

COLOR RATES:
2 color:

	1 ti	6 ti	12 ti	18 ti	24 ti	36 ti
1 page	7,780.	7,470.	7,315.	7,160.	7,000.	6,845.
	48 ti	54 ti	60 ti			
1 page	6,690.	6,615.	6,535.			

4 color:

	1 ti	6 ti	12 ti	18 ti	24 ti	36 ti
1 page	9,720.	9,330.	9,135.	8,945.	8,750.	8,550.
	48 ti	54 ti	60 ti			
1 page	8,360.	8,260.	8,165.			

CIRCULATION:
A.B.C. 12-31-85—211,542
Rate Base: 200,000.

FREQUENCY DISCOUNT
Ads for New York, Chicago and California editions may be
combined to earn frequency discount and may be combined with national ads to earn frequency discount in the
less-than national advertising only.

15. MECH. REQUIREMENTS
**For complete, detailed production information, see
SRDS Print Media Production Data.**
Printing Process: Web Offset.
Trim size: 8-3/16 x 10-7/8; No./Cols. 3.
Binding method: Saddle-stitched.
Colors available: Publisher's Choice; Matched; 4 color
process (AAAA/MPA); Special Standards; 5-Color
Process, Sheen Inks.

DIMENSIONS-AD PAGE

1	7 x	10	1 col.	4-5/8 x	4-7/8
2 cols.	4-5/8 x	10	1/2 col.	2-1/4 x	4-7/8
1/2	7 x	5	Spread	15 x	10
1 col.	2-1/4 x	10			

16. ISSUE AND CLOSING DATES
Published monthly. On sale 25th of month prior to issue
date.

FIGURE 9–5 Example of Magazine Promotional Piece with Selected Demographics

The highest income magazine

Based on 1985 SMRB data, MONEY has a higher median household income than does any other major magazine.*

At an income of $40,498, MONEY is a far tastier advertising entree than the second place finisher, *Bon Appetit* at $37,699. And the MONEY income story doesn't end there.

MONEY delivers a greater concentration of p/m readers with household incomes of $50,000+ or $75,000+ or $100,000+ than *any* other major magazine.

In short, MONEY readers can afford to buy what you advertise. Moreover, your ad in MONEY becomes part of what may be the publishing phenomenon of the decade, and what is already the fastest growing major magazine in America.

MONEY. Where unparalleled income can help determine your marketing outcome.

Money
America's Financial Advisor

FIGURE 9-6 Syndicated Research Services Comparisons

Research Service	Magazines Surveyed	Effective Sample	Relative Error	Survey Technique	Features of Technique	Possible Weaknesses of Technique	Corporate Clients	Magazine Clients	Agency Clients
SMRB	110 (total list)	20,000	8.9%	"Through the book"	a. Issue specific b. Time specific by "aging" factor c. Memory aids d. Frequency determined by 2-phase interview	a. Misses late readers b. May understate out-of-home reading c. Interviewee's memory loss penalizes monthlies	40	100	350+
MRI	185-190 (core list) 285 (total list)	20,000	8.8%	Recent reading	a. Not issue specific b. Time specific by publishing cycle. c. Frequency determined by asking. New interviewees monthly	a. Tends to pick up more casual readers b. Prone to readership inflation due to title confusion, ego-building, yea-saying, etc.	22	165	350+

SOURCE: Reprinted with permission Advertising Age, November 31, 1985, p. 32. Copyright Crain Communications, Inc.

Discrepancies between the Two Services. Perhaps the major concern of advertisers, as well as the area of harshest criticism, is that the two syndicated readership services produce different readership numbers for the same issue of the same magazine. MRI audience estimates for weekly magazines range from 15 to 22 percent higher than those from SMRB. For monthly books, the MRI numbers are 30 to 50 percent higher. Both sets of numbers can't be right.

The discrepancies have given rise to what might be called the "Great Magazine Audience Fiddle." Agencies adjust audience numbers on the basis of qualitative factors such as long copy, or whenever publishers can spin a convincing story, or whenever they don't believe the numbers. In 1985, an MPA survey of 109 agencies showed that 27 subscribed to MRI alone, 30 subscribed to SMRB alone, 8 did not subscribe to either service, and 26 subscribed to both services. Publishers pick and choose the most favorable numbers, while advertisers remain uncertain of audience size.

The Gold Standard

In an effort to resolve the discrepancies between services, the Advertising Research Foundation formed a magazine audience validity committee that designed a "Gold Standard" for measuring magazine audiences. Important features include:

1. Personal interviews.
2. Issue-specific and time-specific measures.
3. Full-issue review copies.
4. Smaller samples of publications per interview.
5. Allowance to measure multiple issues of the same magazine and magazines easily confused with each other.

Underlying activities like the Gold Standard rules is the clear need to develop a system that resolves discrepancies between the syndicated services. Publishers alone spend over $12 million annually on audience measurement services. One member of the ARF committee predicts that, should the Gold Standard pass its validation tests, "a new service will be developed, or the other two will change, or one will change and one will go out of business or both will go out of business."[4] Expressed in different words, the market for magazine audience estimates will simply not tolerate a continuation of the status quo.

---

[4] Terence Poltrack, "A Meeting of Minds on Reader Research," *Marketing and Media Decisions,* October 1985, p. 142.

HOW ADVERTISERS BUY MAGAZINES

Buying space in a magazine involves several steps, and the advertisers must make many decisions. Let's follow the process from the decision to buy space in a magazine (*Time*) to the publication of the advertisement.

Where?

Perhaps the first question that the advertiser must answer is this: Where will the advertisement run? *Time* (like many other major magazines) offers various possibilities including:

1. Full national circulation.
2. Eleven regional editions.
3. Thirteen major spot markets.
4. Over 37 supplemental spot markets.
5. Fifty state editions bought individually or in combination with metro editions.
6. Four major demographic editions.
7. Fifteen international editions.

In addition, the advertiser can buy **split-run** editions, which allow several different advertisements to be run in the same issue. The advertiser can also buy circulations of 2.9 and 2.0 million that are matched demographically to the full national circulation of 4.6 million. Many of these editions have special requirements. For instance, supplemental spot market editions are available only every other week.

What Format?

Having decided on the edition (in the example, we will buy the full circulation), we must next decide on the format of our advertisement. The first question is one of size. Magazines normally sell space by the fractional page. However, many publications offer other alternatives, such as inserts (either booklets or single cards), gatefolds, and **cover positions.** Normally only the second, third, and fourth covers of consumer magazines are available for advertising space.

Assume that we have decided on a full-page advertisement. Now we must decide on color or black and white. Costs for color vary widely from magazine to magazine, but an extra charge of 10 to 15 percent for two-color and 20 to 30 percent for four-color is usual. Magazines such as *Time* also offer bleed color (no margins) for a premium of about 15 percent over regular color.

How Much?

Once the size and format of our advertisement have been decided, our next step is to determine how much we will spend. The one-page, four-color rate for *Time* costs more than $87,000; it is obvious why advertisers want to take steps to reduce their costs. The major way to cut per-unit costs is through discounts given larger advertisers. Magazine rates, like newspaper rates, are subject to rebate and short rate adjustments. See Chapter 8 for a full discussion of these adjustments.

Common Magazine Discounts

Frequency Discounts. These are offered for the number of pages (or page equivalents) run during a year or other contract period. Sometimes frequency discounts are figured on dollar volume rather than insertions. The dollar volume discount is often used when an advertiser is using regional buys. *Time* uses a dollar volume discount schedule, as follows:

Dollar Volume	Discount
$ 325,000– 544,999	2%
$ 545,000–1,084,999	4
$1,085,000–1,624,999	6
$1,625,000–2,174,999	7
$2,175,000–2,174,999	8
$2,715,000–3,254,999	9
$3,255,000–3,794,999	10
$3,795,000–4,344,999	11
$4,345,000–4,884,999	12
$4,885,000–5,434,999	12.5
$5,435,000–5,974,999	13
$5,975,000 or more	13.5

Multiple-Page Discounts. Advertisers wishing to run several pages in the same issue are normally given special discounts.

Multiple-Edition Discounts. An advertiser buying more than one regional/demographic edition gets a discount for each extra edition bought.

Standby (Remnant) Space. In *Time,* an advertiser who gives the publisher complete flexibility in placing his ads is charged 65 percent of the national cost per thousand.

Most magazines offer discounts similar to these. In taking advantage of these discounts, however, an advertiser must be certain that his advertising strategy calls for frequency rather than reach. Multiple insertions that gain discounts rather than fulfill advertising and marketing goals constitute a shortsighted savings for the advertiser.

An advertiser who plans to advertise in a publication throughout a coming year should consider signing a space contract with the publisher. Normally such a **contract** gives the advertiser some protection from rate increases. Signing a contract does not always mean that rates cannot be increased during the year, but it may mean that the magazine will agree to give four or six months notice instead of five to eight weeks. With the uncertainties of inflation, publishers are less willing to lock themselves into long-term advertising rates than they were several years ago. However, the advertiser should inquire about a contract even if it is not mentioned in the publisher's rate information.

THE MAGAZINE NETWORK

Another potential cost savings for the larger magazine advertiser is the magazine network. Networks allow an advertiser to purchase space in several magazines simultaneously at a significant savings over buying them individually. There are two types of networks:

1. *The publisher network.* Here a publisher combines several related magazines (alone or in cooperation with other publishers), all of which an advertiser can buy at the same time. The Petersen Action Group, an example of such a network, offers the following:

Car Craft	*Motorcyclist*
Circle Track	*Motor Trend*
Dirt Rider	*Photographic*
4 Wheel & Off-Road	*Pickups & Mini Trucks*
Guns & Ammo	*Sea Magazine*
Hot Rod	*Skin Diver*
Hunting	

Being a member of a magazine network normally does not prevent a magazine from selling advertising space individually.

2. *The independent network.* The independent network contracts with several publishers to sell advertising on a regional basis. The advertisements are usually bound as an insert, but conform to the style of the individual magazine. One example is the News Network (a combination of *Newsweek, Sports Illustrated, Time,* and *U.S. News & World Report*), which, at the beginning of 1986, was available in over 100 markets.

SCHEDULING MAGAZINE ADVERTISING

The advertiser—after deciding on the vehicle, format, and price of the advertising—must determine the schedule. The scheduling decision is made according to the advertising and marketing goals discussed earlier.

The mechanical problems of scheduling require careful planning by the advertiser. A checklist for scheduling such as the following might be helpful in planning magazine advertising.

Closing Dates. The **closing date** is the date by which an advertisement must reach the publisher in order to be carried in a particular issue. Often a magazine has different closing dates for color advertisements, regional editions, and special services such as split runs. Some magazines accept a limited number of advertisements on short notice (five days as compared to five to seven weeks); however, there is a significant price increase for this service. Most magazines do not accept cancellations after the closing date.

Mechanical Requirements. The advertiser must make certain that his advertisement conforms to a magazine's mechanical requirements. Most major magazines' requirements are listed in the SRDS Print Media Production Data. However, it is a good idea to get mechanical information directly from the publisher prior to making a mechanical layout.

Addresses. Many magazines have different addresses for their advertising sales offices and their printing operations. Don't assume that advertising material should be sent to the advertising sales office.

Insertion Orders. Carefully check the insertion order to make sure it includes the issue to carry the advertisement, the size of the ad, and the cost. If a prior contract has not been signed, an insertion order/contract may be combined in the order.

THE GUARANTEED CIRCULATION

Most magazines guarantee their paid circulation to advertisers. Normally a magazine makes this guarantee on its average six-month circulation. If a magazine fails to meet its guarantee, the advertiser is due a rebate of some portion of the advertising dollars he invested during the past six months. Guarantees are set conservatively, and rebates are seldom given, but when they are, it is damaging to the publisher's reputation.

People magazine introduced a new wrinkle on the idea of the rebate in the fall of 1979. *People* computes ad charges on the basis of issue-by-issue circulation instead of its average six-month circulation. When the per-issue circulation goes below the base, the advertiser receives credits. When the per-issue circulation goes above the base, the magazine gets credits. At the end of a six-month period, the advertiser will be credited for any circulation shortfall. On the other hand, if the magazine has credits, the advertiser will not be charged further. In this system, an advertiser accrues credits even when the magazine meets its base for the six-month period if the specific issues used fail to meet the average circulation.

THE FUTURE OF THE CONSUMER MAGAZINE

In the beginning of this chapter, we discussed the bright future of magazines. However, no medium can be successful if it is allowed to become stagnant. The opportunities and accompanying problems for magazines in the 1980s are multiple and diverse.

Special Interest.   Development of new, special-interest magazines will continue in the 1980s. As education and income continue to increase, the opportunities for leisure activities will become more plentiful. Magazines devoted to hobbies and special interests should prosper in this environment.

Inflation.   There seems to be no end in sight to increases in the cost of paper, postage, and labor. Publishers will be forced to manage scarce resources more efficiently and look for additional revenue in the future. Magazines may cut back on the quality of paper for all or a portion of their pages. Further reduction in page size may be a possibility, especially for publications with nonstandard page sizes. Alternative delivery systems may become more popular if second-class postage rates continue to rise.

Competition from Cable Television.   The new broadcast technology (see Chapter 6) will bring the opportunity for broadcast audience segmentation. Audience fragmentation into small special-interest groups through electronic communications can be a major threat to the special-topic magazine. However, some observers think broadcast segmentation will complement magazines by creating superficial, preliminary interest in topics, which can then be developed in depth by specialized publications. In any case, the magazine of the future will have to find a way to compete with this new technology.

The City Magazine. Perhaps the ultimate specialty magazine is the city publication. Begun in 1948 with *San Diego Magazine,* the city book has grown in number to over 100. In 1985, a readership survey of 30 city and regional magazines measured a very affluent demographic profile; average household income exceeded $75,000, average household net worth was more than $300,000, investment portfolios averaged $156,000, and in addition to owning homes with an average value of $157,000, one household in five owned a second home.[5]

Originally, city books were created as a means to express political, cultural, and local issues in magazine format; they have succeeded in reaching the powerful, wealthy, and influential strata in their respective societies. However, their performance in attracting national advertisers, and in appealing to younger readers who represent the next generation of influentials, has not been uniformly good. Nevertheless, city magazines are expected to remain a significant medium among advertisers seeking a high-income, well-educated, geographically concentrated audience.

BUSINESS MAGAZINES

In the previous section, we discussed magazines directed to the ultimate consumer. In this section, we examine magazines intended for the industrial, middleman, and professional groups within the marketing channel. Figure 9–7 outlines the categories of magazines discussed in this chapter (except farm publications, which are treated separately in the last section of the chapter).

FIGURE 9–7 Magazines and the Marketing Channel

---

[5] Jeremy Schlosberg, "The Glittering World of City Magazines," *American Demographics,* July 1986, pp. 22–25.

The general category of business publications involves industrial, merchandising, and professional publications intended for groups in the marketing channel short of the ultimate consumer.

The general business press comprises some 2,500 major publications, accounting for advertising revenues of more than $2.6 billion per year. As compared to consumer publications, business magazines are generally lower in circulation, higher in CPM, and more precisely targeted to a specific audience. Like consumer magazines, they sell advertisers on audience selectivity, long reading life, and close association between readers' advertising and editorial interests. However, it would be a mistake to characterize the business press as simply magazines directed to nonconsumers. Despite many similarities between business and consumer magazines, the business press has a number of unique features.

Marketing Strategy for Business Publications

The typical business publication advertisement is different from a consumer advertisement in several significant ways. First, it is usually directed to a small, knowledgeable audience of experts. The types of product "puffery" and general media strategy used to reach a general consumer audience are inadequate in successful business advertising.

The purpose of most consumer advertising is to create long- or short-term sales. Business advertising is more often designed to complement personal selling. With current estimates of the direct cost of a sales call at over $230,[6] it is imperative that products be introduced to prospects before a sales call. Business advertising does this.

Competition from Other Media

The dollars allocated to any particular consumer medium often could have purchased advertising in any number of competing vehicles. Business publications tend to compete in a much narrower arena. The major competitor of business publications is direct mail because it offers many of the advantages of the business press. However, the higher cost of direct mail and, in the minds of some, its lower prestige, work against direct mail in competing with business publications. Yet, while estimates are difficult to obtain, direct mail probably brings in more business advertising dollars than do business publications.

Circulation

Many business publications do not charge for subscriptions. Such magazines are said to have **controlled circulations** since the publisher deter-

---

6 "Survey: Business Sales Calls," *Marketing News,* August 1, 1986, p. 1.

mines who is to receive the publication and thereby "controls" the circulation. Magazines may also offer a combination of paid and controlled circulation. For instance, *Marketing and Media Decisions* is sent free to those who "plan, approve, and implement media buys." Others can subscribe for $45 a year. In the last several years, many controlled circulation magazines have gone to a paid basis to offset increased costs.

Earlier in this chapter we mentioned that magazines are audited. The three major organizations—VAC, BPA, and ABC—also audit business publications to verify circulation figures. While all three audit controlled circulation, the ABC has special requirements, which must be met before it will agree to audit a business publication. The publication to be audited by ABC must meet one of three conditions:

1. Have at least 70 percent of its total distribution as paid circulation.
2. Have at least 70 percent of its circulation as paid and choose also to report further nonpaid circulation to the field served.
3. Have at least 70 percent nonpaid direct request (issues provided without charge in response to reader requests) or a combination of at least 70 percent paid and nonpaid direct request.

See Figure 9–8 for an example portion of the ABC report for a business publication in this category. In addition, business publications with more than 50 percent paid circulation must report percentage of renewals of paid subscription.

Another feature of the circulation of business publications is the use of the Standard Industrial Classification (SIC), which was established by the U.S. Office of Management and Budget, to report their circulation (see Figure 9–9). The SIC is a seven-digit code that classifies all industries and subcategories of industries; however, for most purposes, only the first four levels are used. The Business Publications SRDS lists the basic two-digit code for many industrial publications to allow advertisers to identify the circulation breakdowns of these magazines.

The Business Publications SRDS also requires that most magazines fill out a sworn statement to verify their circulation figures. It breaks down circulation into census areas, paid and nonpaid circulation, and a business analysis, which divides circulation into various groups. Magazines are required to provide a notarized statement twice a year.

Industrial publications are often characterized as either vertical or horizontal. A **vertical publication** covers all aspects of an industry. A **horizontal publication** covers one job that cuts across several industries (see Figure 9–10).

In 1986, Simmons Market Research Bureau performed the first through-the-book readership study of an industrial market, the metalworking industry (SIC 33–38). SMRB had earlier done a readership study for the food service industry, but used a mail questionnaire method of

FIGURE 9–8 Section of the ABC Report for a Business Publication with a Majority of Nonpaid Circulation

2. Paid Circulation & Non-Paid Circulation to Field Served by Issues and Non-Paid Removals & Additions:

Issue	Paid	Non-Paid	Total	Non-Paid Removed	Non-Paid Added
Jan.	1,571	2,606	4,177	12	11
Feb.	1,571	2,603	4,174	15	12
Mar.	1,558	2,605	4,163	10	12
Apr.	1,531	2,601	4,132	24	20
May	1,553	2,604	4,157	15	18
June	1,558	2,594	4,152	30	20

3(a). Business/Occupational Analysis Of Circulation For The May, 19-- Issue:

Paid subscription circulation of this issue was 1.09% less than average total paid subscription circulation for period. Non-paid circulation to field served of this issue was 0.08% greater than average for period.

					Classification by Title & Occupation			
Classification by Business & Industry	**Paid Subs.**	**Non-Paid**	**Total**	**%**	**A**	**B**	**C**	**D**
1. Manufacturers of Coatings & Resins............	723	1,427	2,150	51.93	175	432	1,289	254
2. Manufacturers of Raw Materials & Equipment ...	30	1,065	1,095	26.45	32	87	859	117
3. Wholesalers & Retailers of Chemical Coatings & Resins..........	152		152	3.67	17	61	57	17
4. Manufacturers' Agents; Brokers; Importers & Exporters	157	52	209	5.05	5	21	181	2
5. Research & Testing Laboratories; Consultants; Educational Institutions; Government Agencies; Technical & Public Libraries	188	57	245	5.92	15	40	171	19
6. Others Allied to the Field	264	3	267	6.45	21	35	194	17
Total Qualified	1,514	2,604	4,118	99.47	265	676	2,751	426
Qualification Not Determined	22		22	0.53				22
Total Paid Subscription Circulation and Non-Paid Circulation To Field Served For The May, 19-- Issue	**1,536**	**2,604**	**4,140**	**100.00**	**265**	**676**	**2,751**	**448**

Key to Classification by Title, Occupation and/or Function

A - Subscriptions in Company Name
B - Owners, Presidents, Vice Presidents & General Managers
C - Superintendents, Chemists & Technical Directors
D - Branch Managers, Salespeople & Other Personnel

3(b). Analysis of Non-Paid Circulation To Field Served By Age Of Source Data For May, 19-- Issue:

	Qualified Within							
SOURCE	**1 Year**	**%**	**2 Years**	**%**	**3 Years**	**%**	**Total**	**%**
Non-Paid Circulation to Field Served:								
Direct request from recipient:								
Written	1,042	45.88	123	51.46	66	7,021	1,231	47.27
Telemarketing	173	7.62					173	6.64
Direct request from recipient's company:								
Written	844	37.16	116	48.54	28	29.79	988	37.94
Telemarketing	22	0.97					22	0.85
Communication other than request:								
Written	8	0.35					8	0.31
Telemarketing								
Business directories								
Lists	182	8.01					182	6.99
Other Sources								
Total Non-Paid Circulation To Field Served	**2,271**	**100.00**	**239**	**100.00**	**94**	**100.00**	**2,604**	**100.00**
Percent	**87.20**		**9.17**		**3.63**		**100.00**	

Management Production

SOURCE: "How to Read an ABC Business Publication Publisher's Statement," Audit Bureau of Circulations.

FIGURE 9-9   An Example of the Standard Industrial Code

20	Food
202	Dairy products
2021	Creamery butter

data collection. The metalworking study, commissioned by *Iron Age,* produced controversial findings because of the data collection method used. However, it represents a fundamental change in the data business publishers offer advertisers about readers. Before this study, readership data were collected (and, some say, "cooked") by the publishers themselves. Research done on the circulation of a publication by a reputable third party, such as SMRB, may do much to reassure advertisers that the audiences they wish to reach in the business press are actually available.

FARM MAGAZINES

Although the smallest in number, circulation, and advertising revenues, the farm press, like its larger contemporaries, has experienced significant increases in advertising revenues during the last several years. In 1984, these revenues exceeded $181 million.

In many respects, farm publications have followed the same pattern as consumer magazines during the last decade. During the 1960s, several

FIGURE 9-10   Horizontal and Vertical Business Publications

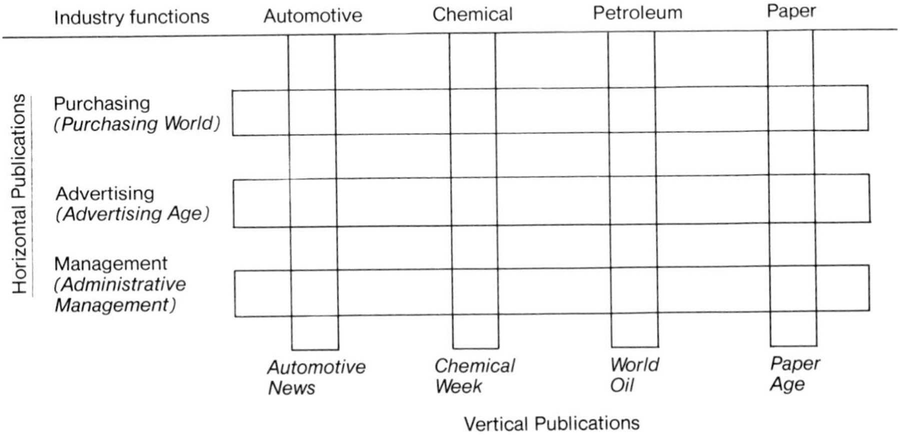

specialized farm journals were founded that began to compete effectively with the more general farm journals. Also, the large-circulation farm magazines were hurt by reductions in the number of farm families and by the growing sophistication and specialization of agribusiness. With the advent of the "consolidated farm," magazines that treated the farm family as a unique lifestyle became increasingly unnecessary. The college-educated, higher-income farm family was concerned with modern fashion, world events, and farm commodity prices. The farm family was reading *The Wall Street Journal, McCall's,* and *Agri Finance.*

Forecast of Changes in Agriculture

In forecasting the changes that may be expected in U.S. agriculture during the next several decades, five major factors have been identified.

1. Exports will be even more important than they are today as communications improve and nations lower their trade barriers.
2. U.S. farms will be large, commercial, family-operated enterprises.
3. U.S. farms will employ additional mechanization.
4. Productivity will continue to increase because of more careful use of soil and water, crops and animals modified by biotechnology, and computer science applied to farm operations.
5. Farm families will enjoy all the amenities of city dwellers, while retaining the sense of belonging to a group apart that works with soil, water, and seed to provide food to the people of the world.[7]

By the late 1960s, the major farm publications had almost eliminated features about homemaking and had begun to emphasize the business aspects of farming. They also eliminated rural subscribers who were not farmers, thus cutting circulation but offering a more valuable audience to advertisers. They followed the lead of consumer magazines by aggressively selling regional and demographic editions to compete with the new regional publications. Some of the larger farm magazines have gone a step further and offered regionalized editorial material as well as advertising. For instance, *Progressive Farmer* offers "All Cotton," "East Cotton," and "West Cotton" editions tailored to the needs of advertisers concerned with this particular crop and with east-west regional differences in its production.

---

[7] Wayne D. Rasmussen, "The Challenge of Change," *U.S. Agriculture in a Global Economy,* U.S. Department of Agriculture, 1985, p. 11.

Marketing Strategy for the Farm Press

Today the farm press offers advertisers market segmentation, which is often more sophisticated than the market segmentations developed by either consumer or business publications. Target marketing of farm publications is necessary for two reasons. First, the farm audience is extremely diversified by climate, crops, and soil condition. Second, agricultural businesses have shown a willingness to use a variety of media to reach their customers. In competing for the agribusiness advertising dollar, farm magazines must position themselves against radio, direct mail, outdoor, and, in many major farm markets, television and newspapers.

To compete for this fragmented farm market, farm publications have developed extensive regional and demographic editions. A farm magazine may simultaneously offer regional editions, crop editions, and a general publication. Farm magazines may even increase their frequency of publication during peak growing seasons or send special editions to certain reader segments. For instance, *Farm Journal* publishes 14 times a year—monthly except for two issues in January, February, and March, and a combined June-July issue.

Unlike the advertising in consumer magazines, in which national advertising is supplemented by regional/demographic advertising, most farm magazine advertising is placed on a regional basis. The only major category of farm advertisers that routinely uses national runs is farm equipment. Chemical companies, the largest category of farm advertisers, must adjust their advertising to various crop and geographic conditions. In fact, most farm advertisers would like even more specialized editions or major farm publications than are available at present.

Despite the demographic/regional breakouts offered by the major farm publications, specialized magazines have flourished in the agricultural sector. It could be said that most of the regional/demographic editions offered by the major farm publications have been a result of the growth of small, specialized farm magazines. Here, the large-circulation farm publications have followed the same patterns as the major consumer publications. However, farm publications differ from consumer publications in that they offer both advertising and editorial material on a regional basis. Regionalized editorial material is rarely offered in business publications and almost never offered in consumer magazines.

The number of specialized farm magazines has more than doubled in the last decade. The trend in these smaller circulation farm publications is toward both regional and vocational specialization. Magazines such as *Avocado Grower* and *Charolais Journal* are typical of the newer narrow-interest publication.

Structure of the Farm Press

The farm press is divided into four categories:

1. *General-circulation farm magazines.* The largest of the big three is *Farm Journal* (circulation 1 million). The other two are *Successful Farming* and *Progressive Farmer.*
2. *Regional farm magazines.* These publications aim specifically at farmers in different parts of the country. Examples are *Michigan Farmer* and *Buckeye Farm News.*
3. *Vocational farm magazines.* These publications are also called crop-specific/livestock-specific magazines. Often, a single magazine combines both regional and vocational elements, such as the *New Mexico Stockman* and *Pecan South.*
4. *Agribusiness publications.* These magazines address the complexities of farming as a business. They include both business (*Agri Finance*) and technological (*Crops and Soils Magazine*) publications.

REVIEW QUESTIONS

1. Discuss consumer, farm, and business publications from the perspective of the advertisers using each type.
2. Discuss the transition of magazines from a mass medium to a "class" medium. Are there exceptions to this trend?
3. Discuss the Media Imperative concept as a device for selling magazine advertising.
4. How does the Audit Bureau of Circulations differ from the major syndicated magazine readership services?
5. Discuss advertising flexibility as it relates to magazines. In what respect are magazines an inflexible advertising medium?
6. What is a magazine network?
7. In what ways is the magazine rebate different from the newspaper rebate?
8. Why are magazines concerned with the growth of cable television?
9. Name three types of business magazines and give an example of each.
10. In what ways have the farm magazines shown patterns of development similar to those of the consumer magazines during the last several years? How have they differed from consumer magazines?
11. How are business publications different from consumer magazines?

APPENDIX*

TOP 10 CONSUMER MAGAZINE ADVERTISERS 1985

(000)

1.	$56,709.1	National Paragon Corp.
2.	35,898.1	R.J. Reynolds Industries Inc.
3.	20,895.0	Philip Morris Cos. Inc.
4.	13,719.8	CBS Inc.
5.	11,704.5	Bat Industries PLC
6.	8,741.2	Franklin Mint
7.	6,952.7	American Can Co.
8.	5,901.1	Nutrition Headquarters
9.	5,339.0	Brown-Forman Co.
10.	5,003.4	Abernathy & Closther Ltd.

* As reported in *Marketing and Media Decisions*, August 1986, pp. 86, 88–89.

BASIC DATA FOR CONSUMER MAGAZINES
SELECTED YEARS—1960–1985

	1985	1984	1983	1982	1980	1970
Number, including farm publications	1,859	1,816	1,759	1,644	1,506	1,182

Advertising in major magazines

	1985	1984	1983	1982	1980	1970
Pages (per year)	152,100	153,600	133,000	120,800	115,300	76,990
Dollars (millions per year)	$4,920	$4,668	$3,421	$3,222	$2,374	$1,169

Circulation per issue

ABC audited magazines (millions)	1985	1984	1983	1982	1980	1970
Single copy	81	82	83	86	91	70
Subscription	243	233	222	217	174	173
Total	**324**	**315**	**305**	**303**	**265**	**243**

SOURCE: James B. Kobak

FINANCIAL PROFILES OF MAGAZINE PUBLISHING
1983-1985
(Amounts expressed as a percentage of total magazine revenues)

	Percentages		
	1983	**1984**	**1985**
Total number of magazines reporting	154	172	169
Revenue			
Net advertising revenues	49.87	51.91	49.70
Gross subscription revenues	33.70	32.97	33.29
Gross single copy revenues	16.43	15.12	17.01
Total magazine revenues	**100.00**	**100.00**	**100.00**
Advertising expenses	9.15	9.47	9.38
Circulation expenses	25.07	24.83	26.87
Editorial costs	8.40	8.66	8.51
Manufacturing and distribution expenses	36.90	36.55	36.19
Other operational costs	3.27	3.31	3.29
Administrative costs	6.32	5.89	6.11
Total magazine costs	**89.11**	**88.71**	**90.35**
Operating profit (before taxes)	**10.89**	**11.29**	**9.65**

SOURCE: *Magazine Publishers Association*

CONSUMER MAGAZINES ADVERTISING RATE INDEX

	Unit Rates	Cost per Thousand	Consumer Price Index
1970	100	100	100
1977	119	123	156
1978	120	135	168
1979	140	146	187
1980	156	162	212
1981	173	179	234
1982	189	195	249
1983	203	212	258
1984	224	227	269
1985	241	242	279
1986 (est)	255	256	287
1970–77 Increase	19%	23%	56%
1977–86 Increase	114%	108%	84%

SOURCE: *James B. Kobak*

CONSUMER MAGAZINES CIRCULATION PRICE INDEX

	Average Single Copy Price		Average Yearly Subscription Price		Consumer Price Index
	$	Index	$	Index	
1970	$ .63	100	$ 7.16	100	100
1977	1.11	176	13.39	187	156
1978	1.21	192	14.86	208	168
1979	1.33	211	16.30	225	187
1980	1.48	235	16.75	234	212
1981	1.62	257	18.06	252	234
1982	1.80	286	20.28	283	249
1983	1.97	313	21.53	301	258
1984	2.07	329	22.61	316	269
1985	2.10	333	23.15	323	279
1986 (est.)	2.16	343	23.84	333	287
1970–1977 Increase	76%		87%		56%
1977–1986 Increase	95%		78%		84%

SOURCE: *James B. Kobak*

SUGGESTED ADDITIONAL READING

BARTOS, RENA. "Daniel Starch: The Founding-est Father." *Journal of Advertising Research* 26, no. 1 (February/March 1986), pp. 50–54.

Bylaws and Rules, Audit Bureau of Circulations, August 1985.

"Four-Color Insert Program Helps Sell Catalogues." *Marketing News,* September 27, 1985, p. 13.

HOUSTON, FRANKLIN S., and DIANE SCOTT."The Determinants of Advertising Page Exposure." *Journal of Advertising* 13, no. 2 (1984), pp. 27–33.

"Integrated Marketing Urged for Magazine Publishers." *Marketing News,* April 12, 1985, pp. 4–5.

LILL, DAVID; CHARLES GROSS; and ROBIN PETERSON."The Inclusion of Social-Responsibility Themes by Magazine Advertisers: A Longitudinal Study." *Journal of Advertising* 15, no. 2 (1986), pp. 35–41.

"Little Old Lady Rides Again to Promote Magazines." *Marketing News,* June 7, 1985, p. 18.

"Rural America—On the Trail of the White-Collar Settlers." *The Economist,* November 8, 1986, pp. 37–38, 43.

SOLEY, LAWRENCE, and LEONARD N. REID. "Ad Readership as a Function of Headline Type," *Journal of Advertising* 12, no. 1 (1983), pp. 34–38.

SOLEY, LAWRENCE, and LEONARD N. REID. "Satisfaction with the Information Value of Magazine and Television Advertising." *Journal of Advertising* 12, no. 3 (1983), pp. 27–31.

ZINKHAN, GEORGE M., and BETSY D. GELB. "What Starch Scores Predict." *Journal of Advertising Research* 26, no. 4 (August/September, 1986), pp. 45–50.

CHAPTER TEN

Out-of-Home Advertising

I've chosen to confine myself to one medium . . . the lowly poster: object of environmentalist's wrath and the creative director's disdain . . . this maligned medium is, I contend, the ultimate synthesis of the creative idea, and its history is the history of advertising itself.*

John O'Toole

Outdoor is considered to be the oldest form of advertising and one of the most ancient forms of communication. The ancient Egyptians posted roadside commercial messages on stone tablets called stelae. Later the Romans and Greeks set aside space in public places for ads and announcements of sports contests.[1]

In the United States, the growth of outdoor advertising coincided with the development of automobile travel. Early in this century, outdoor advertising moved away from the bill posting of the 1800s to become a standardized, self-regulated industry. By the 1930s, it had a strong trade association, the Outdoor Advertising Association of America (OAAA), and an organization to provide outdoor circulation figures, the Traffic Audit Bureau (TAB).

OUTDOOR ADVERTISING TODAY

Today outdoor advertising is a major medium with revenues greater than network radio and farm publications and about equal to those of women's magazines. Annual outdoor revenues are about $1.3 billion; about 70 percent comes from national advertisers. Co-op outdoor alone produced about 10 percent of the industry's gross revenue. At the same time,

---

* "The Great Outdoors," James Webb Young Fund Address, University of Illinois, March 5, 1985.

[1] *The First Medium,* Institute of Outdoor Advertising, 1975, p. 2.

almost 80 percent of outdoor advertisers are local merchants and companies advertising in local markets. From 1967 to 1985, outdoor advertising grew at an annual rate of more than 8 percent.

A major concern of the outdoor advertising industry is criticism from special-interest groups and legislative bodies. Some of this criticism may be warranted. However, the organized outdoor industry thinks, with some justification, that the public often confuses outdoor with nonstandardized or on-premise signs. In recent years, the industry has attempted to educate the public and lawmakers about the outdoor industry.

OUTDOOR AS A REGULATED INDUSTRY

Self-Regulation

Because of the criticism directed at outdoor advertising, the industry has a self-regulation program stronger than that of any other medium. The initiative for this industry-wide effort is provided by the OAAA, although many local outdoor firms also engage in public education programs. These self-regulation efforts have been successful; in nearly all instances, member organizations adhere to the OAAA regulations regarding outdoor advertising practices. Unfortunately for these OAAA members, the public does not always distinguish between members and nonmembers in its call for legal restrictions on outdoor advertising.

Legal Regulation

The major federal legislation affecting outdoor advertising is the Highway Beautification Act, which was passed by Congress in 1965. It was known as the "Lady Bird Bill" because Mrs. Lyndon Johnson lobbied for the bill when it was being considered by Congress. The act was intended to regulate and control both outdoor advertising and junkyards.

The act requires a 660-foot buffer along interstate and major federal highways, with some exemptions in industrially zoned areas and near businesses being advertised. It provides penalties of up to 10 percent of federal highway funds for states found to be in noncompliance. It also provides that "just compensation" be paid for removed signs. The act is administered by the Federal Highway Administration.

The major obstacle to implementation of the act has been the failure of Congress to allocate funds to fully compensate sign owners. It would cost an estimated $400 million to remove the 200,000 offending signs that fall under the provisions of the act. In the last 10 years, Congress has budgeted a little over $200 million, but this money has been earmarked for junkyard screening as well as outdoor poster removal. In recent years,

Congress has been reluctant to allocate funds, and its attention has been repeatedly turned to dismantling existing billboards (boards).

What does the general public think about the industry? A study by the University of Michigan's Survey Research Center showed that 64.5 percent of those polled favored "reasonable regulation" of outdoor advertising, while only 19 percent were in favor of banning outdoor ads. And according to the Federal Highway Administration, in the 20 years since the Beautification Act passed, the number of signs has declined from 4.4 per mile to 1.7.[2]

One proposal considered by Congress that would ban outdoor advertising within five years outside of newly restricted "commercial" areas implicitly recognizes that the plan represents confiscation of property. The five-year interval is based on the depreciable life of a billboard under the present tax code (only economic assets may be depreciated).

The lack of coherent action by Congress has left the outdoor industry in a difficult position. Owners of outdoor advertising companies do not know which of the following Congress will decide to do:

1. Fund additional poster removal.
2. Put the program in a holding pattern by leaving present signs alone.
3. Drop the program altogether by repealing the Act.
4. Require the removal of certain classes of signs or signs in specified locations.

In the meantime, the outdoor industry must deal with local and state legislation, which sometimes contradicts federal regulations.

In the future local legislation may present a bigger problem than federal legislation. The outdoor industry generally takes the position that it can operate successfully under a fair federal control program. However, since the outdoor industry depends on standardized, national advertising, local rules that specify varying sizes of outdoor posters would be impossible to deal with. For this reason, some in the outdoor industry favor federal legislation that would take precedence over any local laws.

TYPES OF OUTDOOR ADVERTISING

The outdoor industry has three categories: posters (or paper), painted bulletins, and one-of-a-kind spectaculars.

---

[2] Lisa Phillips, "Industry Battles Beauty and Beast Images," *Advertising Age,* December 12, 1985, p. 20.

Posters (Highway Billboards)

The basic **poster** sizes are 24- and 30-sheet posters and bleed posters. The standard poster panel is built to accommodate all three sizes; therefore, in major markets, an advertiser should be able to use one of them. The 30-sheet poster is the most widely used size and has replaced the 24-sheet as the standard unit. There is no difference in advertising costs for the three sizes, although production costs are greater for the larger types.

In some markets, two smaller posters are available. These are the **junior panel** or 8-sheet poster, which has a copy area 5 feet by 11 feet, and the 3-sheet poster, which measures 46 inches high by 30 inches wide. These posters are generally used for pedestrian traffic and are often placed in shopping center parking lots or on the sides of buildings. Because of their smaller size and their unavailability in some markets, these posters are used more often by local advertisers. At the same time, the smaller posters, particularly the 8-sheet size, have attractive characteristics. The 8-sheet board, at one quarter the cost of a 30-sheet poster, delivers 77 percent of the visibility, as much viewer recall, and about equal copy readership.[3] And the 8-sheet size is one of the industry's hottest offerings, growing in number by 75 percent from 1980 to 1985.

Painted Bulletins

The **painted bulletin** is an individually designed and painted sign. Because bulletins are painted one at a time, they offer greater opportunities for creativity and individuality than posters. The size of painted bulletins can be increased by the use of extensions that can add up to 200 square feet of space. Normal limits on extensions are 5 feet 6 inches at the top and 2 feet at the bottom and sides. When extensions are used, the sign is known as an *embellished bulletin*. In some cases, a high-gloss paper may be used. Figure 10–1 shows the mechanical specifications for the various sizes of outdoor posters. Advertisers often buy rotary plans, in which the message is moved from one location to another, to increase audience reach. Figure 10–2 is an example of a typical rotary bulletin plan.

Spectaculars

The final category of outdoor advertising is the spectaculars. These custom-built displays are usually large, with extensive use of lighting,

---

[3] "Nothing Small about Eight-Sheet Efficiencies," *Marketing and Media Decisions*, March 1985, pp. 92–94.

FIGURE 10-1 Mechanical Specifications for Outdoor Posters

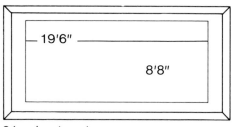

19'6"

8'8"

24—sheet poster

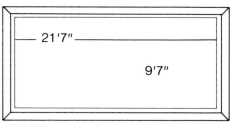

21'7"

9'7"

30—sheet poster

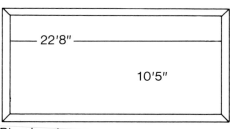

22'8"

10'5"

Bleed poster

48'

14'

Painted bulletin

FIGURE 10-2 A Typical Rotary Bulletin Plan

Atlanta Metro Rotary Bulletin Plan

RATE SCHEDULE:

THREE YEAR CONTRACT	$1,161.00 Per Mo.
TWO YEAR CONTRACT	$1,225.50 Per Mo.
ONE YEAR CONTRACT	$1,290.00 Per Mo.

MAGNA–FACE BULLETIN
COPY AREA: 14' X 48'

The rates indicated above reflect a 5% continuity discount for two year and 10% for three year noncancellable contracts, respectively. Rate protection is provided throughout the term of noncancellable contracts.

Three year contracts cancellable at the end of the first and second year shall not have rate protection beyond the anniversary dates and the monthly rate shall be as follows: First year $1,290.00; second year $1,225.50; third year $1,161.00.

Advertising agency commissions will be allowed on the net rate after applicable discounts.

THE BASE MONTHLY RATE INCLUDES:

- Three copy changes per year*
- All night illumination
- Sixty day rotation
- Cost of fabrication, painting, and rotation of up to 100 sq. ft. of cut-out extension is included in the initial copy design.*

*Repaints and cut-out allowances may not be accumulated, nor will credits be issued for unused repaints or cut-out square footage.

SHORT TERM CONTRACTS:

Rates furnished upon request, based on availability.

PRINTED BULLETINS:

Advertisers furnishing 14' x 48' printed posters to be displayed on a 60 day basis for a minimum of 12 consecutive months will receive a $50.00 monthly allowance.

CUT–OUT EXTENSIONS:

The fabrication, painting and rotation of up to 100 square feet of flat surface cut-out extension for the initial copy is included in the contract cost, provided the contract term is a minimum of 12 months. The cost for additional square footage during the contract term will be $9.00 Gross (subject to agency commission) or $7.50 Net (not subject to agency commision) per square foot.

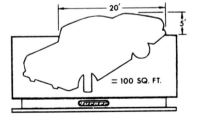

CUT–OUT LIMITATIONS: Side 2' 6"   Bottom 2' 0"   Top 5' 0"

ILLUMINATED AND CUT–OUT LETTERS, TRIVISION, AND OTHER SPECIAL TREATMENT:

Prices will be quoted upon request.

Courtesy of Turner Advertising Company

movement, and intricate designs. Because of the high cost of construction and maintenance, only the largest advertisers customarily contract for spectaculars, and then only in the most heavily traveled locations. Spectaculars are bought for specific locations, and their cost is determined by production costs and, to a lesser extent, traffic flow.

In recent years, outdoor signs have been developed that offer greater durability, lower maintenance costs, and higher visibility than traditional paper posters. These new outdoor signs combine certain elements of paper posters, painted bulletins, and spectaculars. One example is 3M's Panagraphics, which places a series of lamps behind a translucent, vinyl-type material called Penaflex. Like paper, the sign is relatively easy to change, has the durability of paint, and distributes light more evenly for better night visibility than the usual spotlight illuminated posters.

A variation of nighttime illumination has been developed that looks like an ordinary sign by day. However, during times when illumination is required, a computer-driven slide projector, mounted on an automatic boom, projects slides back onto the billboard. Slides are changed every 20 seconds or so.[4]

PLANTS

Outdoor advertising is purchased through individual operators or **plants.** Approximately 600 plant operators in the United States offer outdoor advertising in more than 900 markets. A plant usually leases locations for its poster panels and then sells this space to advertisers. Many larger plants offer some creative services, but this is not generally a plant function. National outdoor campaigns are purchased through one or more national outdoor buying organizations. Using one of these services allows the advertiser to buy several markets and pay only a single bill and deal with one company instead of several plants.

OUTDOOR AS AN ADVERTISING MEDIUM

Strengths

Broad Reach and High Frequency Levels. Outdoor is a high-intensity medium since it generates high levels of coverage as well as multiple exposures. It is also excellent for reaching all segments of the population—only the very young and very old are not prime prospects for

---

[4] "Billboards Go On-Line . . . ," *Venture,* July 1983, p. 10.

outdoor advertising. Note in Figure 10–3 that outdoor advertising is efficient in reaching almost all market segments.

Flexibility. Since outdoor advertising can be purchased in almost every community, the media planner has flexibility in choosing the geographic pattern. The medium can be used selectively to accommodate specific market problems or in a general national campaign.

FIGURE 10–3   Outdoor Reach and Frequency by Selected Demographic Characteristics (30 days)

	#100 Showing		#50 Showing		#25 Showing	
	R	F	R	F	R	F
Adults	87.2%	24.9	81.9%	13.3	71.4%	7.4
Men	86.1	29.6	81.2	15.7	74.3	8.6
Women	88.3	20.6	82.5	11.0	74.0	6.2

Household Income

	#100 Showing		#50 Showing		#25 Showing	
	R	F	R	F	qR	F
$35,000+						
Adults	90.7%	29.4	85.7%	15.6	79.6%	8.4
Men	89.1	34.2	84.1	18.2	79.5	9.6
Women	92.8	23.7	87.7	12.6	79.6	7.0
$25,000+						
Adults	90.7	29.0	85.4	15.4	79.0	8.4
Men	88.9	33.9	83.7	18.1	78.2	9.7
Women	92.9	23.3	87.5	12.4	79.9	6.9
$15,000+						
Adults	89.2	27.5	84.2	14.6	77.4	8.0
Men	88.6	32.5	83.9	17.2	78.6	
Women	89.9	22.1	84.5	11.8	76.0	6.6

Education

	#100 Showing		#50 Showing		#25 Showing	
	R	F	R	F	R	F
Attended/Graduated college						
Adults	89.6%	27.8	85.4%	14.6	78.1%	8.0
Men	87.9	31.7	83.5	16.7	77.2	9.1
Women	91.7	23.4	87.7	12.3	79.1	6.8
Graduated high school						
Adults	89.5	25.8	84.5	13.6	76.8	7.6
Men	89.1	30.3	84.9	15.9	78.3	8.7
Women	89.7	22.3	84.3	11.9	75.6	6.6

FIGURE 10-3 (concluded)

Employment and Occupation

	#100 Showing		#50 Showing		#25 Showing	
	R	F	R	F	R	F
Professionals/managers						
Adults	91.2%	30.4	87.2%	15.9	81.4%	8.6
Men	89.6	32.8	85.2	17.3	79.3	9.3
Women	94.0	26.1	91.1	13.5	85.3	7.2
Clerical/sales						
Adults	91.7	28.7	87.1	15.1	79.7	8.3
Men	89.7	33.9	84.2	18.1	78.4	9.7
Women	92.6	26.5	88.4	13.9	80.3	7.7
Craftsman/foreman						
Adults	91.6	32.6	88.5	17.0	83.2	9.0
Men	91.4	33.0	88.1	17.2	83.4	9.1
Employed full time						
Adults	90.2	29.4	86.2	15.4	79.3	8.4
Men	89.3	31.6	85.2	16.6	78.9	9.0
Women	91.8	25.4	87.9	13.3	79.9	7.3

Age

	#100 Showing		#50 Showing		#25 Showing	
	R	F	R	F	R	F
Age 18–24						
Adults	91.6%	30.2	87.0%	15.9	80.4%	8.7
Men	90.6	33.5	86.0	17.7	81.2	9.5
Women	92.5	27.0	88.1	14.2	79.5	7.9
Age 25–34						
Adults	92.0	29.8	88.1	15.6	81.7	8.4
Men	92.2	34.0	88.6	17.7	82.4	9.5
Women	91.8	25.6	87.5	13.5	80.9	7.3
Age 35–44						
Adults	86.1	24.1	81.1	12.8	73.9	7.0
Men	84.6	28.3	81.2	14.8	74.7	8.0
Women	87.6	20.0	81.0	10.8	73.0	6.0
Age 45–54						
Adults	86.8	22.5	81.0	12.1	73.1	6.7
Men	86.2	28.0	79.3	15.2	72.8	8.3
Women	87.3	17.3	82.6	9.2	73.4	5.2
Age 55–64						
Adults	82.7	20.1	75.9	11.0	65.5	6.4
Men	80.1	26.5	74.3	14.3	65.7	8.2
Women	85.1	14.5	77.5	8.0	65.2	4.7
Age 65+						
Adults	80.6	16.9	73.3	9.3	64.3	5.3
Men	76.2	20.4	70.0	11.1	59.4	6.6
Women	83.5	14.7	75.4	8.2	67.6	4.6

Courtesy of Institute of Outdoor Advertising

Low Cost per Thousand. Outdoor advertising is the least expensive major medium by a wide margin. Generally, posters achieve a CPM of 30 to 40 cents, while the cost of the more expensive painted bulletins averages about $1 per 1,000.

Impact. One of the greatest strengths of outdoor advertising is its size. Combining visual dominance and color, it offers advertisers excellent opportunities for brand and package identification.

Out-of-Home Audience. Outdoor advertising reaches an audience that is already in the marketplace. It is an excellent medium to complement other advertising as a last reminder before purchase.

Weaknesses

Nonselectivity. Outdoor advertising is a mass medium in every respect. Used correctly, the medium can accomplish many marketing objectives with its wide coverage. However, it is not the best choice for reaching a particular market segment or target audience. Occasionally, painted bulletins may provide such coverage in a particular geographic area of a market, but under normal circumstances, outdoor advertising cannot be used to provide selective demographic coverage.

High Absolute Cost. Despite the low CPMs achieved by outdoor advertising, it is not an inexpensive medium for a multimarket campaign. This is especially true for advertisers who need extensive coverage of the top 10 or top 50 markets. Figure 10–4 shows some comparative cost data.

Short Exposure Time. Outdoor advertising benefits advertisers because it is attractive to a mobile, out-of-home audience. However, this characteristic is also a detriment to communication. Outdoor advertising functions best when it is asked to deliver a visual image—a package, a brand name, or a short slogan. It is not designed to communicate lengthy advertising copy. An outdoor message that must be "read" is not as effective as one that only needs to be "seen."

Audience Measurement. A major problem, which some advertisers think prevents outdoor advertising from achieving equal status with other media, is a lack of verified audience measurement. The Traffic Audit Bureau (TAB) is the circulation-auditing organization for the outdoor industry. The auditing procedure is merely a traffic count in areas adjacent to poster locations.

A simple traffic count is not adequate in determining the overall

FIGURE 10–4 Estimated Outdoor Costs for Large Markets

30-Sheet Metro Area Poster Costs
(#50 Showing)

ADI Market	Market Population Size (000)	Number of Posters		Monthly Cost ($)
		Non-Illuminated	Illuminated	
1. New York				
Richmond/NYC-SI	395	6	6	4,980
Winston Network/New York	7,179	134	—	70,350
Suburban Outdoor/NY	1,107	28	30	22,772
Seaboard/New York	7,072	—	186	97,650
Gannett/NJ Metro	5,240	—	160	69,280
Sunrise/Nassau-Suffolk	2,686	20	5	12,999
Total	**23,680**	**191**	**387**	**278,031**
2. Los Angeles				
Gannett/L.A.	10,600	26	224	115,991
Patrick/L.A.	12,120	26	224	117,062
Martin/L.A. North	270	10	10	6,000
Total	**22,990**	**62**	**458**	**239,553**
3. Chicago				
Patrick/Chicago	6,029	22	142	75,976
Chicago Metro 5/ Chicago Metro 5	1,409	31	44	17,808
Whiteco Metrocom/ Chicago Metro Suburban	1,240	17	39	14,870
Total	**8,678**	**70**	**225**	**34,468**
4. Philadelphia				
Rollins/Philadelphia	1,626	20	56	34,440
H.A. Steen/Philadelphia	3,592	24	54	31,200
Metro/Wilmington	536	76	16	8,920
United/Wilmington Urban	401	8	10	5,180
Total	**6,155**	**68**	**136**	**79,740**
5. San Francisco				
Patrick/San Francisco-Oakland-San Jose	4,304	11	110	53,837
Gannett/San Francisco-Oakland-San Jose	4,746	24	98	53,480
Total	**9,050**	**35**	**208**	**107,677**
6. Boston				
Ackerley/Boston-Worcester	4,566	55	115	68,995
7. Detroit				
Gannet/Detroit	4,100	—	92	46,920
Total	**4,100**	**—**	**92**	**46,920**
8. Dallas-Ft. Worth				
Patrick/ Dallas Metro	1,981	8	56	20,440
Dallas Suburban/ Dallas Suburban	359	32	4	7,560
Patrick/Ft. Worth	1,055	4	32	11,556
Total	**3,395**	**44**	**92**	**39,556**
9. Washington, DC				
Rollins/ Washington Metro Mkt.	3,426	8	94	44,880
Total	**3,426**	**8**	**94**	**44,880**
10. Houston				
Patrick/Houston	3,475	12	106	38,008
Total	**3,475**	**12**	**106**	**38,008**

SOURCE: *Adweek's Marketer's Guide to Media* 10, no. 1 (1987), pp. 166–67.

value of an outdoor poster. To estimate the overall value of a location, the TAB assigns a Space Position Value Rating (SPV) to a poster. The SPV reflects the visibility of the poster, its angle to traffic flow, the number of panels in a location, and the speed of the traffic. The combination of visibility and circulation determines the value of any single poster (see Figure 10–5).

To ensure that the poster positions sold meet minimum requirements for visibility, the TAB has developed the following guidelines to serve as standards for comparisons within a market or against other markets. These guidelines, utilized with the Space Position Valuation Table, ensure that the advertiser buys only positions that meet the standards of the American Association of Advertising Agencies.

If you look closely at Figure 10–5, you will notice that, on a scale of 10 to 1, no SPV scale value of less than 7 meets AAAA standards. In fact, four combinations of panel type and approach, with values ranging from 7 to 9, fall below these standards. In general, the concept of SPV is based on common sense. Long approach distances, slow traffic velocity, and easily seen panel types get high SPV scores because ads placed on such panels are relatively easy to read. Ads placed on panels that are difficult to see, where approach distances are short, and where traffic passes by rapidly earn lower SPV scores because they are difficult to read.

BUYING OUTDOOR ADVERTISING

The Gross Rating Point

The terminology for purchasing outdoor advertising has changed during the last several years. Formerly outdoor's basic unit of purchase was the "100 showing." A 100 **showing** was defined as the number of outdoor posters that would be seen by 100 percent of the mobile population (approximately 96 percent of the total population) in a 30-day period. This definition was unsatisfactory since it was fundamentally an attempt to measure reach (or unduplicated audience) when, in fact, the audience measurement techniques used in outdoor advertising had no practical means of distinguishing new from repeat exposures.

To overcome this problem, the outdoor industry redefined the term *100 showing*. It used the term *100* to define a level of *daily* coverage equal to the population of the market. Therefore, in a market of 100,000 persons, a level of intensity that provided 100,000 exposures was said to be a 100 showing.

This change in terminology provided a definition of what had been measured all along—duplicated audience. In 1972, the outdoor industry adopted its current definition of audience coverage, the gross rating

FIGURE 10–5   Space Position Valuation Table

SPACE POSITION VALUATION TABLE
Code and Scale of Values for Poster Panels

TAB

Form D	APPROACH (VEHICULAR)			TYPES OF PANELS								
	VEHICULAR			Angled Single (AS) / Angled nearest the Line of Travel (AE)		All Other Angled (A)				Parallel Single (PS) / Parallel End of a Group (PE)		All Other Parallel (P)
	Fast Travel	Slow Travel				In a Two Panel Facing		In a Facing With More Than Two Panels				
PEDESTRIAN				CODE	VALUE	CODE	VALUE	CODE	VALUE	CODE	VALUE	CODE	VALUE
Over 125 ft.	Long Approach Over 350 ft.	Over 250 ft.	1AS 1AE	10	1A	10	1A	9	1PS 1PE	8	1P	7
75 to 125 ft.	Medium Approach 200 to 350 ft.	150 to 250 ft.	2AS 2AE	8	2A	7	2A	7	2PS 2PE	6	2P	5
40 to 75 ft.	Short Approach 100 to 200 ft.	75 to 150 ft.	3AS 3AE	6	3A	5	3A	5	3PS 3PE	4	3P	3
	Flash Approach Under 100 ft.	Under 75 ft.	AF	4 3 2 1 0	AF	3 2 1 0	AF	3 2 1 0	PF	2 1 0	PF	1 0

Space position values in shaded areas are below AAAA standards.

Courtesy of Traffic Audit Bureau

point. By using GRP, the medium could sell more easily to national advertisers who were comfortable with this television terminology. As used by outdoor advertising, "a rating point is 1 percent of the population one time." GRPs are based on the daily duplicated audience as a percentage of a market. If three posters in a community of 100,000 population achieve a daily exposure to 75,000 people, the result is 75 GRPs. The formula can be stated as follows:

$$GRP = \frac{\text{Average Daily Effective Circulation (ADEC)}}{\text{Population of the Market}}$$

ADEC is defined as follows:

Daily is 12 hours for nonlighted signs and 18 hours for illuminated signs.

Effective is a measure of audience proximity to a sign rather than communication.

Circulation is a measure of the total number of duplicated people passing a sign rather than the total number of different people.

GRPs are sold in units of 25, with 100 and 50 being the two most often purchased levels. Intensities of more than 100 may be purchased, but this is rare. Some plants still use the term *showing,* although in most cases they also use GRPs. In recent years, the term *showing* has come to mean that an outdoor campaign of some level of intensity was used (e.g., a showing of 50 GRPs). See Figure 10–3 for an example of this usage.

Rate Information

Outdoor advertising is one of the few media for which no Standard Rate and Data volume is available. Advertising rates are published in the *Buyers Guide to Outdoor Advertising,* published twice a year by the Leading National Advertisers. Figure 10–6 shows an example of the information contained in the guide. Note that the guide gives GRP costs, market population discounts, and the number of posters in a GRP allotment and also cross-references overlapping markets.

Individual plants have their own rate cards (see Figure 10–7). The format of these cards is usually similar to that of the standard buying guide. However, the local rate cards often give more local market information as well as CPMs for the various GRP levels. When CPM is computed, remember that we are dealing with daily circulation, so some conversion must be made in the CPM formula to obtain the equivalent of the monthly CPM costs used for other media.

CPM conversion for outdoor:

$$\text{Outdoor CPM} = \frac{\dfrac{\text{Monthly cost}}{30} \times 1000}{\text{Daily circulation}}$$

FIGURE 10-6 **Example of Outdoor Rates and Markets**

NEW YORK   36   **OUTDOOR RATES AND MARKETS**   NEW YORK

PLANT NO.	MARKET NO.	MARKET NAME	COUNTY NAME	POP.	EFF. DATE	GRP/ SHOW	POSTERS NON ILL.	POSTERS ILL.	COST PER MONTH	DIS
5080.0 MIDPT	06800	CATSKILL MT BORSCHT DIST NYC	ULSTER-SULLIVAN	65.2	01/01/87	100	18	6	3876.00	03
						75	14	5	3162.00	03
			SINGLE PANEL RATE BOTH 315-			50	10	4	2402.00	03
						25	7	1	1415.00	03
5170.0 MODJES	06820	CATSKILL MT DIST. MKT NYC	GREENE-ULSTER	196.5	03/01/85	100	18	12	5700.00	
						50	10	8	3420.00	
		–Sub Markets (Sold Separately) CAIRO, NY CATSKILL MKT, NY ELLENVILLE, NY HIGHMOUNT, NY ⸺ON, NY				25	5	4	1710.00	
									145.00	
5110.0 MIDST	10050	CORTLAND COUNTY SYR	TOMPKINS-CAYUGA- CORTLAND	31.4	09/01/85	100	14		2030.00	
						50	8		1160.00	
		–Sub Markets (Sold Separately) CORTLAND, NY DRYDEN, NY GROTON, NY HOMER, NY MCGRAW, NY MARATHON, NY MORAVIA, NY				25	6		870.00	
5110.0 MIDST	10500	CUYLER SYR	CORTLAND	.1	09/01/85	100	1		145.00	
5110.0 MIDST	11150	DEANSBORO SYR	ONEIDA	3	09/01/85	100	2		290.00	
						50	1		145.00	

ADI CODE SEE NOTE TO BUYER	GRP GROSS RATING
**FIRST TWO DIGITS INDICATE STATES	POINTS EXCEPT *** = SHOWING

Courtesy of Leading National Advertisers.

Or using the 100-GRP level for the Ft. Smith Metro Area in Figure 10–7 and a daily circulation of 175,000:

$$\text{Outdoor CPM} = \frac{\frac{\$5,040}{30} \times 1,000}{175,000} = 96 \text{ cents}$$

Advertisers must consider outdoor production costs as well as space costs. In most other media, production costs are a small percentage of total advertising costs. This is not true in outdoor advertising. Production costs for painted bulletins and spectaculars comprise significant portions of total outdoor costs.

Buying Procedures

As mentioned earlier, the "medium" for outdoor advertising is the plant. The agency or advertiser works in much the same way with the plant as

FIGURE 10–7 A Rate Card for Outdoor Advertising

POSTER RATES AND ALLOTMENTS

Market/Population (000)	#100 GRP/showing Panels N-Ill.	Ill.	Cost Per Month	#75 GRP/showing Panels N-Ill.	Ill.	Cost Per Month	#50 GRP/showing Panels N-Ill.	Ill.	Cost Per Month	#25 GRP/showing Panels N-Ill.	Ill.	Cost Per Month
ARKANSAS												
NW Arkansas (227.9)	16	4	$ 4,340	12	3	$ 3,540	8	2	$ 2,570	4	1	$ 1,315
Fort Smith Urban (83.6)	5	5	2,288	4	4	1,926	3	3	1,500	2	2	1,027
Fort Smith Metro (175.5)	14	10	5,040	10	7	3,757	7	5	2,760	4	2	1,416
Little Rock Urban (288.8)	10	11	5,565	8	8	4,320	6	5	3,025	2	3	1,400
Little Rock Metro (428.7)	15	16	7,440	11	12	5,635	8	8	4,000	4	4	2,040
Pine Bluff Metro (90.4)	5	6	1,540	4	5	1,305	3	3	900	2	2	620
Russellville/Dardanelle (93.4)	16	2	3,453	13	1	2,772	8	1	1,838	4	1	1,087
IDAHO												
Coeur d' Alene (67.3)	3	3	1,704	3	2	1,420	2	2	1,136	1	1	589
Kellogg-Wallace (18.1)	3		714				2		477	1		250
INDIANA												
Muncie Metro (125.1)	5	11	2,714	4	8	2,086	2	6	1,425	1	3	730
KANSAS												
Wichita Urban (283.5)	12	16	8,120	9	12	6,090	6	8	4,060	3	4	2,030
Wichita Metro (424.7)	32	20	13,780	24	15	10,335	16	10	6,890	8	5	3,445
NEVADA												
Las Vegas Metro (567.2)	10	18	9,600	8	13	7,299	5	9	4,900	3	4	2,515
Reno Metro (210.0)	4	12	5,040	3	9	3,780	2	6	2,520	1	3	1,260
NEW MEXICO												
Albuquerque Metro (506.5)	16	16	9,495	12	12	7,800	8	8	5,500	4	4	2,975
OHIO												
Columbus (875.1)	15	51	24,090	12	38	18,750	9	26	13,475	4	13	6,715
Columbus Metro (1,243.8)	28	54	27,060	22	41	21,420	16	29	15,750	8	15	8,280
Springfield (145.4)	6	11	3,827	5	8	2,927	4	6	2,251	2	3	1,197
OKLAHOMA												
Okla. City Metro (969.5)	18	46	19,200	13	35	14,400	9	23	9,600	4	12	4,800
Norman (79.3)	4	2	1,522	4	1	1,302	2	1	782	2		525
El Reno (71.0)	3	2	1,155	3	1	940	3		703	2		478
Tulsa Urban (422.8)	8	16	7,080	6	12	5,310	4	8	3,540	2	4	1,800
Tulsa Metro (689.4)	15	25	10,710	11	19	8,080	7	13	5,440	4	6	2,785
Muskogee (107.5)	14	5	3,857	10	4	2,926	7	3	2,140	4	1	1,095
OREGON												
Pendleton (61.5)	2	2	1,105	1	2	859	1	1	573		1	305
TEXAS												
Amarillo Metro (191.4)	18	10	6,496	13	7	4,760	10	6	3,856	7	3	2,620
WASHINGTON												
Spokane Metro (354.3)	12	16	8,763	9	12	6,573	6	8	4,382	3	4	2,302
Walla Walla (48.5)	3	3	1,656	3	2	1,380	2	2	1,105	1	1	573
Walla Walla/Pendleton (110.0)	11	5	3,729				8	3	2,701			

SOURCE: Donrey Outdoor Advertising Co./Donrey Media Group. *National Rates and Allotments 1987.*

with other media. Agency and client first decide whether outdoor advertising can meet marketing and advertising objectives. Then a decision is made concerning the markets and exposure level to be used. Finally, the contracts and insertion orders are completed.

National advertisers and their agencies normally work with a national organization rather than with separate plant operators. Currently the largest such organization is the Out of Home Media Service (OHMS). OHMS serves as the media-buying department for its clients. An advertiser contracts with OHMS to purchase outdoor advertising in specified markets. OHMS also supervises transit advertising media buys. OHMS not only handles the buying of out-of-home media but also conducts field inspections to verify that buys were made properly and to investigate complaints.

The cost of the OHMS services varies with the types of media and with the number of services requested. The agency is billed 3.5 percent of gross billings for total service, which includes both administrative and field services. Administrative services alone cost the agency 2.5 percent of gross billings, and transit is serviced for 2 percent of gross billings. The organization is particularly advantageous to advertising agencies since it frees them from the overhead of a large in-house, out-of-home buying staff.

After the purchase is made, the advertiser should require some proof of performance by the plant. Usually an affidavit, often with accompanying pictures of poster locations, is provided. In addition, regional and national buying services provide on-site inspection of the posters they purchase.

The Agency Commission

The outdoor advertising industry is unique in that it offers a commission of 16.67 percent to advertising agencies. The "bonus" of 1.67 percent over the commission offered by all other media has traditionally been used to encourage agencies to consider the outdoor medium in making media recommendations to their clients.

OTHER FORMS OF OUT-OF-HOME ADVERTISING

Out-of-home advertising usually means posters and painted bulletins. However, there are other types of outdoor advertising. Many advertisers have promoted their products by placing messages on trash containers, bus stop shelters, and freestanding displays in shopping malls. Even more unusual methods, such as skywriting have been used. See Figure 10–8 for other examples of out-of-home advertising.

FIGURE 10–8 Shopping List of Out-of-Home Options

Arrival departure boards	Port-a-panels
Balloons	Roach coaches (mobile display
Banner towing by planes	canteens)
Beetleboards (privately owned Volkswagens)	Sailboats
Book covers	Shopping bags
Bus advertising	Shopping carts
Bus benches	Shopping center specials
Bus shelters	Spectacolor (Times Square)
Cablecar advertising in San Francisco, at resorts	Sports arenas
Clocks in off-track-betting parlors	Sports events sponsorships
Delivery trucks	Stadium signs
Egg cartons	Subway advertising
Greyhound, Trailways, other bus lines	Sugar packets
Holographic displays	T-shirts
Individual spectaculars	Taxicabs
Junior panels	Timetable programs
Kiosks and other public receptacles	Trash baskets
Lavatory advertising	Trucks
Lifeguard chairs at beaches	Three-sheets
Metroforms	Umbrellas
Panagraphic displays	Urban panels

SOURCE: *Media Decisions*, July 1977, p. 71.

One company, Ackerly Airport Advertising of Seattle, holds display concessions at over 85 airports and charges $400 to $1,000 per month for terminal displays for products ranging from luggage to Tabasco Sauce. One client, Classic Motor Carriages, Inc., spends about $45,000 per month for 10- by 25-foot display areas for its finished replica antique cars. Classic estimates that such displays generate almost 1,000 inquiries each month, and these leads account for five percent of company sales.[5]

The problem with these outdoor media is that their impact is largely unmeasurable. The advertiser who uses these methods must rely on intuition to decide what types of displays to use and how much to spend. In addition, there is the public relations problem of environmental pollution associated with such promotions. The potential customer backlash, as well as the clutter associated with massive introduction of outdoor devices, should cause advertisers to carefully weigh costs and benefits from out-of-home advertising.

THE OUTLOOK FOR OUTDOOR ADVERTISING

Outdoor advertising continues to grow at a rate slightly greater than secular inflation. In many markets, the demand for outdoor posters and

---

[5] "Step Right Up," *Inc.*, October 1983, p. 162b.

bulletins is greater than the available space and will continue to be in the foreseeable future. Currently the outdoor industry is a major beneficiary of television's high cost and its exclusion of some product categories. As a result, it is estimated that as much as 30 percent of all outdoor advertising is devoted to liquor and cigarette advertising. These products, with large advertising budgets and limited media in which to place their advertising, have formed the financial base of the outdoor industry. While tobacco and spirits continue to lead outdoor spending, other rapidly growing categories—including insurance, farm products, import cars, dairy products, telephone companies, hospitals, and packaged goods—have assumed greater importance to the industry. In 1984, the largest annual increase in outdoor usage (+360 percent) was credited to retail advertisers. This fact reflects a much-improved marketing performance by outdoor companies in tailoring the medium to the needs of local advertisers. It also reflects a source of potentially lively competition for ad dollars with other media historically dominant among local advertisers, especially with newspapers and radio.

Through the 1980s, it is likely that television advertising costs will continue to increase, and it is unlikely that either cigarette or liquor ads will be permitted in broadcasting. Therefore, the elements for continued success for outdoor advertising will extend through the 1990s. The major barrier to continued growth in ad revenues is that of finding more space to accommodate the existing demand for posters and bulletins.

Despite the strong demand for outdoor advertising, potential problems for the industry exist during the next decade (see Figure 10–9). Public criticism and legislative action can be expected to continue in the coming years. It seems, however, that the intensity of active criticism directed toward the outdoor industry in the 1960s and early 70s has abated. The failure of the Highway Beautification Act to fully achieve its objectives and recent reluctance by Congress to fund the act indicate a lack of public enthusiasm for new limits on outdoor advertising.

The outdoor industry is still faced with various state and local sign ordinances that restrict outdoor advertising. In some cities, more stringent zoning laws have cost outdoor plants thousands of dollars. One of the most restrictive outdoor advertising markets in the country is Washington, D.C., where only 35 posters are allowed in the entire city.[6]

TRANSIT ADVERTISING

Most people give only passing thought to transit advertising and have little understanding of the industry. However, it is prospering, and most

---

[6] "Out-of-Home Explosion!" *Media Decisions,* July 1977, p. 70.

FIGURE 10-9   An Editorial Advocating Billboard Control

The Atlanta Journal

Covers Dixie Like the Dew

Since 1883

James M. Cox Chairman 1939 1957 — James M. Cox Jr. Chairman 1957 1974

Tom Wood, President

Durwood McAlister, Editor   Jim Minter, Managing Editor

4-A   ★★★★★   JANUARY 3, 1980

Billboard Control

ARGUMENTS can be advanced in behalf of billboards along Georgia highways, most notably that they provide information of convenience for the motorist.

But there are billboards and there are billboards. Some are a credit to the product or service that is advertised. And some are an utter disgrace to the state. Some are tasteful and some are atrocious. Some are located in such a way as to blend in with the scenic view and some are blatantly hideous.

Thus there must be rules and regulations regarding billboards. There must be a measure of control, and that control must be effectively enforced by the state.

Because of that we endorse the move by the Georgia Department of Transportation for legislation which would close existing loopholes in billboard control.

The DOT notes that there are some 31,000 billboards along Georgia's primary and interstate highways. Of that number a mere 3,300 are legal, complying with 1971 state law. Classified as illegal are 5,600 billboards. And the remaining 22,000 billboards are rated as non-conforming—which means they were erected before the 1971 law and do not comply with it. The state must purchase non-conforming billboards in order to remove them.

Legislation to be considered by the forthcoming General Assembly would authorize DOT to issue permits for non-conforming signs until those signs could be purchased. Thus only illegal signs would not have a permit and could be identified more readily, thus making them easier to remove.

Proposed legislation would also authorize DOT personnel to go on private property and remove an illegal sign without being personally liable.

We believe in highway billboards that are a credit to the state. But as DOT statistics point out, those in compliance with the 1971 law are definitely a minority.

For that reason we support DOT Commissioner Tom Moreland's efforts to improve billboard control, and we urge local governments to enact zoning ordinances which would further strengthen that control.

industry indicators predict that its prosperity will continue in the 1980s. Annual gross revenues for transit advertising currently exceed $150 million.

Transit advertising is purchased from firms called operators that have leased space from municipal authorities. The largest operator is Metro Transit Advertising (MTA), which operates in several of the top 20 markets. In some respects, the operator functions much like the outdoor plant. It receives printed material from agencies (through specialty printing houses) and maintains space inside and outside vehicles and in transit stations.

The operator pays a 15 percent agency commission (not the 16.67 percent paid by outdoor). There is an industry-supported rate guide, published by Transit Advertising Association, which is the major source of transit rates in the same way that the LNA's *Buyer's Guide* is the major source of outdoor rates.

Transit Categories

The transit medium is divided into three major categories:

Car Cards.   **Car cards** are displayed inside mass transportation vehicles, primarily buses and subway trains. The increased use of mass transportation systems has improved the appeal of car cards to advertisers. Ridership of mass transportation systems has increased because of the high cost of driving. And the demographics of public transportation has improved. Today, with the introduction of such systems as the Bay Area Rapid Transit (BART) system in San Francisco and new or renovated transportation systems in Washington, D.C., and other markets, advertisers can use car cards to reach a more upscale audience.

Despite the development of a broader audience, car cards and transit advertising must be considered a mass medium. There are few practical opportunities to reach a specific market. In this respect, the strategy for transit advertising is usually similar to that used in outdoor advertising. Because of this similarity, the term *out-of-home* is being used increasingly to designate the broad concept of nontraditional media.

Car cards are 11 inches by 28 inches in most markets and are sold on the basis of a "full run." A full run means that every vehicle (or car, in the case of subways) in the system has one card. An advertiser may also purchase half run (every other car) or double runs (two cards in every car). Minimum contracts for car cards are generally 30 days, with discounts based on 3-, 6-, and 12-month contracts.

Costs are based on six-month average ridership of a system. Circulation figures are compiled by the Transit Advertising Association (TAA) and are simply a matter of counting passengers. As with outdoor advertising, the circulation figures supplied by TAA are estimates of the

---

FIGURE 10–10 Basic Sizes of Outside Signs

Traveling displays	21 inches × 44 inches (basic unit)
	21 inches × 36 inches
	21 inches × 17 inches
Queen size	21 inches × 88 inches
King size	30 inches × 144 inches
Rear end	21 inches × 72 inches
Front end	11 inches × 42 inches

---

potential audience, since there is no way of telling from these figures what segment of the audience saw any particular car card.

Outside Space (Traveling Displays). Outside space is purchased on the back, front, and sides of mass transportation vehicles but extends to a wider audience of pedestrians and other riders. In most respects, outside transit posters are comparable to outdoor advertising. They are seen by the broadest possible audience; their viewing time is short, necessitating a concise message. Audience measures, when they exist, report potential rather than real impact.

There are several sizes of outdoor signs. At one time, the only standard-size exterior sign was the 21- by 44-inch traveling display. Some operators still refer to all exterior signs, regardless of their size, as traveling displays. In recent years, operators have offered two additional widths of traveling displays: the so-called king- and queen-size outside posters. Figure 10–10 outlines the sizes available for exterior signs. Seldom are all sizes available in any single market, and most multicity advertisers use either the king-size or the 21- by 44-inch traveling display.

Outdoor signs are sold by the unit and also on the basis of showings. However, since circulation figures are only estimated, the advertiser is buying largely on the basis of judgment.

Station Posters. Most station posters are found in the very largest markets. Originally these ads were located in railway stations; hence, the name. There is a wide variety of standardized and custom displays in the various markets. The standard station poster comes in four basic sizes:

	Height (inches)		Width (inches)
One-sheet poster	46	×	30
Two-sheet poster	46	×	60
Three-sheet poster	84	×	42
Six-sheet poster	60	×	144

The most common types of station posters are the one- and two-sheet sizes. The station poster is sold on a per-unit basis or by showings.

The Basic Bus. In recent years, a few advertisers and operators have developed the idea of having a single advertiser take over an entire vehicle for its advertising messages. This concept, called the "basic bus," works best when a firm has several messages to communicate (such as a storyboard layout or before-after advertising) or when it wants to advertise several of its brands.

Transit Strengths

Mass Appeal. Transit advertising not only reaches large numbers of people, but it brings advertising messages to them while they are in the marketplace. It is an excellent method of supplementing other media as well as providing package identification on a reminder basis.

Low Cost. Transit advertising is among the least expensive media. Costs vary by market size, but the average traveling display costs about $60 a month in the top 10 markets, and a car card costs less than $3 per vehicle in the same markets. CPMs range from 15 to 30 cents for all forms of transit advertising. In computing CPMs, the advertiser must remember that there is no evidence concerning advertising exposure; even so, the low absolute costs and CPMs are impressive.

Flexibility. Transit advertising offers the advertiser geographic, format, and intensity flexibility in larger markets. The advertiser can choose from a variety of inside and outside signs available in excellent production quality. In most markets, the advertiser can choose coverages as broad as a 200 showing (in station posters) to a specific bus route for a car card.

Recently, more flexible formats have been tested successfully. For instance, Metro Transit Advertising and the 3M Company have developed a plastic material that adheres directly to the outside of the vehicle. Called Metroform Spectacular, it eliminates frames, cuts down on maintenance costs, and permits the use of large, unstandardized signs.[7] (See Figure 10–11.)

Transit Weaknesses

Lack of Audience Research. Transit advertising suffers from a lack of in-depth audience research. While overall audience estimates are

---

[7] William T. Hadley, "Out-of-Home," *Media Decisions,* November 1977, p. 96.

**FIGURE 10–11   Use of the Free-Form Spectacular to Announce the King
Tutankhamen Exhibit in Los Angeles**

Courtesy of 3M Company; graphic by Norm Gollin Design

available, there is almost no information on demographics, impact, or
reach/frequency levels. From time to time, audience research studies
have been conducted by A. C. Nielsen and other research organizations,
but these have tended to be narrow in scope and to apply only to a single
market.

Lack of Prestige.   Transit suffers from much the same problem of
recognition that is encountered by outdoor, direct mail, and sales promotion. Often these media are not eliminated from a media plan; they are
simply not considered in the first place. While educational efforts by the
TAA and other industry groups have helped upgrade the image of transit
advertising, it remains a poor relation to the major media.

The Outlook for Transit Advertising

The future of transit advertising appears positive. Current annual revenues are estimated at more than $150 million, and this figure should
increase dramatically during the next 10 years. Like outdoor advertising,
transit benefits from the broadcast media's exclusion of cigarettes and
liquor ads. These two product categories account for more than 15 percent
of transit advertising's total revenues. With space becoming an increasing problem in outdoor advertising, it is reasonable to assume that more
advertising dollars will be diverted to transit.

Also, transit advertising will benefit from continuing energy problems. In both numbers and upscale demographics, transit advertising is a
more attractive medium now than it was a decade ago. In the next several

years, transit advertising may have the same problems keeping up with demand that outdoor advertising now faces. However, future expansion of transit advertising should not meet the type of public resistance that has been the bane of outdoor advertising. As more and better mass transportation systems are developed throughout the country, transit advertising can anticipate a more lucrative position in the industry.

REVIEW QUESTIONS

1. Describe the three categories of outdoor advertising.
2. Discuss the use of gross rating points as a measure of outdoor audiences.
3. What is the purpose of the Space Position Valuation?
4. What is the role of the plant in outdoor advertising?
5. Discuss the services provided by the Out of Home Media Service (OHMS) and the commission it receives for these services.
6. How is the success of transit advertising related to future energy conservation?
7. Discuss the major types of transit advertising.
8. What is the role of the operator in transit advertising?
9. Outdoor advertising is sometimes called the "reminder" medium. In what ways is this name accurate? How does outdoor advertising compare with 10- to 15-second TV commercials?
10. In 1985, Gannett Outdoor Co. of Colorado used the rate card below for posters:

GRPs	Circulation	Number of Panels	Cost/Month
25	376,000	21	$ 8,200
50	752,000	39	15,200
75	1,128,000	57	22,200
100	1,504,000	78	30,400

Compute the outdoor CPM for each of the four GRP levels.

SUGGESTED ADDITIONAL READING

ALSOP, RONALD. "Companies Cram Ads in Stores to Sway Shopping Decisions." *The Wall Street Journal*, August 22, 1985, p. 23.

"AMMO Outdoor Poster Reach and Frequency Data, by Demographics, Southern California Markets." Foster and Kleiser Outdoor Advertising, Los Angeles, Calif., 1986.

"Battling AIDS in Ads." *Advertising Age,* August 26, 1985, p. 59.

CARTER, CRAIG C. "Billboard Foes Are on A Tear-'em-Down Tear." *Fortune,* July 21, 1986, p. 88.

CONTE, CHESTER. "Ruckus in Greenville, S.C., Underscores Power of Billboard Industry as Potent Business Lobby." *The Wall Street Journal,* March 10, 1986, p. 42.

"A Creative Guide to Outdoor Advertising." *Institute of Outdoor Advertising,* New York, N.Y., undated.

Donrey Presents AMMO. Donrey Outdoor Advertising Co., Fort Smith, Ark., September 1985.

"8-Sheet Poster Rates, 1986." Foster and Kleiser Outdoor Advertising, Los Angeles, Calif.

HENDERSON, SALLY, and ROBERT LANDAU. *Billboard Art.* San Francisco, Calif.: Chronicle Books, 1981.

Inside Outdoor, published quarterly by Major Media Management Corporation, Eden Prairie, Minn. 55344.

O'TOOLE, JOHN. "The Great Outdoors." James Webb Young Fund Address, University of Illinois, March 5, 1985.

"Out of Home Advertising." *Advertising Age,* Special Report, May 12, 1986, pp. S1–S16.

"Outdoor Advertising." *Advertising Age,* Special Report, December 12, 1985, pp. 13–24.

"The Outdoor Channel" (advertisement). *Marketing and Media Decisions,* January 1986, p. 97.

"Outdoor Company Bares Its Promise." *Advertising Age,* September 21, 1981, p. 20.

Outdoor, The OASA News, published quarterly by OASA, 825 Russell Street, Augusta, Ga. 30904.

"Outdoor Rates and Allotments." Foster and Kleiser Outdoor Advertising, Los Angeles, Calif., 1986.

CHAPTER ELEVEN

Direct Advertising and Sales Promotion

Loctite Corporation . . . developed a new sealant system to prevent porosity leakage in castings. Among potential customers . . . there was little awareness of the product. Direct Mail Corporation sent three mailings to 4,500 decisionmakers at 1,600 plants . . . the mailings produced more than $1 million in sales. With out-of-pocket expenses of $10,000 . . . that's a damn good return on our money.*

David P. Garino

In a survey of consumer audiences, A. C. Nielsen Company (Northbrook, Ill.) found that almost one third (31 percent) of respondents were still using at least one specialty they had received 12 months earlier.†

Specialty Advertising Fact Sheet

DIRECT MARKETING

In the next decade, direct marketing faces a period of problems and opportunities unlike those of the other major media. On the positive side, direct marketers see the need for greater efficiency in home management and business procurement leading to more direct purchasing. A growing number of women who work out of home will require time-saving methods of purchasing such as direct marketing. In business settings, purchasing agents and buyers find that direct marketing meets their needs for simpler, less costly, and quicker methods of evaluating products from rival suppliers. And direct marketing facilitates buying for those customers who simply prefer to consider products and select purchases in the comfort and safety of their own home or office. Well over $150 billion worth of goods and services are bought direct each year. According to the Direct Marketing Association, 41 percent of adult males and half the

---

* "Osherow Gives Junk Mail a Good Name with String of Successes for Business Clients," *The Wall Street Journal*, November 13, 1980, p. 26.

† Specialty Advertising Fact Sheet, 1983.

adult females in the United States order at least one product by direct mail each year.[1]

On the negative side, direct marketers see problems, which may grow worse in the future. Despite the large expenditures for direct marketing (over $15 billion for direct mail alone in 1985), the public and many advertisers regard direct marketing with suspicion. The unfavorable attitude and the "junk mail" stereotype hurt the credibility of most areas of direct marketing. In addition, cost increases in the production and distribution of direct marketing materials place added pressure on the medium's profitability. Finally, but sadly, the terminology used in direct marketing is still widely misunderstood by advertisers.

Terminology of Direct Marketing

Direct marketing is a term for marketing including distribution and/or advertising that occurs directly between the seller and the consumer. Direct marketing requires no retailer or supplementary middleman to reach the consumer. It can be promoted through direct channels or in traditional advertising media. This sometimes creates a misunderstanding. Direct mail is often confused with other related advertising terms. Therefore, it is necessary to make a clear distinction between what direct mail is and is not.

> *Mail-order advertising.* Mail-order advertising refers to goods that are distributed directly from the seller to the buyer through the mails. The solicitation for such goods can be through any one advertising medium or any combination of advertising media, including direct mail. Many magazines carry classified sections for such mail-order advertising.
>
> *Direct advertising.* Direct advertising is any form of promotion that passes directly from the seller to the buyer without first being placed in a medium. Political candidates, small retail stores, and car dealers often place their selling messages on car windshields as a form of direct advertising.
>
> *Direct mail advertising.* Direct mail advertising is advertising distributed directly to prospects by mail. It is the largest category of direct advertising. Some advertising practitioners prefer the term *direct-by-mail.*

Advantages of Direct Advertising and Direct Mail

The major appeal of direct marketing for most advertisers is its selectivity, which can take many forms. For some advertisers, the appeal of

---

[1] Bob Stone, "Now, a Bigger Bargain," *Advertising Age,* May 30, 1983, p. M28.

direct advertising is its flexibility of format; other advertisers use direct advertising because they cannot reach a widely scattered market segment efficiently through the traditional media; still other advertisers need the timing flexibility of direct advertising. The Direct Mail/Marketing Association has outlined 10 major differences between direct advertising and other media:

Selectivity.   Direct advertising can be used to reach specific individuals or markets with greater control than can be obtained with any other medium. An appeal can be directed to 100 handpicked millionaires just as readily as to a very select professional group of 100,000 book buyers. In many cases, lists can be obtained with postage guaranteed up to 98 percent accuracy. How else, or how better, could a promotion be limited, yet assure absolute coverage, than through a direct approach by mail to recent customers, or past customers, or recommended customers?

Personalization.   Direct advertising can be made personalized to the point of being confidential. Whether a letter, order blank, confidential price list, or product information—regardless of the appeal or number of people to be reached—a first-class mailing can do it. Not all direct mail is of a confidential nature, but when a confidential approach is needed, only this medium can provide the means.

Low Clutter.   Direct advertising is a single advertiser's individual message; it does not compete with other advertising and/or editorial matter. At the moment of reception, or when a piece of direct advertising reaches the reader, it has his or her complete attention. It will stand or fall on its appeal, just as will any other advertisement—but at least it will have a better chance because there is less competition for the reader's attention.

Few Format Restrictions.   Direct advertising does not have the limitations on space and format of other advertising media. Almost no limit exists as to the size, shape, style, number of colors, and all of the other elements that enter into the makeup of direct mail and printed promotion. Direct advertising formats range from the small poster stamp and miniatures to booklets, brochures, and broadsides as big as the top of a desk, to accommodate any length of message or size of illustration. The piece can be made to fit the story, and the possibilities are as boundless as the designer's ingenuity.

Flexibility.   Direct advertising permits greater flexibility in materials and processes of production than any other medium of advertising. Production of direct advertising includes every phase of reproduction known to the graphic arts—printing, lithography, photo-offset, rotogravure, steel engraving, silk screen, Multigraph, mimeograph, Multilith, and so on. Added to these are the processes of die cutting, scoring, punching, tabbing, swatching, varnishing, laminating, mounting, and all kinds of binding and folding. Because of these facilities, and because each piece is individually produced, greater latitude exists in the use of materials—all kinds of papers, inks, plastics, and so on. These are the reasons why direct advertising can be custom made, can fit any pattern, and can outdo any other form of advertising in physical presentation.

Novelty and Realism.   Direct advertising provides a means for introducing novelty and realism into the interpretation of the advertiser's story. Cutouts, pop-ups, and odd shapes and patterns are employed to good advantage by users of direct mail advertising. If a folder or booklet is desired in the shape of a bottle, box, or barrel, the effect is easy to obtain. Even invisible colors and perfumed inks are used in some printed pieces for novelty and as powerful attention getters.

Quick Response.   Because direct advertising can be produced quickly, advertisers can use it for a quick promotion or an emergency mailing to take advantage of a situation. With direct mail, advertisers don't have to wait for a publication date.

Research Possibilities.   Direct advertising can be controlled for specific research jobs, to reach small groups, and to test ideas, appeals, and reactions. Before big campaigns in which other media may be employed, confidential questionnaires can be used for these research purposes. Next to personal contact, direct mail affords the best medium for research and individual contact.

Precise Timing.   Direct advertising can be dispatched for accurate and in some cases exact timing, both as to departure of the pieces and as to their receipt. Material can be mailed according to a set plan. Even departure schedules are available at the post office to help achieve good timing. Dealer material can be scheduled to reach dealer counters according to plan. Sales, holiday promotions, and stockholders' meetings as well as distributor, jobber, dealer, and consumer promotions can be timed for maximum results.

Invitation to Respond.   Direct advertising provides more thorough means for the reader to act or buy through action devices that cannot be used by other media. The business reply card and envelope make it easier for the recipient of direct advertising to take action. Complete order blanks and other action enclosures can also be used.[2]

---

[2] Reprinted with permission from the Direct Mail/Marketing Association, Inc., from its publication *The Direct Mail/Marketing Manual,* Release No. 1201, May 1975.

Disadvantages of Direct Advertising and Direct Mail

These 10 items give ample evidence of the versatility and selectivity of the medium. However, direct mail advertising is not suitable for many advertising purposes. Advertisers need to consider several potential disadvantages before they make a commitment to direct mail.

Cost per Thousand. While most media sell time and space at a CPM of $5 to $25, direct mail can easily run $1,000 per 1,000 addresses. For example, a first-class mailing costs $220 per 1,000 just for postage. Naturally the advertiser must consider factors other than cost:

Are prospects widely scattered?
Would personalized copy benefit the product?
Is long copy required to tell the story?
Is product sampling feasible through direct mail?
Is the market for the product relatively small?

Any one of these factors may mean that direct mail would be an appropriate medium.

Updating Mailing Lists. The per-exposure cost of direct mail mandates even greater efficiency than other media. Maintaining a current mailing list is expensive and time-consuming due to the mobility of the U.S. population. An out-of-date list is not only inefficient in reaching prospects, it often destroys the personal contact that your message is attempting to convey. It is difficult to convince a prospect that you can solve his immediate problems when the envelope that carried your message has been forwarded from a previous address.

Improper Timing. It is surprising how many users of direct mail do not take advantage of the control they have over the timing of their message. Commonsense rules, such as not mailing on the first of the month when the recipient is most likely receiving bills, are often ignored to the advertiser's detriment.

Improper Format. Some advertisers fail to utilize the medium fully by sending an inappropriate message. There is no set of rules that fit every direct mailing piece. However, some rules of thumb may be helpful:

First-class postage generally gets better response than bulk mail.
Stamped envelopes get better response than metered mail.
Messages on envelopes work for mass mailing, such as sweepstakes, but are generally inappropriate for selling most consumer goods.
Mimeographed or machine-copied messages are usually ineffective. Consumers equate your product with the quality of the message that announces it.

Messages to businesses usually get opened (often by a secretary); messages sent to home addresses are less likely to be seen.

Format

The most common direct mail format is the letter and for the majority of advertising messages, the letter remains the most appropriate choice. However, a format should be chosen only after full consideration has been given to the alternatives available to the direct mailer. Some of the major formats and their advantages are discussed in Figure 11–1. Two of these formats, the computer letter and the catalog, are sufficiently important that they deserve special discussion.

The Computer Letter

One of the major technological breakthroughs in direct marketing is the computer letter. Developed in the mid-1970s, this system connects printers directly to a computer and is capable of high-quality, high-speed production. Such systems can also personalize each letter with address, name, and other individual information from the computer's data base.

Use of the computer letter demands extremely detailed, careful planning in order to avoid glaring errors. A computer letter should read like a personal letter. A letter with a mechanical "tone" is no better than a printed message and can be worse if it contains silly errors. One of the major errors made by computer letters is to pick up the addressee's name and insert it incorrectly in the body of the letter. Let's look at an actual example of how this can destroy a direct message.

Addressee: Mr. John Jones, Instructor Radio

Computer letter: Dear Mr. Radio:
    In a few days the Radio family will be receiving
a . . .

Needless to say, the "Radio" family received the accompanying product sample with something less than enthusiasm. Since a personalized computer letter costs up to three times more than a nonpersonalized printed message, the damage caused by such errors may be not only silly or insulting but also expensive.

The Catalog

Between 1980 and 1985, the mail-order catalog business boomed. During that period, the number of catalogs increased even more rapidly. One measure of the growth in competition can be found in the volume of

FIGURE 11–1   Some Major Direct Mail Formats

BROADSIDES

Broadsides are large folders, used advantageously when the average folder is not adequate to convey the story and a booklet is not the form needed or wanted; when a smash effect is sought, for a special announcement, or for a special emphasis of certain appeals; when a large surface is required for pictorial and bold copy expression; or when the psychology of bigness is desired.

BOOKLETS

Booklets should be used when broadsides are not adequate to convey the longer story or lack sufficient prestige value or appropriateness for certain printed promotion jobs.

Catalogs, house organs, sales booklets, instruction books, directories, price lists, etc. are some of the functional purposes of booklets (and books).

BROCHURES

Brochures are for the glamorous phases of direct advertising and should be used when an elaborate presentation of company, product, or service is called for; when there is a need or desire to go beyond the ordinary booklet and broadside format for richness, power, and impressiveness in size, illustration, color, materials, bindings, etc.; or when the presentation of a story must match the bigness of the selling job and must reflect the stature and dignity of the company responsible for its production.

CIRCULARS

The circular, or flier, is the usually inexpensive form to adopt when you want to get across a strong message in a flash. Circulars are generally flat pieces up to the size of the broadside category. The circular provides an opportunity for big, smash headlines, black and white, or full color. It can tell its story quickly, "loudly," and inexpensively.

LETTERS

Letters are perhaps the most widely used of all direct advertising forms. Letters perform almost every function in direct advertising. In fact they are used for a wider variety of purposes than any other advertising form. They can be used alone or in conjunction with practically every other form of direct advertising. Letters lend a personal touch to direct mail. They are the most adaptable, the most personal, and the most flexible of all forms of direct advertising. For the mailer with a small list, the cost of printed matter, which involves typesetting and printing press work, may be prohibitive. Letters are economical in small quantities and large ones.

FOLDERS

Folders are the most commonly used of all printed advertising forms because they are the most flexible and comparatively inexpensive. Size, shape, and style are unlimited. In format, folders bridge the gap between personal letters and the booklet. That is the best rule to remember when considering the use of folders.

MAILING CARDS

Mailing cards provide an inexpensive physical form of direct advertising, yet they have great utility. Mailing cards can be used for brief announcements (not

FIGURE 11–1 *(concluded)*

confidential); when budgets do not allow for a more expensive format; when a teaser idea is used to introduce a campaign; when single messages or thoughts are needed to influence prospects or obtain leads; when quick reminders are effective; when the element of time is most important; or when notices, announcements, instructions, invitations, and other short direct messages lend themselves to this inexpensive, open, quick-reading format.

UNUSUAL FORMS

Cutouts, pop-ups, novelties, gadgets, and sample pieces can be used when realism is wanted; when it is important to make a fast, single impression to gain the prospect's immediate interest; when you want to show things that cannot be shown by other forms of advertising; when original, individual, and effective presentations of products, services, or their features can be achieved through forms that are different, unusual, but extremely appropriate and forceful.

BLOTTERS

The blotter is an inexpensive type of direct mail used to carry short, strong sales messages, with or without illustrations; product or service information, directions for use, and so on. Blotters are also used at times as miniature house organs. Blotters and calendars are leading forms of "reminder" direct mail.

SOURCE: Reprinted with permission from the Direct Mail/Marketing Association, Inc., from its publication *The Direct Mail/Marketing Manual*, Release No. 1201 and 3001, November 1976.

catalogs delivered through the U.S. mails. Between the dates mentioned, the number of catalogs grew from under 5 billion to 12 billion. As a result of sharpened competition, catalogers are adopting new strategies, and some are simply opting out. Montgomery Ward & Co. ended distribution of its catalogs in 1985, after 113 years. Others are dropping nonrespondent addresses more quickly, while increasing their mailings to good customers. Still others who have traditionally relied on catalog sales are opening retail outlets to augment or replace the catalog channel. Finally, catalog marketers are redesigning this traditional format, from one that merely offers an attractive listing and display of products to a booklet that includes feature articles related to the product assortment.

Two other emerging alternatives to the catalog are the "magalog" and telemarketing. The name, *magalog*, has been given to those catalogs that accept paid advertising. Opinion is divided among catalogers over the wisdom of including paid ads for products that are not stocked in their books. One advantage is the advertising revenues this practice generates. Another is a favorable association with similar merchandise; companies like Spiegel, Bloomingdale's, and The Sharper Image are enthusiastic about the prospects. The principal disadvantage is that the paid advertising may detract from the image or noteworthiness of the cataloger's products. Thus, L. L. Bean, Eddie Bauer, and Land's End oppose the practice, at least for their own catalogs.[3]

Telemarketing is an evolutionary form of the door-to-door salesman channel and captures many of the improved technological efficiencies and advantages of direct mail. Sophisticated data bases permit the telephone marketer to personalize the sales message, and the widespread use of consumer credit cards facilitates a prompt method of taking an order. The sales representative may inform buyers about related products and special sale items. At present, almost as much is spent on telemarketing as is invested in direct mail advertising. Costs per thousand average about $2,500 for calls made during evening hours and as much as four times that for calls made during normal business hours.

One of the most effective strategies in direct response marketing blends a combination of catalog and telemarketing. Catalogers who combine their mail-delivered books with a toll-free telephone order system and who accept credit card orders have made the purchase of higher priced items so convenient that they almost become impulse purchases. At the same time, consumers who wish to fully evaluate catalog descriptions of products before buying are able to do so and still enjoy the advantage of speedier deliveries.

The Mailing List

The success of direct mail requires that three major elements work together: the format and message of the mailing piece, the product offered, and the mailing list. It would be a mistake to rank any of these elements as more important than the others. However, common sense indicates that a product offered to nonprospects will have no chance of success, however creative the message.

The biggest mistake made by inexperienced direct mail advertisers is to use an out-of-date, inappropriate, or duplicate-address list. It is crucial to remember that lists have a high wear-out factor. For some lists, this may mean that as many as 25 percent of addresses must be changed annually. It does no good to obtain a list, usually at considerable expense, unless provisions are made to keep it current.

Sources of Mailing Lists

In-house List. If it is feasible, advertisers can save money by building their own lists either from standard sources (city directories, Chamber of Commerce membership, etc.) or from customer account lists in the case of

---

[3] "Magalogs Become a Mega-Craze," *Marketing and Media Decisions,* October 1985, p. 80.

retailers. However, national manufacturers can rarely obtain a list of the consumers who buy their products. Techniques such as obtaining data from warranty cards enclosed in products are helpful for research, but rarely allow a complete list to be compiled.

Many retailers have done away with in-store credit in favor of bank credit cards. While shifting the credit function normally saves the retailers money, it causes them to lose contact with their customers. In cases where no in-house list is available, the advertiser should turn to a direct mail professional.

The List Broker.   The most common source of mailing lists is the list broker. List brokers function in the same way as other brokers in bringing buyers and sellers together. Most major list brokers are members of the Mailing List Brokers Professional Association. The list broker has knowledge of the thousands of lists available and can direct the advertiser to those most appropriate to his product or promotion.

A list broker does not sell lists, but rather rents them for a specified number of mailings. The actual list is not given to the advertiser. The mailing piece and the mailing list are delivered to a separate firm that specializes in folding, addressing, and mailing large commercial promotions. These mailing firms are called *letter shops*. Some printing firms have their own letter shops. In any case, the printer and the letter shop must work closely together. The list broker is normally paid a 20 percent commission by the *list owner*. The costs of lists vary greatly, but $40 to $75 CPM is an average range. The only names known to the advertiser on a brokered list are the names of those who respond.

The list broker should be regarded as more than someone who deals only with the mechanics of a mailing. A list broker can offer professional advice about the total direct mail program. The direct mail advertiser should use the expertise of the list broker in much the same way as advertising agencies use the expertise of the media reps.

The List Compiler.   The list compiler is another source of lists. Unlike the list broker, who rents lists, the compiler sells them. Normally, an advertiser that buys a list is a regular direct mailer. A firm may want to expand a present customer list, or a new firm may purchase a list as the first step in building an in-house list. In either case, the advertiser should make sure that the list under consideration is current and is made up of the right market segment. List costs are usually based on a price per 1,000 names. In the case of smaller lists, the entire list must usually be purchased. Figure 11–2 shows an example of a list compiler's catalog.

Standard Rate and Data.   The most available source of list brokers and compilers is the *Standard Rate and Data Service Direct Mail List*

FIGURE 11–2   List Compiler Catalog

Quantity	List	Price
13,889	Wig & Hair Piece Dealers	$35/M
5,681	Window Cleaning Services	$35/M
22,648	Window & Door Dealers	$35/M
6,403	Window Shade & Venetian Blind Dealers	$35/M
500	Wine, Liquor & Beer Bottlers	$100/F
54,514	Wine & Liquor Stores	$35/M
2,609	Wholesalers	$100/F
1,560	Wire & Steel Spring Manufacturers	$100/F

WOMEN

By Profession

Quantity	List	Price
16,080	Accounting	$45/M
10,249	Advertising	$45/M
2,852	Arts	$45/M
30,000	Athletics	$45/M
64,492	Banking	$45/M
3,300	Broadcasting	$45/M
573,088	Business & Professionals Database	$45/M
16,128	Certified Public Accountants	$45/M
18,307	Engineers & Scientists	$45/M
186,060	Executives in Business	$45/M
45,711	At Top Corporations	$45/M
70,000	Garden Clubs	$45/M
17,908	Government	$45/M
9,179	Hospital Administration	$45/M
14,992	Insurance	$45/M
15,646	Investors	$45/M
27,839	Medicine	$45/M
20,367	Pesonnel	$45/M
15,569	Psychiatry & Psychology	$45/M
4,587	Public Relations	$45/M
7,192	Publishing	$45/M
105,973	Real Estate	$45/M
9,129	Retailing	$45/M
5,006	Scientists	$45/M
59,000	Social Scientists	$45/M
199,940	Wealthy Women at Home Address	$55/M
46,796	Women's Clubs	$40/M
326,395	Executive Female Universe	$40/M
10,000,000	Female Heads of Household	$40/M
159,597	American Museum of Natural History Women Members	$75/M
81,956	The Atlantic Magazine Women Subscribers	$65/M
225,000	Cosmetique Beauty Club Hotline Members	$55/M
103,354	Family Computing Magazine Women Subscribers	$70/M
92,126	Inc. Magazine Women Subscribers	$90/M
336,505	Ms. Magazine Subscribers	$55/M
135,000	National Association for Female Executives	$85/M
200,000	Savvy Magazine Subscribers	$65/M

WEALTHY EXECUTIVES & PROFESSIONALS AT HOME ADDRESS 1,800,000 @ $40/M

The most affluent group of Americans ever presented in a single database. Includes 67,000 Board Members of S & P corporations as well as other prominent leaders in industry and the professions. Selectable by age, sex, function and available with home telephone numbers (70%).

FIGURE 11-2 *(concluded)*

Quantity	List	Price

FEMALE HEADS OF HOUSEHOLDS 10,000,000 @ $40/M

A growing segment of the population, these decision makers and spenders are selectable by the following factors: age, estimated income, dwelling type, occupation, ethnic background, number of children, length of residence, estimated home value and telephone numbers.

Quantity	List	Price
165,622	Shape Magazine Subscribers	$55/M
436,759	U.S. News & World Report Magazine Women Subscribers	$65/M
10,000	Women's Clothing Manufacturers	$35/M
18,000	Wholesalers	$35/M
83,246	Women's Ready To Wear Stores	$35/M

YACHT OWNERS (The real thing!) 173,000 @ $40/M

This is the largest list available of owners of *genuine* yachts. Selection capabilities include individual vs corporate ownership, length of yacht, year built and material.

Quantity	List	Price
15,114	Wood Kitchen Cabinet Manufacturers	$35/M
1,058	Wood Pallet & Skid Manufacturers	$100/F
24,160	Wood Products Manufacturers	$35/M
30,000	Executives	$40/M
11,727	Word Processing Equipment and Supplies	$35/M
2,921	Wrecking & Demolition Contractors	$35/M
7,000	Writers at Home Address	$40/M

X Y Z

Quantity	List	Price
1,500	X-Ray Apparatus & Supply Dealers	$100/F
1,081	X-Ray Laboratories	$100/F
10,889	Yacht & Boat Dealers (See also Boats)	$35/M
173,000	Owners (Selectable by size, please request data)	$40/M
6,300	Supplies	$35/M
7,291	Yarn & Knitting Shops	$35/M
2,310	YMCA's & YWCA's, YMHA's & YWHA's	$100/F
6,446	Youth Centers Organizations	$35/M
2,640	Zoologists	$100/F
504	Zoos, Aquariums & Botanical Gardens	$100/F

Note: Prices indicated are either cost per thousand names ($/M) or flat price for entire list ($/F).

Rates and Data. Under the volume's separate listings for list brokers and compilers, hundreds of lists and their prices are enumerated.

Direct Marketing Association

One of the most aggressive media trade associations is the Direct Marketing Association (DMA). The association has recently inaugurated a three-year, $1.5 million campaign of consumer education and lobbying to tell the direct marketing story. The two major problems that this campaign is attempting to overcome are (1) the idea that unsolicited direct mail is an invasion of privacy and (2) the ill will that has been engendered by the minority of fraudulent mail-order schemes.

Regulation of Direct Marketing

Legislators at both the state and national level continue to advocate various forms of direct mail regulation, including the restriction of certain types of mailing lists. This trend toward more legislation assumes that the use of a person's name without permission is an invasion of privacy and that unwanted mail slows down the postal distribution system.

The DMA has sought to counteract this adverse trend by research and public relations. According to one study, only 5 percent of respondents did not like any direct mail; 33 percent enjoyed all direct mail; and 85 percent had no general dislike for direct mail. The same study showed that 83 percent of respondents received less than 10 pieces of direct mail per week.[4]

Similar complaints and research findings are reported by DMA in the telemarketing area. A SMRB study done in 1984 for the Association showed that 51 percent of those called listened to the complete telephone sales message and only 7 percent consistently hung up. Nevertheless, legislative proposals to limit telemarketing are being considered in 33 states.[5]

The major DMA public relations program has been the Mail Preference Service, or MPS. Initiated in 1971, the service provides a "name removal form." Consumers who complete this and return it to DMA have their name passed on to major direct marketers who remove that name from the list. It is not necessary for consumers to use the DMA form. They can simply write a letter to DMA asking that their names be removed from the mailing lists of association members. The service also provides an "add-on" form for requests to place a name on specific types of lists. Advertising promoting the MPS has appeared in major magazines during recent years, and in the 1982–85 period, the number of requests for add-ons were about four times greater than the number requesting removal. The DMA ended the add-on service in 1985.

In 1985, DMA began the research needed to offer a similar service to consumers for telemarketing. Called TPS, for Telephone Preference Service, the procedure was tested using newspaper advertising phone bill inserts and 800 numbers in Knoxville, Tennessee, and Salt Lake City; in a five-week period, the ad generated about 200 requests in each city.[6]

---

[4] *Study of Consumer Attitudes toward Direct Mail—A Summary,* Direct Mail Advertising Association, 1962, pp. 3 and 8.

[5] "Will New Laws Hang Up Telemarketers?" *Marketing and Media Decisions,* May 1985, p. 47.

[6] *Ibid.,* p. 48.

The Outlook for Direct Marketing

The future of direct mail marketing appears to be positive, though there are warning signals on the horizon. The growing trend toward local marketing strategy can only help direct markets. The continually rising costs of traditional media make direct mail a more practical alternative than it has been.

Computers are helping identify, produce, and distribute direct mail pieces. Computers are being utilized in all phases of advertising and marketing to find profitable consumer groups and segment them from the general population. As the delineation of these groups becomes more specific, direct mailers can increasingly make a case for CPM/*prospect* efficiencies in comparison to other media. It is only a matter of time before the problems of the computer letter, discussed earlier, are solved. Already computers are being placed on line with formats other than the letter. Simple folders can be printed by computer printing systems, and soon more elaborate formats will utilize these systems.

Direct mail and direct marketing in general should benefit from concerns about energy conservation and increased demand for shopping convenience. In the future, the percentage of in-home shoppers should rise. Conservation, combined with the female work force, expands the advantages of direct mail to a larger portion of the population.

On the negative side, direct marketing must continue to upgrade its image and work to keep down costs. The efforts of the DMA, outlined earlier, seem to be a step in the right direction. Whether these efforts will be enough to forestall anti-direct marketing attitudes by the public and legislatures remains to be seen. Also, despite the use of sophisticated computer techniques, direct mail is an expensive means of reaching large groups of consumers. However, under certain circumstances, direct mail can be a useful supplement to or substitute for traditional media.

SALES PROMOTION

Strictly speaking, sales promotion is not advertising. The major difference between sales promotion and advertising is that sales promotion is direct promotion between the advertiser and the customer, whereas advertising operates through an interpersonal, intervening medium of communication. Sales promotion consists of a wide range of techniques designed to help sell a product and to complement traditional media advertising. Sales promotion ideas are as endless as the companies that employ them. The major trade show, the "Can you draw me?" matchbook, and the handsomely designed point-of-purchase display are all forms of sales promotion.

Sales promotion, especially premiums and specialty promotions, is clearly related to advertising and is often included in a firm's advertising budget. Furthermore, the sales promotion program, like the advertising program, should be planned and coordinated with the overall marketing and advertising goals of the firm. One estimate of the importance of sales promotion for packaged goods firms can be found in Figure 11–3.

This section discusses the three major forms of sales promotion closest to advertising: specialty advertising, premiums, and point-of-purchase.

Specialty Advertising

At a typical meeting of the Specialty Advertising Association International (SAAI), more than 20,000 different items are on display. Advertising specialties range from beer mugs and ball caps to one-of-a-kind sculptures and lead crystal stemware. In 1985, industry sales were $4 billion, and survey after survey shows that businesses as well as the general public have a positive regard for specialty advertising items. Yet,

FIGURE 11–3 Promotion's Rising Share of the Marketing Dollar

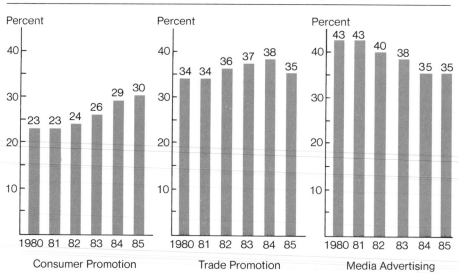

Consumer promotion spending by package-goods companies is on the rise, primarily at the expense of media advertising, as marketers embrace promotion techniques designed to build long-term sales as well as spot sales. Spending on promotion to the retail trade had held relatively steady. Figures above show percent of total marketing dollars. Figures may not add to 100 due to rounding. *SOURCE: Donnelley Marketing.*

SOURCE: Reprinted with permission of *Advertising Age*, July 13, 1986, p. 65. Copyright Crain Communications, Inc.

for all its successes, the specialty advertising industry is not fully understood by either the public or advertisers.

What Is Specialty Advertising? Specialty advertising has several characteristics that distinguish it from other forms of advertising and sales promotions. It consists of a wide array of items, usually imprinted with the name of the advertiser. These items are free gifts given with no obligation to selective target markets. In this regard, the specialty item is different from the advertising premium, which usually is received only after a product has been purchased.

Specialty advertising is a complement to traditional promotion and is rarely the central focus of an advertising campaign. Specialties have the advantage of long life and should continually remind the customer of the advertiser's product. Since everyone enjoys a gift, specialties are an excellent method of building consumer goodwill.

The major disadvantage of the specialty item is its cost. Specialty items are not for mass distribution. Even the smallest gift is expensive on a CPM basis and should be used carefully to achieve a specific goal. However, the long life of many specialty items reduces their cost significantly since it eliminates the need for frequent repetition that exists in mass media advertising. It is important to exercise control over the distribution of specialty items to guarantee that legitimate prospects are receiving them.

Specialty advertising is generally divided into four major categories. In 1985 each category accounted for the following percent of the industry's sales:

1. Novelties or advertising specialties, about 55 percent.
2. Advertising calendars, 12 percent.
3. Writing instruments, 16 percent.
4. Executive gifts, 17 percent.

Novelties. The novelty category is by far the most extensive in number of items. Almost any item can be used as an advertising specialty, but advertising specialties generally have these two characteristics: (1) they are relatively inexpensive and (2) they are imprinted with the name of the advertiser (see Figure 11–4).

Calendars. Calendars meet the qualifications of the novelty category. However, historically they are treated as a separate category. Each year, millions of calendars are distributed for advertising purposes. Calendars have the advantage of daily communication with the recipient and represent one of the most practical gifts in the specialty category. Calendars are available in three basic formats: wall, desk, and pocket. The wall

FIGURE 11–4   A Specialty Advertising Case Study

The Humble, Texas, Police Department sought to promote a positive community image at a nominal cost. Specialty advertising provided an arresting way.

To position itself in the community while separating itself from the harsh image of the police department in a nearby metropolis, the department staffed a booth at the annual one-day Main Street Festival to answer questions for citizens.

The specialty advertising counselor combined humor in the specialty and the copy to show the small-town friendliness of the Humble Police Department. Distributed at the booth were colorful 9-inch plastic flyswatters imprinted "Official weapon of the Humble Police SWAT Team." The telephone number was printed below for easy reference.

The chief and members of the department were pleasantly overwhelmed at the warm response. Rather than shying away from the booth, citizens were attracted by the flyswatters. Thus, the desired positive exposure was achieved.

And inexpensively, too! The specialties were first distributed in 1983 at a cost of $90; the order was repeated (and doubled) in 1984 at a cost of only $150.

SOURCE: *Ideasworth* 6, no. 1 (1985), Specialty Advertising Association International.

calendar is usually sent to the home, while desk and pocket calendars are more appropriate for business distribution.

Calendars have become so popular that a clutter problem has developed. Each year, more and more calendars are being used as sales promotion. Normally only a few of these calendars are used; recipients discard the others at a major expense to the advertiser. Unless an advertiser invests in a quality calendar that can compete with others the customer receives, another form of sales promotion should be considered. (See Figure 11–5.)

Writing Instruments. Most adults use a writing instrument at least once a day. Writing instruments are a flexible medium that may be imprinted with an advertiser's name or message. They can be obtained in a wide range of prices and types (e.g. highlighter, roller-ball pen, porous-point pen) and in a variety of shapes.

Executive Gifts. Executive gifts differ from other forms of specialty items in that they are more expensive and do not carry the name of the advertiser. Gifts in this category are usually given by the manufacturers or wholesalers to their retail customers rather than to the general public.

FIGURE 11–5   A Specialty Advertising Case Study

Consumer promotion

Calendar draws 10% response

Intercoastal Communities Inc. had a list of 10,000 leads — persons who had either visited one of its three mobile home communities in central Florida or had made inquiries. The firm was interested in maintaining contact with them and in securing referrals.

A 12-sheet calendar was developed for this purpose. The copy theme, "Florida is . . . Love at first sight," was carried out in the photography that appeared on the front of each page. These illustrations represented typical Florida lifestyles and scenes that might be expected to appeal to senior citizens. Mailed to the target audience, the calendar was accompanied by a reply card to be used if additional information was desired or for referrals.

Response to the calendar mailing exceeded 10%. The Ft. Lauderdale firm sold 50 units and secured 155 referrals as a result of the promotion.

SOURCE: *Ideasworth* 6, no. 3 (1985), Specialty Advertising Association International.

Christmas is the customary time to give these gifts. Executive gifts can be as ordinary as a pen and pencil set or as unusual as a smoked ham. Often a company will give the same type of gift year after year, such as items of glassware, and thus become identified with a specific kind of gift.

Structure of the Specialty Advertising Industry.   The specialty industry is divided into three types of organizations: suppliers, jobbers, and direct-selling houses.

Suppliers.   The supplier is the source of the many specialty items available. Some suppliers specialize in a particular type of specialty, but most offer a wide array of merchandise. Suppliers may manufacture items, but more often they simply buy merchandise, which they then imprint. These items are sold through jobbers for distribution to the advertising client.

Jobbers. Jobbers (or distributors) are independent salespeople who contact business for the sale of specialty items. The typical jobber has contacts with a wide range of suppliers, and most jobbers offer almost any type of merchandise an advertiser might want to use as a specialty. A good jobber is not only a salesperson, but someone who can work with a client to develop the most appropriate idea for a company's promotional program.

Direct-Selling Houses. The direct-selling house is a firm that combines the function of the supplier and the jobber. It manufactures specialty items and sells them through its own sales force. Occasionally a direct-selling house will sell to independent jobbers to cover areas or customers missed by its own sales force. For the client, there is really no difference between dealing with a direct-selling house and dealing with a jobber. The distinction is important, however, within the industry.

Selection of the Specialty Item. The major failure of specialty advertising is choosing an item without proper planning. The advertiser should develop the specialty advertising program in the same way he develops other aspects of the advertising program. When he contemplates a specialty sales promotion, he should ask, "Will it contribute to the overall marketing plan?" Only when the answer to this question is yes should the advertiser go forward.

Actual selection of the specialty item should meet several criteria:

It should be related to the product or to the company's promotional program.
It should have utility to the receiver, preferably in a way related to a job activity (for instance, copyfitting guides for printers, miles-per-gallon charts for traveling salespeople).
It should be of good quality; shoddy merchandise not only disappoints the receiver, but may reflect poorly on the product of the advertiser.
It should be practical to distribute and easy to imprint.

Premium Advertising

The advertising premium differs from the specialty item in that it is not a free gift. It is given as a reward for some action by the consumer. Usually the requirement for receiving a premium is to purchase the product. However, premiums are also given as traffic builders, such as a T-shirt for test-driving a car or a small appliance for viewing some real estate. In either case, the premium should remind the customer of the product and should appeal to the same audience as the product.

Like all advertising programs, premium advertising programs should be conducted with the marketing objectives in mind. Among these objectives are the following:

Overcoming price competition by lower priced brands.
Encouraging purchases, or traffic, during slack seasons.
Introducing a new product.
Giving an edge to parity products.

Advertising premiums are designed to increase sales either by promoting products to consumers or by providing incentives at the wholesale or retail level. Premiums are normally used to deal with a specific problem during a relatively short period. In other cases, premiums are a long-term complement to the product. In rare cases, such as baseball trading cards, the premium becomes as important as the product and is promoted as a separate product. Premiums normally supplement general media advertising by providing an added buying incentive. Consequently, one of the primary considerations in selecting a premium is that it should lend itself to advertising and merchandising.

Types of Advertising Premiums. As with advertising specialties, there is a wide selection of premiums from which an advertiser can choose. In this chapter we discuss some of the major categories. We should note that a premium may fall into several of these categories since they are not mutually exclusive.

Factory Pack Premiums. The factory pack is the oldest and still the most popular type of premium. Since it is included with the product, it has the advantage of intimate association with the product and immediate reward for the buyer. In some cases, factory packs are in the package—towels and dishes in boxes of detergent. In other cases they are attached to the package, such as toothbrushes packaged with toothpaste. Sometimes the premium is the package. Glass jelly jars or decorated liquor bottles are examples.

Self-Liquidating Premiums. In recent years, advertisers have turned to premiums that pay for themselves or can actually provide a profit. Self-liquidators are normally offered for proof-of-purchase and cash. The cost to the consumer covers the expense of handling and mailing as well as the cost of the premium itself. Self-liquidating premiums can be as inexpensive as a T-shirt or a toy, but may include expensive watches, bicycles, or clothing items. In recent years, both Marlboro and Budweiser have set up subsidiaries to sell advertising premiums.

Traffic-Building Premiums. It is unrealistic to expect a premium to play a major role in the purchase of high-priced goods. However, premiums may be helpful in getting consumers to inspect such products. A wide variety of premiums can be used for this purpose, including self-liquidators such as the Texaco toy fire engines and the Firestone Christmas records.

Continuity Premiums. Continuity premiums build in value as the customer purchases more of the product. Among the more familiar continuity premiums are grocery store trading stamps and merchandise coupons such as those offered by Raleigh cigarettes. Continuity premiums may also be used as factory packs, for examples in cases where a set of towels or dishes may be obtained after frequent purchases of a product.

Sweepstakes and Contests. Normally a sweepstakes promotion is one in which prizes are awarded as a result of chance. In a contest, prizes are awarded on the basis of skill; however, the terms *contest* and *sweepstakes* are often used interchangeably. Publisher's Clearinghouse and *Reader's Digest* conduct two of the best-known sweepstakes.

The advertiser should consider some of the problems associated with sweepstakes and contests before sponsoring either. Care must be taken to assure that the contest or sweepstakes is conducted fairly and that no state or federal regulations are violated. In addition, an advertiser must remember that contests and sweepstakes result in many more dissatisfied "losers" than winners.

Dealer Premiums. While most premiums are designed for consumers, many are used to encourage trade support by wholesalers and retailers. Usually a variety of gifts or cash prizes are offered based on sales performance. Some companies issue catalogs and offer dealer incentives as continuity premiums. In some cases, dealer premiums include foreign travel or automobiles.

Point-of-Purchase

Point-of-purchase advertising is the last opportunity for a company to promote its product before a customer makes a purchase. Ideally, point-of-purchase ads should supplement other media advertising and also promote impulse purchasing. Often point-of-purchase ads will duplicate the creative message from a firm's advertising and promote tie-ins with celebrity endorsers. Not all store signs and displays are point-of-purchase advertising. Generally only manufacturer-supplied displays are included in this category. (See Figure 11–6.)

FIGURE 11-6 A Point-of-Purchase Marketing Case Study

Advertiser: Time-Life "How to Do It" books

Type of display: Manual rotation book display

Marketing objectives:

1. To carry out the overall promotional theme "Time-Life Books Show America 'How to Do It' " and to gain off-shelf space on a permanent basis for additional sales by centralizing the five book categories in the Time-Life Books "How To" series in one display.
2. To upgrade the display of the Time-Life "How To" series by stressing the image of quality related to the company and the product line itself.

In test markets retailers reported that centralization of titles and easy visual and manual access to books, along with the attractiveness of the display, promoted increased sales and in some cases multiple purchases of the books in the series.

Courtesy of Point-of-Purchase Advertising Institute, Inc.

Point-of-purchase ads are usually handled directly by a company's sales force. The success of a point-of-purchase display depends on the aggressiveness of a company's sales force in obtaining space from retailers and, of course, on the promotional value of the display. As the sale of consumer goods grows more dependent on self-service, point-of-purchase ads will grow in importance.

Because of the number of displays available to retailers, manufacturers must provide point-of-purchase ads whose value is commensurate with the space required. Many proprietary drug manufacturers ship their products within point-of-purchase displays that give a more integrated appearance to the products and conserve space for the retailer. Combining product and display also enhances the chances of the display being used by the retailer.

In most cases, a point-of-purchase display is free to the retailer. However, when a display involves considerable expense, the manufacturer and the retailer sometimes share the cost. In either case, the retailer must be convinced of the promotional benefits of any point-of-purchase display, or it won't be used.

In the last few years, point-of-purchase techniques have been combined with certain aspects of out-of-home promotion to use the strengths of both media. In the spring of 1980, On-Line Media introduced video monitors to deliver an advertising message to customers in supermarket checkout lines. The network, called the OMI System, displays a six-minute look of 3-, 5-, and 10-second commercials. CPM levels are in the $1 to $1.50 range. Similar systems have also been introduced in other locations such as shopping malls and hotel lobbies.

Couponing

Couponing has been a major area of sales promotion for decades. It is difficult to find a company in the food, soft drink, or soap/detergent category that does not use couponing regularly. In 1985, packaged goods producers issued 180 billion coupons with a face value of $50 billion, and consumers redeemed about 4 percent, or 6.5 billion, of these.[7] Figure 11–7 shows the growth in coupons, face values, and costs of redemption. Figure 11–8 shows the methods of distributing coupons.

Couponing has several purposes: (1) to offer price incentives to customers without tampering with the actual product purchase price, (2) to gain new customers or retain present customers, and (3) to introduce a new brand or a product innovation. Couponing, however, is not inexpensive. The average handling charge paid to retailers is about seven cents, up from three cents as recently as 1974.

In addition to legitimate costs, a major problem for coupon users is the misredemption of coupons. Every year, millions of coupons are probably redeemed illegally. Some unethical retailers send in hundreds of coupons that were not used to purchase the product. This practice costs manufacturers hundreds of thousands of dollars annually. Before undertaking a coupon promotion, the prudent marketer should consult one of the several coupon houses that specialize in coupon promotion and security, such as Manufacturers Coupon Control Center, an A. C. Nielsen/Dun & Bradstreet venture.

The marketing strategy of the advertiser largely determines the type of coupon distribution used. The most common method is newspaper advertising which includes the coupon and freestanding inserts containing coupons. Newspaper coupons reach both present and potential users

---

[7] "The Costly Coupon Craze," *Fortune,* June 9, 1986, p. 84.

FIGURE 11-7   Growth in Coupon Use

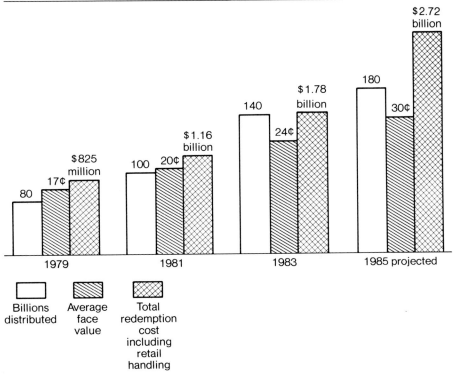

Billions
distributed

Average
face
value

Total
redemption
cost
including
retail
handling

Estimate based on clearing house data.

SOURCE: Reprinted from "System Keeps Track of Coupons," *Marketing News* 13 (September 1985), p. 20. Published by the American Marketing Association.

FIGURE 11-8   Percent of Coupons Distributed by Media

	1977	*1978*	*1979*	*1986*
Daily newspaper	56.9%	55.6%	52.3%	22.3%
Sunday newspaper	8.5	7.7	9.5	
Freestanding insert	11.8	13.4	14.9	59.9
Total newspaper	77.3	76.7	76.7	82.2
Magazine	12.5	11.4	12.2	8.6
Direct mail	3.0	3.0	3.2	4.4
In/on pack	8.2	8.9	7.9	4.8
Coupons distributed (billions)	62.2	72.7	81.2	180.0

SOURCE: *Marketing and Media Decisions,* April 1980, p. 30, and April 1986, p. 156.

of a product. Often an advertiser wants to encourage repeat purchases or keep customers in the face of new or more aggressive competition. In such situations, the in-pack coupon might be the ideal solution.

Sources of Sales Promotion Information

Direct Mail Marketing Association
6 East 44th Street
New York, NY 10017

National Premium Sales Executives
1600 Route 22
Union, NJ 07083

Point-of-Purchase Advertising Institute
60 East 42nd Street
New York, NY 10017

Promotion Marketing Association of America
420 Lexington Avenue
New York, NY 10017

Specialty Advertising Association International
1404 Walnut Hill Lane
Irving, TX 75062

REVIEW QUESTIONS

1. What are the prospects for growth in direct marketing? Why do you think this?
2. What are the major advantages and disadvantages of direct mail? What medium is the most direct competitor?
3. What is the role of the list broker? How does this differ from the role of a list compiler?
4. Compare and contrast advertising and sales promotion. What factors are likely to be present when these two functions are mutually enhancing?
5. What is the major difference between specialty and premium sales promotion?
6. Give an example of the following premiums.
    a. Factory pack.   *d.* Continuity.
    b. Self-liquidating.   *e.* Sweepstakes.
    c. Traffic building.   *f.* Contests.
7. What is the major medium for couponing? What are typical coupon redemption rates?

8. Consult the current SRDS Direct Mail rate book and find the costs, sources, and any other important decision factors for a mailing list comprised of names of the following:

    a. Attorneys in Pacific Coast states.

    b. Inventors of patented inventions.

    c. Female physicians living east of the Mississippi River.

    d. Fast-food franchisers.

    e. Members of sororities at universities in Indiana.

SUGGESTED ADDITIONAL READING

Alvin B. Zeller, Inc., 1987 Catalog of Mailing Lists. Alvin B. Zeller, Inc., 37 East 28th Street, New York, NY 10016.

"Are Purchases from Direct Mail Increasing?" Cahners Advertising Research Report No. 160.1, Cahners Publishing Company, Boston, MA, 1985.

BAGLEY, DAN S. *Specialty Advertising: A New Look.* Specialty Advertising Association International, 1978.

"Boom Time for Cataloguing Is Quieting Down." *Marketing News,* August 2, 1985, pp. 11, 13.

BULKELEY, WILLIAM. "Catalog Merchants Try New Strategies as the Field Crowds with Competitors." *The Wall Street Journal,* January 20, 1986, p. 21.

"Catalog Fallout." *Fortune,* January 20, 1986, pp. 63–64.

"Direct Marketing." *Advertising Age,* Special Report, February 6, 1986, pp. 13–31.

"Direct Marketing Next Tidal Wave to Make Its Impact Worldwide." *Marketing News,* October 10, 1986, p. 3.

"Direct-Response Technique Targets High-Tech Farmers." *Marketing News,* December 6, 1985, p. 3.

NABER, JAMES H. "The Sales Promotion Explosion." The James Webb Young Fund Address, University of Illinois, October 21, 1986.

Need Sales Leads? American Business Lists, Inc., Omaha, NE 61827, March 1986.

"Premiums and Promotions." *Advertising Age,* Special Report, May 5, 1986, pp. S1–S33.

RAJU, P.S., and MANOJ HASTAK. "Pre-Trial Cognitive Effects of Cents-Off Coupons." *Journal of Advertising* 12, no. 2 (1983), pp. 24–33.

Rave Reviews: 27 Award-Winning Specialty Advertising Promotions. Specialty Advertising Association International, 1986.

"Revamping Mailing Increases Response." *Marketing News,* October 11, 1985, p. 8.

"Sales Promotion." *Advertising Age,* Special Report, February 6, 1986, pp. 13–31.

SHOEMAKER, ROBERT W., and VIKAS TIBREWALA. "Relating Coupon Redemption Rates to Past Purchasing of the Brand." *Journal of Advertising Research* 25, no. 5 (October/November 1985), pp. 40–47.

STEPHENS, NANCY, and BRUCE D. MERRILL. "Targeting the Over Sixty-Five Vote in Political Campaigns." *Journal of Advertising* 13, no. 3 (1984), pp. 17–20, 49.

STONE, BOB. "Direct Marketing Flow Chart." *Advertising Age,* January 18, 1982, p. 57.

Trade Shows in Black and White: A Guide to Marketers. The Trade Show Bureau, New Canaan, CT, 1986.

WENTZ, LAUREL. "Saatchis Keen on Direct Mail," *Advertising Age,* September 15, 1986, p. 70.

CHAPTER TWELVE

International Advertising Media

Imagine a market with more consumers than America and Europe combined. Where imports grew by 38% in 1984. Where 100 million people watch an evening TV programme and there are 104 TV stations. With 1,300 newspapers with a combined readership of 200 million, 3,000 periodicals and 1,667 radio stations. Where the domestic advertising industry has grown by 50% per annum in the last 5 years. Whose export advertising has increased by over 82% in 1984 alone. A market which is anxious to do business with you. It's called China. Shouldn't you be there?*

> From an advertisement jointly
> sponsored by *South* magazine and the
> China National Advertising Association
> for Foreign Economic Relations and Trade

"Be sure to use our heavy-duty mouth detergent every morning" . . . "You can buy this safe children's aspirin at your local narcotics store" . . . "This book says break the car's front arm before attaching the wheel of a fly."†

> Yuri Radzievsky

Advertising beyond the borders of the United States has become a common task for domestic advertising agencies for several reasons. A U.S. client may wish to market its product overseas. An overseas client may want to stimulate sales in the United States. And a client in any country may want to expand the market for a successful product to other countries.

In almost every market in the world, the task of advertising is

---

* *Advertising Age,* June 9, 1986, p. 58.

† "The 'Invisible Idiot' and Other Monsters of Translation," *Viewpoint,* Fall 1983, p. 10.

essentially the same—to communicate product information in an attractive and persuasive manner, and thereby stimulate demand. However, the components used in advertising, such as words, colors, symbols, creative execution, and media, must be harmonized with differing cultures, customs, languages, levels of economic development, legal systems, and infrastructure in order to accomplish the advertising task effectively. The purpose of this chapter is to sensitize you to the differences between domestic advertising and advertising practices in other countries. Particular emphasis is placed on differences in the media function beyond the borders of the United States.

GLOBAL MARKETING STRATEGIES

In the mid-1980s, global marketing strategies acquired a special prominence. Major marketers of autos, pharmaceuticals, consumer packaged goods, industrial products, and financial services recognized more completely the advantages of global markets. Global markets provided the added efficiencies inherent in large-scale markets and a synergy to marketing programs where the summed result was greater than simply the "sum of the parts."

Global marketing strategies are founded on the premise that human wants and needs have a number of important similarities regardless of cultural differences. These strategies highlight regularity in consumer demand, and modify marketing programs to account for cultural and other differences found in different countries. In contrast, country-specific marketing strategies emphasize the unique characteristics of each particular market and relegate intermarket similarities to a secondary role in market planning.

Multinational marketing and advertising strategies fall into one (or a combination) of five types.

1. One product/one message—worldwide.
2. Product extension—communications adaptation.
3. Product adaption—communications extension.
4. Dual adaption.
5. Product invention.[1]

One Product/One Message

This strategy of uniform advertising across national boundaries emphasizes common human nature. Proponents argue that this approach is the

---

[1] Stephan Robock and Kenneth Simmonds, *International Business and Multinational Enterprises,* 3rd ed. (Homewood, Ill.: Richard D. Irwin, 1983), pp. 429–47.

simplest and the most profitable. Students are often surprised that this approach works. In fact, it works quite well for a limited number of product categories—for example women's cosmetics, tobacco products, and relatively sophisticated industrial products.

When this strategy works, the cost savings for advertising can be enormous. However, critics are quick to suggest that this is not only a simple but also a simple-minded way to advertise in more than one national market. Many attempts to use a single product/message combination in different markets have failed disastrously. For example, Pet milk encountered problems in French markets where the word "pet" means to break wind. Similar difficulties attended the introduction in Germany of a hair-curling iron called "Mist-Stick," due perhaps to the fact that *mist* means *excrement* in German. It was discovered after product introduction that "Nonox," a gasoline additive; "Joni," a facial cream; and "Fundavit," a vitamin line, each referred to or were highly suggestive of female genitalia in Java, India, and Spain.[2]

Of course, not all such errors are committed by U.S. firms operating abroad. Foreign corporations make mistakes in the United States, too. Koff beer, Siff beer, and Zit chocolates have not yet swept the domestic market, though their exporters had hoped for success. Perhaps the classic Japanese advertising malaprop can be found in a line of men's trousers marketed in the U.S. under the brand name "Trim Pecker."[3]

Product Extension-Communications Adaptation

In this strategy, the multinational marketer offers identical or at least highly similar products to markets that use a common product in different ways. While the product is common to the markets and users share certain basic characteristics, the advertising message must differ to be effective. For example, a bicycle might be advertised as a recreational product in the United States, a military training device in Eastern Europe, a basic transportation product in Africa, and a commercial delivery vehicle in Southeast Asia. Fish hooks and hand-held fertilizer spreaders are promoted as hobby-related products in the United States, but have commercial uses elsewhere in the world. Television sets, radios, and even newspapers are purchased by villages as common property in some underdeveloped countries; they are used as media for the dissemination of public or government messages. In Central America, a Collins machete is not only (or even primarily) a camper's tool.

---

[2] David A. Ricks, *Big Business Blunders* (Homewood, Ill.: Dow Jones-Irwin, 1983), pp. 41–44.

[3] Donald B. Miller, "What Does Global Marketing/Advertising Really Mean?" *Advertising World,* April 1985, p. 10.

Product Adaption-Communications Extension

In this strategy, the message remains the same, or at least greatly similar, but the advertised product is modified to meet local conditions in overseas markets. This strategy places primary responsibility for meeting local needs on the producing company, while the advertising function enjoys more extensive economies of scale. For example, condensed Campbell soups did not sell well in Great Britain, where canned soup is traditionally sold in a "ready to heat" dilution. Britons thought the condensed form provided only half the quantity for the same price. By altering the water content and can size, Campbell avoided a market failure. U.S.-based fast food franchises find greater consumer acceptance by changing ingredient proportions and menu assortments to match foreign flavor and dietary preferences, but they continue to use messages featuring the "Colonel" and the "golden arches." Detergent companies prosper when they blend soap powders to give good results in local water conditions. Appliance manufacturers modify products to operate with the different electrical power types found in other countries. Industrial products are altered to have the different safety characteristics or engineering specifications required outside the United States.

Dual Adaption

On occasion, both product and message must be altered. At first glance, this seems to represent a country-by-country strategy, and sometimes only a market offering developed specifically for a single market will work. More often, however, major elements in the product and message mix can be standardized. When standardization can be maintained, even for only a portion of the marketing mix, economies and efficiencies can be realized.

In Europe, greeting cards are exchanged on different occasions and holidays than in the United States. And Europeans prefer to write their own messages in cards, while the American tradition calls for a pre-printed message. To be successful in European markets, U.S. greeting card marketers altered not only the advertising messages but also the product by leaving the interior of the card blank. In spite of a need for dual adaption, these marketers were able to preserve many aspects of both message and product that had worked well at home. David Ricks describes a problem faced by the overseas marketer of copying machines in a country where the government held a monopoly on the manufacture of paper. This particular paper had sufficient variation in physical properties to render the machines inoperable, but due to "national" pride, importing standardized paper was not an acceptable solution. The situation called for redesigning machine tolerances *and* emphasizing compatibility with the national paper—a dual adaption strategy.[4]

Product Invention

When, for cost or other reasons, a product and message offering cannot be modified to suit the needs of a particular overseas market, a firm may still be able to participate in that market. Any successful firm has expertise in meeting the basic needs of its market, and such expertise may help the company "invent" a product in the form another market requires. By using different materials, product designs, or marketing channels, or by making other departures from the traditional marketing mix, a firm may be able to capitalize on its particular expertise to offer a "new" product that can succeed elsewhere.

A common problem U.S. consumer goods manufacturers face when attempting to market their products to other countries is the lower levels of household income abroad. American goods simply cost too much to be bought in large quantities. A slightly different way of expressing the problem is that labor-saving products do not offer consumers or businesses an automatic reason for buying where labor is inexpensive and capital is scarce. For example, a labor-saving agricultural machine may have little appeal in a market with widespread unemployment among farm workers.

But by inventing a product that serves the same basic need the firm is already meeting in other markets, it may be able to overcome the local market obstacle. Here, there is no automatic answer to the question of using a communications extension to advertise the invented product. However, since the invented product design is based on the firm's knowledge of basic product function, the basic advertising appeal may be effective.

FACTORS TO CONSIDER WHEN PLANNING ADVERTISING IN OTHER COUNTRIES

Factors that are second nature in creating advertising for a domestic market, or that can be conveniently and cheaply settled by consulting "ordinary" advertising research, must be thoroughly and systematically considered when dealing with foreign markets. The most important of these considerations are presented below.

---

[4] Ricks, *Big Business Blunders*, pp. 25–26.

Culture

Culture may be defined as the nonbiological conditions of human life. It is made up of people's patterns of thinking, behaving, feeling, and reacting. It is learned and shared with others of the cultural group. It includes a value system. Its boundaries are often roughly defined by nationality, though many countries contain more than one culture, and a single culture may span more than one nation. It serves as a loose collection of social rules, and violations are often met with social, emotional, and/or economic penalty.[5]

To be effective, advertising must be designed to stimulate demand in ways consonant with the culture(s) of its audience. When advertising outside the parent culture, the marketer must be especially careful to be informed about relevant aspects of the other culture, to be sensitive to differences between cultures, and to create and place the advertising message in a way that conforms to the cultural structures of the market. Failure to do this usually results in severe market penalties.

Language

One of the most salient aspects of any culture is its language. Many scholars have concluded that language is the most important element in identifying a person's cultural identity. It is the heart of successful communication among people. Effective advertising communication depends on a thorough knowledge of the language or languages used in a market.

In transnational advertising, problems often arise when ad copy is translated into another tongue. Improper or imperfect translations can change advertising copy in ways that range from humorous to obscene and from inane to insulting. None of these "accidental" alterations accomplish the advertiser's intended objectives. Some are so inappropriate that the advertiser is driven from the target market. Advertisers must translate the copy into a second language keeping in mind idioms, slang, and local usage and pronounciation.

In the United States, advertising copy frequently captures the contemporaneous appeal of the vernacular form of language. This is an especially dangerous obstacle to correct translation. Several examples have already been mentioned where a literal translation from American copy produced unintended messages. While accurate translation is always important to extending advertising messages, and should always be done by thoroughly competent translators, extending successful U.S.

---

[5] Adapted from Bernard Berelson and Gary A. Steiner, *Human Behavior, An Inventory of Scientific Findings* (New York: Harcourt Brace Jovanovich, 1964), pp. 644–45.

slogans and themes is particularly dangerous. From the number and severity of the horror stories based on poorly translated copy, a special corollary to "Murphy's Law" seems to apply here. However, the use of language experts, local people, and the practice of **back-translation** can usually prevent mistranslation. This process first translates to the second language, say, from English to French. Then a different expert "back translates" from French to English, to guarantee that the original intent is preserved.

Law

The legal frame within which advertising is practiced varies widely among countries. These differences affect what messages advertising may carry, when advertising may be placed, the media that may carry advertising, and even the structure of the ad agencies that are licensed to conduct advertising.

Of special importance are the legal variations that restrict or regulate advertising media in other countries, and these will be discussed in greater detail later in the chapter. Other markets restrict copy possibilities and impose other regulations on advertising that are much different from those in this country.

Economic Development

It is conventional to group the nations of the world into three classifications, based on the extent of their economic development. These categories are usually listed as developed, developing, and underdeveloped. Examples of countries falling into these categories might be Japan, Korea, and Thailand, respectively. The United States, Western Europe, and some countries in the Far East are considered developed. Central European and some South American nations are categorized as "developing." Much of the southern hemisphere (with the important exceptions of Australia and New Zealand), the so-called Third World nations, are considered underdeveloped.

Economic development is itself an index comprised of many factors that include average individual economic well-being, the distribution of individual wealth, and public sector variables such as transportation, communications, industrial diversification, and education. The extent to which the public sector has been developed is collectively called the level of infrastructure.

Advertising must work within the confines of a market's economic development. It would be foolish to plan an advertising campaign that relied on television for a market that had few television stations or sets. Equally ineffective would be a campaign based on long copy for a market where literacy rates were low. Yet, even the most undeveloped markets have media, and by using these, the advertiser can disseminate commercial information.

For economically underdeveloped nations, some special conditions apply. John Hill makes the point that in less developed countries, about 10 percent of the population lives in urban areas. This 10 percent is most likely to be educated, affluent, have a "modern" world view, and to contain the innovators and early adopters of imported products. To reach the larger percentage of population, the marketer must operate outside major urban areas, too. Suburban areas (10 to 15 miles outside cities) contain an additional 20 percent of the population, while about 70 percent of the population lives in rural areas. Advertising taken from an urban area to the remainder of the country will encounter progressively more people, greater individual poverty, more traditional outlooks, a longer interval before product adoption, greater numbers of nonusers, a more rudimentary infrastructure, and a necessarily greater reliance on nonwestern nontraditional media, including loudspeaker trucks, mobile movies, and riverboats fitted with loudspeakers.[6]

Religion

Another powerful aspect of a market environment is found in a market's religious practices and groupings. Every religion makes unequivocal statements about what its members should consider right and wrong, and these statements are applied to food, dress, courtship, occupational choice, recreation, business practices, public architecture, and a host of other matters. Advertising messages must be consistent with prevailing religious strictures if they are to inform and persuade.

In some markets, advertising must operate within a multiplicity of religious beliefs. For instance, it is not enough to know that the predominant religion in a market or country is Islam. The advertiser also needs to know if Suuni Moslem or Shiite Moslem practices prevail and what portions of the population belong to each. In Israel, you might think that the Jewish religion predominates, but that view obscures important differences. One advertiser of bikini-style swimwear used poster advertising at Tel Aviv bus stops and found that the ads got mixed reactions. Relatively secular Jews found the ads interesting, while more fundamentalist Jews thought the posters obscene and repeatedly trashed them. Advertising illustrations of refrigerators that show a ham among the contents run into trouble throughout the Middle East, since several of the religions practiced there forbid the consumption of pork.

---

[6] John S. Hill, "Targeting Promotions in Lesser-Developed Countries: A Study of Multinational Corporation Strategies," *Journal of Advertising* 13, no. 4 (1984), pp. 39–48.

Technology

Some technological differences in foreign markets are part of the infrastructure, others are a feature of the particular market's economic development. Advertising designed for one market should be evaluated for compatibility with another market's technical condition. One way to do so is to examine the entire marketing mix in a framework that has stood the test of a quarter century of use. Proposed by Richard Robinson, this scheme to check advertising and product suitability is shown in Figure 12–1.

Political System

The political system and government structure in an overseas market can be a major influence on advertising. Variations in political systems and governments can determine who may distribute goods, who may retail them, what media may be used to advertise them, what restrictions apply to imports, what tariffs will be charged, and what products or suppliers will be banned from this market.

Most markets can be characterized as capitalistic, socialistic, or a mixture of the two, although to do this tends to combine politics with economics. Capitalistic markets tend to be more fully developed, in an economic sense, and permit greater freedom in the use of advertising,

---

FIGURE 12–1 Technical Conditions and Consequences in Foreign Markets

Condition	Consequence
Level of technical skills	Product simplification
Level of labor cost	Automation or manualization of the product
Level of literacy	Remarking and simplification of the product
Level of income	Quality and price change
Level of interest rates	Quality and price-change (Investment in quality might not be financially desirable.)
Level of maintenance	Change in tolerances
Climatic differences	Product adaptation
Isolation (heavy repair difficult and expensive)	Product simplification and reliability improvement
Differences in standards	Recalibration of product and resizing
Availability of other products	Greater or lesser product integration
Availability of materials	Change in product structure and fuel
Power availability	Resizing of product
Special conditions	Product redesign or invention

SOURCE: Reprinted from Richard D. Robinson, "The Challenge of the Underdeveloped National Market," *Journal of Marketing* 25 (October 1961), p. 22. Published by the American Marketing Association.

while socialistic markets are likely to impose greater restrictions on advertising and to be less well developed.

The Advertising Industry

In other markets, advertisers need to recognize any differences in the way the advertising industry is configured. For example, what is the monetary volume of advertising handled by the country's ad agencies? Is this large enough to provide the necessary advertising experience? What about agency ownership? Is this restricted to nationals? How about agency compensation? While a nominal commission of 15 percent is the single most common scheme, some countries have different rates for each medium. In other places, bribes, kickbacks, and what is sometimes called "la mordida" (the bite) are prevalent.

One way U.S. agencies can operate overseas is to acquire all or part of a foreign agency. Another is to establish a branch office or subsidiary in the overseas market. A third is to rely on the services of an agency native to the market. Advertisers and their agencies are not always free to choose among these three alternatives. In some countries, foreign ownership is prohibited; in others it is permitted, while elsewhere it is restricted, often to a minority ownership share. In most of the communist world, ad agencies are state monopolies.

From the standpoint of ad quality, U.S. advertisers and agencies are more comfortable using native agencies for markets in the developed countries and more inclined to depend on their own resources when the market is not well developed. However, local input is more valuable when advertising to a totally unfamiliar market than when the market is more familiar. Major advertising agencies often try for the best of both (local knowledge and extensive account experience) by acquiring agencies in other nations or by participating in joint ventures with them. Figure 12–2 indicates some of this activity. Research done among ad agencies in Western Europe confirms that the joint venture between U.S. and native participants is more productive than either of the other two alternatives, native agency or U.S. subsidiary.[7]

MEDIA CHARACTERISTICS IN INTERNATIONAL MARKETS

In addition to what you have learned about each major advertising medium in the context of U.S. advertising, it is important to know

---

[7] Anthony F. McGann and Nils-Erik Aaby, "United States Influence on Advertising Agency Productivity in Western Europe," *ADMAP*, September 1975, pp. 316–24.

FIGURE 12-2   U.S. Agencies' International Acquisitions in 1985

U.S. Agency	Type of Agreement	Foreign Agency	Country	Billings (millions)
NW Ayer	Acquisition	William Wilkens	W. Germany	$ 62.5
	Acquisition	Berefelt & Delsol Reklambyra	Sweden	$ 2.0
Ted Bates	Majority	Scholz & Friends	W. Germany	$ 48.2
Leo Burnett Co.	Acquisition	Larsen Advertising	New Zealand	$ 2.0
	Majority	Marsden & Hartmann	Switzerland	$ 14.0
	Minority	AD S.A.	Switzerland	Not available
	Acquisition	Star	Italy	$ 15.0
	Acquisition	Euro	Greece	$ 5.0
DDB	Minority	Verba	Italy	Not available
FCB	Affiliation	Yaratim	Turkey	Not available
Grey Advertising	Acquisition	Grierson Cockman Craig & Druiff	U.K.	$ 14.0
	Majority	Konsell Partner	W. Germany	$ 24.0
	Minority	Trace	Spain	Not available
Hill, Holliday	Joint venture	Magnus Nankervis & Curl	Australia	$ 18.6
	Merger	Aspect Advertising	U.K.	$ 30.0
Ogilvy & Mather	Majority	Schellenberg	W. Germany	$ 15.0
	Majority	DC-3	Portugal	$ 1.0
Saatchi & Saatchi	Minority	R.C.P.	Spain	$ 7.7
	Acquisition	Grandfield Rork Collins	U.K.	$ 98.0
	Cooperative	Asahi Advertising	Japan	$163.0
Scali, McCabe	Majority	Cascades	France	$ 15.0
TBWA	Acquisition	Voelker & Vorwerk	W. Germany	Not available
	Acquisition	Valero y Associados	Spain	Not available
JWT	Acquisition	GDD	Spain	$ 12.3
Wells Rich	Minority	Holmes Knight Ritchie	U.K.	$ 25.2

SOURCE: Reprinted with permission *Advertising Age*, January 27, 1986. Copyright Crain Communications, Inc.

something about how each medium fits in a global advertising context. To do this, an overview of each medium is presented.

Television

Television is a popular form of entertainment wherever it is found in the world. In terms of television viewing, Japan leads the world. There, the average *person* watches about seven hours of TV per day. This figure is almost twice as high as it is in the United States, Japan's closest rival. The worldwide popularity of television as a source of entertainment is difficult to underestimate. In 1986, it was estimated that there are 70 million TV sets in the People's Republic of China, where some 300 million viewers are guaranteed for a broadcast of a Chinese program titled "One World." At the same time, in Europe, a satellite TV channel owned by

---

FIGURE 12–3   The World's Favorite TV Programs

Country	Top American Show(s)	Top Local Show
Australia	*Cagney & Lacey* *Hill Street Blues* *Dynasty* and *Dallas*	**A Country Practice:** Drama dealing with medical and veterinary practices in a country town.
Belgium	*Dynasty*	**The Weather:** Twice a week, Armand Pien (who could be Belgium's answer to Willard Scott) gives 12-minute reports on the state of the skies, mixing scientific reports with off-beat pranks and humorous anecdotes. Viewers seem to love sending him bizarre fruits and vegetables, which he proudly displays.
Brazil	*Magnum, P.I.* and *Cover Up* (packaged together)	**Roque Santiero:** Story of a mythical town and a martyred sculptor of religious statues who disappears during a bandit attack. The townspeople assume he died defending the town and erect a monument honoring him, but the sculptor turns up, alive and well, years later.
Canada	*Dallas*	**Hockey Night in Canada:** National Hockey League game of the week (seasonal).
Chile	*Dynasty*	**Shabados Gigantes:** All-day Saturday magazine/variety-type program consisting of comedy sketches, game segments, travel vignettes, and variety-type entertainment.
Denmark	*Dollars* *(Dynasty)*	**Matador:** Drama depicting the changes a small town undergoes after World War II.
England	*Dallas*	**Coronation Street:** Working-class soap opera revolving around the store, pub, garage, and residences on Coronation Street.
Finland	*Dallas*	**Levyraati (Music Panel):** A panel of celebrities and ordinary people judges popular music according to danceability, rhythm, and lyrics.
France	*Dallas*	**La Derniere Seance:** Old movie double features (complete with newsreels and short subjects of the period) with current celebrity interviews during intermission.
Italy	*Dynasty* and *Dallas*	**Quark:** Scientific program dealing with such topics as nuclear physics, biology, and psychology.

Rupert Murdoch (called the Sky Channel) was available to 12.5 million viewers. The weekly cume for the channel was estimated at 8 million persons. In Norway and Sweden where, parenthetically, the governments prohibit advertising on native television broadcasts, 98 percent of viewers with access to Sky watched it at least once during a three-month period. Coca-Cola, IBM, Quaker, Levi-Strauss, McDonald's, Unilever,

FIGURE 12–3 *(concluded)*

Country	Top American Show(s)	Top Local Show
Japan	*Little House on the Prairie* (only foreign show in prime time)	***Miotsukushi:*** 15-minute morning soap opera (8:15 to 8:30) about a couple in a seaside village where marriages are still arranged by the parents of the bride and groom.
Mexico	*El Auto Incredible (Knight Rider)*	***The Years Go By:*** A 30-minute weekday soap opera. The plot: Rodolfo falls in love with and marries Maria, only to be transferred to another job in another city. There, Rodolfo meets a rich woman, pretends to be single, and marries her, too. However, the rich woman turns out to be rude and spoiled and has an affair with another man, causing Rodolfo to leave her and go back to Maria.
Netherlands	*Dynasty* and *Hotel*	***1-2-3:*** A quiz show. Contestants are given clues as to the identity of objects (prizes), which range from a drinking glass to a new car.
South Africa	*Three's Company*	***Kampus:*** Afrikaans-language program about life on a college campus. The plot revolves around a girl who gets pregnant.
South Korea	*CHiPS*	***A Farmer's Diary:*** The longest-running Korean program, the drama presents a realistic view of contemporary life in rural Korea: The exodus of the young from the farms to Seoul and the farmer's grief over his rising debts and falling farm prices.
Spain	*V,* which sparked a nationwide lizard craze.	***Saturday Night Movie***
Switzerland	*Dallas*	***Music und Gaste (Music and Guests):*** A talk/variety show that often blends performances by stars such as Elton John with *interviews* with space scientists and other intellectuals.
West Germany	*Dallas* and *Dynasty*	***Derrick:*** Police drama about two detectives (Mr. Derrick and Mr. Klein) catching murderers.

SOURCE: Reprinted with permission *Advertising Age,* December 2, 1985, p. 54. Copyright Crain Communication, Inc. Reports from *Advertising Age* correspondents based on ratings (where available), TV network reports, and advertiser reports of audience levels.

and Gillette were among the advertisers who paid an average of $3,100 for 30-second, prime-time spots on Sky.[8]

U.S. television programming is popular throughout much of the world. But local programming is also extensive (see Figure 12–3).

---

[8] "Profile of Sky-Watchers," *International Advertiser,* June 1986, p. 22.

Types of Overseas Advertising. In overseas markets, television advertising opportunity falls into one of three categories:

1. Competitive commercial broadcasting.
2. Commercial monopolies.
3. Noncommercial broadcasting.

These are listed in declining order of opportunity and increasing extent of regulation. There seems to be a global movement toward more freedom for television advertising, and markets that once flatly banned TV ads are, in the late 1980s, moving toward a more commercial, competitive position. This movement is the result of two powerful forces: the transnational reach of the new, satellite-based transmission technology and the desire of governments and private sector monopolists to offset high TV production costs with advertising revenues. A recent study of European TV estimated that if all countries permitted as much TV advertising as Italy and the United Kingdom, the change might net these other countries as much as $3 billion in additional revenue per year.[9] Figure 12–4 illustrates the availability of this medium to advertisers in European nations and also indicates the extent of development for the cable TV industry.

Time charges for TV advertising in other countries are often lower than in the United States. For certain countries, the difference is dramatic. In 1986, CCTV, China's national television network, priced a 30-second, prime-time spot at $5,000. With an audience of 300 million viewers, this equates with a CPM of less than two cents! Remember, however, that the only real customer for many of the advertised products was the Chinese government—that is, the effective audience was much smaller than the number of viewers.

China is not typical of many of the underdeveloped countries of the world. The Chinese market features widespread TV ownership and a national network with a signal that reaches virtually the entire country. Elsewhere in the underdeveloped parts of the globe, television advertising is costly, heavily regulated, and capable of reaching only a small fraction of the population.

Radio

As with television, radio advertising in other countries usually fits into one of three classes: competitive/commercial, monopolistic/commercial, and noncommercial. As with all broadcasting, advertising opportunity not only is a function of government regulation and competitive environ-

---

[9] Andrew C. Brown, "Europe Braces for Free-Market TV," *Fortune,* February 20, 1984, p. 82.

FIGURE 12–4   Availability of TV in Europe

Country	Households in Millions	Households with TV	Total No. of Ad Minutes per Day*	Households with Cable
Austria	2.7	91.9%	20	10%
Belgium	3.425	96.0%	0†	75%
Denmark	2.094	N.A.‡	0	0
Finland	1.831	96.0%	12–42	6–7%
France	19.6	95.0%	54	1%
Greece	2.95	95.0%	57	0
Ireland	.927	90.9%	80	27%
Italy	18.5	74.0%	740	0
Netherlands	5.132	98.0%	39§	65%
Norway	1.6	84.0%	0	14%
Portugal	3.057	86.7%	99	0
Spain	9.8	95.2%	80	0
Sweden	3.32	N.A.‡	0	1%
Switzerland	2.54	86.1%	20	40–59%
United Kingdom	19.4	97.0%	144	7%
W. Germany	25.3	97.0%	40	2%

* For national TV networks only, not including private cable TV such as Sky Channel.

† Limited institutional advertising; no brand or product advertising.

‡ Not available.

§ A total of 12 minutes (6 minutes per channel) was added in July.

SOURCE: "How Pan-European Is Europe?" *International Advertiser,* September 1985, p. 8.

ment, but also depends on a broadcasting industry and relatively widespread ownership of receivers.

Radio has several characteristics that set it apart from television as an advertising medium, however. First, radio broadcasts reach the entire world. This is especially significant for marketers operating in Third World countries where TV does not deliver broad penetration levels. Second, radio receivers cost considerably less to buy, on average, than television sets. Markets with lower levels of consumer income are more likely to have consumers who can afford to buy radios than televisions. Third, radio broadcasts probably command higher attention among overseas audiences than is common in the United States. The medium, denegrated in this country as "musical wallpaper," is the focus of its listeners' attention in many other lands. Fourth, by virtue of its long history of reaching across national boundaries, radio broadcasting is a more truly international medium. As such, it has never been as constrained by local regulation as television. Radio Luxembourg historically has reached large audiences in Central European markets where TV advertising has never been allowed. Voice of America broadcasts are listened to avidly in the Soviet Union and, although noncommercial in nature, they easily cross a border that TV could not penetrate. The so-called "pirates" of the

North Sea anchor transmitting-station ships in international waters and broadcast popular radio programs into Denmark, Britain, and other countries with impunity, despite regulations in the receiving markets that forbid such broadcasts. Finally, radio time (almost) always costs less than TV, and when lower costs are combined with its other advantages, radio becomes a very effective medium for reaching audiences in developing and underdeveloped nations.

Print Media

In other countries, the role and prominence of newspapers and magazines is much different than in the United States. Some markets are known for their very large number of very highly competitive newspapers. Lebanon, for example, has historically had one of the greatest assortments of newspapers per capita of any nation. Advertisers, however, translate this fact into a "lowest number of readers per paper" figure and rightly conclude that, in this situation, newspapers are a truly "local" medium. By way of contrast, Japan is a market characterized by very few but genuinely national newspapers. An ad in the largest Japanese daily will reach over half of the country's affluent households and over 80 percent of the nation's influential opinion makers.

Some publications are effective in reaching prospects in more than one country or market. Since these publications tend to be both prestigeous as well as widely distributed, they represent an especially attractive way for multinational advertisers to reach audiences in several countries simultaneously. Figure 12–5 shows a sample of this type of international publication, along with global CPM values.

In Western Europe, the United Kingdom leads in the number of newspapers published, while honors for the most magazines goes to West Germany. Figure 12–6 provides a summary of the publications and audiences for selected European countries in 1985.

With the exception that centimeters are used to indicate length rather than the more familiar units of inches and SAU numbers, rate cards for many overseas publications are quite similar to those for American publishers. Figure 12–7 illustrates this similarity for an Arabic magazine, *Sayidaty,* that closely resembles *Ladies' Home Journal* in this country.

A fundamental problem with print media advertising in other countries involves uncertain circulation figures. In the United States, independent audits of newspaper and magazine circulation have been a familiar part of this industry for three quarters of a century. In other markets, such verification is more often absent than present.

You may have noticed that the rate card in Figure 12–7 indicated that the publisher is a member of Audit Bureau of Circulations. Associations such as the International Advertising Association have worked to establish a set of standards and practices for international advertising. Standards for audience measurement figure prominently in these efforts. In spite of these helpful attempts to standardize and verify audience numbers, audience measurement remain a problem for advertisers in many parts of the world, where audience estimates vary in quality from "somewhat imprecise" to "largely imagined."

Advertisers can encounter other problems and surprises peculiar to individual markets and publishers. Some magazines "overbook" advertising for a particular issue, sometimes by as much as 100 percent. They then hold a lottery just prior to publication to decide which ads will run in the issue. In Southeast Asia, some newspaper publishers operate with equipment that dictates a maximum number of pages per issue. Should too many ads be sold, the publisher delays the surplus to another issue. And unlike the short lead times we associate with newspaper advertising in this country, some Asian papers use closing dates that are months before publication.

Cinema

Advertising shown in movie theaters represents only a tiny fraction of U.S. advertising, but in other countries, cinema advertising is a major advertising medium. Especially in Europe, cinema advertising has a long history. For instance, Greta Garbo appeared in a cinema commercial for a Swedish department store in 1919.[10]

Several aspects of cinema advertising should be considered in planning advertising for this medium:

1. The medium serves as a television substitute where commercial TV is unavailable. Filmed ads, like their TV counterparts, combine sight, sound, and color. And attention levels in theaters may be much higher than those commanded by television ads in households.

2. Audience demographics for movie audiences frequently describe an attractive prospective customer group. In European countries, moviegoers are young, upscale, and more difficult to reach by television than average.

3. In the rare instances when audience reactions are measured, cinema advertising seems to produce remarkably high levels of communications success. Values for measures like ad recall and brand awareness are exceptionally high.

---

[10] Kim B. Rotzoll, "The Captive Audience: The Troubled Odyssey of Cinema Advertising," Advertising Working Papers, University of Illinois, 1984, p. 2.

FIGURE 12–5 Advertising Age's Global Media Lineup

Title/Publisher	Major Printing Plants for Int'l. Editions	Paid N. American Circulation (% chg. from 6/84-6/85)	Paid Foreign Circulation by Region (% chg. from 6/84-6/85)	Paid Global Circulation (% chg. from 6/84-6/85)	Cost of Worldwide B&W Page ($/1986)	Global CPM B&W Pg. ($/1986)	Top Worldwide Advertisers 1985
Dailies:							
Financial Times of London Financial Times Ltd. London	London Frankfurt Bellmawr, N.J.	8,830[2] (+51.8)	Europe: 204,071[3] (+1.2) Middle East/Africa: 4,019 (−16.6) Asia/Pacific: 2,875 (+2.8) Latin America: 189 (−52.4) West Indies: 188 n.a.	229,423[10] (+6.0)	full: 25,984 qtr: 6,496	113.00	Illi Morgan Guaranty Bank Standard Chartered Pan American Mercedes Benz
International Herald Tribune New York Times & Washington Post	8 cities around the world	2,264 (+9.4)	Europe: 125,793 (+5.0) Middle East/N. Africa: 8,839 (−20.7) Asia/Pacific: 25,062 (+4.0) Sub-Saharan Africa: 1,838 n.a. Other: 843 (+78.6)	164,639 (+4.5)	full: 29,044 qtr: 7,261	176.41	IBM, AT&T Intercontinental Hotels R.J. Reynolds Trade Development Bank
Wall Street Journal Dow Jones & Co. New York	Hong Kong Singapore Heerlen, Neth.	1,990,025 (+1.5)	Asia: 28,383 (+2.4) Europe: 32,027 (+26.0)	2,050,435 (+1.9)	full: 96,312 qtr: 24,078	46.97	Bankers Trust[4] IBM, CitiCorp Wang Laboratories Pan American
Weeklies:							
Business Week McGraw Hill New York	Philadelphia, PA	795,409 (+2.6)	Europe: 45,222 (+10.5) Asia: 21,190 (+1.0) Latin America: 16,291 (−6.7) Other: 1,363 (−19.6)	878,276 (+2.6)	full: 32,142	36.60	DHL[4] Citiband Philips Daewoo, Fujitsu
The Economist The Economist Newspaper London	Singapore London Connecticut	104,736 (+3.4)	Europe: 127,806 (+11.4) Asia/Pacific: 25,088 (+27.8) Africa: 7,981 (+16.4) Middle East: 7,769 (+31.2) Central & S. Am: 5,037 (+12.0)	278,417 (+10.1)	full: 5,550[5]	19.93	AT&T Singapore Airlines Lockheed Citibank Lufthansa
Guardian Weekly Guardian Publications Manchester	Montreal Lincoln (U.K.)	24,236 (−1.4)	Europe: 16,638 (−0.9) Asia: 12,572 (+3.2) Middle East/Africa: 5,450 (+5.4) Latin America: 1,312 (+2.7) Other: 397 n.a.	60,585 (0.2)	full: 957	15.82	Tyndall Managers Gartmore Amnesty International Bumpus Haldane Maxwell W.T. Fry
Newsweek Newsweek Ltd. New York	Zurich Tokyo Hong Kong Daytona Beach	3,059,410 (+0.7)	Atlantic: 301,507 (−0.3) Latin America: 50,111 (+8.7) Asia: 183,455 n.a. S. Pacific: 125,000[6] n.a.	3,719,483 (+3.5)	full: 82,470[5]	19.36	Rupperts Int'l.[4] British American Tobacco Singapore Airlines Rolex Watches Distillers Co.
Time Time Inc. Publications New York	Toronto Miami, Fl. Weert, Neth. Melbourne Hong Kong	5,037,151 (+0.9)	Atlantic: 531,239 (+1.2) Asia: 267,243 (+6.2) S. Pacific: 140,867 (+0.1) Latin America: 90,744 (−9.5)	6,057,244 (+0.9)	full: 114,740	18.94	Rothmans Int'l.[4] Singapore Airlines Philip Morris Rolex Watches IBM

Publication / Publisher / Location	Printed in	U.S. circulation	Overseas circulation	Overseas circulation by region	Circulation figure	Page cost[5]	Top advertisers
Monthlies:							
International Management McGraw-Hill Publications Overseas Corp. Lausanne, Switzerland	Singapore St. Gallen, Switz.	n.a.[9]	109,920 (−45.6)	Europe: 84,303 (+19.7) Middle East: 25,617 (+16.0)	full: 7,855	71.40	N.V. Philips Dresdner Bank Lufthansa Thai Airways British American Tobacco
National Geographic Nat'l Geographic Society Washington, D.C.	Corinth, MS	9,266,615 (+2.8)	10,449,396 (+2.4)	Atlantic: 686,538 (+0.4) Pacific: 382,312 (+1.3) Latin America: 92,031 (+1.9) Other: 21,900 (−33.5)	full: 115,520	11.05	Canon Cameras AT&T Nikon Inc. Olympus Corp. Nissan Motor Co.
Reader's Digest Reader's Digest Assn. Pleasantville, N.Y.	26 cities around the world	19,745,000 (+1.1)	30,324,000 (+0.1)	Atlantic: 7,268,000 (−0.5) Pacific: 2,167,000 (−0.6) Latin America: 1,144,000 (−9.6)	full: 207,275	6.84	Nissan Motor Co.[4] Toyota Motor Sales Unilever General Motors Corp. Procter & Gamble
Scientific American Scientific American Inc. New York	Old Saybrook, CN	557,701 (+0.5)	654,489 (+0.3)	Europe: 65,548 (−0.4) Asia/Pacific: 20,506 (−5.6) Central & S. Am.: 5,221 (−17.3) Africa: 2,360 (−8.5) Middle East: 1,066 (−29.4)	full: 21,000	32.31	McDonnell Douglas Hewlett-Packard Hughes Aircraft AT&T Hitachi
South South Publications Ltd. London	London	5,867 (−24.2)	80,200 (+10.3)	Middle East/Africa: 30,432 (+7.3) Asia/Pacific: 18,802 (+36.6) Europe: 13,849 (+2.8) Latin America: 11,250 (+6.4)	full: 3,174	39.57	Bank America Citibank Lufthansa N.V. Philips Airbus Industries
WorldPaper[7] World Times Inc. Boston	18 countries around the world	U.S. edition starts in January n.a.	689,500 (−8.7)	Latin America: 237,000[8] (−23.3) East Asia: 368,500 (+22.4) Middle East: 84,000 (−29.7)	full: 24,255 qtr: 8,975	35.00	AT&T Jim Beam IBM Pan American Hertz
Other:							
Fortune Time Inc. Publications New York	Zurich, Switz.	632,393 (+2.5)	733,225 (+3.3)	Europe: 56,153 (+1.5) Asia: 35,697 (+1.9) Other: 8,982 (+15.9)	full: 28,040	38.68	IBM AT&T General Motors Corp. Volkswagen Ford Motor Co.
Harvard Business Review Harvard Business Review Boston	Glasgow, KY	214,576 (+1.3)	241,082 (+0.4)	Europe: 11,504 (−6.6) Asia/Pacific: 7,569 (−5.9) Central & S. Am.: 3,149 (−18.2) Middle East/Africa: 3,121 (−15.9) Other: 1,163 n.a.	full: 7,200	29.86	IBM AT&T General Motors Corp. N.V. Philips Thai Airways

[1] In all U.S. and international editions.
[2] As of November 1985.
[3] All circulation figures as of December 1984.
[4] All advertisers in category are for non-U.S. editions.
[5] Page cost is for 1985.
[6] An insert in Australia's *Bulletin* with *Newsweek*.
[7] Distributed as a newspaper supplement.
[8] All circulation figures as of October 1985.
[9] Not applicable
[10] As of June 1985.

SOURCE: Reprinted with permission *Advertising Age*, December 2, 1985, p. 56. Copyright Crain Communications, Inc.

FIGURE 12–6   Magazines and Newspapers

Country	Number of Magazines	Reach* in %	Number of Newspapers	Circulation in Millions
Austria	150	64	110	5.3
Belgium	129	70	91	3.5
Denmark	31	85	48	1.8
Finland	56	95	193	3.7
France	900	87	127	13.5
Greece	50	48 (per mo.)	210	No audit
Ireland	60	48	62	2.5
Italy	250	68	80	5.2
Netherlands	96	93	71	4.6
Norway	35	80	199	2.5
Portugal	200	24 (per mo.)	500	3.0
Spain	200	38 (per 6 mo.)	120	3.2
Sweden	150	94	182	4.7
Switzerland	58	85	294	3.4
United Kingdom	1,150	75	1,400	47.0
West Germany	2,500	90	341	27.0

* Cumulative reach of magazines surveyed. Percentage is per issue except where noted.
SOURCE: *International Advertiser*, September 1985, p. 10.

4. The use of TV commercials in movie theaters, as contrasted with commercials made expressly for cinema, is probably a mistake in markets familiar with both media. As a rule, cinema audiences expect higher quality (sound, color, and creative execution) for both feature films and ads than is tolerated by TV audiences.
5. Attendance at film showings is declining in many markets. Several factors have caused this decline, including an increase in urban crime and stiff competitive pressure from cable television and video cassette technology.
6. The number of theaters has declined sharply in many markets. For example, in 1947, there were 1,300 cinemas theaters in Belgium. By 1983, this number had slipped to only 580.[11] More recent evidence suggests that the decline has been arrested and may have even been reversed in some markets.

Other Media

In other countries, several additional media have a role to play in advertising. These include direct marketing, out-of-home media, and sales promotion.

---

[11] Philip Reber, *The Advertiser's Guide to European Media,* Young & Rubicam Europe, June 1983, p. 14.

FIGURE 12–7   Example Rate Card

SAYIDATY

سيدتي

SAYIDATY ("My Lady") is the leading Arabic magazine devoted exclusively to Arab family life. Each weekly, four-color issue contains articles on fashion, cosmetics, education and the arts, subjects of vital interest to the modern Arab woman, whose sophistication, fashion flair and purchasing power are widely known. In addition, **SAYIDATY** annually offers its readers a number of popular special issues highlighting international fashions, mother and child care, home decorating tips, and more. **SAYIDATY** has a paid circulation of 96,787 as certified by the Audit Bureau of Circulations, Ltd. (January-June 1985).

Published weekly on Monday by **Saudi Research & Marketing (U.K.) Ltd.**, London, United Kingdom.

Gate fold front cover		
3 page	$17,544	No Frequency Discount
4 page	$20,467	No Frequency Discount
Centerspread folder		
4 page	$21,052	No Frequency Discount
6 page	$31,579	No Frequency Discount
8 page	$42,106	No Frequency Discount
Insert 1 page	$ 7,603	No Frequency Discount
Insert 2 pages	$12,281	No Frequency Discount

Inserts must be less than size of full page.

MECHANICAL REQUIREMENTS

AD SIZE	WIDTH	DEPTH
Trim size	22.0 cm (8-11/16 in.)	28.5 cm (11-3/16 in.)
Type area	19.8 cm (7-11/16 in.)	26.0 cm (10-1/4 in.)
Back cover	19.8 cm (7-11/16 in.)	26.0 cm (10-1/4 in.)
Inside front/ back cover	19.8 cm (7-11/16 in.)	26.0 cm (10-1/4 in.)
Double/center- spread	41.5 cm (16-5/16 in.)	26.0 cm (10-1/4 in.)
Full page	19.8 cm (7-11/16 in.)	26.0 cm (10-1/4 in.)
1/2 page spread	41.5 cm (16-5/16 in.)	13.0 cm (5-1/8 in.)
1/2 page	19.8 cm (7-11/16 in.)	13.0 cm (5-1/8 in.)
1/3 page	6.5 cm (2-5/8 in.)	26.0 cm (10-1/4 in.)

REQUIRED MATERIALS: Require 120-line screen film positive plus velox for black and white ads; require 133-line screen color separation positives (right-reading, emulsion side down) plus color proof for color ads. Ads must be in Arabic. Materials cannot be returned. Required materials must be received 5 weeks prior to requested issue date. Cancellations must be received in writing 6 weeks prior to publishing date for black and white ads and 12 weeks prior to publishing for color ads.

BLEED AND PREFERRED POSITION CHARGES: Bleed ads accepted for full page only. Size 23 cm x 29.5 cm. Add 10% to above rate. Preferred position (when available): Add 10% to above rate. Rates and specifications for supplements on request.

ADVERTISING RATES

	FREQUENCY				
BLACK AND WHITE	1-6	7-13	14-26	27-38	39 +
Full page	$ 2,924	$ 2,844	$ 2,764	$ 2,683	$ 2,063
Double page spread	$ 5,848	$ 5,688	$ 5,527	$ 5,359	$ 5,190
1/2 page spread	$ 3,539	$ 3,443	$ 3,348	$ 3,246	$ 3,143
1/2 page	$ 1,609	$ 1,565	$ 1,521	$ 1,477	$ 1,433
1/3 page	$ 1,170	$ 1,141	$ 1,112	$ 1,075	$ 1,039
BLACK AND WHITE PLUS ONE COLOR					
Full page	$ 3,626	$ 3,524	$ 3,422	$ 3,319	$ 3,217
Double page spread	$ 7,252	$ 7,047	$ 6,843	$ 6,638	$ 6,433
1/2 page spread	$ 4,386	$ 4,262	$ 4,138	$ 4,014	$ 3,912
1/2 page	$ 1,989	$ 1,938	$ 1,886	$ 1,828	$ 1,770
ONE PAGE COLOR PLUS ONE PAGE BLACK AND WHITE					
Double page spread	$ 7,603	$ 7,391	$ 7,179	$ 6,967	$ 6,755
FOUR COLOR					
Full page	$ 4,679	$ 4,547	$ 4,416	$ 4,284	$ 4,153
Centerspread	$10,527	$10,234	$ 9,942	$ 9,650	$ 9,357
Double page spread	$ 9,357	$ 9,094	$ 8,831	$ 8,568	$ 8,305
Inside front cover	$ 4,971	$ 4,832	$ 4,693	$ 4,555	$ 4,416
Inside back cover	$ 4,679	$ 4,547	$ 4,416	$ 4,284	$ 4,153
Back cover	$12,281	No Frequency Discount			
1/2 page spread	$ 5,673	$ 5,512	$ 5,351	$ 5,191	$ 5,030
1/2 page	$ 2,574	$ 2,501	$ 2,427	$ 2,354	$ 2,281
1/3 page	$ 1,872	$ 1,821	$ 1,770	$ 1,718	$ 1,667

Member ABC

SOURCE: Saudi Research and Marketing Company, January 1, 1986, rate card.

Direct Marketing. In some markets, the number and quality of technical and business publications is low. Particularly in these markets, direct mail advertising can offer an effective advertising medium. The development of direct mail permits business-to-business advertising to escape from the historical inefficiency of placing ads in newspapers where only a small percentage of readers are the intended audience.

Of course, direct marketing is not reserved for business advertising alone, but is widely used by marketers of consumer goods. The development of strong trade associations, such as the European Direct Marketing Association, offers direct marketers a clear voice and the combined weight of its members in addressing industry problems. This association provides not only industrywide services but also training programs, publications, study trips, and an escort service to individual members visiting foreign countries.

Perhaps the most severe problem faced by direct advertisers abroad is the wide variation in postal regulations from country to country. For instance, Chilean postal regulations divide the cost of postage between sender and receiver. Since recipients of unsolicited direct mail advertising might not welcome the opportunity to pay for this material, direct mail advertising is almost nonexistent in this market. There is really no substitute for evaluating postal regulations on a by-country basis. However, marketers may purchase expediting services from firms that specialize in maintaining current postal rates and regulations.

Out-of-Home Media. Outdoor media in foreign markets exhibit at least as much variety as we see in this country. Across the remainder of world markets, the variety is greater. Figure 12–8 shows examples of the familiar outdoor poster in a Middle East setting. Billboards are an important medium in other parts of the world, where literacy rates are low, because they can convey messages pictorially. So can the ads that surround nearly every soccer stadium in the world. In the least-developed lands where the typical household does not contain broadcast receivers, and where illiteracy and poverty combine to severely restrict access to print media, the advertiser really has no alternative but to take the message to the people by trucks, riverboats, posters, and other forms of out-of-home media.

Sales Promotion. Sales promotions overseas include the same tactical considerations and employ many of the same items as those used in this country. Perhaps the most important difference between the domestic market and others is that sales promotion acquires added importance in markets that restrict other media. One form of sales promotion, the trade show exhibit, is one of the few media available to industrial goods marketers selling to customers behind the Iron Curtain. Trade shows are equally important to transactions between Eastern European firms. Both

FIGURE 12–8   Outdoor Advertising in the Middle East

An Idea Exchange From Saudi Arabia—
Tihama Outdoor Advertising

Tihama's art studio is staffed by qualified commercial designers and architectural draftsmen, who offer their services to customers on order.

Tihama's working crew will install and maintain the client's signs, and as a team, they may be commissioned on installation jobs on order.

Mr. Tarek H. Shatta, manager of Tihama Advertising, was kind enough to send us some samples of his company's outdoor advertising as well as photos of Tihama's various divisions.

Tihama Outdoor Advertising is only a part of the diverse company, which also provides public relations, marketing research and advertising in its daily and weekly newspapers in Saudi Arabia.

Tihama covers every possible kind of outdoor signage: lamp posts, football stadiums, buses and highways. They also produce neon signs, brass and other metal building signs, illuminated and non-illuminated plastic signs; and have a silk screen printing facility.

Tihama produces incentive items, designs exhibits, constructs arches and monuments and provides installation and maintenance.

Western and Eastern sellers rely on this "medium" since so few others are available to carry advertising messages in Central and Eastern Europe.

COUNTRY-SPECIFIC CONSIDERATIONS

The advertiser contemplating an overseas campaign must be aware of cultural, economic, and media factors that influence advertising abroad.

These general factors (discussed above) are helpful in adopting the proper mental framework for planning an overseas advertising project. Several factors are not sufficient, however, to produce the detailed kind of knowledge necessary for success in an overseas campaign; detailed, market-specific data are also required.

Sadly, other nations' governments often don't provide market data of the quality and extensiveness available in the United States. We take it for granted that a current edition of the *Statistical Abstract of the United States* will be available any time we need to learn the population of a particular urban area. Further, a SRDS rate book can be counted on for current media prices. This level of public and private sector research simply doesn't exist in many countries.

In some South American countries, a "census" of population only enumerates the urban portion of the population; the remainder is "estimated."

Whether for want of market research or to benefit from a thorough awareness of local conditions, the multinational advertiser usually must acquire a detailed study of the country in question. Sometimes this can be obtained from a bank or other financial institution with experience in the foreign market. Another excellent source for such data is an advertising agency with comparable experience. Figure 12–9 shows a portion of such a study. Some foreign governments will assist advertisers in doing primary research about the market. In the worst case, an advertiser has to complete needed research without assistance before undertaking to plan an ad campaign.

FIGURE 12–9   A Young & Rubicam Study of Sweden

Swedish media are characterised by the lack of commercial television and radio in the country so giving newspapers with 36 percent, direct mail 30 percent, and consumer magazines 15 percent the lion's share of media expenditure. The boom sectors of Sweden's media are the video market with 450,000 VCRs now in use and text-TV with nearly 160,000 homes receiving the service. Text-TV offers a "TV Newspaper" with current information, what's on, sports events, and so on. Cable TV is already under test in certain districts and pay-television is under discussion as a possible alternative for the financing of national TV and radio. Tele-X will be launched in 1986 with three channels. The possibility of Sweden having a commercial television service looks remote although the subject is still being discussed by the country's politicians.

Print media have mixed fortunes. Consumer magazines look set for a circulation fall while the daily press is expected to hold on to its sales with ad space increasing, especially for those papers selling to the large conurbations. Direct marketing, an important slice of Sweden's ad total, is expected to grow this year.

FIGURE 12–9 *(continued)*

SWEDEN

Global Market Statistics

Total Population:	8,323,033
Households:	3,324,956
1982 Gross Domestic Product:	SK 616,666,000,000

Media Planning Statistics

Source:	1982 Orvesto
Universe:	All adults aged 15-70 years
Total Universe:	5,245,000
Men:	2,615,000
Women:	2,627,000
Housewives:	2,207,000

Household Possessions

	%
Television B/W total	100
Colour TV	88
Deep Freeze	89
Washing Machine	74
Dishwasher	38
Car	63
Radio	99
Car Radio	66
Video	13

TELEVISION

There is no commercial television in Sweden.

RADIO

There is no commercial radio in Sweden.

CONSUMER MAGAZINES

Background

The consumer magazine market in Sweden is dominated by four major publishers accounting for around 2/3 of the market.

Circulation and Distribution

Apart from three titles which are distributed solely on subscription, Swedish consumer magazines are distributed directly to subscribers and via newsstand sales, with the latter accounting for some 70% of total magazine circulation. Total inland circulation amounts to five million copies. Quarterly circulation audits are produced by the independent organisation, Tidningsstatistik AB.

Buying Conditions

Basic advertising rates are non-negotiable, although volume discounts are available, based on gross expenditure levels, and ranging from 3% for US$ 8,800 to 12% for US$ 123,000. Pre-payment discounts are not offered, and agency commission is 3%. Surcharges of around 10% are made for special position, such as facing matter or inside cover positions, and these too are not negotiable. Colour surcharges average 13% for a second colour, 33% for full colour, with bleed surcharge of around 15%. Ratecards incorporate a premium for fractional sizes with a half page typically costing 61% of the full-page rate.

No regional editions are available, but mechanical splits, based on regional distribution, are available for the major titles. Deadlines for mono and two-colour are two months before issue date for booking and cancellation and five weeks for delivery of material; three months for booking and cancellation of full colour, and eight weeks for material.

Restrictions

Advertising alcoholic drinks is prohibited. For tobacco, only the pack may be shown on a limited space (max 3/4 of a page) and a health warning must be included.

NEWSPAPERS

Background

Of the 154 newspapers in Sweden, 14 are published by the major newspaper publishing houses, and have established a market share of almost 40%.

Circulation and Distribution

Sweden's newspapers have a combined weekday circulation of approximately 4.7 million and 150 of the 154 titles are distributed with a combination of subscriptions and newsstand sales, the latter accounting for 1/3 of circulation. The remaining four titles, all evenings, are distributed exclusively via newsstands and account for a substantial 1.1 million circulation. Like magazines, quarterly circulation audits are prepared by Tidningsstatistik AB.

Buying Conditions

Rates are non-negotiable, but ratecards incorporate discounts based on volume or gross expenditure levels, which can be as high as 40%. No pre-payment discounts are offered; agency commission is 3%.

The surcharge for special positions is normally 10%, and is also non-negotiable.

A number of regional papers have joined together to offer

Publishing Houses and Main Titles

Publisher	Market Share %	No of Titles	Main Titles
Ahlen and Akerlund	36	9	Husmodern Aret Runt Min Varld
Hemmets Journal	10	10	Hemmets Journal
Allers Forlag	15	2	Allers Hant i Veckan
Tifa	12	2	Hemmets Veckotidning
Saxon and Lindstrom	12	5	Svensk Damtidning
ICA-forlaget	15	2	ICA-kuriren Hem and Fritid

FIGURE 12–9 *(continued)*

SWEDEN

Major Swedish publishing houses, market share and titles

Publisher	Market Share %	No of Titles	Main Titles
Dagens Nyheters AB	42	2	Dagens Nyheter Expressen
Aftonbladet AB	17	1	Aftonbladet
Goteborgs Posten AB	13	2	Goteborgs Posten
Sydsvenska Dagbladet	10	2	Sydsvenska Dagbladet
Svenska Dagbladet	9		Kvallsposten
Nya Wermlands-Tidningen	7	8	Nya Wermlands-Tidningen

combined rates for their advertising space. Regional editions are also offered by a few of the national/metropolitan newspapers. For mono, the deadline for booking is three weeks prior to issue date, with one week required for cancellation or delivery of material. The two-colour booking deadline is three weeks, with a similar period for cancellation, and two weeks for material, while full colour requires eight weeks for booking and five weeks for cancellation or delivery of material.

Restrictions
Like consumer magazines, the advertising of alcoholic drinks is forbidden, and tobacco advertising is limited to pack shots.

CINEMA
Background
Since 1981 the size of the cinema audience has been increasing, but it is now expected to stabilise. The proportion of higher age groups among cinema-goers has also slightly increased. There are 593 cinemas showing advertising in Sweden.

Advertising Environment
Advertising is shown before each programme an average of twice daily in major cinemas. The cinema is half-darkened during the advertising programme, and only 83% of the audience are seated by the mid-point of the advertising reel.

Buying Conditions
Cinema advertising sales in Sweden are handled by two contractors, Filmkontakt (FK), with 290 cinemas, and Forenad Filmreklam (FFR), with 303 cinemas. Although advertisers can select individual cinemas it is not possible to follow the circuit of a major feature film.
Time is sold in a two-weekly period, and commercials are rotated within the advertising programme, so that no specified position can be negotiated.
There are no volume discounts and agency commission is 3%. Bookings need to be made at least eight months in advance.

Planning
Cinema-only campaigns are feasible in Sweden for a campaign aimed primarily at the 15 to 24 age group, and a standard weight campaign for an established product would consist of national coverage for an eight week duration, generating 158.6 GRPs among adults aged 15 to 24 years.

The national level of net reach derived from cinema advertising is estimated to rise from 11% of all adults for a two week period, through 17% for four weeks and 32% for 12 weeks, to 44% after 24 weeks. Among the prime cinema group of 15 to 24 year olds, the corresponding reach figures are 29% after two weeks, 45% after

four, 71% after 12 weeks increasing to 86% after 24 weeks. In this age group, reach levels are significantly higher for men, with a two-week figure of 35%, as compared to 26% for women. The differential narrows after four weeks (5% and 38%), and 12 weeks (76% and 65%), until 24 weeks at 89% for men and 83% for women.

Cinema Only Planning Levels

	Minimum	Standard	Maximum
No of markets	National	National	National
No of cinemas	593	593	593
Campaign duration (weeks)	4	8	12
Approx. No of showings per cinema	12	12	12
Approx. adult GRP (14-24)	86.4	158.6	234.3
Net reach	45	61	71
Budget for 60" Commercial	US$ 80,570	US$ 145,050	US$ 217,560

Research and Control
Cinema data is collected in the six-monthly Testologen survey and analyses are made available for demographic classifications and campaign length.
Control of cinema campaigns is done by Semka and competitive expenditure in the medium is collected by Biografstatistik AB.

Restrictions
As with other media, alcoholic drinks are banned, and tobacco product advertising limited to pack shots.

OUTDOOR
Background
There are around 43,000 poster sites in Sweden.

Sites and Sizes
These range from 70cm by 50cm; a single product could be allocated up to 4,200 of the smaller sites and 1,200 of the larger ones.

Media Expenditure: Gross advertising expenditure during 1983 is estimated to be as follows.·

The average cost for two weeks is US$26 for the 70cm by 50cm site; US$74 for the 300cm by 140cm site.

Buying Conditions
Two major contractors offer outdoor sites on a national basis. There are also a number of smaller contractors for additional sites in the metropolitan areas.
Sites are sold for two-week periods, and, dependent upon campaign size and the time of year, rates are sometimes negotiable. Ratecards also incorporate volume discounts, and agency commission of 3%.

Planning
A poster-only campaign is possible in Sweden, and a standard weight campaign for an established product would consist of a two-week flight in 1,200 sites nationally.

Research and Control
Research on outdoor audience levels is produced by one of the

FIGURE 12–9 *(concluded)*

SWEDEN			

Outdoor-only planning levels

	Minimum	Standard	Maximum
No of markets	National	National	National
% of national market	100	100	100
Approx. No of sites	498	621	1,121
Duration	14 days	14 days	14 days
Approx. cost	US$ 19,000	US$ 23,900	US$ 38,200

contractors, about ten times a year, covering its own sites. Competitive advertising is monitored by Reklamstatistik AB and there is an outdoor ad. control body AB Konsumentdata.

Restrictions
Advertising for alcoholic drinks and tobacco products is forbidden.

MEDIA EXPENDITURE

Total Expenditure 1982

Medium	SK million	US$ million	% of total
Television	—	—	—
Radio	—	—	—
Three Consumer Magazines	937	125.6	15
Newspapers	2,196	294.4	36
Outdoor	154	20.6	2
Cinema	31	4.2	2
Direct Mail	1,773	237.7	30
SP, display material exhibitions etc.	908	121.7	15
Total	6,000	804.2	100.0

Y & R Sweden: Ann Gerd Hager, Riddargarten 19, Box 14082. S-104 40 Stockholm Tel: 226900 Telex: 10342

SOURCE: "The Advertisers' Guide to European Media," Young & Rubicam Europe, June 1983, pp. 85–89.

REVIEW QUESTIONS

1. Describe the five basic global marketing strategies. Give an example of a U.S. company or brand that uses each strategy.

2. Construct a profile of the culture in Japan. What sources did you consult? Will this cultural profile affect U.S. advertising in Japan?

3. Select an ad campaign theme currently used in the United States and have a classmate (or other person) who speaks a Western European language translate it to the second language. Try to get both literal and same-meaning translations. Are these different? Are there chances that the translation could be misunderstood in the European country?

4. Make a list of the Third World countries. Select two from this list and summarize the state of economic development in each.

5. What are the major religions in Canada, Chad, and Colombia? Will they affect advertising in these countries? In what way?

6. Characterize the political systems in Israel, Turkey, Italy, and Morocco.

7. Use the data in Figure 12–4 to determine which of the listed nations seems most promising for effective TV advertising. Discuss your reasons.

8. Why is cinema advertising so important in Europe but not in the United States?

9. See if your school's library has current editions of *British Rate and Data* or *Canadian Advertising Rates and Data*. If it does, compare CPMs for a British,

Canadian, and U.S. daily newspaper published in a major metropolitan market.

SUGGESTED ADDITIONAL READING

"Beware of the Pitfalls of Marketing in Developing Countries." *Marketing News,* March 1, 1985, pp. 3, 6.

Catalog of Publications. Organization for Economic Co-Operation and Development (OECD), 2, rue Andre-Pascal, 75775 Paris CEDEX 16.

FARLEY, JOHN U. "Are There Truly International Products—and Prime Prospects for Them?" *Journal of Advertising Research* 26, no. 5 (October/November 1986), pp. 17–21.

HILL, JOHN S. "Targeting Promotions in Lesser-Developed Countries: A Study of Multinational Corporation Strategies." *Journal of Advertising* 13, no. 4 (1984), pp. 39–48.

"Israeli Agency Tests the Waters with First Direct-Mail Effort." *Marketing News,* August 2, 1985, p. 14.

"Leavitt: Global Companies to Replace Dying Multinationals." *Marketing News,* p. 15.

MADDEN, CHARLES S.; MARJORIE J. CABALLERO; and SHINYA MATSUKUBO. "Analysis of Information Content in U.S. and Japanese Magazine Advertising." *Journal of Advertising* 15, no. 3 (1986), pp. 38–45.

Media International. The international advertising and marketing magazine published by Alain Charles Publishing, 27 Wilfred Street, London SW1 6PR.

PLUMMER, JOSEPH T. "The Role of Copy Research in Multinational Advertising." *Journal of Advertising Research* 26, no. 5 (October/November 1986), pp. 11–15.

PRIDGEN, DEE. "Satellite Television Advertising and the Regulatory Conflict in Western Europe." *Journal of Advertising* 14, no. 1 (1985), pp. 23–29, 56.

ROTZOLL, KIM B. "Advertising in China." Advertising Working Papers, Department of Advertising, University of Illinois, undated.

SEMENIK, RICHARD J.; NAN ZHOU; and WILLIAM L. MOORE. "The Environment for and Chinese Managers' Attitudes toward Advertising in China." *Journal of Advertising* 15, no. 4 (1986), pp. 56–62.

"Standardization Not Standard for Global Marketers." *Marketing News,* September 27, 1985, pp. 3, 4.

"Toll-Free Calling Offered by Global Marketers." *Marketing News,* November 22, 1985, pp. 29, 34.

"Understanding the Five Nations of Latin America." *Marketing News,* October 11, 1985, p. 10.

WILSON, CLAIRE. "Crisis Looms over French TV." *Advertising Age,* March 10, 1986, p. 56.

"The World's Top TV Programs." *Advertising Age,* December 2, 1985, p. 54.

CHAPTER THIRTEEN

Media Selection and Allocation Methods

*Pity the poor radio sales rep who comes calling on Debbie
Smith. Smith, a senior buyer at N. W. Ayer, Inc., sits in front of
an AT&T personal computer, her hands flipping across the keyboard. In almost instant response, the color monitor in front of
her flashes up . . . the quarter-hour ratings for all radio stations
in the Philadelphia market, then a comparison of how two stations fare among different age groups and against males and
females.**

Rich Zahradnik

In the last several chapters (Chapters 6 through 12), we discussed the
principal characteristics of each major advertising medium. It is not
possible to know too much about the media, and profession-oriented
students will continue to add to their knowledge and experience in order
to understand the communications potential of each medium. Nevertheless, careful reading of these chapters will provide a basic understanding, and a core of knowledge on which to build.

This chapter presents the management applications of this knowledge. In order to translate basic media characteristics into advertising
actions, you must be able to evaluate media alternatives, select the media
best suited to a particular client's strategy, organize these into a coherent
and coordinated system, and assess the results.

In this chapter, we discuss methods for evaluating and choosing
media. The next two chapters (14 and 15, in turn) present actual media
plans and how to assess advertising results.

---

* "Media's Micro Age," *Marketing and Media Decisions,* April 1986, p. 34.

LINEAR PROGRAMMING

Components of Linear Programming

Over the last three decades, the professional advertising literature has reflected a growing use of mathematical models for media selection.[1] Perhaps the most prominent media selection technique has been linear programming.

Objective Function. Linear programming is a family of techniques that develop optimal solutions to problems that can be expressed in special ways. The first requirement is that the goal or objective can be expressed as a linear equation, known as an *objective function*. In linear programming, the objective function is usually designed either to maximize a result or else to minimize one. An example maximization problem might be to "maximize the combined audience for a group of media vehicles." A minimization problem is often found in the need to "minimize the cost" of a particular advertising task.

Constraints. The second requirement for linear programming is that the *constraints* imposed on the solution also be expressed as linear equations or functions. In many media selection problems, the advertising budget sets a limit on the amount of media that may be chosen. When the budget limitation is imposed, it is usually called a "budget constraint." Examples of other limitations imposed on real-world selection problems include the need to use no more than so many units of particular vehicles. For example, an advertiser may set a maximum value for daytime TV in order to prevent the entire TV budget from being spent in this (relatively) inexpensive daypart. Limits or constraints are often imposed that require the solution to contain at least so many of other units or vehicles. An example of this kind of limitation would be when a selection must contain so many pages or spots in relatively expensive vehicles.

Feasibility Space. If the objective function and linear constraints can be combined to form a closed area, called a *feasibility space*, the third requirement for linear programming has been met. Then, a well-devel-

---

[1] See, for example, P. Kotler, "On Methods: Toward an Explicit Model for Media Selection," *Journal of Advertising Research,* no. 4 (1964), pp. 31–41; B. Brown, "A Practical Procedure for Media Selection," *Journal of Marketing Research,* no. 4 (1967), pp. 262–69; B. Brown and M. Warshaw, "Media Selection by Linear Programming," *Journal of Marketing Research,* no. 2 (1965), pp. 83–88; A. Charnes, W. W. Cooper, J. K. Devoe, D. B. Learner, and W. Reinecke, "A Goal Programming Model for Media Planning," *Management Science* 14 (1968), pp. B423–30.

oped body of mathematical theory states that an optimal solution will be found at one of the corner points of the feasibility space. This fact greatly reduces the number of possibilities that must be examined in the search for a "best" answer to the problem.

Graphic Solutions to Linear Programming

In the least complicated kinds of problems suitable for linear programming, it is possible to obtain a solution by graphing the problem. This level of problem complexity is exemplified when a planner is choosing optimal amounts of advertising in two media. Since the graphic method also illustrates important terms and concepts in linear programming, an example is presented in Figure 13–1.

Simplex Solutions to Linear Programming

You can readily imagine that the problem of selecting an assortment of media classes and vehicles for an actual advertising campaign is much more complicated than the problem (in Figure 13–1) of selecting the correct number of ads for two magazines. And as the problem becomes more complex, the power and usefulness of graphic solutions are diminished.

In the real world of advertising, media selection problems are almost never as simple as this example. In fact, real media selection problems are almost always so complex as to defy graphic solutions. There are simply too many cornerpoints.

Let's look at a more realistically complicated problem. Let's say that the media objective for a particular campaign is to earn a target of 3,800 Gross Rating Points during a particular month among women between the ages of 18 and 49 in a particular market. The media plan calls for the exclusive use of spot television. The budget in this market for one month is $300,000. Your problem is to achieve the target level of GRPs in this month by the careful selection of television stations and dayparts for your 30-second spots, but you are not authorized to exceed the monthly budget. Further, several restrictions have been imposed on the buy. First, you must achieve a minimum of 1,000 GRPs from ads to run during prime time, and a minimum of 500 GRPs from ads to be aired during late evening broadcasts. Finally, you must make the purchase so as to earn no more than 100 GRPs during the daytime broadcasts of any single station. These restrictions were imposed so that there would be adequate coverage of those people in the target market who are away from home during the day. Costs, availabilities, and ratings for the stations in the market are presented in Figure 13–2.

FIGURE 13-1   Benefit-Maximizing Mix for Two Media Vehicles

Sunset Farms, a producer of retail pork products for a regional market, had decided to allocate the print media budget of $200,000 between two magazines: *Southern Living* (SL) and *Southern Outdoors* (SO). SL has a paid circulation of 1,200,000 and a single-page, four-color ad cost of $30,000. SO has a paid circulation of 750,000 and a four-color, full-page space cost of $20,000. Company executives wish to maximize the exposure of their ads during a 12-month campaign. They assume that audience duplication is not a problem. Both magazines will publish 12 issues during the campaign, and company executives insist that each magazine carry a minimum of one, four-color, full-page ad in 2 of the 12 issues. They further believe that an ad in either magazine will be equally effective in producing sales for Sunset.

This problem of media allocation can be stated as a linear programming problem of the form:

$$\text{Maximize readers per dollar, } Z = \frac{1,200,000(SL)}{30,000} + \frac{750,000(SO)}{20,000}$$
$$= 40(SL) + 37.5(SO)$$

Subject to the following constraints:

$SL \geq 2$
$SO \geq 2$
$\$30,000(SL) + \$20,000(SO) \leq \$200,000$

In graphic form, the problem can be expressed as:

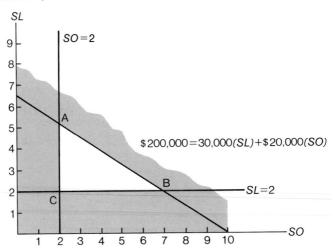

The feasibility space is the triangle, ABC.

Cornerpoint coordinates SL	SO	Objective function Z = 40(SL) + 37.5(SO)
A......5.33*	2	Z_A = 213.2 + 75 = 288.2
B......2	7*	Z_B = 80 + 262.5 = 342.5
C.....2	2	Z_C = 80 + 75 = 155.0

By inspecting values for the objective function Z we can see that it has a maximum value of 342.5 readers per dollar, and this is achieved by placing the four-color, full-page ad in two issues of *Southern Living* and seven issues of *Southern Outdoors*.

* Found by substituting in the equation for the budget constraint.

FIGURE 13–2 Daypart Cost per 30-Second Commercial and Rating among Women 18–49

Television costs/ratings/availabilities

Station	Affiliation	Daytime	Early Evening	Prime Time	Late Evening
A	ABC	$340/7	$1,260/19	Not available	$ 400/4
B	CBS	$212/5	$1,400/21	Not available	$ 580/6
C	NBC	$300/6	$1,320/20	$2,140/15	$1,000/9
D	Independent	$145/3	$ 700/10	$1,400/13	$ 680/8

Television cost per Gross Rating Point: Women 18–49

Station	Affiliation	Daytime	Early Evening	Prime Time	Late Evening
A	ABC	$48.57	$66.32	—	$100.00
B	CBS	42.40	66.67	—	96.67
C	NBC	50.00	66.00	$142.67	111.11
D	Independent	48.33	70.00	107.69	85.00

This table shows, for example, that the independent station in this market will sell a 30-second spot during daytime television for $145 and that this daypart has an average rating of 3. Similarly a late evening 30-second spot on the NBC station costs $1,000 and has an average rating of 9.

An Example of *Simplex*. Fortunately, a method of linear programming called the *simplex method* has been developed that efficiently solves linear programming problems, even when a very large number of variables and constraints are to be considered. The simplex calculations are often performed on computers when the problem is large, though they may be done by hand.

Simplex solutions consider all the possible, feasible solutions, variable by variable, and are therefore systematic. They employ a system of calculation based on the coefficients in the objective function and the constraints. And while potential problems are associated with the method (these will be discussed later in this chapter), simplex offers a clear way to identify the optimum solution.

Personal Computer Solutions to Simplex. The authors decided to apply the simplex method to the problem outlined above. Using a personal computer and a commercially available simplex program,[2] the problem was solved in seven minutes. This interval included every step and procedure required of the analyst, beginning with the task of turning

---

[2] This program was purchased from Optimal Software, P.O. Box 8531, Corpus Christi, Texas 78412-0531. Retail price for the floppy disk that includes the simplex program and four other sets of programs is $19.95.

on the computer and concluding with the printing of a hard-copy record of the solution.

The solution indicated by simplex is as follows:

Station	Daypart	Rating	Number of 30-Second Spots	Cost (Dollars)	GRP
C	Early evening	20	99.15	$130,878.00	1,983
D	Prime time	13	76.92	107,688.00	1,000
D	Late evening	8	62.50	42,500.00	500
A	Daytime	7	14.29	4,858.60	100
B	Daytime	5	20.00	4,240.00	100
C	Daytime	6	16.67	5,001.00	100
D	Daytime	3	33.33	4,832.85	100
		Total	322.86	$299,998.45	3,883

You can see that by the purchase of about 323 commercial spots on the plan described above, the target level of GRPs is achieved (actually, slightly exceeded) without violating any of the restrictions and without exceeding the budget. The solution indicates that portions of a commercial are to be purchased, which it is impossible to do, but the number of spots for each station and daypart can be rounded to the nearest whole number without doing real harm to the optimality of the solution. Thus we would actually purchase 99, not 99.15, 30-second spots during the early evening period on station C.

Something else is implied by the above solution. As part of answering the question of how many commercials to buy, on which stations, during which dayparts, we have almost accidentally solved the problem of how to distribute our advertising budget allocation efficiently among the possible media vehicles. And by the same process we used above, it is possible to include other media classes, other objectives, or other constraints to produce a combined media purchase.

It is important for people who use computer routines in solving problems to understand the method being used. You should recognize that the simplex method does not alter the general linear programming situation. That is, optimal solutions are always found at a cornerpoint of a bounded feasibility space. You should also recognize that the simplex method is not necessarily "simple." Nevertheless, thousands of students and professionals use the method every day. You are encouraged to learn more of this method, through coursework and/or reading. A list of suggested sources of information on simplex is presented at the chapter's end.

Sensitivity Analysis

It is clear that linear programming, especially when enhanced by computer processing for the simplex method, is a powerful tool in selecting a media mix. Perhaps not so clear, but equally important, is the fact that linear programming solutions are very much captive of the decision maker's input. For example, if the constraints are wrong or foolish, the solutions are also likely to be wrong or foolish.

One additional aspect of linear programming, called sensitivity analysis, provides an additional reassurance to the media purchaser. The analyst could ask questions such as the following:

What would happen to the solution if the budget were increased to $400,000?

What would be the effect of a new set of station-by-daypart ratings?

What would the TV buy become if a limit of 1,000 GRPs were imposed on early evening broadcasts?

The prudent media planner can imagine many other such questions relating the sensitivity of the solution to changing conditions, objectives, or judgments. And while sophisticated procedures exist for assessing sensitivity, the most straightforward approach to this part of linear programming is to substitute the new values, recalculate the new optimal solution, and compare the results. In the final analysis, no "black box," computer program, or computational method can relieve the decision maker of responsibility for a decision.

MORE ADVANCED APPROACHES TO CHOOSING MEDIA

In using models for technical problems, we often simplify "reality" so that its various aspects can be better understood. In the technical problem of advertising media selection (and the corresponding budget distribution among vehicles), we often simplify to improve our managerial abilities. Linear programming does this in two dramatic ways. First, it requires objective functions and constraints to be *linear* functions. Second, it considers the bounds of the feasibility space to be *inviolate*. Since neither of these simplifications reflects the way the advertising would really work, it is important to recognize that decision methods exist for making the media selection-budget distribution problem more realistic. And as you may suspect, this added realism comes at a price. In both instances, linearity and boundary rigidity, extra realism means more complicated analysis. However, our discussion will be limited to conversational descriptions of such methods.

Nonlinear Programming

In advertising many objectives are accurately modeled by nonlinear functions. For example, if we chart the reach of an advertising campaign as a function of the number of ads, we (realistically) expect to find something like the pattern shown in Figure 13–3. This pattern happens because of audience duplication. As we place increased numbers of advertisements in media, we begin to have people in the audience who have been exposed to our message more than once. The problem of audience duplication will be handled in greater detail later in this chapter. For the moment, though, imagine what this type of response does to the implied assumptions of linear programming!

Other real circumstances produce discontinuities in objective functions or constraints. For example an advertiser may have virtually saturated the newspapers in a market at an average CPM of $20. To include another class of media in the campaign, say metropolitan magazines, may produce a much different average CPM of $35. While each of the two portions of such a cost curve are linear, together they produce a function called a step function or a "piecewise" linear combination. In these examples, and in many other aspects of media planning, linear programming can produce grotesque oversimplifications. One way of producing added realism is to let the actual, nonlinear functions bound the feasibility space. Then, in principle, one must mathematically search the corner-points to find an optimal solution. You should not imagine that this is an easy calculation. However, you should be aware that computational methods and computer programs are available for nonlinear programming. Experience is the best guide for determining when the added complexity of these methods is warranted.

FIGURE 13–3   Reach as a Function of the Number of Ads

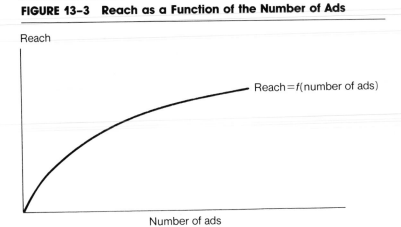

Goal Programming

In practice, objectives and constraints are not often stated with the rigidity implied by linear programming. For example, a budget constraint might be set at $300,000 plus or minus 10 percent. This means that instead of a single straight-line constraint, we really have an "envelope" or family of budget constraints with a minimum value of $270,000 and a maximum value of $330,000. This improvement in realism makes traditional linear programming methods almost impossible to work.

Goal programming, as developed by Charnes[3] and by Lee,[4] provides a way of handling flexible aspects of media selection realistically. Lee,[5] for example, used goal programming to select from among 47 media vehicles in seven media classes when some budget overexpenditure was permitted (5 percent) and when several measures of effectiveness and exposure were permitted to vary within specified limits. While Lee has developed both graphic and simplex approaches to goal programming, a full description of these approaches is beyond the scope of this text. However, you should recognize that goal programming is a way in which advertising problems can be formulated more realistically.

MEASURING AUDIENCE DUPLICATION FOR AN ASSORTMENT OF MEDIA

Anytime a media plan calls for more than one insertion in a single medium, audience duplication becomes an issue for the media planner. In Chapter 5, we discussed the notion of frequency and how *reach* differs from the *duplicated audience* for a media buy.

Audience duplication is a fact in nearly every advertising campaign. Some audience duplication is desirable, and this fact is expressed in frequency goals greater than one. In many actual campaigns, you will see examples where media planners call for monthly GRP levels of 250. As you know, this implies a monthly frequency of 2.5 if the reach is 100 percent of the market. If the reach is less than 100 percent, the implied monthly frequency is even greater. In other instances, multiple exposures above some target level for frequency can be wasteful. But whether audience duplication is "good" or "bad" in a particular media plan, the essential point here is that it must be considered in the media selection and scheduling process.

---

[3] Charnes et al., "Goal Programming Model for Media Planning," pp. B423–30.

[4] S. M. Lee and L. J. Moore, *Introduction to Decision Science* (New York: Petrocelli/Charter, 1975), pp. 196–231.

[5] S. M. Lee, *Goal Programming for Decision Analysis* (Philadelphia: Auerbach, 1972), pp. 250–59.

The Agostini Method

One of the first attempts to estimate audience duplication systematically appeared in the very first issue of the *Journal of Advertising Research*. The author, J. M. Agostini, proposed a method for estimating audience duplication for advertising carried in an assortment of magazines.[6] He suggested that C, the net (or unduplicated) coverage was:

$$C = A \frac{1}{1 + \frac{KD}{A}}$$

where:

A = duplicated audience for all vehicles used
D = sum of the *duplicated* readership of all pairs
K = Agostini's constant, 1.125

You will notice that the value for A in a set of vehicles is simply the sum of each vehicle's readership. And subsequent research by Claycamp and McClelland[7] has shown that the value for K is not constant, but varies, dependent on the media consumption of the audiences for the particular set of vehicles chosen. Nevertheless, it is instructive to work through an example of the rather primitive Agostini model.

Assuming that a set of five magazines have the readership indicated:

Magazine	Readership
A	20,000
B	30,000
C	40,000
D	30,000
E	20,000
Total	140,000

Next, the pairwise audience overlap is:

A−B, 5,000	B−C, 1,000	C−D, 1,000	D−E, 4,000
A−C, 2,000	B−D, 2,000	C−E, 5,000	
A−D, 3,000	B−E, 1,000		
A−E, 2,000			

---

[6] J. M. Agostini, "How to Estimate Unduplicated Audiences," *Journal of Advertising Research* 1, no. 1 (March 1961), pp. 11–14.

[7] H. J. Claycamp and C. W. McClelland, "Estimating Reach and the Value of K," *Journal of Advertising Research* 8, no. 2 (June 1968), pp. 44–51.

Here, 5,000 readers of magazine A also read magazine B, etc. On reflection you will notice that this is the complete list of magazine pairs, since the A—B overlap is identical to the B—A overlap. The sum of these pairwise duplicated readership values, which is the term D in Agostini's formula, is 26,000. By inserting the various values, we can now solve for C, the net audience.

$$C = 140,000 \, \frac{1}{1 + \dfrac{1.125(26,000)}{140,000}}$$

$$= 140,000 \, \frac{1}{1 + .209}$$

$$= \frac{140,000}{1.209} = 115,798$$

Because of the importance of audience duplication estimates, and because of substantial dissatisfaction among media people with the too simplistic Agostini method, more comprehensive methods for estimating audience duplication have been developed. Two prominent improvements, the Metheringham method and the beta-binomial method, will be discussed here.

The Metheringham Method

In 1964, in an article published in the *Journal of Advertising Research*, R. A. Metheringham proposed the method of estimating net audience coverage that bears his name.[8] This method is implemented in two stages:

1. The probability is estimated that a single individual in the target audience is exposed to one, two, three, etc., vehicles in the vehicle assortment up to every vehicle used. The general relationship between number of vehicles, M, and probability of exposure to N of the M vehicles is graphed in Figure 13-4. Intuitively, the probability that some individual will be exposed to all 12 of the vehicles in an assortment containing 12 vehicles is much lower than the probability that the individual will be exposed to 1, 2, or 3 of the 12 vehicles.

2. The probabilities generated in the first stage are converted to information about the proportion of the total audience exposed to one, two, three, . . . M exposures.

Let's take the problem we used to illustrate the Agostini method and

---

[8] R. A. Metheringham, "Measuring the Net Cumulative Coverage of a Print Campaign," *Journal of Advertising Research* 4, no. 4 (December 1964), pp. 23–28.

FIGURE 13–4

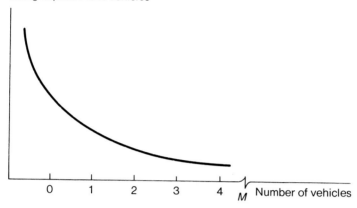

Probability of an individual
being exposed to *N* vehicles

apply Metheringham's method to it. For purposes of this explanation, assume that a single advertisement/insertion was carried in each of the five magazines A through E.

Now the probability that any audience member was "exposed" to the ad in at least one vehicle is 1.0. Notice that *exposure to the ad* is a different and more relaxed criterion than *readership of the ad*. You should recognize in this and subsequent steps that exposure to the ad is assumed to be synonymous with readership of the magazine issue.

The average probability of exposure to any two vehicles is given by the formula:

$$\text{Average}\ P2\ \text{vehicles} = \frac{1}{10}\ [p(A, B) + p(A, C) + p(A, D) + p(A, E) + p(B, C) \\ + p(B, D) + p(B, E) + p(C, D) + p(C, E) + p(D, E)]$$

The probability of any magazine pair is equal to the audience overlap divided by the combined audience for that pair. Therefore, the probabilities are as follows:

Pair	Overlap	Combined Readership	= Probability
AB	5,000	(20,000 + 30,000)	.100
AC	2,000	(20,000 + 40,000)	.033
AD	3,000	(20,000 + 30,000)	.060
AE	2,000	(20,000 + 20,000)	.050
BC	1,000	(30,000 + 40,000)	.014
BD	2,000	(30,000 + 30,000)	.033
BE	1,000	(30,000 + 20,000)	.020
CD	1,000	(40,000 + 30,000)	.014
CE	5,000	(40,000 + 20,000)	.083
DE	4,000	(30,000 + 20,000)	.080

Therefore,

$$\text{Average probability of any two vehicles} = \frac{1}{10} \begin{aligned} &(.100 + .033 + .060 + .050 + .014 \\ &+ .033 + .020 + .014 + .083 + .080) \end{aligned}$$

$$= \frac{.487}{10} = .0487$$

In a similar way we would compute the average probability that an individual audience member would be exposed to any three vehicles, any four vehicles, and all five vehicles. To calculate these probabilities, we would need the duplicated audience for all nonredundant combinations of three vehicles, the same figure for all nonredundant four-vehicle combinations, and finally the number of people who read all five vehicles. Experience suggests that these probabilities would be very close to zero for this problem. And, obviously, the computational details for these probabilities are extensive, though not particularly difficult.

The Beta-Binomial Method

On closer inspection, advertising scholars recognized that the means for generating probabilities of audience exposure in the first stage of Metheringham's method is called the *beta* distribution by statisticians. The second stage then uses what statisticians call a *binomial* distribution to calculate the proportion of the total audience exposed to one, two, three, . . . M exposures.

For students not familiar with complicated statistical notation, it is important to recognize that the beta-binomial distribution can be used to answer the question of *net* audience coverage in campaigns with multiple insertions in a single vehicle and multiple vehicles. Further, R. S. Headen[9] and others have shown that the beta-binomial can be readily converted for broadcast media. They have also shown that this method does not require information about pairwise audience overlap.[10] This feature is of particular interest to those buying large amounts of spot TV, since the pairwise audience overlap values required by Metheringham's method are often unavailable.

A calculation of net audience coverage is provided in Figure 13–5. In this example, the beta-binomial procedure is used directly, rather than in the somewhat roundabout way originally suggested by Metheringham. The direct beta-binomial procedures produce results practically identical with those obtained by Metheringham's method.

---

[9] R. S. Headen, Jay E. Klompmaker, and Jesse E. Teel, Jr., "Predicting Audience Exposure to Spot TV Advertising Schedules," *Journal of Marketing Research* no. 1 (1977), pp. 1–9.

[10] Ibid., p. 6.

FIGURE 13–5 **Example Calculation of Net Audience Coverage**

In this example, four publications and varying numbers of insertions are used to illustrate the beta-binomial method.

Publication	Insertions	Single-Issue Readership (Percent)	Noncoverage
A. Sentinel	3	40	60
B. Journal	2	30	70
C. Bugler	1	20	80
D. Diario	2	30	70
	$\Sigma = 8$		

Step 1
The first step is to calculate the average noncoverage of the group of four publications in the schedule. To do this, we must weight each publication's noncoverage percentage by the number of insertions, or:

$$\overline{X} = [3(.60) + 2(.70) + 1(.80) + 2(.70)] \div 8$$
$$= [(1.8) + (1.4) + (.8) + (1.4)] \div 8$$
$$= 5.4 \div 8 = \underline{.675}$$

In subsequent calculations, we'll call this value, K_1.

Step 2
The second step is to calculate the average noncoverage of each pair of publications. In actuality, these paired noncoverages are obtained from syndicated research services or by primary research. Again, the pairwise noncoverage figures will be weighted by the number of insertions.

Publication	#Ads	Paired Readership (Percent) A	B	C	D
A	3	50	60	30	40
B	2		40	40	40
C	1			30	40
D	2				40

In the half-matrix above, the values in the diagonal represent the two-issue coverage of the publication. For example, the two-issue coverage of A is 50 percent.

Weighting the paired noncoverage can seem like a baffling process. Perhaps the clearest way to determine weighting factors is to consider how many different actual ways the paired coverage can occur.

Let's take the pair, AB. There are 3 insertions in A and 2 in B. Thus exposure to A_1B_1 is a way, as are exposure to A_2B_1, A_3B_1, A_1B_2, A_2B_2 or A_3B_2. As you can see, the weighting factors for each pair are simply the product of the number of insertions in each. The exception to this rule is for 2 insertions in a single publication; here the weight is the number of unique combinations, or 1 way. The weighting factors in this example are:

AB 6	AC 3	AD 6
	BC 2	BD 4
		CD 2
AA 3	BB 1	DD 1

FIGURE 13-5 *(concluded)*

The weighted pairwise noncoverage of the schedule is then:

$\overline{X}$ = [6(.40) + 3(.70) + 6(.60) + 2(.60) + 4(.60) + 2(.60)
    + 3(.50) + 1(.60) + 1(.60) ÷ 28

= [(2.4) + (2.1) + (3.6) + (1.2) + (2.4) + (1.2)
    + (1.5) + (0.6) + (0.6)] ÷ 28

= [15.6] ÷ 28 = .557

In subsequent calculations, we'll call this value, K_2.

Step 3
The next step is to compute the two parameters for the beta binomial distribution for our schedule. To do this, we arbitrarily name these parameters S and T and compute each as follows:

$$S = \frac{K_1^2 - K_1 K_2}{K_2 - K_1^2} = \frac{(.675)^2 - (.675)(.557)}{.557 - (.675)^2}$$

$$= \frac{.456 - .376}{.557 - .456} = \frac{.080}{.101} = .792$$

$$T = \frac{S}{K_1} = \frac{.792}{.675} = 1.173$$

Step 4
The fourth step is to use the two parameters calculated above in the expansion formula for beta binomial distributions, to calculate K_n the net noncoverage of the entire schedule when n is the number of insertions. This formula is:

$$K_n = \frac{S(S+1)(S+2)(S+3)\dots(S+n-1)}{T(T+1)(T+2)(T+3)\dots(T+n-1)}$$

In this example:

$$K_8 = \frac{(.792)(1.792)(2.792)(3.792)(4.792)(5.792)(6.792)(7.792)}{(1.173)(2.173)(3.173)(4.173)(5.173)(6.173)(7.173)(8.173)}$$

$$= \frac{22,071.86}{63,182.57} = .349 \text{ or } 35 \text{ percent noncoverage.}$$

Therefore, the net coverage of the 8-insertion schedule is

$$1.00 - .349 = .651 \text{ or } 65 \text{ percent}$$

A review of recent literature and actual practice suggests that while net audience coverage can be practically estimated via beta-binomial, other methods are also used. The binomial distribution derives its name from the fact that it relates to situations in which only two outcomes (hence "bi") are possible. In the advertising coverage examples, a person (or household) was either "exposed" or "not exposed." While exposure is important to advertising planning, other outcomes, such as "interest" or "intention to purchase," are also important. Here a *multinomial* distribution may be more useful than a binomial distribution in answering a real advertising management question.

As you can surmise, multinomial distributions are more complex than binomial distributions. And a detailed discussion of these is beyond the scope of this text. You should recognize, however, that procedures exist for estimating advertising coverage that permit more than two outcomes. When the situation seems to require them, these procedures can be employed with the help of qualified analysts to produce practical information.

BUILDING THE MEDIA SCHEDULE

In this chapter so far, we have discussed two of the important requirements for building a media schedule. Boiled down to simple terms, the foregoing material has been directed toward the answers to two questions:

> Which vehicles?
> What effective audience?

We should point out that these requirements exert a mutual influence. That is, the vehicle selection problem is to some extent influenced by audience overlap, while net audience coverage is certainly influenced by vehicle selection. In practice, an assortment of vehicles is often chosen on a trial basis; then net audience coverage is estimated, and, if necessary, the assortment is revised. This recursive process continues until both questions have satisfactory answers. The *timing* of the advertising insertions is the remaining decision area in this discussion.

MANAGERIAL OBJECTIVES

In reaching decisions about the timing of advertising, it is of paramount importance that the managerial objectives of the advertising campaign be incorporated into the decision process. First, the intended reach and frequency for the campaign must be considered. Perhaps less obviously, other managerial objectives should also play an important role in the schedule.

Reach-Dominant Situations

For certain advertising projects, the principal objective is to maximize *reach* within a specified target audience. This situation is most likely to occur when the advertising is for a product class that is characterized by highly interested and well-informed prospective buyers. Often advertising for specialty goods has a reach-dominated objective—for example,

DeBeers Consolidated Mines, Ltd., advertising diamond engagement rings to women 18–24 years of age. DeBeers assumes that this audience is highly sensitized to such products. The advertising objective is not so much to create large numbers of reminder-type advertisements as to reach the largest possible percentage of this audience with an appealing, impressive message. In situations like this, a relatively large number of vehicles are scheduled, at relatively low numbers of insertions per vehicle. Also, emphasis is placed on the long-lived media classes, such as magazines.

Frequency-Dominant Situations

In contrast, some advertising is focused on the creation of large numbers of impressions per audience member. A high-frequency objective may be appropriate when the product is likely to appeal to a broad group of prospects and when many reminder-type impressions are desirable. This kind of objective may be implied by advertising for the typical fast-food franchise. In such situations, the media schedule usually contains a relatively smaller number of vehicles and a larger number of insertions per vehicle. Also, greater use of the "perishable" media, particularly the electronic and outdoor media, is consistent with a high-frequency objective.

The General Case—Reach and Frequency

In most advertising, both reach and frequency are important objectives. Even in the situations described in the foregoing discussion, the reach-dominant projects are likely to have target frequencies greater than one, while the frequency-dominant projects are likely to be concerned with obtaining adequate reach.

In the discussion of media selection and audience duplication, Gross Rating Points served as example objectives. GRPs are a measure that combines both reach and frequency. They are, therefore, an appropriate way to state the objective for advertising in some general-audience media. And GRP levels, when combined with constraints in the form of minimum frequency and minimum reach, can be adequate statements of the objectives of a campaign.

Audience and Customer Variables

When reach, frequency, and GRP level are used in combination as advertising objectives, the implied assumption is that audience members are homogeneous with respect to the advertised product. Yet common sense and research evidence suggest that this is not true. Some members of the audience are more inclined than others to respond to a campaign or to buy the advertised product. For instance, young adult women may be one important group of prospects for diamond products. Perhaps another important group comprises married males in the 34 to 49 age group who are likely to buy diamond products for their wives. Other good and poor groups could be specified for these products or for most other products.

One way in which to take account of this inequality among audience members is by *weighting*. We can use weighting to reflect differences in audience characteristics, such as demographic variations. Other bases for differential weighting include differences in propensities to purchase the product class and differences in past purchase patterns.

Weighting influences not only the selection of vehicles but also the scheduling decision. Differences in the audience composition by daypart for broadcast media are an obvious example. Also, weighting can influence the scheduling of print advertising when periodic audience differences are detectable. For example, most daily newspapers have a "best food day," when grocery shoppers expect to find the most complete array of grocery advertising. Ads run on this day reach an audience group who are predisposed to look for "specials." These ads may produce better results than ads run for grocery products on other days.

Product Considerations

For many products, there is a distinct seasonal pattern in sales. Snow tires and tire chains sell briskly in the fall and early winter and shortly after major snowstorms. Sales of bathing suits, skis, vacations to warm climates, fashion apparel, fresh produce, and many other products follow seasonal trends. Marriages tend to occur more frequently in spring and summer, while warm, somewhat heavier foods are most popular during fall and winter.

The schedule of advertising for products with seasonal sales patterns tends to occur in one or more of three patterns. The most obvious scheduling pattern is to place a large proportion of the total advertising effort just before and in the early portions of the "season." Audiences are especially attentive to appeals at that time. And tie-in promotions linked to holidays such as Thanksgiving, Christmas, and the Fourth of July strive to reach audiences during the preparations for these festive occasions. A second scheduling pattern is to place advertising weight just after a major seasonal event has occurred. Thus, ads for tire chains might be frequent just after the first major snowfall, and might be placed in the most time-flexible media, such as radio and newspapers. Similarly, ads for World Series or "Star Wars" paraphernalia might be run shortly after the series began or the movie was shown. Finally, a countercyclical or counterseasonal scheduling pattern may be used. Ads for vacations in warm places, emphasizing low off-season rates, may be run in summer.

Competitors' Schedules

When the influence of competing advertising is being weighed, the scheduling decision usually requires the consideration of a basic trade-off. Ads placed at the "usual" time (such as the best food day) tend to reach more highly interested prospects, but at a time when competition for their attention is greater. Ads placed countercyclically tend to operate with fewer competing messages, but reach audiences that are less interested and are therefore harder to influence. As a rule, ads with frequency-dominated objectives tend to be scheduled along with competitors' ads, while ads with reach-dominated objectives can be scheduled with less regard to competitors' schedules.

ANOTHER MANAGERIAL CONSIDERATION

Capital budgeting was described in Chapter 4 as one method of developing the advertising allocation. In some instances, the capital budgeting process can be influential in scheduling decisions. Recall that a basic element in the capital budgeting decision is the time shape of the cash flow. Thus, both cash outflows in the form of media purchases and cash inflows in the form of sales returns are significant elements in the calculation. To the extent that advertising schedules are linked to sales, scheduling decisions for advertising can be used to refine the capital budgeting process. And while such calculations are more commonly made in client organizations, media people should be aware of these implications. The effect of incorporating the media schedule into the capital budgeting process is to delay media expenditures to their actual dates (rather than to assume that these expenditures occur at the beginning of the budget period). This refinement has the effect of increasing the rate of return on the advertising project.

REVIEW QUESTIONS

1. What is a major limitation on the use of graphic solutions to solve real-world media selection problems?
2. In the simplex example for buying television time, a budget constraint of $300,000 was imposed. What general steps would you follow to assess the sensitivity of the solution to this constraint?

3. Linear programming simplifies the problem of media selection in two major ways. What are these?

4. What are some advantages and disadvantages of using the Agostini method to measure audience duplication?

5. What are the basic differences between the Agostini and Metheringham methods?

6. Discuss an advertising media situation in which product considerations are dominant.

7. Diamond engagement rings are mentioned in this chapter as a product where advertising is planned in a reach-dominant way. Select one other consumer good and one industrial product where reach is the dominant advertising factor. Explain why reach is so important for these two products.

8. Select a product where seasonal sales and advertising factors are paramount. Then outline a countercyclical or counterseasonal advertising schedule and explain why you think it might work.

9. Consult current SMRB sources and find out how many U.S. adults, aged 18–49 read a single issue of *The Wall Street Journal*. How many read two issues?

10. What is the net unduplicated audience for *The Wall Street Journal* and *New York Times* daily edition?

SUGGESTED ADDITIONAL READING

BASS, FRANK M., and RONALD T. LONSDALE. "An Exploration of Linear Programming in Media Selection." *Journal of Marketing Research* 3 (May 1966), pp. 179–88.

CANNON, HUGH M. "Evaluating the Profile-Distance Approach to Media Selection." *Journal of Advertising* 14, no. 1 (1985), pp. 4–9.

GIGES, NANCY. "Forecasters Can Tell Weather to Advertise." *Advertising Age,* January 31, 1985, p. 38.

HEFLIN, DEBBORA, and ROBERT C. HAYGOOD. "Effects of Scheduling on Retention of Advertising Messages." *Journal of Advertising* 14, no. 2 (1985), pp. 41–47, 64.

"How Do Media Buyers Make Decisions?" *Advertising World,* June 1985, pp. 10–32.

JOYCE, TIMOTHY. "How ABC Data Is Used in Total Audience Estimates." ABC news release, October 31, 1985, pp. 10.

LECKENBY, JOHN D., and SHIZUE KISHI. "The Dirichlet Multinomial Distribution as a Magazine Exposure Model." *Journal of Marketing Research* 21 (February 1984), pp. 100–106.

LECKENBY, JOHN D., and MARSHALL D. RICE. "A Beta Binomial Network TV Exposure Model Using Limited Data." *Journal of Advertising* 14, no. 3 (1985), pp. 25–31.

LECKENBY, JOHN D., and MARSHALL D. RICE. "The Declining Reach Phenomenon in Exposure Distribution Models." *Journal of Advertising* 15, no. 3 (1986), pp. 13–20.

LEE, SANG M. *Goal Programming for Decision Analysis.* Especially Chapter 10, "Optimization of Advertising Media Scheduling," pp. 250–59, New York: Auerbach Publishers, Inc., 1972.

"Media Weight Tests: Tips on Split Cable, Matched Markets." *Marketing News,* January 4, 1985, p. 5.

RICE, MARSHALL D., and JOHN D. LECKENBY. "Estimating the Exposure Distribution of Magazine Schedules in Limited Data Situations." In *Proceedings of the 1985 Conference of the American Academy of Advertising,* Nancy Stephens, ed., pp. R95–R99.

RUST, ROLAND T., and ROBERT P. LEONE. "The Mixed-Media Dirichlet Multinomial Distribution: A Model for Evaluating Television-Magazine Advertising Schedules." *Journal of Marketing Research* 21 (February 1984), pp. 89–99.

RUST, ROLAND T.; ROBERT P. LEONE; and MARY R. ZIMMER. "Estimating the Duplicated Audience of Media Vehicles in National Advertising Schedules." *Journal of Advertising* 15, no. 3 (1986), pp. 30–37.

SHOCKER, ALLAN D. "Limitations of Incremental Search in Media Selection." *Journal of Marketing Research* 7 (February 1970), pp. 101–3.

SIMON, HERMANN. "ADPULS: An Advertising Model with Wearout and Pulsation." *Journal of Marketing Research* 19 (August 1982), pp. 352–63.

TURK, PETER B. "Due Notice for an Unsung Media Strategy Hero: A Linear Compensatory Allocation Model." In *Proceedings of the 1986 Conference of the American Academy of Advertising,* Ernest F. Larkin, ed., pp. R57–R61.

The Media Plan

If the planning process sounds commonplace, or what any good media department would do, Lowe Marshalk's media staff heartily disagrees. ". . . I remember a number of times at [another agency] when we handed over a big, thick media plan to the vice president of marketing, only to hear 'Lots of work, guys, but I don't buy off on your target audience . . .' and of course, if the client throws the target audience out, then you can take the media plan and throw it in the garbage can, too . . ."*

Marianne Paskowski

The media plan is a concise description of the objectives, planning, and proposed implementation of the media strategy. The media plan serves two major purposes:

1. It gives a written summary of the media to be bought and the rationale for scheduling them. At this stage the media plan allows all parties (client, creative, account management) to react to the media department's strategy.
2. After its approval, the media plan becomes a guide to the media department in implementing the media program. In this respect the media plan should be specific enough to allow media buyers to make their commitments to space and time purchases with no confusion.

In this chapter, the general requirements for an idealized media plan are discussed. Then, actual media plans for a national brewery at the onset of a campaign featuring a new spokesperson, a regional marketer of a retirement community, and a local restaurant are presented. You will be able to see how these actual plans conform to theory, and also how they depart from it.

_____

* "The World's Most Unpretentious Media Department," *Marketing and Media Decisions,* July 1986, pp. 49–50.

368

COMPONENTS OF THE MEDIA PLAN

Media plans follow a number of formats adapted to the individual marketing and media needs of the advertisers. However, most media plans have certain elements in common.

General Statement of Product Background

The media plan may include a short summary of the product and the major competition as well as some historical sales trend. The product development portion of this section is normally very short. When the media plan is part of a larger discussion of campaign strategy, the product development information would be included in a longer separate section.

Marketing Considerations

The media strategy must be formulated as part of the client's larger marketing and advertising objectives. The media plan does not examine the client's overall marketing program. It does, however, highlight those aspects of the marketing program that must be accomplished through advertising and, more specifically, through the media plan. In this section, the media plan may offer the justification and rationale for the thrust of the media program—for instance, why certain media vehicles were chosen to reach a particular target segment.

Creative Considerations

The media plan next considers how the creative and media strategies complement each other. Again, there is no lengthy discussion of the creative rationale, but it should be noted that creative requirements are considered in development of the media plan.

The Media Platform

After the preliminary statements on the purposes of the media strategy and its coordination with other aspects of the advertising program, the media portion of the campaign is outlined. In the context of an advertising campaign report, the media portion sometimes starts with the media platform. However, it is worthwhile to restate the marketing and advertising objectives so that the media platform can be presented within this larger environment.

While postscheduling research is usually not presented as part of the media plan, it may be mentioned at the conclusion of the plan. A media schedule can rarely be measured without also considering the effectiveness of the advertising messages. Consequently, the results of the total advertising effort, including both creative and media considerations, are normally measured both during and after a campaign. Astute advertisers will consider methods for postadvertising research as they plan their advertising and will make provisions for such research.

Note that the media plan is designed to work from the general objectives to specific tactical decisions. The most frequent mistake of the novice media planner is to move directly to the media schedule without the necessary preplanning. Ideally the media schedule should flow directly from the marketing/advertising objectives and strategy and should be the easiest section of the media platform to execute.

The remainder of this chapter will discuss the general components of the media platform and three actual media plans. Note how these plans develop from overall objectives to specific, tactical buying recommendations. Also observe the research foundation for each step of the plan.

THE MEDIA PLATFORM

Media plans must take into account specific conditions that will be encountered in advertising a particular product or service. Therefore, each media plan is unique for a product and for the time during which the plan will be implemented. There are, however, certain general formats that media plans normally follow. The media planner should use the outline presented here as a guide to develop a specific media plan.

Section I.   Overall Objectives

The media plan should introduce the broad media-planning concepts and demonstrate how they complement both the overall marketing objectives and the general creative plan. In essence this section provides a review of corporate advertising/marketing objectives and forces the media planner to focus the media function on overall corporate planning.

Statement of Media Philosophy.   The media plan follows the introductory section with a statement of overall media objectives and outlines what the media schedule should accomplish in concert with other marketing and promotional areas.

Section II.   Media Strategy

The planning of media strategy is crucial to the success of the overall media program. Here the media planner begins the process of identifying the appropriate target market(s) and developing the media strategy most suited to reaching them.

Prospect Identification. The media planner begins the process of prospect segmentation. At this point, the various consumer groups are identified in terms of demographics, product usage characteristics, and/or lifestyle criteria. Prospects are also identified geographically, both in broad regions (e.g., Southeast) and in smaller socioeconomic units (e.g., particular suburbs). Regardless of the manner in which prospects are identified, the categories should be compatible with similar categories used by the media in identifying their readers and viewers.

Timing Considerations. The timing of media buys is a crucial factor in overall media planning and advertising budgeting. In this regard, factors such as flighting and seasonal sales trends must be considered.

Creative Considerations. The media/creative team must arrive at necessary compromises between the media that are most appropriate to carry the message and those media that reach the target audience most efficiently.

At this stage, the media planner begins specific planning for future media scheduling. Even at this time the media plan should be based on the information available concerning the marketing and competitive situation. However, there is also some "thinking out loud" as the media planner experiments with alternative approaches to the media schedule. Most media departments provide their planners with flowcharts for use in the initial planning stages. These flowcharts are largely for internal agency use and are not sent to either clients or the media as part of the media-buying process. They are most often used in buying television.

Section III. Media Tactics

In the media tactics section the media planner begins to outline the specific principles of the media function which are designed to implement both overall corporate objectives and the overall media strategy.

Advertising Impact

1. *Gross rating point levels.* The first step in media tactics is to decide what level of advertising weight is to be applied against various market segments and in various geographic locales. GRPs have become the standard measure for general levels of advertising, but other measures may be more appropriate in specific cases (e.g., total exposures in magazines).

2. *Reach versus frequency.* Once the general weight of advertising

FIGURE 14–1 General Media Plan and Its Justification

Medium	Budget (percent)	Media Vehicle Types	Justification
Television	$2,000,000 (50%)	Daytime soaps, barter syndication (Donahue, Douglas)	TV provides brand name awareness and excellent package identification; it reaches both women 25-49 (primary market) and women 50 + (secondary market)
Magazines	1,600,000 (40%)	Women's service books (*Family Circle*); specialized, upscale women's books (*Self*)	Magazines will be used to reach upscale and working women missed by a major portion of television advertising
Newspapers	400,000 (10%)	Dailies and major suburban papers	Newspapers will be used to complement other advertising with follow-up couponing in major markets

has been decided, the next step is to analyze the pattern of exposure of the various target markets. These reach/frequency levels may be in terms of target segments, media, or both.

3. *Competitive impact.* Many advertising plans state goals in terms of some competitive strategy (taking away share points from a major competitor). The media planner should show how the campaign will meet such competitive goals.

Principles of Media Selection and Justification. After general guidelines have been developed (Section IIIA), the media planner considers the more specific media factors, which ultimately lead to the media schedule.

1. Selection of general media types and their justification. The media planner can present this section in a number of ways, but the example given in Figures 14–1 and 14–2 is typical.

2. Scheduling strategy. After discussing the media to be used (Section IIIB), the media planner must delineate the scheduling strategy that will be used in each medium. This discussion should be regarded as an

FIGURE 14–2 Budget Allocation Chart

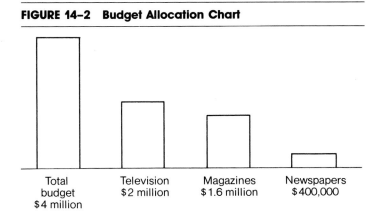

| Total budget $4 million | Television $2 million | Magazines $1.6 million | Newspapers $400,000 |

introduction to the media schedule. It should briefly highlight the major factors of the media strategy to be employed.

3. Budget summary. The way in which the budget is discussed in Section IIIB1 may make a separate budget summary subsection unnecessary. Even in such cases, however, the media planner may use the budget summary subsection to examine the budget constraints affecting the media plan. Usually budget problems of a major nature will be resolved before media planning is begun. On the other hand, if adequate advertising dollars are not available to carry out the overall advertising objectives, this should be noted by the media planner.

Section IV. The Media Schedule

The media schedule is a "calendar" of media buys. Depending on the diversity of the media types, the number of vehicles within these media, and the length and size of advertisements, the schedule may be simple or complex. At a minimum the following information is normally included in the media schedule:

1. Identification of each media vehicle to be used—*Time,* "The Cosby Show."
2. Time or space to be bought in each media and any special criteria for the buys—full position, four-color, ROP.
3. Dates advertisements and commercials are to run (and often insertion dates to media).
4. Cost—total for medium and per insertion with the exception of package buys in broadcast.

This information is sometimes included in media schedules:

FIGURE 14-3   Print Media Request

OGILVY & MATHER INC.	MAGAZINE PRINT MEDIA REQUEST

DATE _____

ESTIMATING _____   1 – NATIONAL   CLIENT _____

TRAFFIC _____   PRODUCT _____

FORWARDING _____   2 – REGIONAL   ESTIMATE _____

BUYER _____   3 – TEST   REVISION _____

OTHER _____   CANCELLATION _____

☐ MAGAZINE   ☐ SUPPLEMENT   ☐ TRADE

PUBLICATION	CIRC. 000	SPACE	ISSUE DATE	SPACE CLOSING DATE	GROSS COST

POSITION – SPECIAL INSTRUCTIONS

1. Circulation, total audience, or prospects reached by each vehicle.
2. Cost per thousand, gross rating points, cost per rating point, or weighted CPM by vehicle, medium, or entire schedule.
3. Coverage areas (broadcast).

From the media schedule actual media buys are made. In larger agencies the process begins with the account team (or account executive) notifying the media planner that media buys previously agreed upon should be made. The media planner prepares a media request form, which starts the buying mechanism (see Figures 14-3 and 14-4).

FIGURE 14–4 Network Buying Request

OGILVY & MATHER INC.
Advertising

2 EAST 48 STREET, NEW YORK 10017
(212) MURRAY HILL 8 6100

NETWORK BUYING REQUEST

FROM: _____

Date: _____

TO: BROADCAST (N.Y.)_____
BROADCAST (.L.A.)_____
ASSISTANT MEDIA DIRECTOR_____
ACCOUNT EXECUTIVE_____

☐ GROSS

CLIENT_____
PRODUCT_____ DAYPART_____ BUDGET $_____ ☐ NET

INSTRUCTION: ☐ BUY ☐ CHANGE ☐ PREPARE BUY FOR REVIEW ☐ ORIGINAL or REVISION # _____

WEIGHT DISTRIBUTION TARGET

☐ SPEND TO BUDGET

☐ SPEND TO GRP'S

☐ NOTIFY PLANNING GROUP OF OPPORTUNITIES

REACH OBJECTIVE

☐ HIGH

☐ MEDIUM

☐ LOW

AGE	TOTAL	18-34	35-49	50+	25-49	18-49		TEENS	CHILDREN
MEN							M		2-5
WOMEN							F		6-11

INCOME	-$5M	$5-10M	$10-15M	$15M+	FAMILY SIZE	1-2	3-4	5+

	A	B	C	D
COUNTY SIZE				

PRE-EMPTION POLICY: ☐ ACCEPT MAKE GOOD ☐ DURING FLIGHT ☐ OTHER TIMES ☐ ACCEPT CREDIT ☐ NOTIFY PLANNER

INCLUSIVE DATES _____ TOTAL # WKS _____

GROSS RATING POINT BASIS ☐ HOUSEHOLD ☐ WOMEN ☐ MEN ☐ CHILDREN OTHER _____

COST PER RATING POINT $_____ $_____ $_____ $_____ $_____

DATES		GRP's		WEEKLY BUDGET	NO. OF	SPECIAL· INSTRUCTIONS
START	END	30's	:60's	(GROSS)	WEEKS	
		TOTAL				

REMARKS

ASSISTANT MEDIA DIRECTOR
SIGNATURE _____

ATTACH LATEST FLOW CHART

Courtesy of Ogilvy & Mather, Inc.

Copies of the media request form are sent to traffic and creative as well as media, so that all aspects of the buy can be coordinated. From the media request forms, insertion orders are submitted based on previously executed contracts with the media.

Contracts and Insertion Orders. The purchase of media involves two steps: contracting for time and space and submitting the advertisement or commercial insertion instructions to the given medium. The contract sets the price that the medium will charge over a set period. In some cases the contract also specifies or fixes the amount of time and space to be bought. In other cases, especially with newspapers, the final rate is computed after all the media buys have been made. In these cases the contract indicates the final discounts available and the price to be paid at each billing period.

The insertion order accompanies the advertisement or commercial (see Figure 14–5). It gives the date the advertisement is to run, reaffirms the cost, outlines any special requirements already agreed upon by the medium and the advertiser, and sometimes gives the advertising run to that time for discount purposes.

Section V. Summary

The summary is designed to show how the proposed media schedule accomplishes the advertising objectives. It should address the manner in which the media plan aids the client in meeting competitive challenges. Often the specific marketing goals (e.g., shift in a certain percentage market share) are reiterated here, and the methods by which the media strategy will aid in accomplishing these goals are discussed.

The media plan summary is an overview of anticipated accomplishments, reasonable chances of success, and potential pitfalls in the media portion of the advertising program. As mentioned at the beginning of this chapter, the media plan should both sell a client on the media program and guide the media department in implementing the plan.

MEDIA PLAN 1—NATIONAL CLIENT

Coors—The premium beer of the Adolph Coors Company.

Agency—Foote, Cone & Belding.

1. MEDIA OBJECTIVES

1985 marked the start of the "Coors is the One" campaign, also known as the "Distinctiveness" campaign, for Coors premium beer. Also introduced with this campaign was spokesperson, Mark Harmon.

FIGURE 14–5

Ogilvy & Mather Inc.	PLEASE SEND INVOICES TO OGILVY & MATHER INC. P.O. BOX 1596 GRAND CENTRAL STATION NEW YORK, N.Y. 10017

Advertising

2 EAST 48 STREET   NEW YORK 10017   (212) 688-6100

INSERTION ORDER

TO PUBLISHER OF:

ORDER NO.   **B**   112978

DATE

RATE

AGENCY COMM.   %

CASH DISC.   %

PLEASE INSERT THE ADVERTISING OF

DATE OF ISSUE	SPACE	P.O.	AD. NO.	CAPTION

Please advise at once if instructions are not clear.
Please check reproduction material against proof
to make sure it corresponds in every respect.
Please acknowledge receipt by return mail.
Schedule and instructions given above are subject
to the same conditions as in our contract.

A copy of each issue of your publication containing each
advertisement should be sent promptly to the advertiser as
well as to our office.

Ogilvy & Mather Inc.

Per _____

Member of
AMERICAN ASSOCIATION OF ADVERTISING AGENCIES

8-6E REV. 8-76
PRINTED IN U.S.A

The focus of the 1985 campaign was different from earlier themes and different than competitors' messages. The account team believed that Coors was not just different, but better. This belief led to the conviction and the creative strategy of having something to say, not just something to sell.

The campaign incorporated an attempt to rekindle the Coors mystique and made a statement about the product, the efforts, and the company. It was a highly visual representation of the product and company philosophy, and it relied heavily on longer than average television spots to accomplish its objectives.

In 1986, the client and agency account group were very pleased with the campaign results and decided to continue the direction established in 1985.

2. MEDIA STRATEGY

Target Audience

For 1985, the proposed target audience is Men Legal Age (LA)–34.
There are two reasons for the proposed target.

1. To position Coors more closely with the Premium category and major competitor, Budweiser.
2. To plan and place media to be in concert with the Coors Creative objective of a young feel and image as well as maintaining Coors current drinkers.

Data Source

The following user information is based on "Demographic Profile of the Beer Market 26-State Coors Marketing Area," July 1984.

Premium Category versus Total Beer

Men by far, consume most beer for the industry and especially the Premium category.

	Users		Volume Contribution	
	Total Beer	Premium	Total Beer	Premium
Male	80%	83%	87%	90%
Female	20	17	13	10

The LA–34 age segment is key especially in terms of volume, and most importantly for Premium.

Age	Composition of Past Two-Week Users		
	Total Beer	Premium	Index of Premium to Total Beer
LA–24	22%	26%	118
25–34	34	36	106
35–49	25	22	88
50+	19	16	84

The difference is more acute when Premium users are compared to the total population:

	Total Population	Premium	Index Premium to Population
LA–24	16%	26%	163
25–34	24	36	150
35–49	25	22	88
50+	35	16	46

Age	Volume Contribution Past Two Weeks		
	Total Beer	Premium	Index of Premium to Total Beer
LA–24	25%	29%	116
25–34	34	36	106
35–49	24	21	88
50+	17	14	82

Again, compared to the total population, the volume contribution very keenly skews to the younger age segments.

	Total Population	Premium	Index Premium to Population
LA–24	16%	29%	181
25–34	24	36	150
35–49	25	21	84
50+	35	14	40

Coors Comparison to Premium Category Competition

Coors source of volume is older than both the Premium category and Budweiser.

	Premium Brands Composition of Past Two Week Volume				
Age	Category	Coors		Budweiser	
	Percent	Percent	Index	Percent	Index
LA–24	29	25	86	32	110
25–34	36	34	94	36	100
35–49	21	24	114	20	95
50+	14	17	121	12	86

The difference in volume distribution within the LA–24 and 25–34 sub-segments further highlights Coors deficiency among the youngest drinkers.

	Category		Coors			Budweiser		
	Total Percent	Percent within LA–34	Total Percent	Percent within LA–34	Index to Category	Total Percent	Percent within LA–34	Index to Category
LA–24	29	45%	25	42%	93	32	47%	104
25–34	36	55	34	58	105	36	53	96
35–49	21	100%	24	100%		20	100%	
50+	14		17			12		

Geography

Media will be used to cover a 26-state Coors Marketing Area. Unlike last year, the 6-Southeast Expansion states will not be considered as part of the Base CMA.

Base (26 States)		
Arizona	Montana	Alabama
Arkansas	Nebraska	Eastern Tennessee
California	New Mexico	Florida
Colorado	Nevada	Georgia
Idaho	Oklahoma	North Carolina
Iowa	Texas	South Carolina
Kansas	Utah	Virginia
Louisiana	Washington	Washington, D.C.
Mississippi	Western Tennessee	
Missouri	Wyoming	

Market Analysis Allocation

Each DMA will be ranked according to the approved weighting as follows: Note that the Base area includes all the SE markets for 1985.

Base CMA	
Coors BDI	60%
Coors category CDI	20
Media efficiency	20
Market value	100%

The next step is to rank the DMA's and then separate them into groups of markets with similar importance/volume potential. Further adjustments were made manually by the Brand Group, resulting in some markets moving from one group to another. Factors contributing to a manual adjustment include market potential, profits, distributors' input, and other factors.

Spending Methodology Allocation

In 1985, the budget will be allocated on a weight basis.

The specific budget allocation of the total budget to DMA's will be made as follows:

- According to its market value/groupings.
- Allocated on a target rating point goal per group per quarter.

Response Function
Goal:

Attitude Reinforcement/Sales Maintenance

- Maintain current drinkers by increasing Coors' presence in the marketplace.

Considerations:

- Decline in sales
- Maintaining current Coors drinkers is more important than going after a new target.

Maximum Value Frequency Level:

$5\times$ over a 4-week period. Incremental effectiveness diminishes at $4\times$/week level.

Curve:

S-shape, building faster than initial exposures to emphasize the current base of Coors drinkers.

Weights:

Communication Frequency	Weight	Incremental Percentage Point Gain
0×	0.00	—
1×	0.15	+15
2×	0.30	+15
3×	0.55	+25
4×	0.85	+30
5×	1.00	+15

Incremental exposure value begins to gain proportional to weekly frequency; declines as we approach four exposures per week.

3. MEDIA RATIONALE

Media Mix

Television will be the primary medium utilized because it provides the best combination of cost efficiency and message communication. The base unit will be 30 seconds.

Daypart selection will consist of Weekend and Prime Sports via Network, Cable, Syndicated and Spot TV and Prime, Early Fringe, and Late Fringe via Spot TV.

Radio will be the secondary medium utilized to build frequency at efficient costs.

Both television and radio will be scheduled year-round with heavier activity scheduled around promotional and high sales periods during the year. The media efficiency of TV versus radio will help to determine the local media mix by market.

Medium	Weight	Communication Weights Comments
TV :30	1.00	Strongest medium in visual and audio impact.
TV :10	.65	Strong in audio/visual impact but less than a :30 due to its brevity. Can be localized for key markets.
Radio :60	.60	Supports the campaign musically but doesn't convey the "refreshment" theme as well as a visual medium.
Outdoor	.35	Increased emphasis due to its ability to emphasize the visual theme through the use of its size and flexibility of locations.
Magazines (P4C)	.15	The static, silent nature of this smaller print medium lessens our ability to communicate the campaign.
Newspapers	.05	Not an effective medium to communicate the campaign theme.

The Coors media mix will be determined based on the following media weights:

Medium	Noticing (Stage I)	Communication (Stage II)
Net/Spot TV :30	.52	1.00
Spot TV :10	.28	.65
Radio :60	.42	.60
Outdoor	.32	.35
Magazine (P4C)	.40	.15
Newspaper (SAU #13)	.28	.05

**1985 Media Cost Comparison
Men 18–34**

Vehicle	Gross CPM	Noticing Weight	Noticing CPM	Communication Weight	Communication CPM	Percentage Difference versus Spot TV
Spot TV :30 Fringe/sports/ prime*	$28.10	.52	$54.04	1.00	$ 54.04	—
Network TV :30 Sports	30.00	.52	57.69	1.00	57.69	+ 7%
Spot TV :10 Fringe/sports/ prime	16.86	.28	60.21	.65	92.64	+ 71
Spot radio :60 Music	12.40	.42	29.52	.60	49.21	− 9
Outdoor 100 Showing	7.40	.32	23.13	.35	66.07	+ 23
Magazine Pg. 4/C Bld.	22.00	.40	55.00	.15	366.67	+ 579
Newspapers (SAU #13)	24.00	.28	85.71	.05	1,714.29	+3,072

* Based on a quarterly 5%0 split of Sports/Prime and Early/Late Fringe

Television Dayparts

For the 1985 media plan, FCB and ACC agreed to the following quarterly daypart mix goals.

Daypart	1ST Quarter	2ND Quarter	3RD Quarter	4TH Quarter	Average
Sports/Prime*	50	50	50	50	50
Early/Late Fringe	50	50	50	50	50
	100	100	100	100	100

* Prime would be purchased to a higher percentage in those quarters where lots of sports programming is not available. This is especially true in second quarter and early third quarter—April–July.

Media Mix Comparison Using Constant Dollars

Several TV/Radio mixes were examined to determine what effect radio has on improving the Net Effective Reach. As radio increases, the Net Effective Reach builds until radio hits a point between one third and one half of the weight.

Media Mix	Gross TRPs			Comm. TRPs			Gross R/F	Comm. R/F	Percent NER	NER Percent Change versus All TV
	TV	R	Total	TV	R	Total				
All TV	481	—	481	250	—	250	86/ 5.6	79/3.2	41	—
¾ TV	419	140	559	218	35	253	93/ 6.0	82/3.1	42	+ 2.4
⅔ TV	395	195	590	205	49	254	93/ 6.3	83/3.1	42	+ 2.4
½ TV	334	334	668	174	84	258	94/ 7.1	83/3.1	43	+ 4.9
⅓ TV	254	516	770	132	130	262	93/ 8.3	81/3.2	42	+ 2.4
¼ TV	207	622	829	108	157	265	92/ 9.0	80/3.3	42	+ 2.4
No TV	—	1,092	1,092	—	275	275	76/14.4	60/4.6	35	− 15.0

Cost Base: Prototype Plan based on $25 million budget.
Radio CPP—22.90
TV CPP—51.94

Optimum 4-Week Effective Weight for Branded Advertising

Per our analysis of weight levels based on ½ TV, ½ Radio, and ⅔ TV, ⅓ Radio, and All TV, we estimate in 1985, with the quicker response function for the Coors brand, that the optimum 4-week effective weight level is at 225 Total Rating Points (TRPs) adjusted for noticing and communication weights.

This is the level at which incremental Net Effective Reach equals incremental dollar expenditure.

Media Weight Levels
½ TV, ½ Radio Markets

Optimum 4-Week Effective Weight—225 TRPs (adjusted for Noticing and Communication Weights):

4-Week Communication TRPs	Percent of Increase	4-Week Net Effective Reach	Percent of Increase	Index
100	—	16	—	—
150	+ 50	25	+ 56	112
200	+ 33	34	+ 36	109
250	+ 25	42	+ 24	96
300	+ 20	48	+ 14	70
200	—	34	—	—
225	+ 12	38	+ 12	100

This translates to 600 gross TRPs of ½ TV and ½ Radio. The gross reach and frequency is 93 and 6.5, the adjusted numbers are 80 and 2.8.

Maximum 4-Week Effective Weight for Branded Advertising

Per our analysis we estimate that the maximum 4 week effective weight level is at 550 TRPs, adjusted for noticing and communication weights.

This number allows us to approach 70 percent Net Effective Reach. These weight levels will only occur in top market groupings.

Maximum 4-Week Effective Weight—550 TRPs (adjusted for Noticing and Communication Weights):

TRPs	Percent of Change	Percent Net Effective Reach	Percent of Change	Index	Index Percent Drop
350	—	54	—	—	—
400	+ 14	59	+ 9	64	—
450	+ 13	63	+ 7	54	− 16
500	+ 11	66	+ 5	45	− 17
550	+ 10	70	+ 6	60	+ 33
600	+ 9	72	+ 3	33	− 45

This translates to 1,450 gross TRPs of ½ TV and ½ Radio mix. The gross reach is 96 and 15.1. Adjusted reach and frequency is 93 and 5.9.

4. MEDIA PLAN

Scheduling Guidelines

The following guidelines will be used for all quarterly schedules:

- Maximum advertising schedule per quarter is 10 weeks.
- Hiatus weeks are taken after post-offs.*
- Only support one post-off if schedule allows only 2 weeks to advertise. (Don't support both post-offs with one week each.)
- After post-off week skew towards seasonality.

Quarterly Scheduling Priorities

Quarter One Priorities

1. St. Patrick's Day post-off (Branded Advertising)
2. Seasonality

Quarter Two Priorities

1. Memorial Day post-off (Themed Advertising)
2. 4th of July post-off (1 week Branded Advertising)
3. Seasonality

Quarter Three Priorities

1. Labor Day post-off (Themed Advertising)
2. 4th of July post-off (1 week Branded Advertising)
3. Seasonality

Quarter Four Priorities

1. Halloween post-off (Themed Advertising)
2. Christmas post-off (Themed Advertising)
3. Thanksgiving post-off (Branded Advertising)

Quarterly Scheduling

Media weight within a quarter will be skewed to cover the following *confirmed* post-off periods.

---

* Post-off is the industry term for promotions involving price reductions.

Dual Post-Offs with Themed Advertising		
Event	*Month*	*Weeks*
Memorial Day	May	20, 21
Labor Day	August	34, 35
Halloween	October	42, 43
Holiday	December	50, 51
Dual Post-Offs with Branded Advertising		
St. Patrick's	March	10, 11
4th of July	July	26, 27
Thanksgiving	November	47, 48

The dual post-offs with themed advertising will include Coors and Coors Light in the TV and Radio spots.

Timing Seasonality

Media weight will be allocated in each DMA on a quarterly basis based on category seasonality, adjusted for media efficiency.

	Quarter			
Base and SE	*1*	*2*	*3*	*4*
Monthly seasonality	93	110	107	90
Media Cost Index	90	107	93	110
Opportunity Index	103	102	115	80
A ÷ B				
Percent of weight (C X .25)	25	26	29	20
Percent of dollars (D X B)	23	28	27	22

Category Seasonality

Month	*J*	*F*	*M*	*A*	*M*	*J*	*J*	*A*	*S*	*O*	*N*	*D*
Percent year	7.4	7.4	8.5	8.6	9.3	9.6	9.0	9.4	8.5	8.1	7.3	7.4
Index	89	89	102	104	112	116	108	113	102	98	88	84
Quarterly Index		93			110			107			90	
Media Cost Index												
Spot TV (73)		87			109			91			113	
Spot Radio (27)		100			100			100			100	
Weighted average		90			107			93			110	

Coors
1985 Scheduling Strategy

Media	1st quarter			2nd quarter			3rd quarter			4th quarter		
Week beginning	January	February	March	April	May	June	July	August	September	October	November	December
Category/Seasonality	89	89	102	104	112	116	108	113	102	98	88	84

Month week-beginning numbers:
- January: 31 7 14 21 28
- February: 4 11 18 25
- March: 4 11 18 25
- April: 1 8 15 22 29
- May: 6 13 20 27
- June: 3 10 17 24
- July: 1 8 15 22 29
- August: 5 12 19 26
- September: 2 9 16 23 30
- October: 7 14 21 28
- November: 4 11 18 25
- December: 2 9 16 23

Week numbers: 1–52

Rows:
- Dual post-off
- Brand post-off
- 10 weeks of advertising
- 9 weeks
- 8 weeks
- 7 weeks
- 6 weeks
- 5 weeks
- 4 weeks
- 3 weeks
- 2 weeks
- 1 week

MEDIA PLAN 2—REGIONAL CLIENT

Palm Village—A retirement community in central Florida.
Agency—Newman & Associates.

MEDIA OBJECTIVE

To create awareness both nationally and locally for this new retirement community. Secondly, to stimulate inquiries among prospective customers prior to and while vacationing in Central Florida area.

MEDIA RATIONALE

National publications will be used more heavily prior to tourist season to create awareness and spark interest in Palm Village. Magazines have been evaluated on a content and CPM basis.

Local/Statewide publications are recommended through the "season" to add impact to local/statewide newspaper advertising effort.

Local/Statewide newspapers will be used on a continuous basis, increasing frequency during the season. Classified ads are recommended in addition to display to create more reach and higher frequency at a lower CPM.

The top *Manufactured Home publications* will be utilized throughout the year, as sales do continue into the off-season.

Radio is recommended during the height of the season only, to reinforce other advertising and to create a higher awareness for Palm Village. The proposed schedule will accomplish our goals based on the 15 spots per station allocation. (Please note: Arbitron ratings are not available for this area.)

Permanent Outdoor boards will help to stimulate traffic as well as create a higher exposure for the community. *A 100 Poster Showing* is recommended during the season to help achieve these goals at this crucial selling period.

Palm Village
Ocala, Florida
Media Plan, August 1986 to August 1987

Month	Monthly Budget	Newspapers	Magazines	Radio	Outdoor	Percent of Total Budget
Aug.	$ 3,994.85	764.12	334.73	—	2,896.00	1.67%
Sep.	8,043.63	2,867.40	853.73	—	4,322.50	3.36
Oct.	27,991.19	5,474.96	18,193.73	—	4,322.50	11.70
Nov.	22,416.65	6,667.00	11,427.15	—	4,322.50	9.38
Dec.	39,300.71	7,222.44	26,755.77	—	4,322.50	16.00
Jan.	31,730.46	6,108.60	17,372.06	2,025.00	6,224.80	13.26
Feb.	27,342.29	6,001.28	12,416.21	2,700.00	6,224.80	11.43
Mar.	22,251.71	6,108.60	7,218.31	2,700.00	6,224.80	9.30
Apr.	24,001.72	6,106.16	10,320.76	1,350.00	6,224.80	10.03
May	9,913.62	4,041.24	1,549.88	—	4,322.50	4.14
Jun.	7,576.92	2,294.44	959.98	—	4,322.50	3.17
Jul.	8,829.36	2,296.88	2,209.98	—	4,322.50	3.69
Aug.	6,872.48	1,590.00	959.98	—	4,322.50	2.87
Totals	$239,265.59	57,543.12	110,572.27	8,775.00	62,375.20	
Percent of total Budget in this medium:		24.04%	46.21%	3.67%	26.07%	

Example Monthly Schedule

Publication February	Insertion Date	Ad Size	Cost per Insertion	Total Cost
Ocala Star Banner	2/1,7,15,21	5c × 10″	$ 553.00	$ 2,212.00
(Circ: 42,210)	2/8,14,22,28	8″ class.	88.48	353.92
	2/1–28	3 lines*	2.44	68.32
Northern classified:				
New York	2/1	4 lines	351.32	351.32
(Circ: 3,188,000)				
Michigan	2/8	4 lines	260.88	260.88
(Circ: 1,902,000)				
Pennsylvania	2/1	4 lines	314.92	314.92
(Circ: 2,898,200)				
Ohio	2/8	4 lines	264.24	264.24
(Circ: 2,446,600)				
Florida	2/1,8,15,22	4 lines	392.20	1,568.80
(Circ: 2,916,700)				
NY/nearby	2/15	4 lines	396.80	296.80
(Circ: 4,115,500)				
Mich/nearby	2/22	4 lines	310.08	310.08
(Circ: 3,611,000)				
Manufactured Home News	2/7	4c × 11″	334.73	334.73
(Circ: 25,000)				
Mobile Home & Park Guide	February	FP B/W	400.00	400.00
(Circ: 40,000)				
Florida Directory of Mobile Homes & Parks	February	FP B/W	119.00	119.00
(Circ: 35,000)				
Florida Living	February	FP B/W	589.90	589.90
(Circ: 25,000)				

Publication February	Insertion Date	Ad Size	Cost per Insertion	Total Cost
Florida Visitor's Guide	February	FP B/W	106.25	106.25
(Circ: 6,000)				
Senior Voice	February	4c × 9½"	445.13	445.13
(Circ: 35,000)				
Today in Ocala	February	½P B/W	275.00	275.00
(Circ: 12,000)				
Elks	February	5" class	1,354.50	1,354.50
(Circ: 1,607,000)				
VFW	February	1/6P class	1,610.75	1,610.75
(Circ: 1,957,000)				
Golden Years	February	1/3P B/W	1,442.05	1,442.05
(Circ: 150,000)				
Modern Maturity—Florida	Feb./Mar.	1/3P B/W	5,738.90	5,738.90
(Circ: 987,000)				
Radio—3 stations—15x per	2/2-28	:60	675.00	2,700.00
station				
Outdoor		16 boards	4,322.50	4,322.50
Outdoor posters		100 showing	1,902.30	1,902.30
				$27,342.29

* Rate Holder

MEDIA PLAN 3—LOCAL CLIENT

Melissa Javelina's—chain of Mexican restaurants that specializes in Sonoran desert cooking. MJ's is celebrating eight years in Miami. **Agency**—Dunlop, Over, Belt and Co.

MEDIA OBJECTIVE

To promote Melissa Javelina's 8th Anniversary celebration with a full media blitz featuring "roll back menu prices to 1978." High awareness of this campaign will be achieved through a media mix of television, radio, and newspaper.

MEDIA RATIONALE

Television will be used primarily for reach, in building this awareness campaign. A goal of 250 HH rating points per week is recommended in order to assure substantial market reach and ample frequency.

Radio is recommended as a frequency supplement to television. A demographic (Adult 25-54) rating point goal of 140 per week is recommended to adequately reach this target audience within a sufficient frequency.

Newspaper will be used as support for the broadcast media. Print will also allow for more detailed information such as price and item and locations.

MJ's
8th Anniversary
Summary of Media Proposal
7/1–18/86
July 1 to 28, 1986

Television	$ 40,594.00
Radio	35,460.00
Newspaper	27,472.33
Total media:	$103,526.33

Miami/Ft. Lauderdale Television
July 1 to 20, 1986

Daypart	Percent of Schedule	GRPs per Week	Cost per Week
Early fringe 4–6P	10%	25	
Early news 6–7P	12	30	
Prime access 7–8P	23	57	
Prime 8–11P	23	57	
Late news 11–11:30P	15	38	
Late fringe 11P–2A	8	20	
Weekend 11A–2A	9	23	
	100%	250	$13,531.00
3 week total:		1,000	$40,594.00

NOTE: Spots are : 10 second commercials.

**MJ's
8th Anniversary Television Plan
Miami/Ft. Lauderdale
July 1 to 27, 1986**

Station	Time Period	Day	Program	ADI HH Rating	Number of Spots per Week
WTVJ(4)	4–5P	T–F	Newlywed Game/ Price Is Right	6	2x
WTVJ(4)	5–5:30P	T–F	Wheel of Fortune	8	2x
WCIX(6)	5–6P	T–F	Laverne & Shirley/ Gidget	5	1x
WPLG(10)	5–6P	T–F	Early News	9	2x
WTVJ(4)	6–7P	T–F	Early News	12	1x
WBFS(33)	5P–Mid	T–F	Various	3	5x
WCIX(6)	7–8P	T–F	Benson/Barney Miller	4	2x
WDZL(39)	7–8P	T–F	Kojak	3	2x
WTVJ(4)	7–7:30P	T–F	Wheel of Fortune	10	2x
WPLG(10)	7–8P	T–F	Million Dollar Chance of a Life- time/Jeopardy	8	2x
WCIX(6)	8–10P	T–F	Movie	4	2x
WTVJ(4)	8–11P	T–Su	Prime rotator	8	2x
WSVN(7)	8–11P	T–Su	Prime rotator	12	2x
WPLG(10)	8–11P	T–Su	Prime rotator	11	1x
WTVJ(4)	11–11:30P	T–Su	Late News	8	2x
WSVN(7)	11–11:30P	T–Su	Late News	8	2x
WPLG(10)	11–11:30P	T–Su	Late News	11	1x
WDZL(39)	11P–1A	T–F	Goodwill Games	4	2x
WCIX(6)	11:30P– 12:30A	T–F	Star Trek	3	1x
WTVJ(4)	11:30P– 12:30A	Fri	Summer Concert Series	6	1x
WCIX(6)	11:30P–1A	Sat	Cannes Film Festival	3	1x
WPLG(10)	Mid–1A	T–F	Hawaii 5-O	4	2x
WBFS(33)	Mid–1A	T–F	Movie	2	1x
WTVJ(4)	1A–3A	T–F	Late Show	2	2x
WTVJ(4)	Noon–6P	Sa/Su	Afternoon rotation	3	2x
WCIX(6)	Noon–6P	Sa/Su	Afternoon rotation	4	1x
WPLG(10)	Noon–6P	Sa/Su	Afternoon rotation	4	3x
WBFS(33)	Noon–6P	Sa/Su	Afternoon rotation	4	1x
WCIX(6)	11:30A–5P	Sun	Afternoon rotation	4	1x

294	51
Rating points per week	Spots per week
Cost per week:	$13,525.00 (G)
3-week total rating points:	882
3-week total spots:	153
3-week total cost:	$40,575.00

MJ's
Radio Advertising Plan

Station	Weekly GRPs 25–54 Adults	Weekly Number of Spots†	Cost/ Week
For 7/1–5/86, repeat 7/22–26/86:			
WAXY-FM	19.4	12X	$ 1,400.00
WLVE-FM	13.3	13X	990.00
WKQS-FM	26.1	11X	1,100.00
WSHE-FM	28.3	10X	1,044.00
WHYI-FM	30.9	12X	1,224.00
WJQY-FM	26.7	12X	1,170.00
Weekly total	144.7	70X	6,928.00
Two-week aggregate	289.4	140X	$13,856.00
For 7/1–27/86:			
Melbourne Radio:			
WMEL-AM	42.4	24X	
WSSP-FM ⎱ *		24X	
WKRT-AM ⎰	62.4	24X	
WYRL-FM ⎱ *		27X	
WMMB-AM ⎰	31.5	27X	
WVTI-FM	33.3	24X	
WSTF-FM	60.0	24X	
WOCL-FM	25.0	12X	
Weekly total	258.2	210X	$ 3,663.00
Four-week aggregate	1,032.8	840X	$14,652.00
Stuart Radio:			
WSTU-AM ⎱ *		27X	
WHLG-FM ⎰	85.5	27X	
WOVV-FM	127.3	18X	
WKGR-FM	42.3	12X	
Weekly total	255.1	84X	$ 1,738.00
Four-week aggregate	1,020.4	336X	$ 6,952.00
Grand total	2,342.6	1,316X	$35,460.00

NOTES:

* Sold in combination.

† Spots rotated 6 A.M.–midnight, M–F, and 8 A.M.–10 P.M., Sa, Su.

**MJ's
Newspaper Advertising Plan**

Newspaper/ Section/Edition	Insertion Date	Size	Cost
Ft. Lauderdale News/Sun Sentinel			
(Showtime)	7/4	FP	$ 2,695.66
	7/11	4c × 10.5″	1,658.86
	7/18	4c × 10.5″	1,658.86
	7/25	4c × 10.5″	1,658.86
Hollywood Sun Tatler			
(Spotlighter)	7/4	5c × 18″	$ 1,429.45
	7/11	3c × 10.5″	476.48
	7/18	3c × 10.5″	476.48
	7/25	3c × 10.5″	476.48
Miami Herald/Broward			
(Entertainment)	7/4	5c × 18″	$ 1,825.45
	7/11	3c × 10.5″	608.49
	7/18	3c × 10.5″	608.49
	7/25	3c × 10.5″	608.49
Miami Herald/			
Neighbors-West Dade	7/3	FP	$ 1,622.75
	7/10	3c × 10.5″	748.96
	7/17	3c × 10.5″	748.96
	7/24	3c × 10.5″	748.96
Florida Today			
(TGIF)	7/4	4c × 10.5″	$ 1,105.91
	7/11	4c × 10.5″	1,105.91
	7/18	4c × 10.5″	1,105.91
	7/25	3c × 10.5″	829.43
Stuart News			
(Entertainment)	7/4	5c × 18″	$ 873.55
	7/11	3c × 10.5″	291.18
	7/18	3c × 10.5″	291.18
	7/25	3c × 10.5″	291.18
The Pompano Observer	7/3	4c × 10.5″	$ 249.60
	7/10	4c × 10.5″	249.60
	7/17	4c × 10.5″	249.60
	7/24	4c × 10.5″	249.60
The Pompano Beach/			
Monday Paper	7/7	4c × 10.5″	$ 254.00
	7/14	4c × 10.5″	254.00
	7/21	4c × 10.5″	254.00
	7/28	4c × 10.5″	254.00
The Jewish Journal	7/3	3c × 10.5″	$ 378.00
	7/10	3c × 10.5″	378.00
	7/17	3c × 10.5″	378.00
	7/24	3c × 10.5″	378.00
Total			$27,472.33

NOTE: Sizes conform to SAU requirements.

REVIEW QUESTIONS

1. What are the two major purposes of the media plan?
2. How does the media plan fit into the total marketing program of a firm?
3. What is the purpose of a media flowchart?
4. How does the media schedule differ from the media strategy section of the media platform?
5. Discuss the purpose of each of the following:
   a. Media request form.
   b. Space or time contract.
   c. Insertion order.
6. In the examples provided in this chapter, list three major differences between:
   a. Coors' national media plan and Melissa Javelina's local media plan.
   b. Coors' national media plan and the Palm Village regional media plan.
7. After studying the three example media plans, suggest an appropriate creative strategy for each.
8. What other local media might be considered for Melissa Javelina's media plan?

SUGGESTED ADDITIONAL READING

ANDERSON, ROBERT L., and THOMAS E. BARRY. "Factors in Media Strategies." In *Advertising Management*. Columbus, Ohio: Charles E. Merrill Publishing, 1979, pp. 261–81.

BOGART, LEO. "Advertising Models and Advertising Realities." In *Strategy in Advertising*. 2nd ed. Chicago: Crain Books, 1984, pp. 333–54.

BRUNO, ALBERT V.; THOMAS P. HUSTAD; and EDGAR A. PESSEMIER. "Media Approaches to Segmentation." In *Advertising Management: Practical Perspectives*. Englewood Cliffs, N.J.: Prentice-Hall, 1975, pp. 313–24.

BURNS, THOMAS J. *Effective Communications and Advertising for Financial Institutions*. Englewood Cliffs, N.J.: Prentice-Hall, 1986.

MARTIN, DAVID N. "A Model Investment." *Marketing and Media Decisions,* September 1986, pp. 87–90.

PATTI, CHARLES H., and JOHN H. MURPHY. "Developing the Media Plan." In *Advertising Management Cases and Concepts*. Columbus, Ohio: Grid Publishing, 1978, pp. 151–208.

PHELPS, STEPHEN P. "Media Planning: The Media . . . Gap." *Marketing and Media Decisions,* July 1986, pp. 148–51.

QUELCH, JOHN A., and PAUL W. FARRIS. "Media Selection." In *Cases in Advertising and Promotion Management*. Plano, Tex.: Business Publications, 1983, pp. 335–99.

SACHS, WILLIAM S. "The Advertising Plan." In *Advertising Management, Its Role in Marketing*. Tulsa: Penwell Publishing, 1983, pp. 137–62.

SIMON, JULIAN L. "Advertising for a National Airline." In *The Management of Advertising*. Englewood Cliffs, N.J.: Prentice-Hall, 1971, pp. 206–34.

"Use Computers to Decide How Much Advertising Is Enough." *Marketing News,* May 24, 1985, p. 19.

Postscheduling Management Techniques

My job is not so much in planning the media, but in executing it, going out and coordinating it with all the different Coke divisions and all of the agencies involved. You really have to be one hell of a diplomat and administrator.

Claire Simpson

Once the media schedule has been prepared, four tasks remain in the advertising process. First, the media must actually be purchased. Second, the schedule must be monitored so that ads appear at the planned time and place. Third, adjustments to the schedule must be made when circumstances require them. Finally, the efficiency of the media plan as well as the success of the advertising campaign should be measured.

SUPERVISING THE ACTUAL MEDIA PURCHASE

In the purchase of broadcast media time, negotiation is the primary basis for transactions. In Chapter 6, an example chronology for buying network television time is presented, as are the procedures for purchasing spot and local television time. Similarly the general negotiation process for radio time purchase is detailed in Chapter 7.

Any business negotiation has the objective of producing an agreement, between buyer and seller, on the terms and conditions of a sale. In order to produce this agreement, each party advances proposals, has them evaluated by the other party, who then offers counterproposals. In theory, this process continues until either a mutually agreeable contract is arrived at or until no further discussion is necessary since agreement seems beyond reach.

_____

* "Coke's Kissinger", *Marketing and Media Decisions*, May 1986, p. 4.

398

GUIDELINES FOR SUCCESSFUL NEGOTIATION

In other areas of business, where negotiations are often public and bitter, and where agreement is often not reached, several guides to successful negotiation have emerged. Some of these are listed below:

1. *Learn to prepare for the negotiation.* Buyers should know the details of the available money and the budget tolerances (over-ages-shortages, if any), the nominal or published rate and discount structure, and the performance of the medium (e.g., show or daypart ratings) insofar as possible. Obviously, the purchase of time in future shows deals with situations for which there is no available rating.

2. *Learn about the persons with whom you will deal.* Especially during the first meeting, try to establish a relaxed, friendly, cooperative atmosphere.

3. *Learn the value of a change in subject.* If it seems that agreement on a particular issue (say, the price of an ad in a particular show or daypart) is not near, table this issue and go on to others. Often resolution of the tabled problem will emerge as part of other discussions.

4. *Learn to be a good listener.* It is good psychology to let a person finish a statement. If the term or condition or price is different from what you will accept, there will be time to discuss the difference *after* the other party finishes presenting the proposal.

5. *Learn that haste makes waste.* Generally, attempts by one party to "hurry" the negotiation are resented by the other, and this resentment can poison the bargaining. A pause in the bargaining, in the form of a coffee or lunch break, or a late afternoon suggestion to pick up talks again in the morning can provide a creative opportunity for both parties to evaluate the progress made so far.

6. *Learn how to be a good questioner.* Try to question the "facts" and the statistical evidence offered by the other party in a way that will let you learn what these data really mean.

7. *Learn to identify which processes and techniques work best.* No one benefits from anger, emotion, and irritation.

8. *Learn to avoid public statements or positions until the agreement is reached.* Public positions are much harder to adjust by compromise than nonpublic positions.

9. *Learn to emphasize areas of common agreement.* These can be the negotiating bridge to areas of remaining differences.

10. *Learn that it never pays to take advantage of the other party.* It is sometimes tempting to seize an unfair short-term advantage.

However, over the interval of many seasons, many campaigns, and many media negotiations, taking unfair advantage (setting aside whatever ethical demerits this may produce) is almost certain to result in present bitterness and future retribution.

As you can see from these suggestions, negotiation is more art than science, and more demanding of interpersonal skills than are other areas of media management. And the problems of television time supplies and radio "network" variations have already been covered.

INTERMEDIA EQUIVALENCIES

For either broadcast or print media schedules, the media plan begins with a statement of objectives. Then the media mix is selected with an eye toward meeting these objectives. An important aspect of this mix is the development of comparable units among media.

The practitioner relies most heavily on GRPs to make intermedia comparisons. If one keeps in mind the substantive, fundamental differences between the broadcast media and other media, this method of comparison can work reasonably well. For instance, consider the recent acceptance of the GRP standard by the outdoor advertising industry, although you will recall that an "outdoor" GRP is different from, say, a "TV" GRP.

In print advertising, the use of cost per thousand seems to emerge as the method of comparing media or media classes. Newspapers thus become more comparable with magazines in spite of the fact that newspapers compete more directly with other media for audiences.

What has largely eluded media planners is general agreement about the print versus broadcast equivalencies. While cost per thousand (of target market members) can be and sometimes is applied to broadcast advertising, the application of ratings to print advertising has never been enthusiastically accepted. In practice, advertising objectives for a single campaign are often set in the form of GRPs for broadcast media and CPM for print media. Further, both reach and frequency objectives are often stated.

In a recent study of intermedia equivalencies, Sissors reviewed nine practical bases for intermedia comparisons.[1] He concluded that the fundamental problem is the absence of an adequate response function and that the major contributing factor is a lack of agreement over what should be measured, especially the "dependent" variables.

---

[1] Jack Z. Sissors, "Problems of Finding an Adequate Response Function for Media Planning," in *Making Advertising Relevant, Proceedings of the 1975 American Academy of Advertising,* ed. L. W. Lanfranco, pp. 152–54.

FIGURE 15–1 Broadcast Verification Form

IN ACCOUNT WITH

REMIT TO

WSB TV 2

P.O. BOX 102198, ATLANTA, GEORGIA 30368 PHONE: 897-7355

REPRESENTATIVE	BRANCH	SALESMAN
ADVERTISER		PRODUCT

INVOICE DATE		INVOICE NO	PAGE NO
AGENCY NO	ADVTSR NO	SALESMAN NO	CONTRACT NO
BILLING METHOD		AGY EST REP P.O. NO	
BILLING WEEK	RATE CARD	FUTURE RATE CARD NO EFF	
CON YR	BROADCAST MONTH	CONTRACT DATES	

TERMS: NET CASH

SCHEDULE								ACTUAL BROADCAST							RECONCILIATION	
LINE NUMBER	DAY(S) OF WEEK	DATES ORDERED		TIME ORDERED		SPOTS P/W	RATE	DAY	DATE	TIME	LENGTH	MAKE GOOD FOR	PRODUCT/MEDIA NUMBER	GROSS CHARGES	IDENTIFICATION	AMOUNT
		START	STOP	START	STOP											

COX Broadcasting Corporation

GROSS SCHEDULED AMOUNT (EXCLUDING MAKE GOOD) $

NET RECONCILIATION $

TOTAL $

WE HEREBY CERTIFY THAT THE TELECASTS LISTED ABOVE WERE MADE THROUGH OUR FACILITIES AS SHOWN ON THE OFFICIAL STATION LOG

TOTAL GROSS CHARGES $

AGENCY COMM $

NET CHARGES $ ← PAY THIS AMOUNT

NET RECONCILIATION

Courtesy WSB-TV, Atlanta, Georgia

MONITORING THE ADVERTISING CAMPAIGN

The second major managerial responsibility for a media schedule is the monitoring activity by which the scheduled times and places are verified. Not only must the advertising appear as planned (and the verification here can be more complicated than a novice would expect), but the adjacent communications must also be scrutinized.

Verification of Broadcast Advertising

For radio and television, verification should take the form of an affidavit signed by a broadcast station official that a particular ad was run at a specified time and entered in that station's program log. This affidavit has been cooperatively expanded by the Radio Advertising Bureau (RAB), the Television Bureau of Advertising (TvB), and the Association of National Advertisers to include not only the air time information but also the price of the commercial and a copy of the script. This combined form is particularly useful in preventing abuses in cooperative retail advertising, discussed more fully later. An example is presented in Figure 15–1.

Recent developments in electronic monitoring have altered the situation, as has deregulation of broadcasting. The FCC no longer requires broadcasters to maintain a log of all broadcast activity. This had been the mainstay of broadcast verification documents. By 1983, commercial firms had refined systems that recognized an imperceptible code affixed to radio or TV advertisements, and relayed this code along with frequency and date/time information to a central computer. The systems were given a somewhat mixed welcome by advertisers, agencies, and the media; and costs for the systems were not fully understood.

There is no argument that electronic verification technology is superior to handwritten logs on the bases of accuracy, quickness, and flexibility. By the end of 1985, electronic verification was offered by several commercial research firms (see Figure 15–2). There is little doubt that electronic verification systems will become the industry norm.

Verification of Print Advertising

For print advertising verification, the usual procedure is for the medium (e.g., the newspaper) to "tear" out the entire page on which the advertisement appears and to furnish this to the advertiser or the agency. In addition, a duplicate of the invoice showing effective prices is sometimes furnished. In certain cases, especially ads that are legal notices, an affidavit is also furnished.

Makegoods, Rebates, and Rip-offs

The verification procedures described so far are incomplete in some respects. They do not, of themselves, monitor the immediate environment in which an ad is broadcast, nor do they completely preclude opportunities for chicanery.

To handle the problem of the messages that surround a particular broadcast ad, broadcasters furnish advertisers with certain guarantees. These are often stated on rate cards or in the SRDS rate books. They can be negotiated as part of the advertising time purchase. Examples of such guarantees by broadcasters, often called "product protection" promises, are these:

"Station will endeavor, but cannot guarantee, to provide product protection of at least 10 minutes."

"Station will use reasonable care at all times to avoid scheduling of advertising in an obviously competitive atmosphere."

"Station will endeavor to provide a minimum of 15 minutes' separation between directly competitive products when both commercials are originated by the station."

"Station guarantees against running competitive products back to back only."

FIGURE 15–2

Whose eyes and ears are monitoring your most expensive TV spots?

Let BAR's videotape recorders be your eyes and ears in the three largest markets. We'll check your schedules every day of the year, 7 a.m. to 3 a.m. Missed spots, wrong copy, poor audio or video, clipped commercials, competitive conflicts ...we'll report them all hot off the tubes. Competitive schedules and copy themes are sent weekly, estimated expenditures monthly.

For details, call your nearest BAR sales office New York (212) 682-8500. Los Angeles (818) 956-5471. Chicago (312) 280-8262.

BROADCAST
ADVERTISERS
REPORTS, INC.
an SFN company

SOURCE: *Marketing and Media Decisions,* October 1985.

Most broadcasters offer advertising credits, or **makegoods,** only when ads for directly competing products are aired back to back and when the station (as opposed to the network and station) originates the advertising message. Management of the media schedule usually involves spot checks of the client's advertising, either by electronic verification or by inspecting broadcasters' logs, to ensure that product protection contract clauses have been observed by the broadcaster. If such promises are not kept, the broadcaster usually provides either a "free" ad in an "equivalent" time or else credits the advertiser with the cost of that particular ad.

In the short run, similar "conflicts" may exist between ads and the surrounding editorial or program material. Examples of such conflicts can be found in a political ad that is aired during a movie portraying politicians as venal, in an ad for an analgesic directly following a news story that analgesics were ineffective in the long-term treatment of tension headache, or a news story listing the five least crashworthy autos immediately preceding an ad for one of the five. Virtually no media enterprise offers product protection guarantees against this eventuality, though its regular occurrence would have unfavorable consequences for the broadcaster's or publisher's advertising revenues. This problem is most often handled in the negotiations for space or time, especially by advertisers who use the medium regularly.

Verification procedures also require the prevention (or, more realistically, the minimization) of **double billing** and **double stapling.** These abuses occur most often in cooperative retail advertising, in the print and broadcast media, respectively. While the details of such scams are varied, they are basically the substitution of an "unauthorized" message or an "inflated" rate for advertising purchased cooperatively by the manufacturer and the retailer. Verification procedures have been tightened by the industry to prevent double billing. However, since this exploitation requires conspiracy between media officials and retailers, such measures as affidavits are only a partial answer. Complete verification procedures should include reasonable measures to detect double billing, especially for advertising campaigns that employ significant amounts of co-op advertising.

ADJUSTING THE SCHEDULE DURING THE CAMPAIGN

In the discussion of media-buying processes presented in Chapter 5, we suggested that it would be foolhardy to construct a media plan in ignorance of what advertisers of similar products are doing. It would be equally foolish to disregard changes in the competitive environment during the life of the campaign.

Changes in the Competitive Environment

As you recall from Chapter 5, the size and timing of competitive pressure were incorporated into the media plan in one of the three ways: wave theory, media dominance, or media concentration. All three methods of dealing with competition reflect the fact that most advertising budgets are not large enough to overwhelm all competition in all media at all times. In fact, there are good managerial reasons for not even attempting to outspend all competitors on all fronts. But depending on the strategy used in building the media plan, changes in the competitive environment during the campaign can produce a situation that requires adjustments to the media plan.

Wave Theory Adjustments.   In wave theory, a large "wave" (or burst or flight) of advertising is followed by a hiatus (or pause). It is hoped that the wave's impact will be sufficient to produce audience impressions that will carry through the hiatus.

Recall also the problem identified in Figure 5–4, where a planned wave theory campaign is simply overwhelmed by competitive expenditures. In this situation, continuing with the planned schedule is likely to produce disappointing results. Among the adjustments that might be considered are the following:

Increasing the budget to "competitive" levels.

Increasing the expenditure during the wave period and increasing the length of the hiatus, so that fewer, larger bursts of advertising match the competition without increasing the total budget.

Switching to an alternative strategy.

Media Dominance Adjustments.   The second strategy, media dominance, permits the advertiser to "beat" the competition in a single medium for a specified time period, then switch to the dominance of a second medium, and so on. Of course, this strategy is likely to have maximum success only if the medium used is, in fact, "dominated."

If, during a campaign planned around media dominance, competitive expenditures are much larger than expected, the planned dominance may not be achieved. In this instance, some of the possible adjustments are these:

Increasing the budget to "competitive" levels.

Rearranging the sequence in which media are to be used. For example, the sequence newspaper–metro magazine–outdoor might become newspaper—outdoor—metro magazine. Such a rephasing of the schedule, even without additional expenditure, may permit the reestablishment of dominance.

Incorporating wave theory into the plan. In the dominated medium, the advertiser might use a burst-then-pause sequence, which creates the impression of "dominance" among the audience.

Switching to an alternative strategy.

Media Concentration Adjustments. The third strategy, media concentration, can also encounter unexpected competitive pressure. Since this strategy requires the selection of a single "best" medium, an unexpected competitive development can turn "best" into "not so good" or worse. Here the alternatives for adjustment include:

Increasing the budget to "competitive" levels.

Selecting another "best" medium.

Incorporating wave theory within the single medium used.

Changes in the Editorial Environment

The development of a media plan must, of course, take account of the editorial environment in which the advertising is to appear. Media planners are required to look beyond the numbers (such as GRP or CPM) to select editorial formats that will be harmonious with the advertising messages.

This editorial ambience can be imagined as the intellectual and emotional river that carries the advertiser's canoe. And as is the case with wilderness explorers, when the direction of the river deviates from the planned route, it may become necessary to leave the river and use another route.

Editorial environments are almost never static. However, changes in these environments can occur at either of two rates: evolutionary and revolutionary. Examples of evolutionary change include the expansion or contraction of a particular section in a newspaper or magazine, minor reformatting of a television news show, and the addition or deletion of a syndicated feature by a local radio station. Revolutionary changes can be produced by major changes in editorial policy (such as the recent decision of two television networks not to accept an advertisement of a major energy corporation) or by external events. Strikes, which force the suspension of publication, or major criticism of a television show by an influential group are examples of such externalities.

Changes in the Client Organization

In a fundamental sense, media planning is a staff function undertaken in support of the client organization's marketing objectives. When these objectives change, the supporting media plans must be reexamined and often recalculated to be consistent with the new objectives. Among the events that can produce revised marketing objectives for the advertiser are a new corporate philosophy, a new chief executive, technological breakthroughs that result in new or modified products, new competitive products, governmental action in the form of product recalls, the granting of patents, and new licensing for production and sale. These and many other events can produce changes in marketing objectives that must, in turn, be reflected in altered media plans.

Regardless of their source, adjustments to a carefully prepared media plan are not without risk. Adjustments that take the form of spending more money for advertising increase the capital investment. In the language of capital budgeting, such decisions increase the cash outflow and thereby increase the overall risk of the capital project. Adjustments that alter the placement, timing, or media mix of the original plan are accompanied with the very real prospect of cancelling out bulk or continuity media discounts, which had been an important part of the plan. And, of course, some media, especially television, have at least short-term limitation on the available inventory of space or time available for sale. Finally, the process of adjustment and replanning is itself a cost-incurring activity.

Prudence requires that adjustment costs be considered before adjustments to the media plan are implemented. But prudence also requires that a media plan that has been seriously invalidated by changes in the competition, the editorial environment, or the advertiser's marketing objectives be reconsidered. Adjustments that can be accomplished at reasonable cost and materially improve the prospects for advertising success are an important part of postscheduling management of the media plan. The calculation of "reasonable" costs can be developed by use of a decision tree of the type discussed in Chapter 2. The measurement of advertising success is the subject of the next section of this chapter.

EVALUATING THE EFFICIENCY OF THE MEDIA PLAN

It may seem evident that for advertising to be successful it must be efficient. And we can intuitively relate to the axiom that advertising, which is a cost-incurring activity, must produce returns above its costs to be economically justified. But to develop a more systematic understanding of advertising success, it is helpful to understand the concept of efficiency.

Definition of Efficiency?

The most useful notion of efficiency is an amalgam of economic theory and simple arithmetic. In this notion **efficiency** is defined as the simple ratio of output to input when both are measured in constant units, say dollars. Thus, if some process costs $10 to perform and produces $15 of returns, its efficiency is $15:$10, or 1.5.

In the physical and mechanical world in which we live, many processes are notoriously inefficient. If we measure the energy value of gasoline and the energy value produced by gasoline engines in autos, we find that the efficiency ratio fall in the range of .15 to .30. That is, less than a third of the energy value of the gasoline we put in a car is converted to energy used to move the car. The balance is wasted, mostly in the form of heat. And one of the most efficient areas of agriculture, fish farming, requires about 1.15 pounds of feed to produce a pound of fish. This is equivalent to an efficiency of 1:1.15, or about 87 percent.

In regard to advertising efficiency in general, and media efficiency in particular, it is relatively easy to measure the input side of the ratio. Net advertising expenditures (after allowances, discounts, and rebates) are combined with the cost of the human resources employed (i.e., wages and salaries) and the administrative or overhead cost required to produce the campaign. The sophisticated practitioner (or student) will then use these dollar inputs to calculate the net present value of the advertising project. This produces a relatively unambiguous measure of the input required for a particular advertising effort.

Unlike the horsepower of auto engines and the weight of catfish, which are outputs amenable to relatively unambiguous measurement, the output of an advertising campaign is often the subject of lively debate and disagreement among the interested parties. This controversy about advertising output can be divided into two problems: What is the proper set of goals or objectives for the ad campaign, and what are the proper methods of measuring the level at which those goals or objectives were realized?

As we suggested in Chapter 1, advertising objectives can be stated on one, two, or three levels: communications output, sales output, or profitability output. Of these three levels, the first two are the most frequently used measure of advertising success. These two are most often measured by syndicated research services or by other "custom job"-type research firms. You may wish to review, from Figure 2–9, the identities and sizes of the major advertising research firms in the United States.

Communicative Efficiency of the Media Plan

In circumstances where the communications level has been chosen to express advertising objectives, the measurement of advertising output or results ideally produces answers to three questions:

1. How may people were exposed to the ad(s)?
2. Who were these people?

3. To what extent were the exposed people involved in the ad(s), and what was the nature of this involvement?

A moment's reflection will suggest that the most familiar media statistics—such as reach, frequency, and Gross Rating Points—are largely methods of answering the first question, the extent of exposure. For the broadcast media, the *rating* and subsequent calculations derived from it are based on the exposure level of the program in which the ad was embedded—not necessarily on the exposure level of the ad per se. In print advertising, analogous measures of exposure as well as problems in calculating actual exposure to the ad (versus exposure to the medium) are found in circulation figures. Traffic counts for outdoor locations measure a similar exposure potential rather than a true exposure figure.

Answers to the second question, about audience identity, most often take the form of demographic profiles of the exposed audience or of subgroups within this audience. From the advertiser's viewpoint, this method is usually more useful than research that reveals the identity (name, address, etc.) of individual audience members, though direct mail can furnish the answer to this question in both forms.

Answers to the third question, about the extent and nature of audience involvement with the ad message, are the most varied and are subject to the highest level of controversy. Here mechanical, physiological, psychological, and many other measures have been employed.

You are already familiar with the most prominent measures of exposure and audience identity, those furnished by Nielsen and Arbitron for broadcast advertising. You are also cognizant of services such as Starch, which provide indications of audience involvement in print advertising. To provide a better overview of how advertising practitioners calculate communicative success, as well as the role that research firms play in furnishing these answers, an appendix to this chapter has been prepared. While this is not an exhaustive list of such research companies, the firms listed and their services are representative of the available measurements of advertising success.

Sales Efficiency of the Media Plan

The second level of advertising objectives, sales results, has the benefit of being measured in the same units as advertising inputs, namely dollars. Thus, the expressions of advertising and media efficiency are more directly formed than the expressions of communication objectives. Sales objectives can also be expressed in terms such as *brand share, market share, repurchase rate,* and other measures that convert to dollar values.

The crucial problem in using sales as a measure of efficiency is the accurate linking of sales to the advertising that produced them. In earlier chapters some methods have been suggested for evaluating sales response and decay and for discounting nonadvertising influences on sales. Here, it is important to recognize that not only the client, ad agency, and media enterprise can combine to produce the data required for such a sales-efficiency test of advertising. Some of the research firms that also offer such measurement services and examples are identified in the appendix.

The cost of research information varies. Some research reports, such as the CARR Report prepared by Cahners Publishing (and some of the media trade associations), are furnished at no cost. The costs of standard reports, such as those of Arbitron or Nielsen, begin at under $100 per copy. However, the cost of custom research begins at about $3,000 to $4,000 for studies using very small samples. The cost for a well-designed custom research project to measure recognition and recall, using a sample of around 300 subjects, is likely to cost $10,000 to $20,000.

Beyond Sales Response

To restate the problems of measuring advertising (and therefore media) efficiency, some dependent variables are less than satisfactory. It is also true that more preferred outcomes are difficult to measure. Nearly all parties agree that exposure measures, such as GRPs, represent only a partial measure of advertising success. On the other hand, attitudes, intentions, and other behavioral measures of inclination to purchase are difficult to measure precisely, and even then are not perfect correlates of sales. Net sales, the most theoretically pleasing dependent variable, is often contaminated by factors other than the current advertising campaign. Such contamination reduces the power of net sales as an output measure for efficiency calculations.

One alternative is to use "owner wealth" measures as the output part of the efficiency calculation. This is easy to do for publicly held firms, since the financial press provides daily figures for the value of common stocks. In this way, the collective wisdom of an information-efficient stock market, after looking at a company's overall success, places a value (price) on its common stock. Thus, not only advertising success, but success in other areas of the firm, is reflected in the price of its stock.

This approach to efficiency is still in its infancy, and not even its enthusiasts claim that it is problem free. It too suffers from some of the measurement contaminants associated with the net sales criterion. And while the possibility is unlikely, this approach could obscure the facts in the firm where poor-to-ordinary advertising is combined with superior performance in other management areas. And in the not-for-profit organization the approach is not possible.

Perhaps the strongest claim for the owner wealth approach is that it brings the question of advertising efficiency into conformity with the "acid test" used by the business community for business success. The units of measurement (dollars) are the same for both sides of the efficiency ratio. And if work progresses in this area, profitability measures of advertising success have great potential as a tool for the overall management of the media function.

APPENDIX:
EXAMPLES OF FIRMS PROVIDING
ADVERTISING MEDIA RESEARCH*

BROADCAST

A. C. Nielsen Company

A. C. Nielsen's data break down into two general areas: The Nielsen Television Index (NTI), which measures national TV viewing, and the Nielsen Station Index (NSI), which measures local TV viewing.

Nielsen now has more than 100 agency users accessing its two general data bases via computer. Most agency subscribers are on-line users, retrieving data with microcomputers or word processors, which are hooked up to the mainframe computers of secondary suppliers like Interactive Market Systems, Donovan, Market Science Associates, and Telmar. In the case of large agencies with their own mainframe computers—about half a dozen—magnetic tapes of the Nielsen data bases are available. In addition, Nielsen offers market data on floppy disks.

The company declined to discuss cost or user charges for any of its services, but sources say its fees for television data are similar to Arbitron's.

Nielsen Television Index, National Television Service

National Overnights—Household ratings and shares and projected household audience for national sponsored network programs. Based on a sample of 1,700 households in markets.

Ranking Report—Weekly report ranking all prime time programs for previous week. Also includes ratings/shares for programs, season to date.

Cume Facility—Designed to allow users to evaluate four-week reach and frequency of various uses of program schedules.

---

* SOURCE: *Marketing and Media Decisions*, April 1986, pp. 40–48.

National Audience Demographic Facility—Designed to allow users to compare programs on any selected target audience.

Preval/Postval—Designed to provide on-line delivery of network TV post-buy evaluation.

PRIZM—Designed to allow users to match television program profiles to product-usage patterns.

Nielsen Station Index, Local Television Service

Metered Market Overnights—Ratings and shares for local stations in 12 markets, based on a sample of 400–500 households varying by market.

Reach and Frequency—Designed to determine the number of different household/people viewing a proposed schedule and how much repeat viewing is included.

Duplication (Only-Only-Both)—Evaluate loyalty or turnover in terms of household/people viewing.

Special Ratings—Designed to evaluate demographic groups of particular interest (i.e., cable households, upper income, etc.).

Special Area Study—Designed to produce data by county grouping, zip code area, etc.

Geo-demographic—Evaluate the marketplace by product usage and lifestyle characteristics.

Arbitron Ratings Company

Like Nielsen, most of Arbitron's 200 subscribers access Arbitron's data base either via microcomputer or dumb terminals linked to a third-party processor. Likewise, computer tapes are available for all data bases if an agency wishes to load its own mainframe. Floppy disks are available as well.

Costs vary from $100 to $10,000, depending on the scope of the project. The average Arbitron's Information on Demand (AID) project is a couple of hundred dollars, according to Arbitron executives.

Unlike Nielsen, AID, in addition to providing access to the national and local television data, also provides radio data.

AID—Television

Reach and Frequency Report—Dissects basic audience rating to show the number of viewers a commercial is attracting.

Audience Share Report—Shows households watching television for specific programs.

Audience Flow Report—Tracks the movement of viewers between the two time periods.

Dayparts Report—Creates up to 100 custom dayparts, piecing together quarter hours.

Promotion AID—Examines audience of given daypart or program, then identifies other dayparts and programs that attract the same audience.

USAID—Provides nationwide audience estimates, based on a one-week sample of 5,000 diaries from each Arbitron's survey sweep.

Meter AID—Provides measurement of TV viewing in the 11 Arbitron meter markets.

Arbitrends II—Access to overnight data from 11 metered markets, accessible for microbased system, allowing user to manipulate data to show trends and rankings. (*Arbitrends I* is the printed report.)

Multimarket—New product based on Arbitrends II allows agencies to look at a program across all metered markets at a given point in time.

Meter/Diary Integrated Report—Combines demographic capabilities of diary information with meter data.

Percent of Duplicated Cume Report—Tells which stations share listeners, which have exclusive audiences, and how much or little of the target audience is shared with others having similar and/or different formats.

Target AID—Produces audience estimates based on lifestyle.

Arbitrends Radio—Most agency subscribers, about 100, subscribe to printed report, with only a dozen subscribing to an on-line version so far. The report provides updates to the standard radio market reports, updating each month rolling averages, giving more current information.

Target AID—Using ClusterPlus and PRIZM geodemographic profiles, Target AID reports audience estimates by lifestyle, as well as age and sex.

AID Radio

Reach and Frequency Report—Uses actual listener diaries to deliver gross impression, gross rating point, net reach, percent of market reached, cost of spot/schedule, cost per thousand, cost per point, average frequency, and cost per thousand net reach.

Audience Duplication Report—Tells which stations or groups of stations share the same audience.

Birch Radio

Birch Radio Ratings are available in printed reports and on line through secondary suppliers like Telmar and IMS and from software packages like Media Management Plus. Agencies pay processor on a bit-by-bit basis. The company publishes four quarterly reports for 215 markets and monthly reports in about 88 markets.

In addition, the company publishes two yearly qualitative reports covering 100 markets. Birch, as opposed to Arbitron, uses telephone interviewing rather than the printed diary methodology. The company says this technique allows it to collect not only demographic information, but social, economic, and product consumption information as well. Birch Radio now has agency, radio station, advertiser and other subscribers.

Birch Radio, like its competitor Arbitron, can also provide PRIZM geodemographic composites of the radio audiences it measures.

A new service, which sprang up this year, Birch Plus, was designed specifically for the microcomputer. It allows agencies to manage the quarterly reports, 12 monthly reports, and 2 qualitative reports. The system has the ability to do ratings, reach and frequency, and produces graphics as well. The system was produced in conjunction with Media Management Plus, hence the name, Birch Plus.

PRINT

Simmons Market Research Bureau, Inc.

Study of Media and Markets—A syndicated media and marketing survey based on 19,000 annual personal interviews with adults 18+ years of age. Hard copy is available in 43 volumes of data. On-line, this information is offered through Interactive Market Systems (IMS), Telmar, Market Science Associates (MSA), and Windsor Systems. Agencies are also offered the option of Xpedite!, which puts all the Simmons volumes on 45 diskettes, and Choices, the complete Study of Media and Markets on hard disk with software to do crosstabs, media cost rankings, and reach and frequency.

Information included audience measurements for 110 magazines, plus newspaper, television, cable, radio, outdoor, and yellow pages usage data; media imperatives/intermedia comparisons, 27 demographic breakouts; self-concept/buying style data; work-related activities; and information on 3,900 brands in some 800 product categories.

Lifestyle and Geodemography—Enhancement data of VALS, and Net/Nutritional Segmentation from additional questionnaires and PRIZM as applied to the Simmons sample.

National College Study 1985—Three volumes of data based on 2,000 interviews with full-time college undergraduates. Available in hard copy plus via the on-lines and Choices. Information includes media usage for

41 magazines, plus college newspapers, daily/weekly newspapers, comic books, radio, TV and cable; 19 demographic breakouts; self-concept/buying styles; attitudes/opinions; corporate image for 38 corporations; product usage for 300 + categories.

STARS-Simmons Teenage Research—Findings from 2,000 interviews with teenagers, 12–19, in SMRB households from the Media and Markets study. Same options as the National College Study, less college newspaper and corporate image reports.

Simmons-Scarborough 1985 Newspaper Ratings Study—Syndicated newspaper audience survey of adults 18 + in 56 ADIs, including the top 50. Four volumes, available in hard copy, through the on-line and via Choices. Measurements, based on a total sample of 73,000 telephone interviews, includes audience data on 177 daily newspaper/newspaper groups and 125 Sunday newspapers/newspaper groups; demographics in 20 categories; and seven breakouts of marketing and related data. In June 1986, Simmons and Scarborough ended this joint research venture. Both firms plan to continue with similar independent research projects.

Mediamark Research Inc.

While MRI has data available on television, radio, cable, and some newspaper media usage among its 20,000 annual sample, its readership scores for approximately 285 magazines, along with its product usage data, provided the anchor for this service.

MRI data is available on line from Interactive Market Systems (IMS), Telmar, Market Science Associates (MSA), and Windsor Systems. Data is made available in book form, and tape for feed into agency mainframes. This access has met with limited success, however, primarily due to the high cost and limited hardware.

Sylvia Cassell, vice president of sales administration, explains that the advent of disks with capacities large enough to hold MRI's data base, along with availability of cheaper PCs, has encouraged them to offer their numbers in new ways. An effort to market the tabulated magazine data on floppy disks did not fully meet the advertiser and agency needs, according to Cassell. So MRI is making available its magazine and demographic respondent data on floppies for IBM-compatible PCs to allow for a more customized use of the company's findings.

This will be followed in June or July with product usage data on floppies. The company's special studies—Business-to-Business, Upper Deck measuring the affluent market, and local Mediamarket studies of New York, Chicago, Los Angeles, San Francisco, Philadelphia, Boston, Washington, D.C., Cleveland, St. Louis, and Detroit—are currently available on line and may be offered via floppy for PC use if demand warrants.

Mendelsohn Media Research, Inc.

MMR's Survey of Adults and Markets of Affluence combines product and service usage data with readership habits for 86 publications in households with $50,000+ income. Findings are based on a national sample of 7,046 responding adults, contacted by mail in April, May, and June. The study is available in hard copy, on tape, and through the on-line services of IMS, MSA, and Telmar. Gerry Nunziato, assistant vice president, says they are currently studying the option of publishing the data on floppies. Costs for the study are $1,500 for agencies with $100 million or more in billings, $750 for those under $100 million, $750 for advertisers, and $28,500 for subscribing publications (though there are corporate discounts). Costs include the right to access information via the on-lines, though costs of time with the on-lines is figured separately with those services.

REVIEW QUESTIONS

1. What is the primary basis for the transactions required to purchase advertising media? What are some of the ways in which these transactions are facilitated?

2. How would you summarize the progress made to date in developing effective measures of intermedia equivalency?

3. Construct a sound argument for the abolition of makegoods.

4. List the probable reasons why employees of media enterprises might participate in a double-billing scheme. Make a second list of the reasons why national advertisers continue to tolerate a situation in which double-billing can occur.

5. How can a hiatus be used, under a strategy of media concentration, to make adjustments to changes in the competitive environment?

6. Construct a defensible definition of advertising efficiency.

7. Of the three standards for the communicative efficiency of the media plan, which would be the most useful to the advertising client? Why?

8. Use any index in your school's library that indexes *Advertising Age* and look up the news reports about Birch Radio. From your reading, how do you think this firm is different from Arbitron and Nielsen?

SUGGESTED ADDITIONAL READING

ADAMS, ARTHUR J., and MARK M. MORIARTY. "The Advertising-Sales Relationship: Insights from Transfer-Function Modeling." *Journal of Advertising Research* 21, no. 3 (June 1981), pp. 41–46.

BUNN, DEREK W. "Audience Presence during Breaks in Television Programs." *Journal of Advertising Research* 22, no. 5 (October/November 1982), pp. 35–39.

CABALLERO, MARJORIE J., and PAUL J. SOLOMON. "Effects of Model Attractiveness on Sales Response." *Journal of Advertising* 13, no. 1 (1984), pp. 17–23, 33.

CANNON, HUGH M. "A New Method for Estimating the Effect of Media Context." *Journal of Advertising Research* 22, no. 5 (October/November 1982), pp. 41–48.

"Cumulative GRP's Related to Brand Awareness." *Marketing News,* May 16, 1980, p. 10.

EMMRICH, STUART. "Major Study Details Ads' Effect on Sales." *Advertising Age,* June 21, 1982, pp. 1+.

GIGES, NANCY. "New Coupon Trap Set." *Advertising Age,* May 30, 1983, pp. 1+.

LITTLE, JOHN D. C. "Models and Managers: The Concept of a Decision Calculus." *Decision Sciences* 16, no. 4 (April 1970), pp. B466–85.

OSTLE, GLEN, V., and JOHN K. RYANS, JR. "Techniques for Measuring Advertising Effectiveness." *Journal of Advertising Research* 21, no. 3 (June 1981), pp. 19–22.

PFAFF, FRED. "The Simmons-Scarborough Split." *Marketing and Media Decisions,* October 1986, pp. 93–102.

"Rational TV Spots for New Products Earn High Scores." *Marketing News,* January 4, 1985, p. 11.

STEPHENS, NANCY. "The Effectiveness of Time-Compressed Television Commercials with Older Adults." *Journal of Advertising* 11, no. 4 (1982), pp. 48–55, 76.

"Verification Made Easy." *Marketing and Media Decisions,* November 1983, p. 56.

"Who's Ready for Telescan?" *Marketing and Media Decisions,* October 1984, pp. 76–88.

CHAPTER SIXTEEN

Future Trends in Advertising Media: Employment and Opportunities

Mary Kay Buckley has been with Grey Advertising for seven months as an assistant media planner and is about to become a media planner in her own right . . . . She had been told that media was the best place to learn the advertising business, the most feet-on-the-ground part of the business . . . Buckley found that many of the young people looking for media jobs had studied advertising or marketing in college and she believes that was helpful to them because they were familiar with the language of media. The interviewers seem to be looking for young people with some college courses in advertising or marketing.*

"High Hopes for Fledglings"

At the conclusion of each of the chapters dealing with the various mass media (Chapters 6–12), we discussed a particular medium's future outlook. Each of the media faces problems and opportunities; some are unique and some reflect outside forces or intermedia developments. The media planner of tomorrow must be both a specialist and a generalist to deal with these problems and opportunities. Naturally the media planner will continue to be a highly trained specialist in media strategy. However, the media planner, and the business executive with advertising responsibility, will also have to understand the interrelations between advertising media and the firm's basic marketing objectives. This final chapter concentrates on the media management function. In addition, the final section of the chapter discusses academic training and employment opportunities in advertising media planning.

---

* *Marketing and Media Decisions,* March 1984, p. 120.

THE MARKETING REVOLUTION

The post–World War II period was marked by the development of the marketing concept, which supported the idea that the consumer should be the focus of a firm's planning and development. This awareness of the consumer, based on a research orientation and an integration of a firm's marketing activities, has significant application for advertising media.

In recent years advertising has come to be viewed as a segment of marketing. Advertising objectives must flow from the marketing plan, and advertising that operates in ignorance of the firm's general marketing goals will probably fail. The problem with this concept of advertising as complementary to marketing is that it is too often neglected in the day-to-day operations of marketing and advertising agencies. The marketing/advertising marriage is often a shaky one. Advertisers sometimes want to do "their own thing" in the absence of a thorough knowledge of the marketing plan. Unfortunately, the usual result of this attitude is clever, even award-winning, advertising that entertains but rarely sells. The media planner must resist the temptation to be anything but a marketing professional. While any aspect of advertising planning must have its foundation in marketing, this is especially true for the media function.

Marketing, and the financial risks associated with it, have made audience segmentation a vital area of study. The job of the media planner centers on the notion of audience segmentation as it logically proceeds from the consumer orientation of the marketing concept. The media planner must first determine the best prospects and then match these prospects with the advertising media most likely to reach them economically.

The media planner must consider two major aspects of advertising media: those that are external to the advertising function and those that are part of the advertising function but not directly under the control of the media department. The media function is a subcategory of two larger functions, advertising and marketing. Within both marketing and advertising strategy, certain constraints guide the media planner. Generally, it is easier for the media planner to reach compromises among the various parts of the advertising function than to reach compromises between the advertising strategy and the marketing strategy. The marketing plan, on the other hand, generally dictates advertising activities, including media planning.

External Marketing Constraints on the Media Planner

Budget.   Normally the media planner is *given* a budget. Despite the fact that advertising media purchases may account for up to 80 percent of a typical advertising budget, the input of media departments at the initial stages of corporate budgeting remains woefully inadequate.

Target Audience and Competition.   The media planner does not determine who to reach. Normally the client knows who the best prospects are and the degree of competition that will be encountered in attempting to gain them as customers. As the number of prospects or the aggressiveness of competitors increases, the media buyer must become more efficient with the budget allocated.

Price and Distribution.   The choice of distribution channels and the pricing policy of a product often dictate the choice of advertising media. Decisions in these areas often determine the demographic profile of the potential audience. As discussed in Chapter 5, demographic matching is most often utilized in purchasing media time and space.

Specific Product Restrictions.   Legal and regulatory restrictions play a larger role in advertising than ever before. In addition to the obvious broadcast restrictions applying to advertising for such products as liquor and cigarettes, the media buyer must be aware of a number of other restrictions, including those developed by individual media vehicles. For instance, many broadcasters don't accept certain feminine hygiene products, and almost 15 percent of weekly newspapers refuse to carry liquor advertising.

Internal Marketing Constraints on the Media Function

Creative Considerations.   The adoption of some creative strategies eliminates certain media buys. Product demonstrations are difficult in the print media and impossible in radio. A strategy of coupon promotions must be confined to print vehicles.

Qualitative Factors.   Media people are often criticized, and probably with some justification, for an overdependence on numbers. The media buyer must recognize that regardless of what research reveals about reach, frequency, and cost efficiency, the image of the product must be matched with the tone of the various media alternatives.

Message Complexity.   In addition to considering the creative approach and the tone of the advertising message, the media planner must consider its length and complexity. For example, television and outdoor advertising are unsuitable vehicles for long messages, since only a small amount of information can be conveyed in a 10-second television commercial or on an outdoor poster.

Factors Largely Controlled by the Media Planner

Choice of Media Vehicles. The media planner largely determines which media vehicles to purchase. These decisions are based on primary and secondary research and may be made in consultation with other members of the advertising and marketing departments. However, the final decision and responsibility for media choice usually lie with the media planner.

Media Scheduling. A primary responsibility of the media planner is the scheduling of advertising among the media vehicles selected. The skill with which the number and frequency of insertions are determined separates the professional media planner from the novice. The media planner who makes excessive commitments in certain media vehicles will expend the budget before effectively reaching all prospects. The media planner who buys too many vehicles may spread the advertising impact too thin for effective communication.

Allocating the Total Budget to the Various Media Components. It is the media planner who initially decides what proportions of the advertising media budget will be allocated to the various components of the media mix. This decision, of course, is made in consultation with other members of the advertising staff or, in an agency, with the account team.

   In summary, the media planner, like all advertising personnel, should be marketing oriented. This appreciation of the total marketing program by advertisers is not a one-way street. The wise marketing executive, even where an outside advertising agency is employed, should develop a knowledge of and appreciation for the overall advertising program.

THE MANAGEMENT REVOLUTION

Media Planning and the Management Function

In a simplistic fashion, the typical corporation can be characterized as consisting of production, marketing, and finance functions. Corporate management seeks to maximize profitability by operating each of these areas in the most efficient manner possible. While this approach seems like common sense, it is easier to approve in the abstract than to accomplish in reality.

   The management of the advertising function is twofold. First, corporate leadership must be aware of the expense and the accompanying risks of advertising media expenditures. Second, the media function must be creatively managed by those with primary advertising responsibility.

The Media Function as Managed by Executives Outside the Advertising Department

The type of control exercised by corporate management over advertising will vary, but typically the media function is carried out by advertising agencies or other outside organizations. However, the responsibility for the control and approval of media selections, or any other advertising task, is the job of the executive overseeing the advertising program. The person in charge of advertising is often the vice president for marketing or someone in a similar position. Basically the job of this executive is to:

1. Inform the advertising agency of corporate marketing objectives and develop research from which the advertising plan is developed in consultation with the agency.
2. Review and approve the overall advertising strategy developed by the agency.
3. Coordinate the marketing and other promotional activities of the firm with advertising. These include, but are not limited to, public relations, sales promotion, sales management, and distribution. The communications function also includes such tasks as representing the advertising department to top corporate management.

The interest of corporate management in advertising has grown in proportion to the greater investment required and the resulting sales success, especially in television advertising, among national advertisers. With annual corporate advertising expenditures often exceeding $50 million and sometimes representing 10 percent or more of total sales, advertising may be a firm's single largest expenditure.

The media responsibility of corporate management is not confined to ensuring the efficient use of advertising expenditures. Top management must also be aware of the public's reaction to the media in which the firm's advertising appears. Despite disclaimers to the contrary, much of the public regards the purchase of time or space as an endorsement of media editorial or entertainment content.

The Media Function and the Corporate Advertising Department

Too often we assume that when a company employs an advertising agency, there is little to be done by the corporate advertising department. Actually several major functions must be performed by the advertising department even when an outside agency is being used.

Client-Agency Liaison. The corporate advertising department has major responsibility for developing a smooth liaison between the agency and the company. This liaison includes checking to make sure that the agency's work meets the client's requirements and that the media budget is being spent efficiently. The degree of input concerning media expenditures varies widely. A few firms leave the media buying solely to the discretion of the agency, while a firm such as Colgate-Palmolive Company has its own media director to work in concert with its several agencies.

Developing the Marketing Plan.   Ideally, the advertising department should be consulted in the firm's preparation of its overall marketing plan and its advertising budget. Enlightened firms give major input to the advertising department while developing marketing strategy. However, too many firms still complete their marketing strategies without consulting the advertising department and then simply direct the advertising department or the outside agency to draw up a complementary advertising plan.

Choosing an Advertising Agency.   Normally the advertising department is given a major share of the responsibility for choosing an advertising agency. Often the advertising department is asked to prepare a profile of several agencies and a recommendation. The final selection is then based on this recommendation.

Preparing Creative Material.   Often the advertising department is given the task of preparing creative materials that are noncommissionable for an agency. Direct mail pieces, point-of-purchase displays, and various types of specialty items are examples.

The In-House Agency

In the previous discussion we have assumed that the company has hired an outside full-service advertising agency. However, many companies use an in-house agency, which can be one of two major types: (1) an in-house agency that prepares the total advertising program for the firm and, more commonly, (2) an in-house agency that performs some advertising functions and contracts outside for other services, such as media placement. In either case, the size of the internal advertising staff and its breadth of responsibility are much greater than they would be in the more usual client/full-service agency relationship.

TECHNOLOGY AND MANAGING THE MEDIA FUNCTION

Much has been written about the dramatic changes in media technology during the last decade. The media planner and those responsible for the advertising program must be aware of two basic types of technological changes related to advertising media:

1. Those changes affecting the opportunities for using the media more effectively for advertising.
2. Those changes affecting the ways in which the media function itself is carried out.

Advertising and the Changing Media Environment

To some extent every change in media technology has an effect on advertising. However, some recent innovations offer, or will offer, dramatic opportunities and problems for media planners. The following discussion gives an idea of these changes and their potential ramifications for advertising.

Cable and Satellite Communication.   The advent of home cable and satellite distribution of programming brought quality reception to homes in fringe areas and has begun to deliver programming from great distances. The dramatic predictions of the potential consequences of cable include the demise of local stations in favor of a few supernetworks communicating directly to home receivers.[1]

Cable is currently presenting some problems for media planners because of the audience fragmentation that occurs even when cable programming itself is largely ignored. Previously the media planner's decisions were confined to a three-network choice during prime-time. Now the audience is being segmented increasingly among 12 or more channels, including pay television services, which may exclude advertising but siphon off viewers. What makes the problem more acute is that the fragmentation is generally occurring among an upscale audience. A recent survey showed that 50.7 percent of all households with annual incomes of $50,000 or more subscribe to pay cable.[2]

At the end of 1985, cable TV reached about 46 percent of U.S. households, and it is expected to reach a 50 percent penetration in 1986. Yet, in the 10 largest markets, almost 70 percent of households do not have access to cable.[3] Nevertheless, some advertisers and their agencies appear to have mastered this rapidly changing medium. Figure 16–1 shows the client list, cable networks used, and cable billings for Young & Rubicam, the leading cable agency in 1985.

---

[1] Lawrence J. Tell, "Station Break—Independent TV Operators Headed for a Shakeout," *Barron's,* January 6, 1986, p. 13.

[2] Don Veraska and Len Strazewski, "Cable TV Special Report," *Advertising Age,* December 5, 1985, p. 16.

[3] Ibid., p. 15.

FIGURE 16–1 The Top Agency in Cable, by Billings, during 1985

YOUNG & RUBICAM	Key to abbreviations
Clients using national cable: AT&T Cadbury Canada Dry Chiquita Banana Clorox Colgate-Palmolive Disney Productions Dr Pepper Du Pont Ford Corp. Ford Division Frito-Lay General Foods Jamaica Tourist Bureau Johnson & Johnson Kentucky Fried Chicken Kodak Lincoln-Mercury Division Merrill Lynch NYNEX Oil of Olay Olympic Stain/Paint Richardson-Vicks RJR Foods Suzuki U.S. Postal Service Warner-Lambert **Networks used:** A&E, CBN, CNN, CNNHS, TNN, Nickelodeon, TWC, BET, SIN, FNN, Lifetime, MTV, USA, WTBS, ESPN 1985 billings: $45 million Projected 1986: $50-$52 million	**A&E:** Hearst/ABC Video Enterprise Alpha Repertory Television Service. Cultural programing, relaunched as Arts & Entertainment January 1984. **BET:** Black Entertainment Television. Black-oriented sports, features and movies. **CBN:** CBN Cable Network. General interest, all-family drama, sitcoms, westerns. **CNN:** Cable News Network. Ted Turner's 24-hour, all-news channel. **CNNHS:** Cable News Network Headline Service. Brief international and national news update. **ESPN:** Entertainment and Sports Programing Network, a sports channel. **FNN:** Financial News Network. Financial/investments news and stock quotations. **LIFETIME:** Women's service/health and fitness from Hearst/ABC/Viacom Entertainment Services. **MSG:** Madison Square Garden Sports. **MSN:** Modern Satellite Network. General information channel, including the Home Shopping Show. **MTV:** 24-hour contemporary music channel; part of MTV Networks, a subsidiary of Viacom International, Inc. **Nickelodeon:** All-children's programing; part of MTV Networks, a subsidiary of Viacom International, Inc. **SIN:** National Spanish Television Network. All Spanish programing. **SPN:** Satellite Programing Network. Talk shows, movies, how-to. **TNN:** The Nashville Network. Country/western music, with variety, comedy and sports. **TWC:** The Weather Channel: Landmark Communications' 24-hour national, regional and local weather information with special weather features. **USA:** USA Cable Network. Sports, women's talk shows, children's. **VH-1:** Video Hits One, adult music video channel from MTV Networks, a subsidiary of Viacom International, Inc. **WTBS:** Ted Turner's WTBS-TV, Atlanta, superstation.

SOURCE: *Marketing and Media Decisions*, February 1986, p. 100.

The media planner will find the "viewing" audience more and more fragmented because of an increase in the use of the videocassette recorder and pay television. For instance, the problem of fragmentation will increase if projections for rapid growth in pay-per-view TV prove correct. How advertising will fit into pay television systems remains a question. Some see a willingness on the part of a large segment of the population to pay to exclude advertising altogether. Others think that the audience willing and able to pay the full cost of programming is very small and that some type of advertising will eventually enter most of these pay systems. Also, predictions include videotapes with and without advertising messages, with those including advertising priced lower, and the inclusion of a limited amount of advertising between programming on regular pay television.

In December 1977 Warner Communication began an era of two-way cable television with a test system in Ohio. A small cable control mechanism allowed viewers to answer quiz show questions, place orders for merchandise, and participate in straw votes on local political topics. Some restaurant advertisers took reservations from this system, and travel brochures could be ordered during commercials. While a complete evaluation of two-way cable is still some years away, it is evident that television advertisers will be making dramatic adjustments to current advertising practices.

Cable also offers opportunities for realistic research in a home environment. With the coming of two-way cable, researchers can inexpensively document the cable audience and gather information about specific commercials.

The battles over in-home satellite reception also complicate media planning. In 1986, an estimated 1.5 million households had purchased satellite dishes, only to find that HBO, Showtime, and the "superstations" had scrambled signals. Dish owners were faced with the need to purchase a descrambler (at about $400) and also pay a monthly service fee.[4] The media planning problem is created by uncertainty over which of the previously "free" channels will be purchased by which portions of the dish-owning audience.

Print Media Selectivity.   Magazines and, more recently, newspapers have been faced with the problem of competing with the broadcast media for advertising dollars. The print media have long recognized that immediacy and timeliness are attributes that must be conceded to broadcasting. Magazines were the first, followed more recently by newspapers, to respond to the challenge of the broadcast media by building their audiences on in-depth specialization of content that the broadcast media are at present unable to provide.

Selective content is an advantage to a medium only if it can be directed to a selective audience that can then be delivered to advertisers. In the future, as broadcast covers the mass audience, print will succeed through appeals to audience subgroups. Advertisers will expect both

---

[4] "Scrambling for Security," *Advertising Age*, December 5, 1985, p. 27.

magazines and newspapers to offer audience breakouts by geography, demographics, and ultimately perhaps by product preference.

TECHNOLOGY AND THE MEDIA-PLANNING ENVIRONMENT

In addition to the many aspects of media that are currently being changed by new technological developments, technology is changing the methods used by the media planner. It is bringing greater sophistication to the media-buying process. Basically, the media planner is adapting to computer research and the buying opportunities that it makes possible. Media planning has improved dramatically in three major areas in the last few years.

Methodological Improvements.   The selection of the research sample to a great extent determines the value of the information provided by a study. During the last decade, organizations such as the Advertising Research Foundation, faced with industry criticism of media research methodology, have given increasing attention to the problem.

Despite the problems of ascertaining the validity of media research, one must be encouraged by the interest in the topic. Some concrete changes in methodology can be cited. An example is the so-called Extended Sample Frame (ESF), used by Arbitron in placing radio diaries. The technique electronically selects telephone numbers at random. This overcomes the problem of unlisted telephone numbers and includes a more representative sample of the listening population than is obtained when the sample is confined to households with listed telephone numbers.

Improvements in Timeliness of Media Research Information.
Advertisers often complain about the excessive amount of data available. Nielsen and Arbitron together publish more than 300 reports annually at costs that can exceed $100,000 for a large agency. A major problem with media research is that more information can be produced than can be analyzed properly. Much of it is duplicated by other sources. Unfortunately a great deal of this information leaves much to be desired. The current controversies over magazine audience accumulation, out-of-home radio audience, and discrepancies in Nielsen and Arbitron data indicate that improvements in media research are needed. With the continuing growth of syndicated research services, a major job of the media planner is to decide which service to purchase.

Sophistication of Data Analysis.   The computer has created a type of mini-industry devoted to analyzing, restructuring, and modeling the information provided by syndicated research companies. Most major agencies and advertisers subscribe to at least one of these services. Companies such as Telmar, Interactive Market System (IMS), and Marketronics have become as important to media planners as the syndicated services themselves.

By the second half of the 1980s, personal computers had revolutionized many kinds of advertising data analysis, especially media analysis. Of course, computers had long been used for advertising analysis, but the advent of widespread microcomputer use removed layers of misinformation and mumbo-jumbo that had previously existed. Now, analysts produce many of their own analyses, at their own work stations, without having to appeal to someone in a white coat who speaks a mysterious language. The analyses can be obtained from the micro almost instantaneously. By 1986, Ayer, Simmons, Telmar, and Interactive Market System had each staked out important shares as suppliers of software for doing media (and other) analysis via microcomputer.[5]

EDUCATIONAL TRAINING FOR MEDIA PLANNING

Before we discuss the academic background needed for a successful career in media planning, we should first examine the type of skills and personality needed for a career in media. The media-planning function demands both analytical skills and skills in working with people, a combination that is not often found in the same individual. The media buyer and planner must be thorough and careful, but also be able to negotiate effectively in making media purchases and to communicate the media plan to other advertising executives. While no one can give a formula for success in any field, there are four areas that the student should consider in planning a career in advertising media.

1. *Strong Marketing Foundation.* If there is one absolute necessity for a successful career in advertising, it is a strong foundation in basic marketing principles. No one can fully understand advertising without a knowledge of the larger marketing area of which it is a part. Any marketing course would be of some value to the advertising student. However, the basic marketing course, market research, and consumer behavior should constitute the core of any marketing program designed to complement advertising.

2. *Research Emphasis.* All areas of advertising, but especially media, have become increasingly analytical. To interpret and analyze the

---

[5] Rich Zahradnik, "Media's Micro Age," *Marketing and Media Decisions,* April 1986, pp. 34 + .

abundance of data necessary for media planning, the student should have a facility for analytical skills. An introductory course in statistics is essential, and an additional statistics course and a research methodology course would be extremely helpful. The student should keep in mind that the major purpose of research training is to allow decision making and forecasting based on valid and reliable data. Obviously, unless a person has the background to make such judgments, serious error can result.

3. *Practical Experience and Internships.* Advertising is an extremely competitive field, and any practical experience a student brings to the job market is an advantage. Perhaps the best type of experience is summer internships coordinated between employers and colleges, often with academic credit. The college placement office usually has a list of summer jobs and internships, but students should also write employers directly about employment. (See Figure 16–2.)

Students should not limit themselves to advertising agency internships when looking for a part-time job. Media reps, media advertising and circulation departments, and corporate advertising departments all may provide part-time employment. In addition, many campuses have commercial media run by students that require student advertising salespeople. An example is the college newspaper that accepts paid advertising. Finally, directories such as *The Student Guide to Mass Media Internships* are often available at college placement offices; these list both advertising and circulation openings.

4. *Extracurricular activities.* Employers place major importance on outside activities of students as well as grade-point averages. Students should participate in college advertising clubs and volunteer for communication jobs in other organizations. Advertisers are looking for energetic, intelligent, self-starters. This is the image you should project.

EDUCATION FOR A CAREER IN ADVERTISING

Advertising professionals have varying opinions about the best preparation for a career in advertising, but two consistent themes are heard. A broad liberal arts education is beneficial, and some marketing background is helpful. In specialized areas such as account management, the Master of Business Administration degree is often preferred, while those students interested in art may be encouraged to attend an art institute or a department of commercial art.

Most of the largest agencies and many of the smaller ones rely on a combination of college course work and on-job training to prepare the newly hired employee. Especially in media jobs, the rule is that formal training programs are part of the first-year work experience. Figure 16–3 outlines what a new media person should be able to do.

FIGURE 16–2 **Student Internship Opportunity**

LEARN/EARN -- SUMMER '87

DIRECT MARKETING INTERNSHIPS
in New York Metropolitan Area

* Work 8-10 weeks with a top direct marketing firm as a paid intern
* Gain practical hands-on experience related to your goals and interests
* Discover new career options
* Learn about all aspects of direct marketing at weekly seminar sessions

APPLICATIONS DUE FEBRUARY 4, 1987

See Department Chairperson or
Career Office for forms/information

 Sponsored by:
DIRECT MARKETING
EDUCATIONAL FOUNDATION

WOMEN'S DIRECT RESPONSE GROUP
NEW YORK

SOURCE: The Direct Marketing Educational Foundation, Inc., 6 East 43rd Street, New York, NY 10017.

FIGURE 16–3   What Every Media Trainee Should Learn

---

1. The basics of media language and Media Math 101. Trainees should be able to do an eyeball analysis of shares, ratings, and GRPs without a computer or calculator.

2. How to write a media plan, starting from a quick overview of the marketing objectives to a rationale for media choices. How to present the conclusions. Could be taught through role playing or a quick course in acting.

3. The value of research tools in marketing and media analyses to gauge magazine readership and product usage data. How to put that knowledge to work.

4. How to translate learned skills into actual case studies. Some media training programs give students hypothetical case histories for development of media plans. These are later presented to their supervisors for review.

5   Insight into media options through an awareness of the strengths and weaknesses of each medium and an understanding of new developments in each field.

6. How to work with creative and account management teams. Importantly, how to incorporate marketing judgments into strategic media decisions.

7. An intuitive feeling of when it's time to stop analyzing and bring the options to an orderly conclusion. Should be able to put all the bits and pieces in a logical plan and to understand the concept beneath the task.

8. An understanding of marketing concepts such as test marketing and off-price couponing.

9   How to handle diverse assignments, from packaged goods to retail accounts.

10. How to interface with the client, with perhaps a short course on particular client no-no's.

SOURCE: *Marketing and Media Decisions,* February 1986, p. 38.

EMPLOYMENT OPPORTUNITIES

Advertising Agencies.   Entry-level jobs in the media area, like all advertising jobs, are competitive. Over the last several years agency employment has represented a stable market at best. In 1965, 75,000 people were employed in advertising agencies, but this number dropped to 74,000 in 1975. However, the job market is better in media departments than in many other advertising agency departments. A survey conducted by the American Association of Advertising Agencies (4As) showed that of 529 entry-level positions, 214 (40.4 percent) were in the media department of member agencies, with the majority going to people holding only the baccalaureate degree.[6]

Media jobs, both entry-level and more senior positions, tend to pay less than creative or account management jobs. The salary differential between an agency creative director and his counterpart in media often amounts to $10,000 to $20,000. However, media departments offer an excellent opportunity for advancement within agencies.

---

[6] Edward J. Rogers, "A Practitioner's Thoughts on Advertising Education," in *Sharing for Understanding,* (East Lansing, Mich. American Academy of Advertising, 1977), p. 194.

FIGURE 16–4 Agency Executive Compensation

1985 Total Cash Compensation
1,654 top executives—all ad agencies

($73,600 average total compensation)

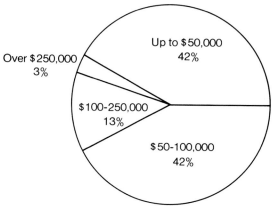

SOURCE: Reprinted with permission *Advertising Age*, May 19, 1986, p. 1. Copyright Crain Communications, Inc.

In 1986, entry level salaries for agency media jobs ranged from $24,000 to $30,000. Top starting media salaries went to those joining agencies located away from New York, Los Angeles, or Chicago. Salary premiums in less-glamourous locations were as high as 30 percent, compared to New York/Los Angeles wages.

Typically the entry-level media position in a larger agency is that of the media **estimator.** The media estimator, sometimes called an assistant media buyer, gathers cost and scheduling information to support the actual media buys done by more experienced personnel. The next level is that of the media buyer. This person negotiates for broadcast buys and supervises the contracting and scheduling of space and time. The coordinator of media strategy is the media planner, who, in consultation with the account team and the client, develops the broad direction of the media strategy for one or several accounts. Depending on the size of the agency, there may be one media planner or several working under an overall media director who is usually an agency vice president. In a small agency these functions are carried out by fewer people, and in some cases a very small agency may elect to have the account executive handle the media-buying function.

Newly hired agency employees are somewhat disappointed by the initial salary levels, and this source of discontent commands industry

---

FIGURE 16–5 Expectations about Career Trajectory

---

1. Assume you are a 22-year-old college graduate who has just been hired as a buyer in the media department at a large advertising agency. At what age do you hope to achieve each of the following titles? (Base = 90)

Title	Median Age
Media planner	24
Group media planner	26
Senior media planner	27
Media director	33
Executive vice president media services	38
Agency management	40

2. Do you feel such guidelines are realistic in measuring your career progress?

Yes	67.8%
No	31.1%
No answer	1.1%

3. Would failing to meet your title goals cause you to change employers?

Yes	65.6%
No	33.3%
No answer	1.1%

4. Which is more important to you, your salary or your title?

Salary	80.0%
Title	15.6%
Equal/NA	4.4%

5. How many job changes do you expect to make in your career?

4

SOURCE: *Marketing and Media Decisions*, May 1986, p. 148–49.

attention.[7] However, those who persevere and succeed in the agency business are well compensated. Figure 16–4 shows the results of a recent survey of agency executive compensation. Figure 16–5 gives an indication of the expectations held by junior agency employees for the time requirements for promotion to agency management.

Nonagency Media Jobs. To the surprise of many students the majority of entry-level advertising media positions are not in advertising agencies. These jobs may lead to agency employment or may themselves provide satisfying lifetime jobs.

---

[7] Lisa Rae Gossels, "Luring the Young to Mad. Ave.", *Advertising Age*, August 4, 1986, p. 18.

Media Time and Space Salespeople. Even the smallest newspaper, magazine, or broadcast station employs media salespeople. At smaller media, these positions not only offer excellent experience, but the salary plus commission for an aggressive space and time seller are usually far above the income obtainable from comparable news and editorial entry-level jobs. Because the turnover is relatively high among smaller media, jobs are often available for a person who is willing to move to a small town.

Sales jobs at media in the top 20 markets, as well as broadcast networks and national magazines, can be lucrative. A top salesperson for a large medium will often earn more than top agency media directors, although the competition to get and hold these jobs is fierce.

Media Representatives. As discussed earlier (see Chapter 5), the media representative, commonly known as a rep, is the middleman between advertising media buyers and sellers. Usually the rep deals directly with advertising agencies, although it is not uncommon for reps to go directly to the client.

The advertising rep holds a specialized job. An individual salesperson normally deals with only one medium, such as newspapers or television. Media planners often depend on reps for detailed media information, so the rep's job is not for an amateur. However, large rep organizations do employ media estimators who perform a function similar to that performed by media estimators in agencies.

Independent Media-Buying Services. Independent media-buying services are employed primarily by companies that do not use full-service agencies and by very small agencies that use them as a media department. Since the independent media buyer survives through skillful negotiation, usually in broadcast time, entry-level positions normally are not available.

THE FUTURE

Media buying and selling offer an exciting and lucrative career for men and women. With the current competition for advertising jobs and the specialized skills needed for media, the student must analyze his talents objectively before pursuing a media career. The relatively rare combination of a faculty for numbers and a people orientation is a prerequisite for success in media. Only those who are willing to work hard and who find fulfillment in analyzing marketing and media information should consider media planning as an occupation.

REVIEW QUESTIONS

1. How does the media function relate to the marketing concept and marketing segmentation?
2. Briefly discuss three external and three internal marketing constraints on the media function.
3. What are some of the major media responsibilities of a corporate advertising department in a firm employing an outside advertising agency?
4. Discuss how the "electronic revolution" will affect (*a*) television, (*b*) print, and (*c*) direct response advertising.
5. Discuss the basic function of the following:
   a. The advertising agency media department.
   b. Media reps.
   c. The individual medium's salespeople.

SUGGESTED ADDITIONAL READING

"Agency Compensation." *Advertising Age,* May 19, 1986, p. 1 +.

"Agency People Offer Some Advice to the Industry's Newcomers." *Adweek,* June 28, 1982, p. 40.

American Association of Advertising Agencies, Committee on Client Service Series, "What Every Account Representative Should Know About . . .
Account Management, 1978.
Agency Management, 1978.
Broadcast Business Affairs, 1980.
Co-op Advertising, 1983.
Cost Control and Profit Responsibility, 1980.
The Creative Function, 1979.
Creative Research, 1978.
Developing New Business, 1981.
Electronic Data Processing, 1981.
Library Research, 1980.
Market Research, 1980.
Media, 1981.
Oral Presentations, 1979.
Organizing the Work, 1980.
Print Production, 1978.
Publicity and Public Relations, 1979.
The Relationship of Copywriting and Research, 1979.
Sales Promotion, 1978.
Television Commercial Production, 1979.
Working with Field Salesmen, 1979.
Writing Plans and Recommendations, 1977.
Yellow Pages Advertising, 1980.

COLFORD, STEVEN W. "Congress Eyes Ad Industry Future." *Advertising Age,* September 30, 1985, p. 40.

COLVIN, GEOFFREY. "Long Hours + Bad Pay = Great Ads." *Fortune,* July 23, 1984, pp. 77–79.

GOLDRING, NORMAN. "Future Lies in a Place Called 'Media.'" *Advertising Age,* November 3, 1986, p. 68.

GOSSELS, LISA RAE. "Luring the Young to Mad. Ave." *Advertising Age,* August 4, 1986, pp. 18, 22.

"High Hopes for Fledglings." *Marketing and Media Decisions,* March 1984, pp. 66–124.

"How Do Reps Represent—And Present—Their Media." *Advertising World,* April 1985, pp. 12–14, 22.

"Is Your Career on Track?" *Marketing and Media Decisions,* May 1986, pp. 148–49.

"Salary Survey: Who Gets How Much, Where and Why." *Adweek,* July 1982, pp. SS3–SS46.

Standard Directory of Advertisers. Wilmette, Ill.: National Register Publishing Company, current edition.

Standard Directory of Advertising Agencies. Wilmette, Ill.: National Register Publishing Company, current edition.

TRACY, ELEANOR JOHNSON. "Envy of Madison Avenue: A Minneapolis Advertising Agency." *Fortune,* March 4, 1985, p. 89.

"The Twists and Turns of Media Training." *Marketing and Media Decisions,* December 1985, pp. 38–41.

"A" counties. Counties located in the 25 largest metropolitan areas.

Adjacency. The time between programs. Commercials during this period are usually sold by local stations.

Advertising allocation. The total funds planned for advertising for a time interval or for an entire campaign.

Advertising Checking Bureau, Inc. Organization that provides advertisers with tear sheets of their advertisements. Often used to verify cooperative advertising.

Advertising decay. The diminishing but still present effect of past advertising on present demand.

Advertising elasticity of demand. The proportional change in demand, given a unit change in advertising expenditures.

Advertising exposure. One person or home exposed to a single medium. Advertising exposures are often accumulated for all media in an advertiser's schedule.

Advertising response. The effect on sales (or some other measure) produced by advertising.

Affiliate. A radio or television station that contracts with a network to carry some portion of the network's programming.

Agate line (or simply **line**). A measurement of newspaper space, one column wide and $\frac{1}{14}$ of an inch deep.

Aided recall. Recall measured with the help of a copy of the publication being studied.

Amplitude modulation (AM). Oldest and most popular form of transmitting radio signals.

Annual discount. Advertising discount based on number of advertisements placed during a 52-week period.

Appropriations budget. A budget containing a fixed level of expenditure and/or revenue.

Arbitron. With A. C. Nielsen, one of the two major broadcast rating services. Also the name of the electronic data-gathering device used to monitor television set usage.

437

Area of Dominant Influence (ADI). A geographic area consisting of all counties in which the home market stations receive a preponderance of total viewing hours. Also referred to as designated market area, or DMA.

Audience composition. The percentage of some market segment within the total audience of a medium.

Audience overlap. The extent to which two or more vehicles share common audience members.

Audience turnover. The rate at which a medium accumulates audience over time. It is determined by dividing the reach by the average audience.

Audilog. The listener diary used by A. C. Nielsen.

Audimeter. The electronic recorder used by A. C. Nielsen to measure set usage.

Availabilities (avails). In broadcasting, the time available for sale by the station.

Average audience rating. The percent of a demographic group that viewed during the average minute of a particular program.

Average issue readership. The number of persons in a target market who will see or read a given issue of a publication.

Average quarter-hour persons. The average number of listeners to a station during any quarter-hour of a daypart.

Average time spent listening. The time an average person listens to a particular radio station.

Away-from-home listening index. A station's proportion of away-from-home audience compared to the typical away-from-home proportion for that market.

"B" counties. Counties with populations over 150,000 that are not "A" counties, as well as counties that are a part of the metropolitan area of cities in these counties.

Back-translation. This process first translates to the second language and then uses a second translator to retranslate back to the first language.

Barter. In media, usually refers to trading space or time by a medium in return for merchandise. In broadcasting, an advertiser may provide a program free of charge to a station in exchange for having the station run the program. The program will normally carry commercials for the advertiser who provides it as well as open time that can be sold by the station.

Billable services. Services not covered by agency commission and therefore billed to clients.

Billing. In media billing, refers to the total amount of money purchases for a client by an advertising agency.

Brand demand. Demand for a particular branded product.

Budget. A financial plan.

Bulk discount. Discount offered to advertisers who contract for a certain quantity of insertions on a monthly or yearly basis.

"C counties. Counties with populations of over 35,000, which are neither "A" nor "B" counties. Also counties that are part of the metropolitan areas of cities in "C" counties.

Capital budget. A financial plan for projects lasting longer than one year which takes into account the time value of money.

Car card. An advertising message that appears within a public vehicle.

Card rate. The time or space cost appearing on a medium's published rate card.

Cash budget. A short-term plan, usually for no longer than a year, for the use of cash.

Cash discount. A 2 percent discount given by media to advertisers for prompt payment. It is calculated after deducting the 15 percent agency commission.

Census. The collecting of information *from every member* of some statistical population.

City zone. The center city of a market. One of the ways in which newspapers report their circulation.

Clearance. Refers to the time that affiliates make available for network programming.

Closing date. The date by which all advertising materials must be at the medium if the advertising is to appear on a certain date.

Coincidental telephone. A data-gathering technique in which interviews are conducted simultaneously with the activity being measured.

Combination rate. A lower rate given to the advertiser for buying two or more media. In the case of one-owner morning and evening newspaper combinations, this is often mandatory.

Continuity. The period of time over which an advertising schedule will run.

Continuity discount. Discount given for consecutive advertising over a set number of weeks.

Continuity of impression. Term associated with flighting. The period during which advertising is reduced but audience still retains the advertising previously communicated.

Contract. In media, a space or time contract sets the price that an advertiser will pay for time or space during some specified period.

Controlled circulation. That portion of a publication's circulation that is delivered free.

Convenience sample. A sample in which the sampling units are chosen on a nonprobability basis.

Cooperative advertising. Advertising placed by retailers but wholly or partly financed by national manufacturers or wholesalers.

Cost per rating point (CPP or CRP). Means of comparing broadcast costs based on delivering one rating point. CPP is often used to compare the costs of reaching 1 percent of a market segment. In this case it may be referred to as the cost per demographic point.

Cost per thousand. The cost of reaching 1,000 circulation. Circulation may be expressed as households, individuals, or some market segment.

Cover positions. Premium positions sold in magazines. First cover—front cover; second cover—inside front cover; third cover—inside back cover; fourth cover—back cover. Only business publications routinely sell their first covers to advertisers.

Coverage. In broadcast, refers to geographic area over which station gets a certain level of listeners or viewers. In print media, it can refer to the geographic area in which the publication has some acceptable level of penetration.

Cumulative audience (cume). The number of different people or households reached by a medium or media over some period of time.

Cumulative readership. The number of persons who will see at least one out of two insertions in a single publication.

Cut-in. A commercial that replaces a network announcement. Often national advertisers will make such substitutions for purposes of local testing.

"D" counties. All counties that are not "A," "B," or "C" counties.

Day-after recall. Recall measured during the day after exposure.

Demarketing. Activities designed to destimulate demand.

Demographic edition. A portion of a magazine's total circulation that can be bought by an advertiser and distributed to some market segment.

Display advertising. Print advertising that includes both copy and pictures. In newspapers the term is used to distinguish it from classified advertising.

Double billing. An abuse most frequent in cooperative retail advertising, in which the participating retailer, with the connivance of the media enterprise, substitutes an unauthorized message or submits an inflated media bill, or both.

Double stapling. A double-billing scam in broadcast advertising in which the cooperating retailer airs an unauthorized advertisement.

Drive time. Periods during morning and evening weekdays when automobile radio usage is considered to be at its highest.

Duplicated audience. The number of people reached two or more times in a media schedule.

Earned rate. The amount an advertiser pays for space and time and figuring all discounts.

Effective Reach. The number of exposures to an advertisement necessary to achieve the campaign objectives.

Efficiency. The ratio of outputs to inputs.

Estimators. Usually entry-level media buyers who figure costs of schedules prior to making actual buys. Also can refer to the many reference books used by media buyers to estimate media costs.

EVPI. Expected value of perfect information.

Exposure. The media making contact with an individual or a household.

Facing. In outdoor advertising, refers to the direction and the number of boards in a location. A double south facing has two boards visible to northbound traffic.

Fifteen and two. Common agency discounts given by media. The traditional agency discount is 15 percent, and 2 percent is given by some media for prompt payment. Often expressed as 15/2.

Flat rate. An advertising rate for which no discounts are available.

Flexible budget. A budget that permits specified variations in revenues and/or expenditures.

Flighting. A concentration of advertising over a short period of time followed by a reduction in advertising and then another burst of advertising.

Frequency. The average number of times an individual or household is exposed to a medium over some period of time.

Frequency discount. Advertising discounts based on the number of insertions during either a month or a year.

Frequency modulation (FM). Fastest growing sector of commercial radio. Offers better sound reproduction than AM radio.

Fringe time. In broadcast, the periods before and after prime time.

Generic demand. Demand for an entire product class.

Gross impressions. The size of the duplicated audience.

Gross Rating Points (GRPs). The total rating achieved by several advertisements or commercials. A duplicated audience measure for the equivalent reach achieved with a particular advertising schedule.

Horizonal publication. An industrial publication directed to a particular job category in several industries. For instance, *Purchasing*.

Households Using Television (HUTs). The number of households tuned in at a specific time.

Hypothesis. Statement of a problem in research form.

Independent station. A broadcast station that is not affiliated with one of the major networks.

In-home readers. Those who read the average issue of a magazine in their home.

Insert. An advertisement, usually prepared by the advertiser, that is provided to a newspaper or magazine. Inserts may be either freestanding or bound into the publication.

Insertion order. Instructions sent by the advertiser or agency to the media outlining how and when an advertisement or commercial is to be run.

Junior panels. Eight-sheet posters available to outdoor advertisers in many large markets.

Local rate. A medium's rate to local advertisers, which is lower than the rate that the medium charges national advertisers. Most common in newspapers.

Macroeconomics. The economics of a nation or a society.

Makegood. An adjustment in which an advertising credit is provided to an advertiser when the ad is aired in violation of the broadcaster's product protection policy.

Management. The process of achieving organizational objectives by planning, organizing, staffing, directing, and controlling.

Market share. The percentage of the total generic market held by an individual brand.

Media schedule. The "calendar" that details the future advertising for a client. Gives the exact date, time, and cost of advertising placements.

Metricity. The ability of a measurement device to produce data that are of interval or ratio quality.

Metro Survey Area. A Metropolitan Statistical Area as defined by the U.S. Department of Commerce.

Microeconomics. The economics of an individual firm.

Network, broadcast. Two or more stations simultaneously broadcasting the same program originating from a single source.

Network, print. Several print media vehicles that can be bought simultaneously whether or not they are commonly owned.

Nonbillable services. Services normally covered by agency commission.

Null Hypothesis. Hypothesis that posits that no actual relationship exists between two (or more) phenomena.

Off-the-card rates. Rates offered to advertisers that do not appear on the rate card. In print media the use of such rates is a very controversial practice and is considered unethical in many quarters.

Opportunity-to-see. Those people who read at least some of a particular issue of a publication.

Out-of-home readers. Those who read the average issue of a magazine outside their home.

Owned and operated stations (O&O). Stations that are not only affiliated with a network but are actually owned by the network.

Package plan. A plan under which an advertiser is offered a lower rate for buying a group of broadcast commercials. Individual stations and networks offer many types of package plans.

Painted bulletin. Outdoor sign whose message is painted rather than papered. Generally used in high-traffic areas and bought for longer periods than are paper posters.

Parameter. Numerical value of some state of nature.

Pass-along readers. Readers of a publication who are not members of the purchasing or subscribing household. See *Secondary readers.*

Penetration. The coverage of a market, an audience, or a segment of the market by a particular medium.

Percent exclusive. That portion of a station's cume audience that only listens to that station.

Percent recycling. The percentage of a station's audience in one time period that also listens in another time period.

Plant. The medium for outdoor advertising. The plant operator is responsible for installing and maintaining outdoor signs on property he owns or leases.

Posters. Highway billboards. Standard units of posters are 24 sheet, 30 sheet, and bleed.

Power share. The number of share points by which a program won or lost its time period.

Preemptible spot. A broadcast commercial that can be replaced on short notice by an advertiser who is willing to pay a higher rate.

Primary data. Facts collected by the decision-making organization.

Primary readers. Readers of a particular magazine where a household member purchased or subscribed to the publication.

Prime time. In TV broadcasting, the 8–11 P.M. time period.

Probability sample. A sample in which the sampling units are chosen on a probability basis.

Rate differential. The practice among most newspapers of charging national advertisers a higher rate than is charged local advertisers.

Reach. The number of different persons exposed to an advertisement or campaign during a specified time period.

Readers-per-copy. The average number of readers of one copy of a publication.

Recall. The process by which consumers notice, remember, and are able to report some or all of an advertising message.

Recall, claimed. An assertion, by a respondent, that an advertisement was seen.

Recent-reading. A reading measurement made without reference to any particular issue of the publication, using only the masthead information.

Regional edition. That portion of a magazine's total circulation that can be bought by an advertiser and distributed in a single area.

Related recall. Recall accompanied by respondents' descriptions of specific portions of the advertisement.

Reliability. The property or ability of a measurement device to produce "repeatable" results.

Representative (Rep). An independent company that acts as the salesperson for a number of media, taking a commission on what it sells.

Retail trading zone. An area outside the city zone, reached by newspaper circulation, whose residents trade in the city.

Run of paper (ROP). An advertisement placed at the discretion of the publisher. In broadcast this is known as run of schedule (ROS).

Run of schedule. In broadcasting, an advertisement placed at the discretion of the station management.

Sampling. The collecting of information from a portion of some statistical population.

Scatter plan. A package buy that emphasizes a number of vehicles or programs, with little weight given to any one of them.

Scientific method. The problem-solving method, used in both the physical and social sciences, in which the problem is defined, pertinent information is collected and analyzed, and a solution is developed and implemented.

Secondary data. Facts collected by others for the decision-making organization.

Secondary readers. Readers who do not buy or subscribe to the medium but receive it on a pass-along basis.

Sets in use. See *Households Using Television*.

Share of audience. The percentage of people with sets in use who are tuned to a particular show.

Shopper. An advertising sheet with little or no editorial material, usually a weekly and distributed free in most cases.

Short rate. Charge made by medium to an advertiser who fails to earn a discount that was granted at the beginning of a contract period.

Showing. In outdoor, formerly a measurement of purchase. Now normally refers to a number of posters in a market that are bought on the basis of Gross Rating Points.

Spill-in. The portion of the television audience in a market viewing programs originating outside that market.

Spill-out. The portion of a television station's broadcast audience who view a program outside the station's designated market area, or DMA.

Split run. When an advertiser runs two different advertisements in the same issue of a publication. Such advertisements can be placed on an every-other-issue basis or on a regional basis.

Spot advertising. When national advertisers buy commercials on a station-by-station basis rather than on a network basis.

Standard Metropolitan Statistical Area. Major U.S. cities and the counties surrounding them.

Starting solution. A system of equations, composed of the objective function and constraint functions, in which all variables appear in all equations. Variables not originally contained in the equations are assigned a coefficient of zero.

Syndication. Broadcast programming that is sold to stations on a market-by-market basis.

Target audience efficiency. The ratio of total time spent listening by the target audience compared to that for the total audience.

Tear sheet. A verification procedure in print advertising in which the publisher furnishes the advertiser (or agency) a copy of the entire page on which the ad appeared.

Through-the-book. Readership estimates made by showing respondents either actual or "skeletonized" copies of the publications studied.

Total survey area. The MSA plus those outside counties that receive moderately strong radio signals from at least two AM stations licensed in the market.

Ultra high frequency (UHF). In television, channels 14–83. UHF stations are often nonaffiliated in major markets, and most UHF stations have weaker signals than VHF stations.

Unaided recall. Recall produced without prompting.

Unduplicated audience. See *Reach*.

Validity. The ability of a measurement device to measure what it claims to measure.

Vertical publication. A business publication that editorially covers an entire industry. For instance, *Automotive News*.

Volume discounts. Discount based on dollars spent during a set period.

Wild code. Impossible or highly implausible values for a variable.

Zero-based budgeting. The development and justification of budget allocations "from scratch," without regard to historical budget allocations.